CW00521920

Essays

BOOK ONE

Cover illustration by Rembrandt:
Self Portrait, 1627, Kassel, Staatliche Museen

Witch Books

2011

Printed in the United States of America

Book design by heatherleeshaw.blogspot.com

ESSAYS

BOOK ONE

Translated by Charles Cotton
Edited by William Carew Hazlitt

WITCH BOOKS

LES ESSAIS
DE MICHEL
DE MONTAIGNE.
Nouuelle Edition
LIVRE PREMIER
Enrichie et Augmentée aux marges
du nom des Autheurs qui y sont citez,
Auec les Versions des passages
Grecs, Latins, & Italiens.

QVE SCAY

A PARIS,
Chez CHRISTOPHLE IOVRNEL, Rue
Vieille Bouclerie au bout du pont St Michel,
à L'image Sainct Iean.
1 6 5 9   N De Larmessin

Contents

Portrait of Montaigne by Dumonstier.

Essays

BOOK ONE

CHAPTER I

THAT MEN BY VARIOUS WAYS
ARRIVE AT THE SAME END

The most usual way of appeasing the indignation of such as we have any way offended, when we see them in possession of the power of revenge, and find that we absolutely lie at their mercy, is by submission, to move them to commiseration and pity; and yet bravery, constancy, and resolution, however quite contrary means, have sometimes served to produce the same effect.⸺[Florio's version begins thus: "The most vsuall waie to appease those minds wee have offended, when revenge lies in their hands, and that we stand at their mercie, is by submission to move them to commiseration and pity: Nevertheless, courage, constancie, and resolution (means altogether opposite) have sometimes wrought the same effect."⸺] [The spelling is Florio's D.W.]

Edward, Prince of Wales [Edward, the Black Prince. D.W.] (the same who so long governed our Guienne, a personage whose condition and fortune have in them a great deal of the most notable and most considerable parts of grandeur), having been highly incensed by the Limousins, and taking their city by assault, was not, either by the cries of the people, or the prayers and tears of the women and children, abandoned to slaughter and prostrate at his feet for mercy, to be stayed from prosecuting his revenge; till, penetrating further into the town, he at last took notice of three French gentlemen,⸺[These were Jean de Villemure, Hugh de la Roche, and Roger de Beaufort.⸺Froissart, i. c. 289. { The city was Limoges. D.W.}]⸺who with incredible bravery alone sustained the power of his victorious army. Then it was that consideration and respect unto so remarkable a valour first stopped the torrent of his fury, and that his clemency, beginning with these three cavaliers, was afterwards extended to all the remaining inhabitants of the city.

*Scanderbeg, Prince of Epirus, pursuing one of his soldiers with purpose
to kill him, the soldier, having in vain tried by all the ways of
humility and supplication to appease him, resolved, as his last refuge,
to face about and await him sword in hand: which behaviour of his gave a
sudden stop to his captain's fury, who, for seeing him assume so notable
a resolution, received him into grace; an example, however, that might
suffer another interpretation with such as have not read of the
prodigious force and valour of that prince.*

*The Emperor Conrad III. having besieged Guelph, Duke of Bavaria,--[In
1140, in Weinsberg, Upper Bavaria.]--would not be prevailed upon, what
mean and unmanly satisfactions soever were tendered to him, to condescend
to milder conditions than that the ladies and gentlewomen only who were
in the town with the duke might go out without violation of their honour,
on foot, and with so much only as they could carry about them. Whereupon
they, out of magnanimity of heart, presently contrived to carry out, upon
their shoulders, their husbands and children, and the duke himself;
a sight at which the emperor was so pleased, that, ravished with the
generosity of the action, he wept for joy, and immediately extinguishing
in his heart the mortal and capital hatred he had conceived against this
duke, he from that time forward treated him and his with all humanity.
The one and the other of these two ways would with great facility work
upon my nature; for I have a marvellous propensity to mercy and mildness,
and to such a degree that I fancy of the two I should sooner surrender my
anger to compassion than to esteem. And yet pity is reputed a vice
amongst the Stoics, who will that we succour the afflicted, but not that
we should be so affected with their sufferings as to suffer with them.
I conceived these examples not ill suited to the question in hand, and
the rather because therein we observe these great souls assaulted and
tried by these two several ways, to resist the one without relenting, and
to be shook and subjected by the other. It may be true that to suffer a
man's heart to be totally subdued by compassion may be imputed to
facility, effeminacy, and over-tenderness; whence it comes to pass that
the weaker natures, as of women, children, and the common sort of people,
are the most subject to it but after having resisted and disdained the
power of groans and tears, to yield to the sole reverence of the sacred*

*image of Valour, this can be no other than the effect of a strong and
inflexible soul enamoured of and honouring masculine and obstinate
courage. Nevertheless, astonishment and admiration may, in less generous
minds, beget a like effect: witness the people of Thebes, who, having put
two of their generals upon trial for their lives for having continued in
arms beyond the precise term of their commission, very hardly pardoned
Pelopidas, who, bowing under the weight of so dangerous an accusation,
made no manner of defence for himself, nor produced other arguments than
prayers and supplications; whereas, on the contrary, Epaminondas, falling
to recount magniloquently the exploits he had performed in their service,
and, after a haughty and arrogant manner reproaching them with
ingratitude and injustice, they had not the heart to proceed any further
in his trial, but broke up the court and departed, the whole assembly
highly commending the high courage of this personage.--[Plutarch, How
far a Man may praise Himself, c. 5.]*

*Dionysius the elder, after having, by a tedious siege and through
exceeding great difficulties, taken the city of Reggio, and in it the
governor Phyton, a very gallant man, who had made so obstinate a defence,
was resolved to make him a tragical example of his revenge: in order
whereunto he first told him, "That he had the day before caused his son
and all his kindred to be drowned." To which Phyton returned no other
answer but this: "That they were then by one day happier than he." After
which, causing him to be stripped, and delivering him into the hands of
the tormentors, he was by them not only dragged through the streets of
the town, and most ignominiously and cruelly whipped, but moreover
vilified with most bitter and contumelious language: yet still he
maintained his courage entire all the way, with a strong voice and
undaunted countenance proclaiming the honourable and glorious cause of
his death; namely, for that he would not deliver up his country into the
hands of a tyrant; at the same time denouncing against him a speedy
chastisement from the offended gods. At which Dionysius, reading in his
soldiers' looks, that instead of being incensed at the haughty language
of this conquered enemy, to the contempt of their captain and his
triumph, they were not only struck with admiration of so rare a virtue,
but moreover inclined to mutiny, and were even ready to rescue the*

prisoner out of the hangman's hands, he caused the torturing to cease, and afterwards privately caused him to be thrown into the sea.--[Diod. Sic., xiv. 29.]

Man (in good earnest) is a marvellous vain, fickle, and unstable subject, and on whom it is very hard to form any certain and uniform judgment. For Pompey could pardon the whole city of the Mamertines, though furiously incensed against it, upon the single account of the virtue and magnanimity of one citizen, Zeno,--[Plutarch calls him Stheno, and also Sthemnus and Sthenis]--who took the fault of the public wholly upon himself; neither entreated other favour, but alone to undergo the punishment for all: and yet Sylla's host, having in the city of Perugia --[Plutarch says Preneste, a town of Latium.]--manifested the same virtue, obtained nothing by it, either for himself or his fellow-citizens.

And, directly contrary to my first examples, the bravest of all men, and who was reputed so gracious to all those he overcame, Alexander, having, after many great difficulties, forced the city of Gaza, and, entering, found Betis, who commanded there, and of whose valour in the time of this siege he had most marvellous manifest proof, alone, forsaken by all his soldiers, his armour hacked and hewed to pieces, covered all over with blood and wounds, and yet still fighting in the crowd of a number of Macedonians, who were laying on him on all sides, he said to him, nettled at so dear-bought a victory (for, in addition to the other damage, he had two wounds newly received in his own person), "Thou shalt not die, Betis, as thou dost intend; be sure thou shall suffer all the torments that can be inflicted on a captive." To which menace the other returning no other answer, but only a fierce and disdainful look; "What," says Alexander, observing his haughty and obstinate silence, "is he too stiff to bend a knee! Is he too proud to utter one suppliant word! Truly, I will conquer this silence; and if I cannot force a word from his mouth, I will, at least, extract a groan from his heart." And thereupon converting his anger into fury, presently commanded his heels to be bored through, causing him, alive, to be dragged, mangled, and dismembered at a cart's tail.--[Quintus Curtius, iv. 6. This act of cruelty has been

doubted, notwithstanding the statement of Curtius.]--Was it that the
height of courage was so natural and familiar to this conqueror, that
because he could not admire, he respected it the less? Or was it that he
conceived valour to be a virtue so peculiar to himself, that his pride
could not, without envy, endure it in another? Or was it that the
natural impetuosity of his fury was incapable of opposition? Certainly,
had it been capable of moderation, it is to be believed that in the sack
and desolation of Thebes, to see so many valiant men, lost and totally
destitute of any further defence, cruelly massacred before his eyes,
would have appeased it: where there were above six thousand put to the
sword, of whom not one was seen to fly, or heard to cry out for quarter;
but, on the contrary, every one running here and there to seek out and to
provoke the victorious enemy to help them to an honourable end. Not one
was seen who, however weakened with wounds, did not in his last gasp yet
endeavour to revenge himself, and with all the arms of a brave despair,
to sweeten his own death in the death of an enemy. Yet did their valour
create no pity, and the length of one day was not enough to satiate the
thirst of the conqueror's revenge, but the slaughter continued to the
last drop of blood that was capable of being shed, and stopped not till
it met with none but unarmed persons, old men, women, and children, of
them to carry away to the number of thirty thousand slaves.

CHAPTER II

OF SORROW

No man living is more free from this passion than I, who yet neither like it in myself nor admire it in others, and yet generally the world, as a settled thing, is pleased to grace it with a particular esteem, clothing therewith wisdom, virtue, and conscience. Foolish and sordid guise! --["No man is more free from this passion than I, for I neither love nor regard it: albeit the world hath undertaken, as it were upon covenant, to grace it with a particular favour. Therewith they adorne age, vertue, and conscience. Oh foolish and base ornament!" Florio, 1613, p. 3] --The Italians have more fitly baptized by this name--[La tristezza]-- malignity; for 'tis a quality always hurtful, always idle and vain; and as being cowardly, mean, and base, it is by the Stoics expressly and particularly forbidden to their sages.

But the story--[Herodotus, iii. 14.]--says that Psammenitus, King of Egypt, being defeated and taken prisoner by Cambyses, King of Persia, seeing his own daughter pass by him as prisoner, and in a wretched habit, with a bucket to draw water, though his friends about him were so concerned as to break out into tears and lamentations, yet he himself remained unmoved, without uttering a word, his eyes fixed upon the ground; and seeing, moreover, his son immediately after led to execution, still maintained the same countenance; till spying at last one of his domestic and familiar friends dragged away amongst the captives, he fell to tearing his hair and beating his breast, with all the other extravagances of extreme sorrow.

A story that may very fitly be coupled with another of the same kind, of recent date, of a prince of our own nation, who being at Trent, and having news there brought him of the death of his elder brother, a brother on whom depended the whole support and honour of his house, and soon after of that of a younger brother, the second hope of his family, and having withstood these two assaults with an exemplary resolution; one of his servants happening a few days after to die, he suffered his constancy to be overcome by this last accident; and, parting with his courage, so abandoned himself to sorrow and mourning, that some thence were forward to conclude that he was only touched to the quick by this last stroke of fortune; but, in truth, it was, that being before brimful of grief, the least addition overflowed the bounds of all patience. Which, I think, might also be said of the former example, did not the story proceed to tell us that Cambyses asking Psammenitus, "Why, not being moved at the calamity of his son and daughter, he should with so great impatience bear the misfortune of his friend?" "It is," answered he, "because only this last affliction was to be manifested by tears, the two first far exceeding all manner of expression."

And, peradventure, something like this might be working in the fancy of the ancient painter,--[Cicero, De Orator., c. 22 ; Pliny, xxxv. 10.]-- who having, in the sacrifice of Iphigenia, to represent the sorrow of the assistants proportionably to the several degrees of interest every one had in the death of this fair innocent virgin, and having, in the other figures, laid out the utmost power of his art, when he came to that of her father, he drew him with a veil over his face, meaning thereby that no kind of countenance was capable of expressing such a degree of sorrow. Which is also the reason why the poets feign the miserable mother, Niobe, having first lost seven sons, and then afterwards as many daughters (overwhelmed with her losses), to have been at last transformed into a rock--

> "Diriguisse malis,"

> ["Petrified with her misfortunes."--Ovid, Met., vi. 304.]

thereby to express that melancholic, dumb, and deaf stupefaction, which benumbs all our faculties, when oppressed with accidents greater than we are able to bear. And, indeed, the violence and impression of an excessive grief must of necessity astonish the soul, and wholly deprive her of her ordinary functions: as it happens to every one of us, who, upon any sudden alarm of very ill news, find ourselves surprised, stupefied, and in a manner deprived of all power of motion, so that the soul, beginning to vent itself in tears and lamentations, seems to free and disengage itself from the sudden oppression, and to have obtained some room to work itself out at greater liberty.

"Et via vix tandem voci laxata dolore est."

["And at length and with difficulty is a passage opened by grief for utterance."--AEneid, xi. 151.]

In the war that Ferdinand made upon the widow of King John of Hungary, about Buda, a man-at-arms was particularly taken notice of by every one for his singular gallant behaviour in a certain encounter; and, unknown, highly commended, and lamented, being left dead upon the place: but by none so much as by Raisciac, a German lord, who was infinitely enamoured of so rare a valour. The body being brought off, and the count, with the common curiosity coming to view it, the armour was no sooner taken off but he immediately knew him to be his own son, a thing that added a second blow to the compassion of all the beholders; only he, without uttering a word, or turning away his eyes from the woeful object, stood fixedly contemplating the body of his son, till the vehemency of sorrow having overcome his vital spirits, made him sink down stone-dead to the ground.

"Chi puo dir com' egli arde, a in picciol fuoco,"

["He who can say how he burns with love, has little fire" --Petrarca, Sonetto 137.]

say the Innamoratos, when they would represent an 'insupportable passion.

"Misero quod omneis
Eripit sensus mihi: nam simul te,
Lesbia, aspexi, nihil est super mi,

> *Quod loquar amens.*
> *Lingua sed torpet: tenuis sub artus*
> *Flamma dimanat; sonitu suopte*
> *Tintinant aures; gemina teguntur*
> *Lumina nocte."*

["Love deprives me of all my faculties: Lesbia, when once in thy
presence, I have not left the power to tell my distracting passion:
my tongue becomes torpid; a subtle flame creeps through my veins; my
ears tingle in deafness; my eyes are veiled with darkness."
Catullus, Epig. li. 5]

Neither is it in the height and greatest fury of the fit that we are in a
condition to pour out our complaints or our amorous persuasions, the soul
being at that time over-burdened, and labouring with profound thoughts;
and the body dejected and languishing with desire; and thence it is that
sometimes proceed those accidental impotencies that so unseasonably
surprise the lover, and that frigidity which by the force of an
immoderate ardour seizes him even in the very lap of fruition.
-- [The edition of 1588 has here, "An accident not unknown to myself."] --
For all passions that suffer themselves to be relished and digested are
but moderate:

> *"Curae leves loquuntur, ingentes stupent."*

["Light griefs can speak: deep sorrows are dumb."
--Seneca, Hippolytus, act ii. scene 3.]

A surprise of unexpected joy does likewise often produce the same effect:

> *"Ut me conspexit venientem, et Troja circum*
> *Arma amens vidit, magnis exterrita monstris,*
> *Diriguit visu in medio, calor ossa reliquit,*
> *Labitur, et longo vix tandem tempore fatur."*

["When she beheld me advancing, and saw, with stupefaction, the
Trojan arms around me, terrified with so great a prodigy, she
fainted away at the very sight: vital warmth forsook her limbs: she
sinks down, and, after a long interval, with difficulty speaks."--
AEneid, iii. 306.]

Besides the examples of the Roman lady, who died for joy to see her son
safe returned from the defeat of Cannae; and of Sophocles and of
Dionysius the Tyrant,--[Pliny, vii. 53. Diodorus Siculus, however (xv.
c. 20), tells us that Dionysius "was so overjoyed at the news that he
made a great sacrifice upon it to the gods, prepared sumptuous feasts, to
which he invited all his friends, and therein drank so excessively that
it threw him into a very bad distemper."]--who died of joy; and of
Thalna, who died in Corsica, reading news of the honours the Roman Senate
had decreed in his favour, we have, moreover, one in our time, of Pope
Leo X., who upon news of the taking of Milan, a thing he had so ardently
desired, was rapt with so sudden an excess of joy that he immediately
fell into a fever and died.--[Guicciardini, Storia d'Italia, vol.
xiv.]--And for a more notable testimony of the imbecility of human
nature, it is recorded by the ancients--[Pliny, 'ut supra']--that
Diodorus the dialectician died upon the spot, out of an extreme passion
of shame, for not having been able in his own school, and in the presence
of a great auditory, to disengage himself from a nice argument that was
propounded to him. I, for my part, am very little subject to these
violent passions; I am naturally of a stubborn apprehension, which also,
by reasoning, I every day harden and fortify.

CHAPTER III

THAT OUR AFFECTIONS
CARRY THEMSELVES BEYOND US

*Such as accuse mankind of the folly of gaping after future things, and
advise us to make our benefit of those which are present, and to set up
our rest upon them, as having no grasp upon that which is to come, even
less than that which we have upon what is past, have hit upon the most
universal of human errors, if that may be called an error to which nature
herself has disposed us, in order to the continuation of her own work,
prepossessing us, amongst several others, with this deceiving
imagination, as being more jealous of our action than afraid of our
knowledge.*

*We are never present with, but always beyond ourselves: fear, desire,
hope, still push us on towards the future, depriving us, in the meantime,
of the sense and consideration of that which is to amuse us with the
thought of what shall be, even when we shall be no more.--[Rousseau,
Emile, livre ii.]*

"Calamitosus est animus futuri auxius."

*["The mind anxious about the future is unhappy."
--Seneca, Epist., 98.]*

*We find this great precept often repeated in Plato, "Do thine own work,
and know thyself." Of which two parts, both the one and the other
generally, comprehend our whole duty, and do each of them in like manner
involve the other; for who will do his own work aright will find that his
first lesson is to know what he is, and that which is proper to himself;
and who rightly understands himself will never mistake another man's work
for his own, but will love and improve himself above all other things,*

will refuse superfluous employments, and reject all unprofitable thoughts and propositions. As folly, on the one side, though it should enjoy all it desire, would notwithstanding never be content, so, on the other, wisdom, acquiescing in the present, is never dissatisfied with itself.
--[Cicero, Tusc. Quae., 57, v. 18.]--Epicurus dispenses his sages from all foresight and care of the future.

Amongst those laws that relate to the dead, I look upon that to be very sound by which the actions of princes are to be examined after their decease.--[Diodorus Siculus, i. 6.]-- They are equals with, if not masters of the laws, and, therefore, what justice could not inflict upon their persons, 'tis but reason should be executed upon their reputations and the estates of their successors--things that we often value above life itself. 'Tis a custom of singular advantage to those countries where it is in use, and by all good princes to be desired, who have reason to take it ill, that the memories of the wicked should be used with the same reverence and respect with their own. We owe subjection and obedience to all our kings, whether good or bad, alike, for that has respect unto their office; but as to esteem and affection, these are only due to their virtue. Let us grant to political government to endure them with patience, however unworthy; to conceal their vices; and to assist them with our recommendation in their indifferent actions, whilst their authority stands in need of our support. But, the relation of prince and subject being once at an end, there is no reason we should deny the expression of our real opinions to our own liberty and common justice, and especially to interdict to good subjects the glory of having reverently and faithfully served a prince, whose imperfections were to them so well known; this were to deprive posterity of a useful example. And such as, out of respect to some private obligation, unjustly espouse and vindicate the memory of a faulty prince, do private right at the expense of public justice. Livy does very truly say,--[xxxv. 48.]-- "That the language of men bred up in courts is always full of vain ostentation and false testimony, every one indifferently magnifying his own master, and stretching his commendation to the utmost extent of virtue and sovereign grandeur." Some may condemn the freedom of those two soldiers who so roundly answered Nero to his beard; the one being asked by him why he bore him ill-will? "I loved thee," answered he, "whilst thou wert worthy of it, but since thou art become a parricide, an incendiary, a player, and a coachman, I hate thee as thou dost deserve." And the other, why he should attempt to kill him? "Because," said he, "I could think of no other remedy against thy perpetual mischiefs." --[Tacitus, Annal., xv. 67.]--But the public and universal testimonies that were given of him after his death (and so will be to all posterity, both of him and all other wicked princes like him), of his tyrannies and abominable deportment, who, of a sound judgment, can reprove them?

I am scandalised, that in so sacred a government as that of the Lacedaemonians there should be mixed so hypocritical a ceremony at the interment of their kings; where all their confederates and neighbours, and all sorts and degrees of men and women, as well as their slaves, cut and slashed their foreheads in token of sorrow, repeating in their cries and lamentations that that king (let him have been as wicked as the devil) was the best that ever they had;--[Herodotus, vi. 68.]--by this means attributing to his quality the praise that only belongs to merit, and that of right is due to supreme desert, though lodged in the lowest and most inferior subject.

Aristotle, who will still have a hand in everything, makes a 'quaere' upon the saying of Solon, that none can be said to be happy until he is dead: "whether, then, he who has lived and died according to his heart's desire, if he have left an ill repute behind him, and that his posterity be miserable, can be said to be happy?" Whilst we have life and motion, we convey ourselves by fancy and preoccupation, whither and to what we please; but once out of being, we have no more any manner of communication with that which is, and it had therefore been better said by Solon that man is never happy, because never so, till he is no more.

> "Quisquam
> Vix radicitus e vita se tollit, et eicit;
> Sed facit esse sui quiddam super inscius ipse,
> Nec removet satis a projecto corpore sese, et
> Vindicat."

["Scarcely one man can, even in dying, wholly detach himself from
the idea of life; in his ignorance he must needs imagine that there
is in him something that survives him, and cannot sufficiently
separate or emancipate himself from his remains"
--Lucretius, iii. 890.]

Bertrand de Guesclin, dying at the siege of the Castle of Rancon, near
unto Puy, in Auvergne, the besieged were afterwards, upon surrender,
enjoined to lay down the keys of the place upon the corpse of the dead
general. Bartolommeo d'Alviano, the Venetian General, happening to die
in the service of the Republic in Brescia, and his corpse being to be
carried through the territory of Verona, an enemy's country, most of the
army were inclined to demand safe-conduct from the Veronese; but Theodoro
Trivulzio opposed the motion, rather choosing to make his way by force of
arms, and to run the hazard of a battle, saying it was by no means fit
that he who in his life was never afraid of his enemies should seem to
apprehend them when he was dead. In truth, in affairs of the same
nature, by the Greek laws, he who made suit to an enemy for a body to
give it burial renounced his victory, and had no more right to erect a
trophy, and he to whom such suit was made was reputed victor. By this
means it was that Nicias lost the advantage he had visibly obtained over
the Corinthians, and that Agesilaus, on the contrary, assured that which
he had before very doubtfully gained over the Boeotians.-- [Plutarch,
Life of Nicias, c. ii.; Life of Agesilaus, c. vi.]

These things might appear strange, had it not been a general practice in
all ages not only to extend the concern of ourselves beyond this life,
but, moreover, to fancy that the favour of Heaven does not only very
often accompany us to the grave, but has also, even after life, a concern
for our ashes. Of which there are so many ancient examples (to say
nothing of those of our own observation), that it is not necessary I
should longer insist upon it. Edward I., King of England, having in the
long wars betwixt him and Robert, King of Scotland, had experience of how
great importance his own immediate presence was to the success of his
affairs, having ever been victorious in whatever he undertook in his own

person, when he came to die, bound his son in a solemn oath that, so soon as he should be dead he should boil his body till the flesh parted from the bones, and bury the flesh, reserving the bones to carry continually with him in his army, so often as he should be obliged to go against the Scots, as if destiny had inevitably attached victory, even to his remains. John Zisca, the same who, to vindication of Wicliffe's heresies, troubled the Bohemian state, left order that they should flay him after his death, and of his skin make a drum to carry in the war against his enemies, fancying it would contribute to the continuation of the successes he had always obtained in the wars against them. In like manner certain of the Indians, in their battles with the Spaniards, carried with them the bones of one of their captains, in consideration of the victories they had formerly obtained under his conduct. And other people of the same New World carry about with them, in their wars, the relics of valiant men who have died in battle, to incite their courage and advance their fortune. Of which examples the first reserve nothing for the tomb but the reputation they have acquired by their former achievements, but these attribute to them a certain present and active power.

The proceeding of Captain Bayard is of a better composition, who finding himself wounded to death with an harquebuss shot, and being importuned to retire out of the fight, made answer that he would not begin at the last gasp to turn his back to the enemy, and accordingly still fought on, till feeling himself too faint and no longer able to sit on his horse, he commanded his steward to set him down at the foot of a tree, but so that he might die with his face towards the enemy, which he did.

I must yet add another example, equally remarkable for the present consideration with any of the former. The Emperor Maximilian, great-grandfather to the now King Philip,--[Philip II. of Spain.]--was a prince endowed throughout with great and extraordinary qualities, and amongst the rest with a singular beauty of person, but had withal a humour very contrary to that of other princes, who for the despatch of their most important affairs convert their close-stool into a chair of State, which was, that he would never permit any of his bedchamber, how familiar soever, to see him in that posture, and would steal aside to make water as religiously as a virgin, shy to discover to his physician or any other whomsoever those parts that we are accustomed to conceal. I myself, who have so impudent a way of talking, am, nevertheless, naturally so modest this way, that unless at the importunity of necessity or pleasure, I scarcely ever communicate to the sight of any either those parts or actions that custom orders us to conceal, wherein I suffer more constraint than I conceive is very well becoming a man, especially of my profession. But he nourished this modest humour to such a degree of superstition as to give express orders in his last will that they should put him on drawers so soon as he should be dead; to which, methinks, he would have done well to have added that he should be blindfolded, too, that put them on. The charge that Cyrus left with his children, that neither they, nor any other, should either see or touch his body after the soul was departed from it,--[Xenophon, Cyropedia, viii. 7.]--I attribute to some superstitious devotion of his; for both his historian and himself, amongst their great qualities, marked the whole course of their lives with a singular respect and reverence to religion.

I was by no means pleased with a story, told me by a man of very great quality of a relation of mine, and one who had given a very good account of himself both in peace and war, that, coming to die in a very old age, of excessive pain of the stone, he spent the last hours of his life in an extraordinary solicitude about ordering the honour and ceremony of his funeral, pressing all the men of condition who came to see him to engage their word to attend him to his grave: importuning this very prince, who came to visit him at his last gasp, with a most earnest supplication that he would order his family to be there, and presenting before him several reasons and examples to prove that it was a respect due to a man of his condition; and seemed to die content, having obtained this promise, and appointed the method and order of his funeral parade. I have seldom heard of so persistent a vanity.

Another, though contrary curiosity (of which singularity, also, I do not want domestic example), seems to be somewhat akin to this, that a man shall cudgel his brains at the last moments of his life to contrive his

*obsequies to so particular and unusual a parsimony as of one servant with
a lantern, I see this humour commended, and the appointment of Marcus.
Emilius Lepidus, who forbade his heirs to bestow upon his hearse even the
common ceremonies in use upon such occasions. Is it yet temperance and
frugality to avoid expense and pleasure of which the use and knowledge
are imperceptible to us? See, here, an easy and cheap reformation. If
instruction were at all necessary in this case, I should be of opinion
that in this, as in all other actions of life, each person should
regulate the matter according to his fortune; and the philosopher Lycon
prudently ordered his friends to dispose of his body where they should
think most fit, and as to his funeral, to order it neither too
superfluous nor too mean. For my part, I should wholly refer the
ordering of this ceremony to custom, and shall, when the time comes,
accordingly leave it to their discretion to whose lot it shall fall to do
me that last office. "Totus hic locus est contemnendus in nobis, non
negligendus in nostris;"--["The place of our sepulture is to be contemned
by us, but not to be neglected by our friends."--Cicero, Tusc. i. 45.]--
and it was a holy saying of a saint, "Curatio funeris, conditio
sepultura: pompa exequiarum, magis sunt vivorum solatia, quam subsidia
mortuorum."--["The care of death, the place of sepulture, the pomps of
obsequies, are rather consolations to the living than succours to the
dead." August. De Civit. Dei, i. 12.]--Which made Socrates answer
Crito, who, at death, asked him how he would be buried: "How you will,"
said he. "If I were to concern myself beyond the present about this
affair, I should be most tempted, as the greatest satisfaction of this
kind, to imitate those who in their lifetime entertain themselves with
the ceremony and honours of their own obsequies beforehand, and are
pleased with beholding their own dead countenance in marble. Happy are
they who can gratify their senses by insensibility, and live by their
death!"*

*I am ready to conceive an implacable hatred against all popular
domination, though I think it the most natural and equitable of all, so
oft as I call to mind the inhuman injustice of the people of Athens, who,
without remission, or once vouchsafing to hear what they had to say for
themselves, put to death their brave captains newly returned triumphant*

from a naval victory they had obtained over the Lacedaemonians near the
Arginusian Isles, the most bloody and obstinate engagement that ever the
Greeks fought at sea; because (after the victory) they followed up the
blow and pursued the advantages presented to them by the rule of war,
rather than stay to gather up and bury their dead. And the execution is
yet rendered more odious by the behaviour of Diomedon, who, being one of
the condemned, and a man of most eminent virtue, political and military,
after having heard the sentence, advancing to speak, no audience till
then having been allowed, instead of laying before them his own cause,
or the impiety of so cruel a sentence, only expressed a solicitude for
his judges' preservation, beseeching the gods to convert this sentence to
their good, and praying that, for neglecting to fulfil the vows which he
and his companions had made (with which he also acquainted them) in
acknowledgment of so glorious a success, they might not draw down the
indignation of the gods upon them; and so without more words went
courageously to his death.

Fortune, a few years after, punished them in the same kind; for Chabrias,
captain-general of their naval forces, having got the better of Pollis,
Admiral of Sparta, at the Isle of Naxos, totally lost the fruits of his
victory, one of very great importance to their affairs, in order not to
incur the danger of this example, and so that he should not lose a few
bodies of his dead friends that were floating in the sea, gave
opportunity to a world of living enemies to sail away in safety, who
afterwards made them pay dear for this unseasonable superstition:--

> "Quaeris, quo jaceas, post obitum, loco?
>   Quo non nata jacent."

["Dost ask where thou shalt lie after death?
Where things not born lie, that never being had."]
                    Seneca, Tyoa. Choro ii. 30.

This other restores the sense of repose to a body without a soul:

> *"Neque sepulcrum, quo recipiatur, habeat: portum corporis, ubi,*
> *remissa human, vita, corpus requiescat a malis."*

> *["Nor let him have a sepulchre wherein he may be received, a haven*
> *for his body, where, life being gone, that body may rest from its*
> *woes."--Ennius, ap. Cicero, Tusc. i. 44.]*

As nature demonstrates to us that several dead things retain yet an
occult relation to life; wine changes its flavour and complexion in
cellars, according to the changes and seasons of the vine from whence it
came; and the flesh of--venison alters its condition in the
powdering-tub, and its taste according to the laws of the living
flesh of its kind, as it is said.

CHAPTER IV

THAT THE SOUL EXPENDS ITS PASSIONS
UPON FALSE OBJECTS, WHERE THE TRUE
ARE WANTING

A gentleman of my country, marvellously tormented with the gout, being importuned by his physicians totally to abstain from all manner of salt meats, was wont pleasantly to reply, that in the extremity of his fits he must needs have something to quarrel with, and that railing at and cursing, one while the Bologna sausages, and another the dried tongues and the hams, was some mitigation to his pain. But, in good earnest, as the arm when it is advanced to strike, if it miss the blow, and goes by the wind, it pains us; and as also, that, to make a pleasant prospect, the sight should not be lost and dilated in vague air, but have some bound and object to limit and circumscribe it at a reasonable distance.

> *"Ventus ut amittit vires, nisi robore densa*
> *Occurrant sylvae, spatio diffusus inani."*

> *["As the wind loses its force diffused in void space, unless it in*
> *its strength encounters the thick wood."--Lucan, iii. 362.]*

So it seems that the soul, being transported and discomposed, turns its violence upon itself, if not supplied with something to oppose it, and therefore always requires an object at which to aim, and whereon to act. Plutarch says of those who are delighted with little dogs and monkeys, that the amorous part that is in us, for want of a legitimate object, rather than lie idle, does after that manner forge and create one false and frivolous. And we see that the soul, in its passions, inclines rather to deceive itself, by creating a false and fantastical a subject, even contrary to its own belief, than not to have something to work upon. After this manner brute beasts direct their fury to fall upon the stone or weapon that has hurt them, and with their teeth a even execute revenge upon themselves for the injury they have received from another:

> "Pannonis haud aliter, post ictum saevior ursa,
> Cui jaculum parva Lybis amentavit habena,
> Se rotat in vulnus, telumque irata receptum
> Impetit, et secum fugientem circuit hastam."

> ["So the she-bear, fiercer after the blow from the Lybian's thong-hurled dart, turns round upon the wound, and attacking the received spear, twists it, as she flies."--Lucan, vi. 220.]

What causes of the misadventures that befall us do we not invent? what is it that we do not lay the fault to, right or wrong, that we may have something to quarrel with? It is not those beautiful tresses you tear, nor is it the white bosom that in your anger you so unmercifully beat, that with an unlucky bullet have slain your beloved brother; quarrel with something else. Livy, speaking of the Roman army in Spain, says that for the loss of the two brothers, their great captains:

> "Flere omnes repente, et offensare capita."

> ["All at once wept and tore their hair."-Livy, xxv. 37.]

'Tis a common practice. And the philosopher Bion said pleasantly of the king, who by handsful pulled his hair off his head for sorrow, "Does this man think that baldness is a remedy for grief?"--[Cicero, Tusc. Quest., iii. 26.]--Who has not seen peevish gamesters chew and swallow the cards, and swallow the dice, in revenge for the loss of their money? Xerxes whipped the sea, and wrote a challenge to Mount Athos; Cyrus employed a whole army several days at work, to revenge himself of the river Gyndas, for the fright it had put him into in passing over it; and Caligula demolished a very beautiful palace for the pleasure his mother had once enjoyed there.

--[Pleasure--unless 'plaisir' were originally 'deplaisir'--must be
  understood here ironically, for the house was one in which she had
  been imprisoned.--Seneca, De Ira. iii. 22]--

I remember there was a story current, when I was a boy, that one of our
neighbouring kings--[Probably Alfonso XI. of Castile]--having received
a blow from the hand of God, swore he would be revenged, and in order to
it, made proclamation that for ten years to come no one should pray to
Him, or so much as mention Him throughout his dominions, or, so far as
his authority went, believe in Him; by which they meant to paint not so
much the folly as the vainglory of the nation of which this tale was
told. They are vices that always go together, but in truth such actions
as these have in them still more of presumption than want of wit.
Augustus Caesar, having been tossed with a tempest at sea, fell to
defying Neptune, and in the pomp of the Circensian games, to be revenged,
deposed his statue from the place it had amongst the other deities.
Wherein he was still less excusable than the former, and less than he was
afterwards when, having lost a battle under Quintilius Varus in Germany,
in rage and despair he went running his head against the wall, crying
out, "O Varus! give me back my legions!" for these exceed all folly,
forasmuch as impiety is joined therewith, invading God Himself, or at
least Fortune, as if she had ears that were subject to our batteries;
like the Thracians, who when it thunders or lightens, fall to shooting
against heaven with Titanian vengeance, as if by flights of arrows they
intended to bring God to reason. Though the ancient poet in Plutarch
tells us--

> "Point ne se faut couroucer aux affaires,
> Il ne leur chault de toutes nos choleres."

["We must not trouble the gods with our affairs; they take no heed
of our angers and disputes."--Plutarch.]

But we can never enough decry the disorderly sallies of our minds.

CHAPTER V

WHETHER THE GOVERNOR OF A PLACE BESIEGED OUGHT HIMSELF TO GO OUT TO PARLEY

Quintus Marcius, the Roman legate in the war against Perseus, King of Macedon, to gain time wherein to reinforce his army, set on foot some overtures of accommodation, with which the king being lulled asleep, concluded a truce for some days, by this means giving his enemy opportunity and leisure to recruit his forces, which was afterwards the occasion of the king's final ruin. Yet the elder senators, mindful of their forefathers' manners, condemned this proceeding as degenerating from their ancient practice, which, they said, was to fight by valour, and not by artifice, surprises, and night-encounters; neither by pretended flight nor unexpected rallies to overcome their enemies; never making war till having first proclaimed it, and very often assigned both the hour and place of battle. Out of this generous principle it was that they delivered up to Pyrrhus his treacherous physician, and to the Etrurians their disloyal schoolmaster. This was, indeed, a procedure truly Roman, and nothing allied to the Grecian subtlety, nor to the Punic cunning, where it was reputed a victory of less glory to overcome by force than by fraud. Deceit may serve for a need, but he only confesses himself overcome who knows he is neither subdued by policy nor misadventure, but by dint of valour, man to man, in a fair and just war. It very well appears, by the discourse of these good old senators, that this fine sentence was not yet received amongst them.

"Dolus, an virtus, quis in hoste requirat?"

["What matters whether by valour or by strategem we overcome the enemy?"--Aeneid, ii. 390]

The Achaians, says Polybius, abhorred all manner of double-dealing in war, not reputing it a victory unless where the courage of the enemy was fairly subdued:

"Eam vir sanctus et sapiens sciet veram esse victoriam, quae, salva fide et integra dignitate, parabitur."--["An honest and prudent man will acknowledge that only to be a true victory which shall be obtained saving his own good faith and dignity."--Florus, i. 12.]--Says another:

"Vosne velit, an me, regnare hera, quidve ferat,
fors virtute experiamur."

["Whether you or I shall rule, or what shall happen, let us determine by valour."--Cicero, De Offic., i. 12]

In the kingdom of Ternate, amongst those nations which we so broadly call barbarians, they have a custom never to commence war, till it be first proclaimed; adding withal an ample declaration of what means they have to do it with, with what and how many men, what ammunitions, and what, both offensive and defensive, arms; but also, that being done, if their enemies do not yield and come to an agreement, they conceive it lawful to employ without reproach in their wars any means which may help them to conquer.

The ancient Florentines were so far from seeking to obtain any advantage over their enemies by surprise, that they always gave them a month's warning before they drew their army into the field, by the continual tolling of a bell they called Martinella.--[After St. Martin.]

For what concerns ourselves, who are not so scrupulous in this affair, and who attribute the honour of the war to him who has the profit of it, and who after Lysander say, "Where the lion's skin is too short, we must eke it out with a bit from that of a fox"; the most usual occasions of surprise are derived from this practice, and we hold that there are no moments wherein a chief ought to be more circumspect, and to have his eye so much at watch, as those of parleys and treaties of accommodation; and

it is, therefore, become a general rule amongst the martial men of these
latter times, that a governor of a place never ought, in a time of siege,
to go out to parley. It was for this that in our fathers' days the
Seigneurs de Montmord and de l'Assigni, defending Mousson against the
Count of Nassau, were so highly censured. But yet, as to this, it would
be excusable in that governor who, going out, should, notwithstanding,
do it in such manner that the safety and advantage should be on his side;
as Count Guido di Rangone did at Reggio (if we are to believe Du Bellay,
for Guicciardini says it was he himself) when the Seigneur de l'Escut
approached to parley, who stepped so little away from his fort, that a
disorder happening in the interim of parley, not only Monsieur de l'Escut
and his party who were advanced with him, found themselves by much the
weaker, insomuch that Alessandro Trivulcio was there slain, but he
himself follow the Count, and, relying upon his honour, to secure himself
from the danger of the shot within the walls of the town.

Eumenes, being shut up in the city of Nora by Antigonus, and by him
importuned to come out to speak with him, as he sent him word it was fit
he should to a greater man than himself, and one who had now an advantage
over him, returned this noble answer. "Tell him," said he, "that I shall
never think any man greater than myself whilst I have my sword in my
hand," and would not consent to come out to him till first, according to
his own demand, Antigonus had delivered him his own nephew Ptolomeus in
hostage.

And yet some have done very well in going out in person to parley, on the
word of the assailant: witness Henry de Vaux, a cavalier of Champagne,
who being besieged by the English in the Castle of Commercy, and
Bartholomew de Brunes, who commanded at the Leaguer, having so sapped the
greatest part of the castle without, that nothing remained but setting
fire to the props to bury the besieged under the ruins, he requested the
said Henry to come out to speak with him for his own good, which he did
with three more in company; and, his ruin being made apparent to him, he
conceived himself singularly obliged to his enemy, to whose discretion he
and his garrison surrendered themselves; and fire being presently applied
to the mine, the props no sooner began to fail, but the castle was

immediately blown up from its foundations, no one stone being left upon another.

I could, and do, with great facility, rely upon the faith of another; but I should very unwillingly do it in such a case, as it should thereby be judged that it was rather an effect of my despair and want of courage than voluntarily and out of confidence and security in the faith of him with whom I had to do.

CHAPTER VI

THAT THE HOUR OF PARLEY DANGEROUS

*I saw, notwithstanding, lately at Mussidan, a place not far from my
house, that those who were driven out thence by our army, and others of
their party, highly complained of treachery, for that during a treaty of
accommodation, and in the very interim that their deputies were treating,
they were surprised and cut to pieces: a thing that, peradventure, in
another age, might have had some colour of foul play; but, as I have just
said, the practice of arms in these days is quite another thing, and
there is now no confidence in an enemy excusable till the treaty is
finally sealed; and even then the conqueror has enough to do to keep his
word: so hazardous a thing it is to entrust the observation of the faith
a man has engaged to a town that surrenders upon easy and favourable
conditions, to the licence of a victorious army, and to give the soldier
free entrance into it in the heat of blood.*

*Lucius AEmilius Regillus, the Roman praetor, having lost his time in
attempting to take the city of Phocaea by force, by reason of the
singular valour wherewith the inhabitants defended themselves,
conditioned, at last, to receive them as friends to the people of Rome,
and to enter the town, as into a confederate city, without any manner of
hostility, of which he gave them all assurance; but having, for the
greater pomp, brought his whole army in with him, it was no more in his
power, with all the endeavour he could use, to restrain his people: so
that, avarice and revenge trampling under foot both his authority and all
military discipline, he there saw a considerable part of the city sacked
and ruined before his face.*

*Cleomenes was wont to say, "that what mischief soever a man could do his
enemy in time of war was above justice, and nothing accountable to it in
the sight of gods and men." And so, having concluded a truce with those*

of Argos for seven days, the third night after he fell upon them when they were all buried in sleep, and put them to the sword, alleging that there had no nights been mentioned in the truce; but the gods punished this subtle perfidy.

In a time of parley also; and while the citizens were relying upon their safety warrant, the city of Casilinum was taken by surprise, and that even in the age of the justest captains and the most perfect Roman military discipline; for it is not said that it is not lawful for us, in time and place, to make advantage of our enemies' want of understanding, as well as their want of courage.

And, doubtless, war has naturally many privileges that appear reasonable even to the prejudice of reason. And therefore here the rule fails, "Neminem id agere ut ex alte rius praedetur inscitia."--["No one should preys upon another's folly."--Cicero, De Offic., iii. 17.]--But I am astonished at the great liberty allowed by Xenophon in such cases, and that both by precept and by the example of several exploits of his complete emperor; an author of very great authority, I confess, in those affairs, as being in his own person both a great captain and a philosopher of the first form of Socrates' disciples; and yet I cannot consent to such a measure of licence as he dispenses in all things and places.

Monsieur d'Aubigny, besieging Capua, and after having directed a furious battery against it, Signor Fabricio Colonna, governor of the town, having from a bastion begun to parley, and his soldiers in the meantime being a little more remiss in their guard, our people entered the place at unawares, and put them all to the sword. And of later memory, at Yvoy, Signor Juliano Romero having played that part of a novice to go out to parley with the Constable, at his return found his place taken. But, that we might not scape scot-free, the Marquess of Pescara having laid siege to Genoa, where Duke Ottaviano Fregosa commanded under our protection, and the articles betwixt them being so far advanced that it was looked upon as a done thing, and upon the point to be concluded, the Spaniards in the meantime having slipped in, made use of this treachery as an absolute victory. And since, at Ligny, in Barrois, where the Count de Brienne commanded, the emperor having in his own person beleaguered that place, and Bertheville, the said Count's lieutenant, going out to parley, whilst he was capitulating the town was taken.

> "Fu il vincer sempremai laudabil cosa,
> Vincasi o per fortuna, o per ingegno,"

["Victory is ever worthy of praise, whether obtained by valour or wisdom."--Ariosto, xv. I.]

But the philosopher Chrysippus was of another opinion, wherein I also concur; for he was used to say that those who run a race ought to employ all the force they have in what they are about, and to run as fast as they can; but that it is by no means fair in them to lay any hand upon their adversary to stop him, nor to set a leg before him to throw him down. And yet more generous was the answer of that great Alexander to Polypercon who was persuading him to take the advantage of the night's obscurity to fall upon Darius. "By no means," said he; "it is not for such a man as I am to steal a victory, 'Malo me fortunae poeniteat, quam victoria pudeat.'"--["I had rather complain of ill-fortune than be ashamed of victory." Quint. Curt, iv. 13]--

> "Atque idem fugientem haud est dignatus Oroden
> Sternere, nec jacta caecum dare cuspide vulnus
> Obvius, adversoque occurrit, seque viro vir
> Contulit, haud furto melior, sed fortibus armis."

["He deigned not to throw down Orodes as he fled, or with the darted spear to give him a wound unseen; but overtaking him, he confronted him face to face, and encountered man to man: superior, not in stratagem, but in valiant arms."--AEneid, x. 732.]

CHAPTER VII

THAT THE INTENTION
IS JUDGE OF OUR ACTIONS

'Tis a saying, "That death discharges us of all our obligations." I know some who have taken it in another sense. Henry VII., King of England, articled with Don Philip, son to Maximilian the emperor, or (to place him more honourably) father to the Emperor Charles V., that the said Philip should deliver up the Duke of Suffolk of the White Rose, his enemy, who was fled into the Low Countries, into his hands; which Philip accordingly did, but upon condition, nevertheless, that Henry should attempt nothing against the life of the said Duke; but coming to die, the king in his last will commanded his son to put him to death immediately after his decease. And lately, in the tragedy that the Duke of Alva presented to us in the persons of the Counts Horn and Egmont at Brussels, --[Decapitated 4th June 1568]--there were very remarkable passages, and one amongst the rest, that Count Egmont (upon the security of whose word and faith Count Horn had come and surrendered himself to the Duke of Alva) earnestly entreated that he might first mount the scaffold, to the end that death might disengage him from the obligation he had passed to the other. In which case, methinks, death did not acquit the former of his promise, and that the second was discharged from it without dying. We cannot be bound beyond what we are able to perform, by reason that effect and performance are not at all in our power, and that, indeed, we are masters of nothing but the will, in which, by necessity, all the rules and whole duty of mankind are founded and established: therefore Count Egmont, conceiving his soul and will indebted to his promise, although he had not the power to make it good, had doubtless been absolved of his duty, even though he had outlived the other; but the King of England wilfully and premeditately breaking his faith, was no more to be excused for deferring the execution of his infidelity till after his death than the mason in Herodotus, who having inviolably, during the time

*of his life, kept the secret of the treasure of the King of Egypt, his
master, at his death discovered it to his children.--[Herod., ii. 121.]*

*I have taken notice of several in my time, who, convicted by their
consciences of unjustly detaining the goods of another, have endeavoured
to make amends by their will, and after their decease; but they had as
good do nothing, as either in taking so much time in so pressing an
affair, or in going about to remedy a wrong with so little
dissatisfaction or injury to themselves. They owe, over and above,
something of their own; and by how much their payment is more strict and
incommodious to themselves, by so much is their restitution more just
meritorious. Penitency requires penalty; but they yet do worse than
these, who reserve the animosity against their neighbour to the last
gasp, having concealed it during their life; wherein they manifest little
regard of their own honour, irritating the party offended in their
memory; and less to their the power, even out of to make their malice die
with them, but extending the life of their hatred even beyond their own.
Unjust judges, who defer judgment to a time wherein they can have no
knowledge of the cause! For my part, I shall take care, if I can, that
my death discover nothing that my life has not first and openly declared.*

CHAPTER VIII

OF IDLENESS

As we see some grounds that have long lain idle and untilled, when grown rich and fertile by rest, to abound with and spend their virtue in the product of innumerable sorts of weeds and wild herbs that are unprofitable, and that to make them perform their true office, we are to cultivate and prepare them for such seeds as are proper for our service; and as we see women that, without knowledge of man, do sometimes of themselves bring forth inanimate and formless lumps of flesh, but that to cause a natural and perfect generation they are to be husbanded with another kind of seed: even so it is with minds, which if not applied to some certain study that may fix and restrain them, run into a thousand extravagances, eternally roving here and there in the vague expanse of the imagination--

> *"Sicut aqua tremulum labris ubi lumen ahenis,*
> *Sole repercussum, aut radiantis imagine lunae,*
> *Omnia pervolitat late loca; jamque sub auras*
> *Erigitur, summique ferit laquearia tecti."*

> *["As when in brazen vats of water the trembling beams of light,*
> *reflected from the sun, or from the image of the radiant moon,*
> *swiftly float over every place around, and now are darted up on*
> *high, and strike the ceilings of the upmost roof."--*
> *AEneid, viii. 22.]*

--in which wild agitation there is no folly, nor idle fancy they do not light upon:--

> *"Velut aegri somnia, vanae*
> *Finguntur species."*

["As a sick man's dreams, creating vain phantasms."--
Hor., De Arte Poetica, 7.]

The soul that has no established aim loses itself, for, as it is said--

    "Quisquis ubique habitat, Maxime, nusquam habitat."

    ["He who lives everywhere, lives nowhere."--Martial, vii. 73.]

When I lately retired to my own house, with a resolution, as much as
possibly I could, to avoid all manner of concern in affairs, and to spend
in privacy and repose the little remainder of time I have to live, I
fancied I could not more oblige my mind than to suffer it at full leisure
to entertain and divert itself, which I now hoped it might henceforth do,
as being by time become more settled and mature; but I find--

    "Variam semper dant otia mentem,"

    ["Leisure ever creates varied thought."--Lucan, iv. 704]

that, quite contrary, it is like a horse that has broke from his rider,
who voluntarily runs into a much more violent career than any horseman
would put him to, and creates me so many chimaeras and fantastic
monsters, one upon another, without order or design, that, the better at
leisure to contemplate their strangeness and absurdity, I have begun to
commit them to writing, hoping in time to make it ashamed of itself.

CHAPTER IX

OF LIARS

*There is not a man living whom it would so little become to speak from
memory as myself, for I have scarcely any at all, and do not think that
the world has another so marvellously treacherous as mine. My other
faculties are all sufficiently ordinary and mean; but in this I think
myself very rare and singular, and deserving to be thought famous.
Besides the natural inconvenience I suffer by it (for, certes, the
necessary use of memory considered, Plato had reason when he called it a
great and powerful goddess), in my country, when they would say a man has
no sense, they say, such an one has no memory; and when I complain of the
defect of mine, they do not believe me, and reprove me, as though I
accused myself for a fool: not discerning the difference betwixt memory
and understanding, which is to make matters still worse for me. But they
do me wrong; for experience, rather, daily shows us, on the contrary,
that a strong memory is commonly coupled with infirm judgment. They do,
me, moreover (who am so perfect in nothing as in friendship), a great
wrong in this, that they make the same words which accuse my infirmity,
represent me for an ungrateful person; they bring my affections into
question upon the account of my memory, and from a natural imperfection,
make out a defect of conscience. "He has forgot," says one, "this
request, or that promise; he no more remembers his friends; he has forgot
to say or do, or conceal such and such a thing, for my sake." And,
truly, I am apt enough to forget many things, but to neglect anything my
friend has given me in charge, I never do it. And it should be enough,
methinks, that I feel the misery and inconvenience of it, without
branding me with malice, a vice so contrary to my humour.*

*However, I derive these comforts from my infirmity: first, that it is an
evil from which principally I have found reason to correct a worse, that
would easily enough have grown upon me, namely, ambition; the defect*

being intolerable in those who take upon them public affairs. That, like examples in the progress of nature demonstrate to us, she has fortified me in my other faculties proportionably as she has left me unfurnished in this; I should otherwise have been apt implicitly to have reposed my mind and judgment upon the bare report of other men, without ever setting them to work upon their own force, had the inventions and opinions of others been ever been present with me by the benefit of memory. That by this means I am not so talkative, for the magazine of the memory is ever better furnished with matter than that of the invention. Had mine been faithful to me, I had ere this deafened all my friends with my babble, the subjects themselves arousing and stirring up the little faculty I have of handling and employing them, heating and distending my discourse, which were a pity: as I have observed in several of my intimate friends, who, as their memories supply them with an entire and full view of things, begin their narrative so far back, and crowd it with so many impertinent circumstances, that though the story be good in itself, they make a shift to spoil it; and if otherwise, you are either to curse the strength of their memory or the weakness of their judgment: and it is a hard thing to close up a discourse, and to cut it short, when you have once started; there is nothing wherein the force of a horse is so much seen as in a round and sudden stop. I see even those who are pertinent enough, who would, but cannot stop short in their career; for whilst they are seeking out a handsome period to conclude with, they go on at random, straggling about upon impertinent trivialities, as men staggering upon weak legs. But, above all, old men who retain the memory of things past, and forget how often they have told them, are dangerous company; and I have known stories from the mouth of a man of very great quality, otherwise very pleasant in themselves, become very wearisome by being repeated a hundred times over and over again to the same people.

Secondly, that, by this means, I the less remember the injuries I have received; insomuch that, as the ancient said,--[Cicero, Pro Ligar. c. 12.]--I should have a register of injuries, or a prompter, as Darius, who, that he might not forget the offence he had received from those of Athens, so oft as he sat down to dinner, ordered one of his pages three times to repeat in his ear, "Sir, remember the Athenians";--[Herod., v.

105.]--and then, again, the places which I revisit, and the books I read over again, still smile upon me with a fresh novelty.

It is not without good reason said "that he who has not a good memory should never take upon him the trade of lying." I know very well that the grammarians--[Nigidius, Aulus Gellius, xi. ii; Nonius, v. 80.]-- distinguish betwixt an untruth and a lie, and say that to tell an untruth is to tell a thing that is false, but that we ourselves believe to be true; and that the definition of the word to lie in Latin, from which our French is taken, is to tell a thing which we know in our conscience to be untrue; and it is of this last sort of liars only that I now speak. Now, these do either wholly contrive and invent the untruths they utter, or so alter and disguise a true story that it ends in a lie. When they disguise and often alter the same story, according to their own fancy, 'tis very hard for them, at one time or another, to escape being trapped, by reason that the real truth of the thing, having first taken possession of the memory, and being there lodged impressed by the medium of knowledge and science, it will be difficult that it should not represent itself to the imagination, and shoulder out falsehood, which cannot there have so sure and settled footing as the other; and the circumstances of the first true knowledge evermore running in their minds, will be apt to make them forget those that are illegitimate, and only, forged by their own fancy. In what they, wholly invent, forasmuch as there is no contrary impression to jostle their invention there seems to be less danger of tripping; and yet even this by reason it is a vain body and without any hold, is very apt to escape the memory, if it be not well assured. Of which I had very pleasant experience, at the expense of such as profess only to form and accommodate their speech to the affair they have in hand, or to humour of the great folks to whom they are speaking; for the circumstances to which these men stick not to enslave their faith and conscience being subject to several changes, their language must vary accordingly: whence it happens that of the same thing they tell one man that it is this, and another that it is that, giving it several colours; which men, if they once come to confer notes, and find out the cheat, what becomes of this fine art? To which may be added, that they must of necessity very often ridiculously trap themselves; for what memory can be *sufficient to retain so many different shapes as they have forged upon one and the same subject? I have known many in my time very ambitious of the repute of this fine wit; but they do not see that if they have the reputation of it, the effect can no longer be.*

In plain truth, lying is an accursed vice. We are not men, nor have other tie upon one another, but by our word. If we did but discover the horror and gravity of it, we should pursue it with fire and sword, and more justly than other crimes. I see that parents commonly, and with indiscretion enough, correct their children for little innocent faults, and torment them for wanton tricks, that have neither impression nor consequence; whereas, in my opinion, lying only, and, which is of something a lower form, obstinacy, are the faults which are to be severely whipped out of them, both in their infancy and in their progress, otherwise they grow up and increase with them; and after a tongue has once got the knack of lying, 'tis not to be imagined how impossible it is to reclaim it whence it comes to pass that we see some, who are otherwise very honest men, so subject and enslaved to this vice. I have an honest lad to my tailor, whom I never knew guilty of one truth, no, not when it had been to his advantage. If falsehood had, like truth, but one face only, we should be upon better terms; for we should then take for certain the contrary to what the liar says: but the reverse of truth has a hundred thousand forms, and a field indefinite, without bound or limit. The Pythagoreans make good to be certain and finite, and evil, infinite and uncertain. There are a thousand ways to miss the white, there is only one to hit it. For my own part, I have this vice in so great horror, that I am not sure I could prevail with my conscience to secure myself from the most manifest and extreme danger by an impudent and solemn lie. An ancient father says "that a dog we know is better company than a man whose language we do not understand."

"Ut externus alieno pene non sit hominis vice."

["As a foreigner cannot be said to supply us the place of a man." ~Pliny, Nat. Hist. vii. I]

And how much less sociable is false speaking than silence?

King Francis I. vaunted that he had by this means nonplussed Francesco Taverna, ambassador of Francesco Sforza, Duke of Milan, a man very famous for his science in talking in those days. This gentleman had been sent to excuse his master to his Majesty about a thing of very great consequence, which was this: the King, still to maintain some intelligence with Italy, out of which he had lately been driven, and particularly with the duchy of Milan, had thought it convenient to have a gentleman on his behalf to be with that Duke: an ambassador in effect, but in outward appearance a private person who pretended to reside there upon his own particular affairs; for the Duke, much more depending upon the Emperor, especially at a time when he was in a treaty of marriage with his niece, daughter to the King of Denmark, who is now dowager of Lorraine, could not manifest any practice and conference with us without his great interest. For this commission one Merveille, a Milanese gentleman, and an equerry to the King, being thought very fit, was accordingly despatched thither with private credentials, and instructions as ambassador, and with other letters of recommendation to the Duke about his own private concerns, the better to mask and colour the business; and was so long in that court, that the Emperor at last had some inkling of his real employment there; which was the occasion of what followed after, as we suppose; which was, that under pretence of some murder, his trial was in two days despatched, and his head in the night struck off in prison. Messire Francesco being come, and prepared with a long counterfeit history of the affair (for the King had applied himself to all the princes of Christendom, as well as to the Duke himself, to demand satisfaction), had his audience at the morning council; where, after he had for the support of his cause laid open several plausible justifications of the fact, that his master had never looked upon this Merveille for other than a private gentleman and his own subject, who was there only in order to his own business, neither had he ever lived under any other aspect; absolutely disowning that he had ever heard he was one of the King's household or that his Majesty so much as knew him, so far was he from taking him for an ambassador: the King, in his turn, pressing him with several objections and demands, and challenging him on all sides, tripped him up at last by asking, why, then, the execution was performed by night, and as it were by stealth? At which the poor confounded ambassador, the more handsomely to disengage himself, made answer, that the Duke would have been very loth, out of respect to his Majesty, that such an execution should have been performed by day. Any one may guess if he was not well rated when he came home, for having so grossly tripped in the presence of a prince of so delicate a nostril as King Francis.

Pope Julius II. having sent an ambassador to the King of England to animate him against King Francis, the ambassador having had his audience, and the King, before he would give an answer, insisting upon the difficulties he should find in setting on foot so great a preparation as would be necessary to attack so potent a King, and urging some reasons to that effect, the ambassador very unseasonably replied that he had also himself considered the same difficulties, and had represented them to the Pope. From which saying of his, so directly opposite to the thing propounded and the business he came about, which was immediately to incite him to war, the King of England first derived the argument (which he afterward found to be true), that this ambassador, in his own mind, was on the side of the French; of which having advertised his master, his estate at his return home was confiscated, and he himself very narrowly escaped the losing of his head.--[Erasmi Op. (1703), iv. col. 684.]

CHAPTER X

OF QUICK OR SLOW SPEECH

"Onc ne furent a touts toutes graces donnees."

["All graces were never yet given to any one man."—A verse in one of La Brebis' Sonnets.]

So we see in the gift of eloquence, wherein some have such a facility and promptness, and that which we call a present wit so easy, that they are ever ready upon all occasions, and never to be surprised; and others more heavy and slow, never venture to utter anything but what they have long premeditated, and taken great care and pains to fit and prepare.

Now, as we teach young ladies those sports and exercises which are most proper to set out the grace and beauty of those parts wherein their chiefest ornament and perfection lie, so it should be in these two advantages of eloquence, to which the lawyers and preachers of our age seem principally to pretend. If I were worthy to advise, the slow speaker, methinks, should be more proper for the pulpit, and the other for the bar: and that because the employment of the first does naturally allow him all the leisure he can desire to prepare himself, and besides, his career is performed in an even and unintermitted line, without stop or interruption; whereas the pleader's business and interest compels him to enter the lists upon all occasions, and the unexpected objections and replies of his adverse party jostle him out of his course, and put him, upon the instant, to pump for new and extempore answers and defences. Yet, at the interview betwixt Pope Clement and King Francis at Marseilles, it happened, quite contrary, that Monsieur Poyet, a man bred up all his life at the bar, and in the highest repute for eloquence, having the charge of making the harangue to the Pope committed to him, and having so long meditated on it beforehand, as, so they said, to have

brought it ready made along with him from Paris; the very day it was to
have been pronounced, the Pope, fearing something might be said that
might give offence to the other princes' ambassadors who were there
attending on him, sent to acquaint the King with the argument which he
conceived most suiting to the time and place, but, by chance, quite
another thing to that Monsieur de Poyet had taken so much pains about: so
that the fine speech he had prepared was of no use, and he was upon the
instant to contrive another; which finding himself unable to do, Cardinal
du Bellay was constrained to perform that office. The pleader's part is,
doubtless, much harder than that of the preacher; and yet, in my opinion,
we see more passable lawyers than preachers, at all events in France.
It should seem that the nature of wit is to have its operation prompt and
sudden, and that of judgment to have it more deliberate and more slow.
But he who remains totally silent, for want of leisure to prepare himself
to speak well, and he also whom leisure does noways benefit to better
speaking, are equally unhappy.

'Tis said of Severus Cassius that he spoke best extempore, that he stood
more obliged to fortune than to his own diligence; that it was an
advantage to him to be interrupted in speaking, and that his adversaries
were afraid to nettle him, lest his anger should redouble his eloquence.
I know, experimentally, the disposition of nature so impatient of tedious
and elaborate premeditation, that if it do not go frankly and gaily to
work, it can perform nothing to purpose. We say of some compositions
that they stink of oil and of the lamp, by reason of a certain rough
harshness that laborious handling imprints upon those where it has been
employed. But besides this, the solicitude of doing well, and a certain
striving and contending of a mind too far strained and overbent upon its
undertaking, breaks and hinders itself like water, that by force of its
own pressing violence and abundance, cannot find a ready issue through
the neck of a bottle or a narrow sluice. In this condition of nature,
of which I am now speaking, there is this also, that it would not be
disordered and stimulated with such passions as the fury of Cassius (for
such a motion would be too violent and rude); it would not be jostled,
but solicited; it would be roused and heated by unexpected, sudden, and
accidental occasions. If it be left to itself, it flags and languishes;

agitation only gives it grace and vigour. I am always worst in my own possession, and when wholly at my own disposition: accident has more title to anything that comes from me than I; occasion, company, and even the very rising and falling of my own voice, extract more from my fancy than I can find, when I sound and employ it by myself. By which means, the things I say are better than those I write, if either were to be preferred, where neither is worth anything. This, also, befalls me, that I do not find myself where I seek myself, and I light upon things more by chance than by any inquisition of my own judgment. I perhaps sometimes hit upon something when I write, that seems quaint and sprightly to me, though it will appear dull and heavy to another.--But let us leave these fine compliments; every one talks thus of himself according to his talent. But when I come to speak, I am already so lost that I know not what I was about to say, and in such cases a stranger often finds it out before me. If I should make erasure so often as this inconvenience befalls me, I should make clean work; occasion will, at some other time, lay it as visible to me as the light, and make me wonder what I should stick at.

CHAPTER XI

OF PROGNOSTICATIONS

For what concerns oracles, it is certain that a good while before the coming of Jesus Christ they had begun to lose their credit; for we see that Cicero troubled to find out the cause of their decay, and he has these words:

> *"Cur isto modo jam oracula Delphis non eduntur,*
> *non modo nostro aetate, sed jam diu; ut nihil*
> *possit esse contemptius?"*

> *["What is the reason that the oracles at Delphi are no longer uttered: not merely in this age of ours, but for a long time past, insomuch that nothing is more in contempt?"*
> *--Cicero, De Divin., ii. 57.]*

But as to the other prognostics, calculated from the anatomy of beasts at sacrifices (to which purpose Plato does, in part, attribute the natural constitution of the intestines of the beasts themselves), the scraping of poultry, the flight of birds--

> *"Aves quasdam . . . rerum augurandarum*
> *causa natas esse putamus."*

> *["We think some sorts of birds are purposely created to serve the purposes of augury."--Cicero, De Natura Deor., ii. 64.]*

claps of thunder, the overflowing of rivers--

> "Multa cernunt Aruspices, multa Augures provident,
> multa oraculis declarantur, multa vaticinationibus,
> multa somniis, multa portentis."

> ["The Aruspices discern many things, the Augurs foresee many things,
> many things are announced by oracles, many by vaticinations, many by
> dreams, many by portents."--Cicero, De Natura Deor., ii. 65.]

--and others of the like nature, upon which antiquity founded most of
their public and private enterprises, our religion has totally abolished
them. And although there yet remain amongst us some practices of
divination from the stars, from spirits, from the shapes and complexions
of men, from dreams and the like (a notable example of the wild curiosity
of our nature to grasp at and anticipate future things, as if we had not
enough to do to digest the present)--

> "Cur hanc tibi, rector Olympi,
> Sollicitis visum mortalibus addere curam,
> Noscant venturas ut dira per omina clades?...
> Sit subitum, quodcumque paras; sit coeca futuri
> Mens hominum fati, liceat sperare timenti."

> ["Why, ruler of Olympus, hast thou to anxious mortals thought fit to
> add this care, that they should know by, omens future slaughter?...
> Let whatever thou art preparing be sudden. Let the mind of men be
> blind to fate in store; let it be permitted to the timid to hope."
> --Lucan, ii. 14]

> "Ne utile quidem est scire quid futurum sit;
> miserum est enim, nihil proficientem angi,"

> ["It is useless to know what shall come to pass; it is a miserable
> thing to be tormented to no purpose."
> --Cicero, De Natura Deor., iii. 6.]

yet are they of much less authority now than heretofore. Which makes so much more remarkable the example of Francesco, Marquis of Saluzzo, who being lieutenant to King Francis I. in his ultramontane army, infinitely favoured and esteemed in our court, and obliged to the king's bounty for the marquisate itself, which had been forfeited by his brother; and as to the rest, having no manner of provocation given him to do it, and even his own affection opposing any such disloyalty, suffered himself to be so terrified, as it was confidently reported, with the fine prognostics that were spread abroad everywhere in favour of the Emperor Charles V., and to our disadvantage (especially in Italy, where these foolish prophecies were so far believed, that at Rome great sums of money were ventured out upon return of greater, when the prognostics came to pass, so certain they made themselves of our ruin), that, having often bewailed, to those of his acquaintance who were most intimate with him, the mischiefs that he saw would inevitably fall upon the Crown of France and the friends he had in that court, he revolted and turned to the other side; to his own misfortune, nevertheless, what constellation soever governed at that time. But he carried himself in this affair like a man agitated by divers passions; for having both towns and forces in his hands, the enemy's army under Antonio de Leyva close by him, and we not at all suspecting his design, it had been in his power to have done more than he did; for we lost no men by this infidelity of his, nor any town, but Fossano only, and that after a long siege and a brave defence.~~[1536]

> "Prudens futuri temporis exitum
> Caliginosa nocte premit Deus,
> Ridetque, si mortalis ultra
> Fas trepidat."

["A wise God covers with thick night the path of the future, and laughs at the man who alarms himself without reason." ~~Hor., Od., iii. 29.]

> "Ille potens sui
> Laetusque deget, cui licet in diem
> Dixisse vixi! cras vel atra
> Nube polum pater occupato,
> Vel sole puro."

["He lives happy and master of himself who can say as each day passes on, 'I HAVE LIVED:' whether to-morrow our Father shall give us a clouded sky or a clear day."--Hor., Od., iii. 29]

> "Laetus in praesens animus; quod ultra est,
> Oderit curare."

["A mind happy, cheerful in the present state, will take good care not to think of what is beyond it."--Ibid., ii. 25]

And those who take this sentence in a contrary sense interpret it amiss:

> "Ista sic reciprocantur, ut et si divinatio sit,
> dii sint; et si dii lint, sit divinatio."

["These things are so far reciprocal that if there be divination, there must be deities; and if deities, divination."--Cicero, De Divin., i. 6.]

Much more wisely Pacuvius--

> "Nam istis, qui linguam avium intelligunt,
> Plusque ex alieno jecore sapiunt, quam ex suo,
> Magis audiendum, quam auscultandum, censeo."

["As to those who understand the language of birds, and who rather consult the livers of animals other than their own, I had rather hear them than attend to them."
--Cicero, De Divin., i. 57, ex Pacuvio]

The so celebrated art of divination amongst the Tuscans took its beginning thus: A labourer striking deep with his cutter into the earth, saw the demigod Tages ascend, with an infantine aspect, but endued with a mature and senile wisdom. Upon the rumour of which, all the people ran to see the sight, by whom his words and science, containing the principles and means to attain to this art, were recorded, and kept for many ages.--[Cicero, De Devina, ii. 23]--A birth suitable to its progress; I, for my part, should sooner regulate my affairs by the chance of a die than by such idle and vain dreams. And, indeed, in all republics, a good share of the government has ever been referred to chance. Plato, in the civil regimen that he models according to his own fancy, leaves to it the decision of several things of very great importance, and will, amongst other things, that marriages should be appointed by lot; attributing so great importance to this accidental choice as to ordain that the children begotten in such wedlock be brought up in the country, and those begotten in any other be thrust out as spurious and base; yet so, that if any of those exiles, notwithstanding, should, peradventure, in growing up give any good hope of himself, he might be recalled, as, also, that such as had been retained, should be exiled, in case they gave little expectation of themselves in their early growth.

I see some who are mightily given to study and comment upon their almanacs, and produce them to us as an authority when anything has fallen out pat; and, for that matter, it is hardly possible but that these alleged authorities sometimes stumble upon a truth amongst an infinite number of lies.

> *"Quis est enim, qui totum diem jaculans*
> *non aliquando collineet?"*

["For who shoots all day at butts that does not sometimes hit the white?"--Cicero, De Divin., ii. 59.]

I think never the better of them for some such accidental hit. There would be more certainty in it if there were a rule and a truth of always lying. Besides, nobody records their flimflams and false prognostics, forasmuch as they are infinite and common; but if they chop upon one truth, that carries a mighty report, as being rare, incredible, and prodigious. So Diogenes, surnamed the Atheist, answered him in Samothrace, who, showing him in the temple the several offerings and stories in painting of those who had escaped shipwreck, said to him, "Look, you who think the gods have no care of human things, what do you say to so many persons preserved from death by their especial favour?" "Why, I say," answered he, "that their pictures are not here who were cast away, who are by much the greater number."--[Cicero, De Natura Deor., i. 37.]

Cicero observes that of all the philosophers who have acknowledged a deity, Xenophanes the Colophonian only has endeavoured to eradicate all manner of divination--[Cicero, De Divin., i. 3.]--; which makes it the less a wonder if we have now and then seen some of our princes, sometimes to their own cost, rely too much upon these vanities. I had given anything with my own eyes to see those two great marvels, the book of Joachim the Calabrian abbot, which foretold all the future Popes, their names and qualities; and that of the Emperor Leo, which prophesied all the emperors and patriarchs of Greece. This I have been an eyewitness of, that in public confusions, men astonished at their fortune, have abandoned their own reason, superstitiously to seek out in the stars the ancient causes and menaces of the present mishaps, and in my time have been so strangely successful in it, as to make me believe that this being an amusement of sharp and volatile wits, those who have been versed in this knack of unfolding and untying riddles, are capable, in any sort of writing, to find out what they desire. But above all, that which gives them the greatest room to play in, is the obscure, ambiguous, and fantastic gibberish of the prophetic canting, where their authors deliver nothing of clear sense, but shroud all in riddle, to the end that posterity may interpret and apply it according to its own fancy.

Socrates demon might, perhaps, be no other but a certain impulsion of the will, which obtruded itself upon him without the advice or consent of his judgment; and in a soul so enlightened as his was, and so prepared by a continual exercise of wisdom-and virtue, 'tis to be supposed those inclinations of his, though sudden and undigested, were very important and worthy to be followed. Every one finds in himself some image of such agitations, of a prompt, vehement, and fortuitous opinion; and I may well allow them some authority, who attribute so little to our prudence, and who also myself have had some, weak in reason, but violent in persuasion and dissuasion, which were most frequent with Socrates,--[Plato, in his account of Theages the Pythagorean]--by which I have suffered myself to be carried away so fortunately, and so much to my own advantage, that they might have been judged to have had something in them of a divine inspiration.

CHAPTER XII

OF CONSTANCY

The law of resolution and constancy does not imply that we ought not, as much as in us lies, to decline and secure ourselves from the mischiefs and inconveniences that threaten us; nor, consequently, that we shall not fear lest they should surprise us: on the contrary, all decent and honest ways and means of securing ourselves from harms, are not only permitted, but, moreover, commendable, and the business of constancy chiefly is, bravely to stand to, and stoutly to suffer those inconveniences which are not possibly to be avoided. So that there is no supple motion of body, nor any movement in the handling of arms, how irregular or ungraceful soever, that we need condemn, if they serve to protect us from the blow that is made against us.

Several very warlike nations have made use of a retreating and flying way of fight as a thing of singular advantage, and, by so doing, have made their backs more dangerous to their enemies than their faces. Of which kind of fighting the Turks still retain something in their practice of arms; and Socrates, in Plato, laughs at Laches, who had defined fortitude to be a standing firm in the ranks against the enemy. "What!" says he, "would it, then, be a reputed cowardice to overcome them by giving ground?" urging, at the same time, the authority of Homer, who commends in AEneas the science of flight. And whereas Laches, considering better of it, admits the practice as to the Scythians, and, in general, all cavalry whatever, he again attacks him with the example of the Lacedaemonian foot--a nation of all other the most obstinate in maintaining their ground--who, in the battle of Plataea, not being able to break into the Persian phalanx, bethought themselves to disperse and retire, that by the enemy supposing they fled, they might break and disunite that vast body of men in the pursuit, and by that stratagem obtained the victory.

As for the Scythians, 'tis said of them, that when Darius went his
expedition to subdue them, he sent, by a herald, highly to reproach their
king, that he always retired before him and declined a battle; to which
Idanthyrses,--[Herod., iv. 127.]--for that was his name, returned
answer, that it was not for fear of him, or of any man living, that he
did so, but that it was the way of marching in practice with his nation,
who had neither tilled fields, cities, nor houses to defend, or to fear
the enemy should make any advantage of but that if he had such a stomach
to fight, let him but come to view their ancient places of sepulture, and
there he should have his fill.

Nevertheless, as to cannon-shot, when a body of men are drawn up in the
face of a train of artillery, as the occasion of war often requires, it
is unhandsome to quit their post to avoid the danger, forasmuch as by
reason of its violence and swiftness we account it inevitable; and many a
one, by ducking, stepping aside, and such other motions of fear, has
been, at all events, sufficiently laughed at by his companions. And yet,
in the expedition that the Emperor Charles V. made against us into
Provence, the Marquis de Guast going to reconnoitre the city of Arles,
and advancing out of the cover of a windmill, under favour of which he
had made his approach, was perceived by the Seigneurs de Bonneval and the
Seneschal of Agenois, who were walking upon the 'theatre aux ayenes'; who
having shown him to the Sieur de Villiers, commissary of the artillery,
he pointed a culverin so admirably well, and levelled it so exactly right
against him, that had not the Marquis, seeing fire given to it, slipped
aside, it was certainly concluded the shot had taken him full in the
body. And, in like manner, some years before, Lorenzo de' Medici, Duke
of Urbino, and father to the queen-mother--[Catherine de' Medici, mother
of Henry III.]--laying siege to Mondolfo, a place in the territories of
the Vicariat in Italy, seeing the cannoneer give fire to a piece that
pointed directly against him, it was well for him that he ducked, for
otherwise the shot, that only razed the top of his head, had doubtless
hit him full in the breast. To say truth, I do not think that these
evasions are performed upon the account of judgment; for how can any man
living judge of high or low aim on so sudden an occasion? And it is much

more easy to believe that fortune favoured their apprehension, and that it might be as well at another time to make them face the danger, as to seek to avoid it. For my own part, I confess I cannot forbear starting when the rattle of a harquebuse thunders in my ears on a sudden, and in a place where I am not to expect it, which I have also observed in others, braver fellows than I.

Neither do the Stoics pretend that the soul of their philosopher need be proof against the first visions and fantasies that surprise him; but, as to a natural subjection, consent that he should tremble at the terrible noise of thunder, or the sudden clatter of some falling ruin, and be affrighted even to paleness and convulsion; and so in other passions, provided his judgment remain sound and entire, and that the seat of his reason suffer no concussion nor alteration, and that he yield no consent to his fright and discomposure. To him who is not a philosopher, a fright is the same thing in the first part of it, but quite another thing in the second; for the impression of passions does not remain superficially in him, but penetrates farther, even to the very seat of reason, infecting and corrupting it, so that he judges according to his fear, and conforms his behaviour to it. In this verse you may see the true state of the wise Stoic learnedly and plainly expressed:--

"Mens immota manet; lachrymae volvuntur inanes."

["Though tears flow, the mind remains unmoved."
--Virgil, AEneid, iv. 449]

The Peripatetic sage does not exempt himself totally from perturbations of mind, but he moderates them.

CHAPTER XIII

THE CEREMONY
OF THE INTERVIEW OF PRINCES

*There is no subject so frivolous that does not merit a place in this
rhapsody. According to our common rule of civility, it would be a
notable affront to an equal, and much more to a superior, to fail being
at home when he has given you notice he will come to visit you. Nay,
Queen Margaret of Navarre--[Marguerite de Valois, authoress of the
'Heptameron']--further adds, that it would be a rudeness in a gentleman
to go out, as we so often do, to meet any that is coming to see him, let
him be of what high condition soever; and that it is more respectful and
more civil to stay at home to receive him, if only upon the account of
missing him by the way, and that it is enough to receive him at the door,
and to wait upon him. For my part, who as much as I can endeavour to
reduce the ceremonies of my house, I very often forget both the one and
the other of these vain offices. If, peradventure, some one may take
offence at this, I can't help it; it is much better to offend him once
than myself every day, for it would be a perpetual slavery. To what end
do we avoid the servile attendance of courts, if we bring the same
trouble home to our own private houses? It is also a common rule in all
assemblies, that those of less quality are to be first upon the place, by
reason that it is more due to the better sort to make others wait and
expect them.*

*Nevertheless, at the interview betwixt Pope Clement and King Francis at
Marseilles,--[in 1533.]--the King, after he had taken order for the
necessary preparations for his reception and entertainment, withdrew out
of the town, and gave the Pope two or three days' respite for his entry,
and to repose and refresh himself, before he came to him. And in like
manner, at the assignation of the Pope and the Emperor,--[Charles V. in
1532.] at Bologna, the Emperor gave the Pope opportunity to come thither*

first, and came himself after; for which the reason given was this, that at all the interviews of such princes, the greater ought to be first at the appointed place, especially before the other in whose territories the interview is appointed to be, intimating thereby a kind of deference to the other, it appearing proper for the less to seek out and to apply themselves to the greater, and not the greater to them.

Not every country only, but every city and every society has its particular forms of civility. There was care enough to this taken in my education, and I have lived in good company enough to know the formalities of our own nation, and am able to give lessons in it. I love to follow them, but not to be so servilely tied to their observation that my whole life should be enslaved to ceremonies, of which there are some so troublesome that, provided a man omits them out of discretion, and not for want of breeding, it will be every whit as handsome. I have seen some people rude, by being overcivil and troublesome in their courtesy.

Still, these excesses excepted, the knowledge of courtesy and good manners is a very necessary study. It is, like grace and beauty, that which begets liking and an inclination to love one another at the first sight, and in the very beginning of acquaintance; and, consequently, that which first opens the door and intromits us to instruct ourselves by the example of others, and to give examples ourselves, if we have any worth taking notice of and communicating.

CHAPTER XIV

THAT MEN ARE JUSTLY PUNISHED
FOR BEING OBSTINATE IN THE DEFENCE
OF A FORT THAT IS NOT IN REASON
TO BE DEFENDED

*Valour has its bounds as well as other virtues, which, once transgressed,
the next step is into the territories of vice; so that by having too
large a proportion of this heroic virtue, unless a man be very perfect in
its limits, which upon the confines are very hard to discern, he may very
easily unawares run into temerity, obstinacy, and folly. From this
consideration it is that we have derived the custom, in times of war, to
punish, even with death, those who are obstinate to defend a place that
by the rules of war is not tenable; otherwise men would be so confident
upon the hope of impunity, that not a henroost but would resist and seek
to stop an army.*

*The Constable Monsieur de Montmorenci, having at the siege of Pavia been
ordered to pass the Ticino, and to take up his quarters in the Faubourg
St. Antonio, being hindered by a tower at the end of the bridge, which
was so obstinate as to endure a battery, hanged every man he found within
it for their labour. And again, accompanying the Dauphin in his
expedition beyond the Alps, and taking the Castle of Villano by assault,
and all within it being put to the sword by the fury of the soldiers, the
governor and his ensign only excepted, he caused them both to be trussed
up for the same reason; as also did the Captain Martin du Bellay, then
governor of Turin, with the governor of San Buono, in the same country,
all his people having been cut to pieces at the taking of the place.*

*But forasmuch as the strength or weakness of a fortress is always
measured by the estimate and counterpoise of the forces that attack it
--for a man might reasonably enough despise two culverins, that would be*

a madman to abide a battery of thirty pieces of cannon--where also the greatness of the prince who is master of the field, his reputation, and the respect that is due unto him, are also put into the balance, there is danger that the balance be pressed too much in that direction. And it may happen that a man is possessed with so great an opinion of himself and his power, that thinking it unreasonable any place should dare to shut its gates against him, he puts all to the sword where he meets with any opposition, whilst his fortune continues; as is plain in the fierce and arrogant forms of summoning towns and denouncing war, savouring so much of barbarian pride and insolence, in use amongst the Oriental princes, and which their successors to this day do yet retain and practise. And in that part of the world where the Portuguese subdued the Indians, they found some states where it was a universal and inviolable law amongst them that every enemy overcome by the king in person, or by his lieutenant, was out of composition.

So above all both of ransom and mercy a man should take heed, if he can, of falling into the hands of a judge who is an enemy and victorious.

CHAPTER XV

OF THE PUNISHMENT OF COWARDICE

*I once heard of a prince, and a great captain, having a narration given
him as he sat at table of the proceeding against Monsieur de Vervins, who
was sentenced to death for having surrendered Boulogne to the English,
--[To Henry VIII. in 1544]--openly maintaining that a soldier could not
justly be put to death for want of courage. And, in truth, 'tis reason
that a man should make a great difference betwixt faults that merely
proceed from infirmity, and those that are visibly the effects of
treachery and malice: for, in the last, we act against the rules of
reason that nature has imprinted in us; whereas, in the former, it seems
as if we might produce the same nature, who left us in such a state of
imperfection and weakness of courage, for our justification. Insomuch
that many have thought we are not fairly questionable for anything but
what we commit against our conscience; and it is partly upon this rule
that those ground their opinion who disapprove of capital or sanguinary
punishments inflicted upon heretics and misbelievers; and theirs also who
advocate or a judge is not accountable for having from mere ignorance
failed in his administration.*

*But as to cowardice, it is certain that the most usual way of chastising
it is by ignominy and and it is supposed that this practice brought into
use by the legislator Charondas; and that, before his time, the laws of
Greece punished those with death who fled from a battle; whereas he
ordained only that they be for three days exposed in the public dressed
in woman's attire, hoping yet for some service from them, having awakened
their courage by this open shame:*

> *"Suffundere malis homims sanguinem, quam effundere."*

["Rather bring the blood into a man's cheek than let it out of his body." Tertullian in his Apologetics.]

It appears also that the Roman laws did anciently punish those with death who had run away; for Ammianus Marcellinus says that the Emperor Julian commanded ten of his soldiers, who had turned their backs in an encounter against the Parthians, to be first degraded, and afterward put to death, according, says he, to the ancient laws,--[Ammianus Marcellinus, xxiv. 4; xxv. i.]--and yet elsewhere for the like offence he only condemned others to remain amongst the prisoners under the baggage ensign. The severe punishment the people of Rome inflicted upon those who fled from the battle of Cannae, and those who ran away with Aeneius Fulvius at his defeat, did not extend to death. And yet, methinks, 'tis to be feared, lest disgrace should make such delinquents desperate, and not only faint friends, but enemies.

Of late memory,--[In 1523]--the Seigneur de Frauget, lieutenant to the Mareschal de Chatillon's company, having by the Mareschal de Chabannes been put in government of Fuentarabia in the place of Monsieur de Lude, and having surrendered it to the Spaniard, he was for that condemned to be degraded from all nobility, and both himself and his posterity declared ignoble, taxable, and for ever incapable of bearing arms, which severe sentence was afterwards accordingly executed at Lyons.--[In 1536]--And, since that, all the gentlemen who were in Guise when the Count of Nassau entered into it, underwent the same punishment, as several others have done since for the like offence. Notwithstanding, in case of such a manifest ignorance or cowardice as exceeds all ordinary example, 'tis but reason to take it for a sufficient proof of treachery and malice, and for such to be punished.

CHAPTER XVI

A PROCEEDING OF SOME AMBASSADORS

I observe in my travels this custom, ever to learn something from the information of those with whom I confer (which is the best school of all others), and to put my company upon those subjects they are the best able to speak of:

> *"Basti al nocchiero ragionar de' venti,*
> *Al bifolco dei tori; et le sue piaghe*
> *Conti'l guerrier; conti'l pastor gli armenti."*

> *["Let the sailor content himself with talking of the winds; the cowherd of his oxen; the soldier of his wounds; the shepherd of his flocks."--An Italian translation of Propertius, ii. i, 43]*

For it often falls out that, on the contrary, every one will rather choose to be prating of another man's province than his own, thinking it so much new reputation acquired; witness the jeer Archidamus put upon Pertander, "that he had quitted the glory of being an excellent physician to gain the repute of a very bad poet.--[Plutarch, Apoth. of the Lacedaemonians, 'in voce' Archidamus.]--And do but observe how large and ample Caesar is to make us understand his inventions of building bridges and contriving engines of war,--[De Bello Gall., iv. 17.]--and how succinct and reserved in comparison, where he speaks of the offices of his profession, his own valour, and military conduct. His exploits sufficiently prove him a great captain, and that he knew well enough; but he would be thought an excellent engineer to boot; a quality something different, and not necessary to be expected in him. The elder Dionysius was a very great captain, as it befitted his fortune he should be; but he took very great pains to get a particular reputation by poetry, and yet he was never cut out for a poet. A man of the legal profession being not long since brought to see a study furnished with all sorts of books, both of his own and all other faculties, took no occasion at all to entertain himself with any of them, but fell very rudely and magisterially to descant upon a barricade placed on the winding stair before the study door, a thing that a hundred captains and common soldiers see every day without taking any notice or offence.

   "Optat ephippia bos piger, optat arare caballus."

   ["The lazy ox desires a saddle and bridle; the horse wants to plough."—Hor., Ep., i. 14,43.]

By this course a man shall never improve himself, nor arrive at any perfection in anything. He must, therefore, make it his business always to put the architect, the painter, the statuary, every mechanic artisan, upon discourse of their own capacities.

And, to this purpose, in reading histories, which is everybody's subject, I use to consider what kind of men are the authors: if they be persons that profess nothing but mere letters, I, in and from them, principally observe and learn style and language; if physicians, I the rather incline to credit what they report of the temperature of the air, of the health and complexions of princes, of wounds and diseases; if lawyers, we are from them to take notice of the controversies of rights and wrongs, the establishment of laws and civil government, and the like; if divines, the affairs of the Church, ecclesiastical censures, marriages, and dispensations; if courtiers, manners and ceremonies; if soldiers, the things that properly belong to their trade, and, principally, the accounts of the actions and enterprises wherein they were personally engaged; if ambassadors, we are to observe negotiations, intelligences, and practices, and the manner how they are to be carried on.

And this is the reason why (which perhaps I should have lightly passed over in another) I dwelt upon and maturely considered one passage in the history written by Monsieur de Langey, a man of very great judgment in things of that nature: after having given a narrative of the fine oration

Charles V. had made in the Consistory at Rome, and in the presence of the Bishop of Macon and Monsieur du Velly, our ambassadors there, wherein he had mixed several injurious expressions to the dishonour of our nation; and amongst the rest, "that if his captains and soldiers were not men of another kind of fidelity, resolution, and sufficiency in the knowledge of arms than those of the King, he would immediately go with a rope about his neck and sue to him for mercy" (and it should seem the Emperor had really this, or a very little better opinion of our military men, for he afterwards, twice or thrice in his life, said the very same thing); as also, that he challenged the King to fight him in his shirt with rapier and poignard in a boat. The said Sieur de Langey, pursuing his history, adds that the forenamed ambassadors, sending a despatch to the King of these things, concealed the greatest part, and particularly the last two passages. At which I could not but wonder that it should be in the power of an ambassador to dispense with anything which he ought to signify to his master, especially of so great importance as this, coming from the mouth of such a person, and spoken in so great an assembly; and I should rather conceive it had been the servant's duty faithfully to have represented to him the whole thing as it passed, to the end that the liberty of selecting, disposing, judging, and concluding might have remained in him: for either to conceal or to disguise the truth for fear he should take it otherwise than he ought to do, and lest it should prompt him to some extravagant resolution, and, in the meantime, to leave him ignorant of his affairs, should seem, methinks, rather to belong to him who is to give the law than to him who is only to receive it; to him who is in supreme command, and not to him who ought to look upon himself as inferior, not only in authority, but also in prudence and good counsel. I, for my part, would not be so served in my little concerns.

We so willingly slip the collar of command upon any pretence whatever, and are so ready to usurp upon dominion, every one does so naturally aspire to liberty and power, that no utility whatever derived from the wit or valour of those he employs ought to be so dear to a superior as a downright and sincere obedience. To obey more upon the account of understanding than of subjection, is to corrupt the office of command ⁓[Taken from Aulus Gellius, i. 13.]⁓; insomuch that P. Crassus, the same

*whom the Romans reputed five times happy, at the time when he was consul
in Asia, having sent to a Greek engineer to cause the greater of two
masts of ships that he had taken notice of at Athens to be brought to
him, to be employed about some engine of battery he had a design to make;
the other, presuming upon his own science and sufficiency in those
affairs, thought fit to do otherwise than directed, and to bring the
less, which, according to the rules of art, was really more proper for
the use to which it was designed; but Crassus, though he gave ear to his
reasons with great patience, would not, however, take them, how sound or
convincing soever, for current pay, but caused him to be well whipped for
his pains, valuing the interest of discipline much more than that of the
work in hand.*

*Notwithstanding, we may on the other side consider that so precise and
implicit an obedience as this is only due to positive and limited
commands. The employment of ambassadors is never so confined, many
things in their management of affairs being wholly referred to the
absolute sovereignty of their own conduct; they do not simply execute,
but also, to their own discretion and wisdom, form and model their
master's pleasure. I have, in my time, known men of command checked for
having rather obeyed the express words of the king's letters, than the
necessity of the affairs they had in hand. Men of understanding do yet,
to this day, condemn the custom of the kings of Persia to give their
lieutenants and agents so little rein, that, upon the least arising
difficulties, they must fain have recourse to their further commands;
this delay, in so vast an extent of dominion, having often very much
prejudiced their affairs; and Crassus, writing to a man whose profession
it was best to understand those things, and pre-acquainting him to what
use this mast was designed, did he not seem to consult his advice, and in
a manner invite him to interpose his better judgment?*

CHAPTER XVII

OF FEAR

"Obstupui, steteruntque comae et vox faucibus haesit."

*["I was amazed, my hair stood on end, and my voice stuck in my
throat." Virgil, AEneid, ii. 774.]*

I am not so good a naturalist (as they call it) as to discern by what
secret springs fear has its motion in us; but, be this as it may, 'tis a
strange passion, and such a one that the physicians say there is no other
whatever that sooner dethrones our judgment from its proper seat; which
is so true, that I myself have seen very many become frantic through
fear; and, even in those of the best settled temper it is most certain
that it begets a terrible astonishment and confusion during the fit.
I omit the vulgar sort, to whom it one while represents their
great-grandsires risen out of their graves in their shrouds, another while
werewolves, nightmares, and chimaeras; but even amongst soldiers, a sort
of men over whom, of all others, it ought to have the least power, how
often has it converted flocks of sheep into armed squadrons, reeds and
bullrushes into pikes and lances, friends into enemies, and the French
white cross into the red cross of Spain! When Monsieur de Bourbon took
Rome,--[In 1527]--an ensign who was upon guard at Borgo San Pietro was
seized with such a fright upon the first alarm, that he threw himself out
at a breach with his colours upon his shoulder, and ran directly upon the
enemy, thinking he had retreated toward the inward defences of the city,
and with much ado, seeing Monsieur de Bourbon's people, who thought it
had been a sally upon them, draw up to receive him, at last came to
himself, and saw his error; and then facing about, he retreated full
speed through the same breach by which he had gone out, but not till he
had first blindly advanced above three hundred paces into the open field.
It did not, however, fall out so well with Captain Giulio's ensign, at

the time when St. Paul was taken from us by the Comte de Bures and
Monsieur de Reu, for he, being so astonished with fear as to throw
himself, colours and all, out of a porthole, was immediately, cut to
pieces by the enemy; and in the same siege, it was a very memorable fear
that so seized, contracted, and froze up the heart of a gentleman, that
he sank down, stone-dead, in the breach, without any manner of wound or
hurt at all. The like madness does sometimes push on a whole multitude;
for in one of the encounters that Germanicus had with the Germans, two
great parties were so amazed with fear that they ran two opposite ways,
the one to the same place from which the other had fled.--[Tacit, Annal.,
i. 63.]--Sometimes it adds wings to the heels, as in the two first:
sometimes it nails them to the ground, and fetters them from moving; as
we read of the Emperor Theophilus, who, in a battle he lost against the
Agarenes, was so astonished and stupefied that he had no power to fly--

"Adeo pavor etiam auxilia formidat"

["So much does fear dread even the means of safety."--Quint.
Curt., ii. II.]

--till such time as Manuel, one of the principal commanders of his army,
having jogged and shaked him so as to rouse him out of his trance, said
to him, "Sir, if you will not follow me, I will kill you; for it is
better you should lose your life than, by being taken, lose your empire."
--[Zonaras, lib. iii.]--But fear does then manifest its utmost power
when it throws us upon a valiant despair, having before deprived us of
all sense both of duty and honour. In the first pitched battle the
Romans lost against Hannibal, under the Consul Sempronius, a body of ten
thousand foot, that had taken fright, seeing no other escape for their
cowardice, went and threw themselves headlong upon the great battalion of
the enemies, which with marvellous force and fury they charged through
and through, and routed with a very great slaughter of the Carthaginians,
thus purchasing an ignominious flight at the same price they might have
gained a glorious victory.--[Livy, xxi. 56.]

The thing in the world I am most afraid of is fear, that passion alone,
in the trouble of it, exceeding all other accidents. What affliction
could be greater or more just than that of Pompey's friends, who, in his
ship, were spectators of that horrible murder? Yet so it was, that the
fear of the Egyptian vessels they saw coming to board them, possessed
them with so great alarm that it is observed they thought of nothing but
calling upon the mariners to make haste, and by force of oars to escape
away, till being arrived at Tyre, and delivered from fear, they had
leisure to turn their thoughts to the loss of their captain, and to give
vent to those tears and lamentations that the other more potent passion
had till then suspended.

> "Tum pavor sapientiam omnem mihiex animo expectorat."

> ["Then fear drove out all intelligence from my mind."--Ennius, ap.
> Cicero, Tusc., iv. 8.]

Such as have been well rubbed in some skirmish, may yet, all wounded and
bloody as they are, be brought on again the next day to charge; but such
as have once conceived a good sound fear of the enemy, will never be made
so much as to look him in the face. Such as are in immediate fear of a
losing their estates, of banishment, or of slavery, live in perpetual
anguish, and lose all appetite and repose; whereas such as are actually
poor, slaves, or exiles, ofttimes live as merrily as other folk. And the
many people who, impatient of the perpetual alarms of fear, have hanged
or drowned themselves, or dashed themselves to pieces, give us
sufficiently to understand that fear is more importunate and
insupportable than death itself.

The Greeks acknowledged another kind of fear, differing from any we have
spoken of yet, that surprises us without any visible cause, by an impulse
from heaven, so that whole nations and whole armies have been struck with
it. Such a one was that which brought so wonderful a desolation upon
Carthage, where nothing was to be heard but affrighted voices and
outcries; where the inhabitants were seen to sally out of their houses as
to an alarm, and there to charge, wound, and kill one another, as if they

had been enemies come to surprise their city. All things were in disorder and fury till, with prayers and sacrifices, they had appeased their gods--[Diod. Sic., xv. 7]; and this is that they call panic terrors.--[Ibid. ; Plutarch on Isis and Osiris, c. 8.]

CHAPTER XVIII

THAT MEN ARE NOT TO JUDGE
OF OUR HAPPINESS TILL AFTER DEATH

[Charron has borrowed with unusual liberality from this and the succeeding chapter. See Nodier, Questions, p. 206.]

> *"Scilicet ultima semper*
> *Exspectanda dies homini est; dicique beatus*
> *Ante obitum nemo supremaque funera debet."*

["We should all look forward to our last day: no one can be called happy till he is dead and buried."--Ovid, Met, iii. 135]

The very children know the story of King Croesus to this purpose, who being taken prisoner by Cyrus, and by him condemned to die, as he was going to execution cried out, "O Solon, Solon!" which being presently reported to Cyrus, and he sending to inquire of him what it meant, Croesus gave him to understand that he now found the teaching Solon had formerly given him true to his cost; which was, "That men, however fortune may smile upon them, could never be said to be happy till they had been seen to pass over the last day of their lives," by reason of the uncertainty and mutability of human things, which, upon very light and trivial occasions, are subject to be totally changed into a quite contrary condition. And so it was that Agesilaus made answer to one who was saying what a happy young man the King of Persia was, to come so young to so mighty a kingdom: "'Tis true," said he, "but neither was Priam unhappy at his years."--[Plutarch, Apothegms of the Lacedaemonians.]--In a short time, kings of Macedon, successors to that mighty Alexander, became joiners and scriveners at Rome; a tyrant of Sicily, a pedant at Corinth; a conqueror of one-half of the world and general of so many armies, a miserable suppliant to the rascally officers of a king of Egypt: so much did the prolongation of five or six months of life cost the great Pompey; and, in our fathers' days, Ludovico Sforza, the tenth Duke of Milan, whom all Italy had so long truckled under, was seen to die a wretched prisoner at Loches, but not till he had lived ten years in captivity,--[He was imprisoned by Louis XI. in an iron cage]-- which was the worst part of his fortune. The fairest of all queens, --[Mary, Queen of Scots.]--widow to the greatest king in Europe, did she not come to die by the hand of an executioner? Unworthy and barbarous cruelty! And a thousand more examples there are of the same kind; for it seems that as storms and tempests have a malice against the proud and overtowering heights of our lofty buildings, there are also spirits above that are envious of the greatnesses here below:

> "Usque adeo res humanas vis abdita quaedam
> Obterit, et pulchros fasces, saevasque secures
> Proculcare, ac ludibrio sibi habere videtur."

["So true it is that some occult power upsets human affairs, the glittering fasces and the cruel axes spurns under foot, and seems to make sport of them."--Lucretius, v. 1231.]

And it should seem, also, that Fortune sometimes lies in wait to surprise the last hour of our lives, to show the power she has, in a moment, to overthrow what she was so many years in building, making us cry out with Laberius:

> "Nimirum hac die
> Una plus vixi mihi, quam vivendum fuit."

["I have lived longer by this one day than I should have done."--Macrobius, ii. 7.]

And, in this sense, this good advice of Solon may reasonably be taken; but he, being a philosopher (with which sort of men the favours and disgraces of Fortune stand for nothing, either to the making a man happy or unhappy, and with whom grandeurs and powers are accidents of a quality

*almost indifferent) I am apt to think that he had some further aim, and
that his meaning was, that the very felicity of life itself, which
depends upon the tranquillity and contentment of a well-descended spirit,
and the resolution and assurance of a well-ordered soul, ought never to
be attributed to any man till he has first been seen to play the last,
and, doubtless, the hardest act of his part. There may be disguise and
dissimulation in all the rest: where these fine philosophical discourses
are only put on, and where accident, not touching us to the quick, gives
us leisure to maintain the same gravity of aspect; but, in this last
scene of death, there is no more counterfeiting: we must speak out plain,
and discover what there is of good and clean in the bottom of the pot,*

> *"Nam vera; voces turn demum pectore ab imo
> Ejiciuntur; et eripitur persona, manet res."*

> *["Then at last truth issues from the heart; the visor's gone,
> the man remains."--Lucretius, iii. 57.]*

*Wherefore, at this last, all the other actions of our life ought to be
tried and sifted: 'tis the master-day, 'tis the day that is judge of all
the rest, "'tis the day," says one of the ancients,--[Seneca, Ep., 102]--
"that must be judge of all my foregoing years." To death do I refer the
assay of the fruit of all my studies: we shall then see whether my
discourses came only from my mouth or from my heart. I have seen many by
their death give a good or an ill repute to their whole life. Scipio,
the father-in-law of Pompey, in dying, well removed the ill opinion that
till then every one had conceived of him. Epaminondas being asked which
of the three he had in greatest esteem, Chabrias, Iphicrates, or himself.
"You must first see us die," said he, "before that question can be
resolved."--[Plutarch, Apoth.]--And, in truth, he would infinitely
wrong that man who would weigh him without the honour and grandeur of his
end.*

*God has ordered all things as it has best pleased Him; but I have, in my
time, seen three of the most execrable persons that ever I knew in all
manner of abominable living, and the most infamous to boot, who all died*

a very regular death, and in all circumstances composed, even to perfection. There are brave and fortunate deaths: I have seen death cut the thread of the progress of a prodigious advancement, and in the height and flower of its increase, of a certain person,--[Montaigne doubtless refers to his friend Etienne de la Boetie, at whose death in 1563 he was present.]--with so glorious an end that, in my opinion, his ambitious and generous designs had nothing in them so high and great as their interruption. He arrived, without completing his course, at the place to which his ambition aimed, with greater glory than he could either have hoped or desired, anticipating by his fall the name and power to which he aspired in perfecting his career. In the judgment I make of another man's life, I always observe how he carried himself at his death; and the principal concern I have for my own is that I may die well--that is, patiently and tranquilly.

CHAPTER XIX

THAT TO STUDY PHILOSOPHY
IS TO LEARN TO DIE

Cicero says--[Tusc., i. 31.]--"that to study philosophy is nothing but to prepare one's self to die." The reason of which is, because study and contemplation do in some sort withdraw from us our soul, and employ it separately from the body, which is a kind of apprenticeship and a resemblance of death; or, else, because all the wisdom and reasoning in the world do in the end conclude in this point, to teach us not to fear to die. And to say the truth, either our reason mocks us, or it ought to have no other aim but our contentment only, nor to endeavour anything but, in sum, to make us live well, and, as the Holy Scripture says, at our ease. All the opinions of the world agree in this, that pleasure is our end, though we make use of divers means to attain it: they would, otherwise, be rejected at the first motion; for who would give ear to him that should propose affliction and misery for his end? The controversies and disputes of the philosophical sects upon this point are merely verbal:

> *"Transcurramus solertissimas nugas"*

> *["Let us skip over those subtle trifles."--Seneca, Ep., 117.]*

--there is more in them of opposition and obstinacy than is consistent with so sacred a profession; but whatsoever personage a man takes upon himself to perform, he ever mixes his own part with it.

Let the philosophers say what they will, the thing at which we all aim, even in virtue is pleasure. It amuses me to rattle in ears this word, which they so nauseate to and if it signify some supreme pleasure and contentment, it is more due to the assistance of virtue than to any other assistance whatever. This pleasure, for being more gay, more sinewy, more robust and more manly, is only the more seriously voluptuous, and we ought give it the name of pleasure, as that which is more favourable, gentle, and natural, and not that from which we have denominated it. The other and meaner pleasure, if it could deserve this fair name, it ought to be by way of competition, and not of privilege. I find it less exempt from traverses and inconveniences than virtue itself; and, besides that the enjoyment is more momentary, fluid, and frail, it has its watchings, fasts, and labours, its sweat and its blood; and, moreover, has particular to itself so many several sorts of sharp and wounding passions, and so dull a satiety attending it, as equal it to the severest penance. And we mistake if we think that these incommodities serve it for a spur and a seasoning to its sweetness (as in nature one contrary is quickened by another), or say, when we come to virtue, that like consequences and difficulties overwhelm and render it austere and inaccessible; whereas, much more aptly than in voluptuousness, they ennoble, sharpen, and heighten the perfect and divine pleasure they procure us. He renders himself unworthy of it who will counterpoise its cost with its fruit, and neither understands the blessing nor how to use it. Those who preach to us that the quest of it is craggy, difficult, and painful, but its fruition pleasant, what do they mean by that but to tell us that it is always unpleasing? For what human means will ever attain its enjoyment? The most perfect have been fain to content themselves to aspire unto it, and to approach it only, without ever possessing it. But they are deceived, seeing that of all the pleasures we know, the very pursuit is pleasant. The attempt ever relishes of the quality of the thing to which it is directed, for it is a good part of, and consubstantial with, the effect. The felicity and beatitude that glitters in Virtue, shines throughout all her appurtenances and avenues, even to the first entry and utmost limits.

Now, of all the benefits that virtue confers upon us, the contempt of death is one of the greatest, as the means that accommodates human life with a soft and easy tranquillity, and gives us a pure and pleasant taste of living, without which all other pleasure would be extinct. Which is the reason why all the rules centre and concur in this one article. And *although they all in like manner, with common accord, teach us also to despise pain, poverty, and the other accidents to which human life is subject, it is not, nevertheless, with the same solicitude, as well by reason these accidents are not of so great necessity, the greater part of mankind passing over their whole lives without ever knowing what poverty is, and some without sorrow or sickness, as Xenophilus the musician, who lived a hundred and six years in a perfect and continual health; as also because, at the worst, death can, whenever we please, cut short and put an end to all other inconveniences. But as to death, it is inevitable:--*

> *"Omnes eodem cogimur; omnium*
> *Versatur urna serius ocius*
> *Sors exitura, et nos in aeternum*
> *Exilium impositura cymbae."*

> *["We are all bound one voyage; the lot of all, sooner or later, is to come out of the urn. All must to eternal exile sail away."*
> *--Hor., Od., ii. 3, 25.]*

and, consequently, if it frights us, 'tis a perpetual torment, for which there is no sort of consolation. There is no way by which it may not reach us. We may continually turn our heads this way and that, as in a suspected country:

> *"Quae, quasi saxum Tantalo, semper impendet."*

> *["Ever, like Tantalus stone, hangs over us."*
> *--Cicero, De Finib., i. 18.]*

Our courts of justice often send back condemned criminals to be executed upon the place where the crime was committed; but, carry them to fine houses by the way, prepare for them the best entertainment you can··

> "Non Siculae dapes
> Dulcem elaborabunt saporem:
> Non avium cyatheaceae cantus
> Somnum reducent."

[*"Sicilian dainties will not tickle their palates, nor the melody of birds and harps bring back sleep."--Hor., Od., iii. 1, 18.*]

Do you think they can relish it? and that the fatal end of their journey being continually before their eyes, would not alter and deprave their palate from tasting these regalios?

> "Audit iter, numeratque dies, spatioque viarum
> Metitur vitam; torquetur peste futura."

[*"He considers the route, computes the time of travelling, measuring his life by the length of the journey; and torments himself by thinking of the blow to come."--Claudianus, in Ruf., ii. 137.*]

The end of our race is death; 'tis the necessary object of our aim, which, if it fright us, how is it possible to advance a step without a fit of ague? The remedy the vulgar use is not to think on't; but from what brutish stupidity can they derive so gross a blindness? They must bridle the ass by the tail:

> "Qui capite ipse suo instituit vestigia retro,"

[*"Who in his folly seeks to advance backwards"--Lucretius, iv. 474*]

'tis no wonder if he be often trapped in the pitfall. They affright people with the very mention of death, and many cross themselves, as it were the name of the devil. And because the making a man's will is in reference to dying, not a man will be persuaded to take a pen in hand to that purpose, till the physician has passed sentence upon and totally given him over, and then betwixt and terror, God knows in how fit a condition of understanding he is to do it.

The Romans, by reason that this poor syllable death sounded so harshly to their ears and seemed so ominous, found out a way to soften and spin it out by a periphrasis, and instead of pronouncing such a one is dead, said, "Such a one has lived," or "Such a one has ceased to live" --[Plutarch, Life of Cicero, c. 22:]--for, provided there was any mention of life in the case, though past, it carried yet some sound of consolation. And from them it is that we have borrowed our expression, "The late Monsieur such and such a one."--["feu Monsieur un tel."] Peradventure, as the saying is, the term we have lived is worth our money. I was born betwixt eleven and twelve o'clock in the forenoon the last day of February 1533, according to our computation, beginning the year the 1st of January,--[This was in virtue of an ordinance of Charles IX. in 1563. Previously the year commenced at Easter, so that the 1st January 1563 became the first day of the year 1563.]--and it is now but just fifteen days since I was complete nine-and-thirty years old; I make account to live, at least, as many more. In the meantime, to trouble a man's self with the thought of a thing so far off were folly. But what? Young and old die upon the same terms; no one departs out of life otherwise than if he had but just before entered into it; neither is any man so old and decrepit, who, having heard of Methuselah, does not think he has yet twenty good years to come. Fool that thou art! who has assured unto thee the term of life? Thou dependest upon physicians' tales: rather consult effects and experience. According to the common course of things, 'tis long since that thou hast lived by extraordinary favour; thou hast already outlived the ordinary term of life. And that it is so, reckon up thy acquaintance, how many more have died before they arrived at thy age than have attained unto it; and of those who have ennobled their lives by their renown, take but an account, and I dare lay a wager thou wilt find more who have died before than after five-and-thirty years of age. It is full both of reason and piety, too, to take example by the humanity of Jesus Christ Himself; now, He ended His life at three-and-thirty years. The greatest man, that was no more than a man, Alexander, died also at the same age. How many several ways has death to surprise us?

> "Quid quisque, vitet, nunquam homini satis
> Cautum est in horas."

["Be as cautious as he may, man can never foresee the danger that
may at any hour befal him."--Hor. O. ii. 13, 13.]

To omit fevers and pleurisies, who would ever have imagined that a duke
of Brittany,--[Jean II. died 1305.]--should be pressed to death in a
crowd as that duke was at the entry of Pope Clement, my neighbour, into
Lyons?--[Montaigne speaks of him as if he had been a contemporary
neighbour, perhaps because he was the Archbishop of Bordeaux. Bertrand
le Got was Pope under the title of Clement V., 1305-14.]--Hast thou not
seen one of our kings--[Henry II., killed in a tournament, July 10,
1559]--killed at a tilting, and did not one of his ancestors die by
jostle of a hog?--[Philip, eldest son of Louis le Gros.]--AEschylus,
threatened with the fall of a house, was to much purpose circumspect to
avoid that danger, seeing that he was knocked on the head by a tortoise
falling out of an eagle's talons in the air. Another was choked with a
grape-stone;--[Val. Max., ix. 12, ext. 2.]--an emperor killed with
the scratch of a comb in combing his head. AEmilius Lepidus with a
stumble at his own threshold,--[Pliny, Nat. Hist., vii. 33.]--
and Aufidius with a jostle against the door as he entered the
council-chamber. And betwixt the very thighs of women, Cornelius Gallus
the proctor; Tigillinus, captain of the watch at Rome; Ludovico, son of
Guido di Gonzaga, Marquis of Mantua; and (of worse example) Speusippus, a
Platonic philosopher, and one of our Popes. The poor judge Bebius gave
adjournment in a case for eight days; but he himself, meanwhile, was
condemned by death, and his own stay of life expired. Whilst Caius
Julius, the physician, was anointing the eyes of a patient, death closed
his own; and, if I may bring in an example of my own blood, a brother of
mine, Captain St. Martin, a young man, three-and-twenty years old, who
had already given sufficient testimony of his valour, playing a match at
tennis, received a blow of a ball a little above his right ear, which, as
it gave no manner of sign of wound or contusion, he took no notice of it,
nor so much as sat down to repose himself, but, nevertheless, died within
five or six hours after of an apoplexy occasioned by that blow.

These so frequent and common examples passing every day before our eyes, how is it possible a man should disengage himself from the thought of death, or avoid fancying that it has us every moment by the throat? What matter is it, you will say, which way it comes to pass, provided a man does not terrify himself with the expectation? For my part, I am of this mind, and if a man could by any means avoid it, though by creeping under a calf's skin, I am one that should not be ashamed of the shift; all I aim at is, to pass my time at my ease, and the recreations that will most contribute to it, I take hold of, as little glorious and exemplary as you will:

> "Praetulerim . . . delirus inersque videri,
> Dum mea delectent mala me, vel denique fallant,
> Quam sapere, et ringi."

> ["I had rather seem mad and a sluggard, so that my defects are
> agreeable to myself, or that I am not painfully conscious of them,
> than be wise, and chaptious."--Hor., Ep., ii. 2, 126.]

But 'tis folly to think of doing anything that way. They go, they come, they gallop and dance, and not a word of death. All this is very fine; but withal, when it comes either to themselves, their wives, their children, or friends, surprising them at unawares and unprepared, then, what torment, what outcries, what madness and despair! Did you ever see anything so subdued, so changed, and so confounded? A man must, therefore, make more early provision for it; and this brutish negligence, could it possibly lodge in the brain of any man of sense (which I think utterly impossible), sells us its merchandise too dear. Were it an enemy that could be avoided, I would then advise to borrow arms even of cowardice itself; but seeing it is not, and that it will catch you as well flying and playing the poltroon, as standing to't like an honest man:--

> "*Nempe et fugacem persequitur virum,*
> *Nec parcit imbellis juventae*
> *Poplitibus timidoque tergo.*"

[*"He pursues the flying poltroon, nor spares the hamstrings of the unwarlike youth who turns his back"*--Hor., Ep., iii. 2, 14.]

And seeing that no temper of arms is of proof to secure us:--

> "*Ille licet ferro cautus, se condat et aere,*
> *Mors tamen inclusum protrahet inde caput*"

[*"Let him hide beneath iron or brass in his fear, death will pull his head out of his armour."*--Propertious iii. 18]

--*let us learn bravely to stand our ground, and fight him. And to begin to deprive him of the greatest advantage he has over us, let us take a way quite contrary to the common course. Let us disarm him of his novelty and strangeness, let us converse and be familiar with him, and have nothing so frequent in our thoughts as death. Upon all occasions represent him to our imagination in his every shape; at the stumbling of a horse, at the falling of a tile, at the least prick with a pin, let us presently consider, and say to ourselves, "Well, and what if it had been death itself?" and, thereupon, let us encourage and fortify ourselves. Let us evermore, amidst our jollity and feasting, set the remembrance of our frail condition before our eyes, never suffering ourselves to be so far transported with our delights, but that we have some intervals of reflecting upon, and considering how many several ways this jollity of ours tends to death, and with how many dangers it threatens it. The Egyptians were wont to do after this manner, who in the height of their feasting and mirth, caused a dried skeleton of a man to be brought into the room to serve for a memento to their guests:*

> "*Omnem crede diem tibi diluxisse supremum*
> *Grata superveniet, quae non sperabitur, hora.*"

["Think each day when past is thy last; the next day, as unexpected,
will be the more welcome."--Hor., Ep., i. 4, 13.]

Where death waits for us is uncertain; let us look for him everywhere.
The premeditation of death is the premeditation of liberty; he who has
learned to die has unlearned to serve. There is nothing evil in life for
him who rightly comprehends that the privation of life is no evil: to
know, how to die delivers us from all subjection and constraint. Paulus
Emilius answered him whom the miserable King of Macedon, his prisoner,
sent to entreat him that he would not lead him in his triumph, "Let him
make that request to himself."--[Plutarch, Life of Paulus Aemilius,
c. 17; Cicero, Tusc., v. 40.]

In truth, in all things, if nature do not help a little, it is very hard
for art and industry to perform anything to purpose. I am in my own
nature not melancholic, but meditative; and there is nothing I have more
continually entertained myself withal than imaginations of death, even in
the most wanton time of my age:

> *"Jucundum quum aetas florida ver ageret."*

> *["When my florid age rejoiced in pleasant spring."*
> *--Catullus, lxviii.]*

In the company of ladies, and at games, some have perhaps thought me
possessed with some jealousy, or the uncertainty of some hope, whilst I
was entertaining myself with the remembrance of some one, surprised, a
few days before, with a burning fever of which he died, returning from an
entertainment like this, with his head full of idle fancies of love and
jollity, as mine was then, and that, for aught I knew, the same-destiny
was attending me.

> *"Jam fuerit, nec post unquam revocare licebit."*

> *["Presently the present will have gone, never to be recalled."*
> *Lucretius, iii. 928.]*

*Yet did not this thought wrinkle my forehead any more than any other.
It is impossible but we must feel a sting in such imaginations as these,
at first; but with often turning and returning them in one's mind, they,
at last, become so familiar as to be no trouble at all: otherwise, I, for
my part, should be in a perpetual fright and frenzy; for never man was so
distrustful of his life, never man so uncertain as to its duration.
Neither health, which I have hitherto ever enjoyed very strong and
vigorous, and very seldom interrupted, does prolong, nor sickness
contract my hopes. Every minute, methinks, I am escaping, and it
eternally runs in my mind, that what may be done to-morrow, may be done
to-day. Hazards and dangers do, in truth, little or nothing hasten our
end; and if we consider how many thousands more remain and hang over our
heads, besides the accident that immediately threatens us, we shall find
that the sound and the sick, those that are abroad at sea, and those that
sit by the fire, those who are engaged in battle, and those who sit idle
at home, are the one as near it as the other.*

"Nemo altero fragilior est; nemo in crastinum sui certior."

*["No man is more fragile than another: no man more certain than
another of to-morrow."--Seneca, Ep., 91.]*

*For anything I have to do before I die, the longest leisure would appear
too short, were it but an hour's business I had to do.*

*A friend of mine the other day turning over my tablets, found therein a
memorandum of something I would have done after my decease, whereupon I
told him, as it was really true, that though I was no more than a
league's distance only from my own house, and merry and well, yet when
that thing came into my head, I made haste to write it down there,
because I was not certain to live till I came home. As a man that am
eternally brooding over my own thoughts, and confine them to my own
particular concerns, I am at all hours as well prepared as I am ever like
to be, and death, whenever he shall come, can bring nothing along with
him I did not expect long before. We should always, as near as we can,*

be booted and spurred, and ready to go, and, above all things, take care, at that time, to have no business with any one but one's self:

> *"Quid brevi fortes jaculamur avo*
> *Multa?"*

> *["Why for so short a life tease ourselves with so many projects?"*
> *--Hor., Od., ii. 16, 17.]*

for we shall there find work enough to do, without any need of addition. One man complains, more than of death, that he is thereby prevented of a glorious victory; another, that he must die before he has married his daughter, or educated his children; a third seems only troubled that he must lose the society of his wife; a fourth, the conversation of his son, as the principal comfort and concern of his being. For my part, I am, thanks be to God, at this instant in such a condition, that I am ready to dislodge, whenever it shall please Him, without regret for anything whatsoever. I disengage myself throughout from all worldly relations; my leave is soon taken of all but myself. Never did any one prepare to bid adieu to the world more absolutely and unreservedly, and to shake hands with all manner of interest in it, than I expect to do. The deadest deaths are the best:

> *"'Miser, O miser,' aiunt, 'omnia ademit*
> *Una dies infesta mihi tot praemia vitae.'"*

> *["'Wretch that I am,' they cry, 'one fatal day has deprived me of*
> *all joys of life.'"--Lucretius, iii. 911.]*

And the builder,

> *"Manuet," says he, "opera interrupta, minaeque*
> *Murorum ingentes."*

[*"The works remain incomplete, the tall pinnacles of the walls unmade."*--*AEneid, iv. 88.*]

A man must design nothing that will require so much time to the finishing, or, at least, with no such passionate desire to see it brought to perfection. We are born to action:

"Quum moriar, medium solvar et inter opus."

[*"When I shall die, let it be doing that I had designed."* --*Ovid, Amor., ii. 10, 36.*]

I would always have a man to be doing, and, as much as in him lies, to extend and spin out the offices of life; and then let death take me planting my cabbages, indifferent to him, and still less of my gardens not being finished. I saw one die, who, at his last gasp, complained of nothing so much as that destiny was about to cut the thread of a chronicle he was then compiling, when he was gone no farther than the fifteenth or sixteenth of our kings:

"Illud in his rebus non addunt: nec tibi earum
jam desiderium rerum super insidet una."

[*"They do not add, that dying, we have no longer a desire to possess things."*--*Lucretius, iii. 913.*]

We are to discharge ourselves from these vulgar and hurtful humours. To this purpose it was that men first appointed the places of sepulture adjoining the churches, and in the most frequented places of the city, to accustom, says Lycurgus, the common people, women, and children, that they should not be startled at the sight of a corpse, and to the end, that the continual spectacle of bones, graves, and funeral obsequies should put us in mind of our frail condition:

"Quin etiam exhilarare viris convivia caede
Mos olim, et miscere epulis spectacula dira

Certantum ferro, saepe et super ipsa cadentum
Pocula, respersis non parco sanguine mensis."

[*"It was formerly the custom to enliven banquets with slaughter, and
to combine with the repast the dire spectacle of men contending with
the sword, the dying in many cases falling upon the cups, and
covering the tables with blood."--Silius Italicus, xi. 51.]*

And as the Egyptians after their feasts were wont to present the company
with a great image of death, by one that cried out to them, "Drink and be
merry, for such shalt thou be when thou art dead"; so it is my custom to
have death not only in my imagination, but continually in my mouth.
Neither is there anything of which I am so inquisitive, and delight to
inform myself, as the manner of men's deaths, their words, looks, and
bearing; nor any places in history I am so intent upon; and it is
manifest enough, by my crowding in examples of this kind, that I have a
particular fancy for that subject. If I were a writer of books, I would
compile a register, with a comment, of the various deaths of men: he who
should teach men to die would at the same time teach them to live.
Dicarchus made one, to which he gave that title; but it was designed for
another and less profitable end.

Peradventure, some one may object, that the pain and terror of dying so
infinitely exceed all manner of imagination, that the best fencer will be
quite out of his play when it comes to the push. Let them say what they
will: to premeditate is doubtless a very great advantage; and besides, is
it nothing to go so far, at least, without disturbance or alteration?
Moreover, Nature herself assists and encourages us: if the death be
sudden and violent, we have not leisure to fear; if otherwise, I perceive
that as I engage further in my disease, I naturally enter into a certain
loathing and disdain of life. I find I have much more ado to digest this
resolution of dying, when I am well in health, than when languishing of a
fever; and by how much I have less to do with the commodities of life,
by reason that I begin to lose the use and pleasure of them, by so much I
look upon death with less terror. Which makes me hope, that the further
I remove from the first, and the nearer I approach to the latter, I shall

the more easily exchange the one for the other. And, as I have experienced in other occurrences, that, as Caesar says, things often appear greater to us at distance than near at hand, I have found, that being well, I have had maladies in much greater horror than when really afflicted with them. The vigour wherein I now am, the cheerfulness and delight wherein I now live, make the contrary estate appear in so great a disproportion to my present condition, that, by imagination, I magnify those inconveniences by one-half, and apprehend them to be much more troublesome, than I find them really to be, when they lie the most heavy upon me; I hope to find death the same.

Let us but observe in the ordinary changes and declinations we daily suffer, how nature deprives us of the light and sense of our bodily decay. What remains to an old man of the vigour of his youth and better days?

> "Heu! senibus vitae portio quanta manet."

> ["Alas, to old men what portion of life remains!"--Maximian, vel Pseudo-Gallus, i. 16.]

Caesar, to an old weather-beaten soldier of his guards, who came to ask him leave that he might kill himself, taking notice of his withered body and decrepit motion, pleasantly answered, "Thou fanciest, then, that thou art yet alive."--[Seneca, Ep., 77.]--Should a man fall into this condition on the sudden, I do not think humanity capable of enduring such a change: but nature, leading us by the hand, an easy and, as it were, an insensible pace, step by step conducts us to that miserable state, and by that means makes it familiar to us, so that we are insensible of the stroke when our youth dies in us, though it be really a harder death than the final dissolution of a languishing body, than the death of old age; forasmuch as the fall is not so great from an uneasy being to none at all, as it is from a sprightly and flourishing being to one that is troublesome and painful. The body, bent and bowed, has less force to support a burden; and it is the same with the soul, and therefore it is, that we are to raise her up firm and erect against the power of this adversary. For, as it is impossible she should ever be at rest, whilst she stands in fear of it; so, if she once can assure herself, she may boast (which is a thing as it were surpassing human condition) that it is impossible that disquiet, anxiety, or fear, or any other disturbance, should inhabit or have any place in her:

> "Non vulnus instants Tyranni
> Mentha cadi solida, neque Auster
> Dux inquieti turbidus Adriae,
> Nec fulminantis magna Jovis manus."

> ["Not the menacing look of a tyrant shakes her well-settled soul, nor turbulent Auster, the prince of the stormy Adriatic, nor yet the strong hand of thundering Jove, such a temper moves."
> --Hor., Od., iii. 3, 3.]

She is then become sovereign of all her lusts and passions, mistress of necessity, shame, poverty, and all the other injuries of fortune. Let us, therefore, as many of us as can, get this advantage; 'tis the true and sovereign liberty here on earth, that fortifies us wherewithal to defy violence and injustice, and to contemn prisons and chains:

> "In manicis et
> Compedibus saevo te sub custode tenebo.
> Ipse Deus, simul atque volam, me solvet. Opinor,
> Hoc sentit; moriar; mors ultima linea rerum est."

> ["I will keep thee in fetters and chains, in custody of a savage keeper.--A god will when I ask Him, set me free. This god I think is death. Death is the term of all things."
> --Hor., Ep., i. 16, 76.]

Our very religion itself has no surer human foundation than the contempt of death. Not only the argument of reason invites us to it--for why should we fear to lose a thing, which being lost, cannot be lamented? --but, also, seeing we are threatened by so many sorts of death, is it not *infinitely worse eternally to fear them all, than once to undergo one of them? And what matters it, when it shall happen, since it is inevitable? To him that told Socrates, "The thirty tyrants have sentenced thee to death"; "And nature them," said he.--[Socrates was not condemned to death by the thirty tyrants, but by the Athenians.-Diogenes Laertius, ii.35.]-- What a ridiculous thing it is to trouble ourselves about taking the only step that is to deliver us from all trouble! As our birth brought us the birth of all things, so in our death is the death of all things included. And therefore to lament that we shall not be alive a hundred years hence, is the same folly as to be sorry we were not alive a hundred years ago. Death is the beginning of another life. So did we weep, and so much it cost us to enter into this, and so did we put off our former veil in entering into it. Nothing can be a grievance that is but once. Is it reasonable so long to fear a thing that will so soon be despatched? Long life, and short, are by death made all one; for there is no long, nor short, to things that are no more. Aristotle tells us that there are certain little beasts upon the banks of the river Hypanis, that never live above a day: they which die at eight of the clock in the morning, die in their youth, and those that die at five in the evening, in their decrepitude: which of us would not laugh to see this moment of continuance put into the consideration of weal or woe? The most and the least, of ours, in comparison with eternity, or yet with the duration of mountains, rivers, stars, trees, and even of some animals, is no less ridiculous.--[Seneca, Consol. ad Marciam, c. 20.]*

But nature compels us to it. "Go out of this world," says she, "as you entered into it; the same pass you made from death to life, without passion or fear, the same, after the same manner, repeat from life to death. Your death is a part of the order of the universe, 'tis a part of the life of the world.

> *"Inter se mortales mutua vivunt*
> *................................*
> *Et, quasi cursores, vitai lampada tradunt."*

[*"Mortals, amongst themselves, live by turns, and, like the runners in the games, give up the lamp, when they have won the race, to the next comer."* Lucretius, ii. 75, 78.]

"Shall I exchange for you this beautiful contexture of things? 'Tis the condition of your creation; death is a part of you, and whilst you endeavour to evade it, you evade yourselves. This very being of yours that you now enjoy is equally divided betwixt life and death. The day of your birth is one day's advance towards the grave:

"*Prima, quæ vitam dedit, hora carpsit.*"

[*"The first hour that gave us life took away also an hour."* Seneca, Her. Fur., 3 Chor. 874.]

"*Nascentes morimur, finisque ab origine pendet.*"

[*"As we are born we die, and the end commences with the beginning."* Manilius, Ast., iv. 16.]

"All the whole time you live, you purloin from life and live at the expense of life itself. The perpetual work of your life is but to lay the foundation of death. You are in death, whilst you are in life, because you still are after death, when you are no more alive; or, if you had rather have it so, you are dead after life, but dying all the while you live; and death handles the dying much more rudely than the dead, and more sensibly and essentially. If you have made your profit of life, you have had enough of it; go your way satisfied.

"*Cur non ut plenus vita; conviva recedis?*"

[*"Why not depart from life as a sated guest from a feast?*" Lucretius, iii. 951.]

"If you have not known how to make the best use of it, if it was unprofitable to you, what need you care to lose it, to what end would you desire longer to keep it?

> "'Cur amplius addere quaeris,
> Rursum quod pereat male, et ingratum occidat omne?'

["Why seek to add longer life, merely to renew ill-spent time, and be again tormented?"--Lucretius, iii. 914.]

"Life in itself is neither good nor evil; it is the scene of good or evil as you make it.' And, if you have lived a day, you have seen all: one day is equal and like to all other days. There is no other light, no other shade; this very sun, this moon, these very stars, this very order and disposition of things, is the same your ancestors enjoyed, and that shall also entertain your posterity:

> "'Non alium videre patres, aliumve nepotes
> Aspicient.'

["Your grandsires saw no other thing; nor will your posterity."
--Manilius, i. 529.]

"And, come the worst that can come, the distribution and variety of all the acts of my comedy are performed in a year. If you have observed the revolution of my four seasons, they comprehend the infancy, the youth, the virility, and the old age of the world: the year has played his part, and knows no other art but to begin again; it will always be the same thing:

> "'Versamur ibidem, atque insumus usque.'

["We are turning in the same circle, ever therein confined."
--Lucretius, iii. 1093.]

"'*Atque in se sua per vestigia volvitur annus.*'

[*"The year is ever turning around in the same footsteps."*
--Virgil, Georg., ii. 402.]

"*I am not prepared to create for you any new recreations:*

"'*Nam tibi prxterea quod machiner, inveniamque*
Quod placeat, nihil est; eadem sunt omnia semper.'

[*"I can devise, nor find anything else to please you: 'tis the same*
thing over and over again."--Lucretius iii. 957]

"*Give place to others, as others have given place to you. Equality is*
the soul of equity. Who can complain of being comprehended in the same
destiny, wherein all are involved? Besides, live as long as you can, you
shall by that nothing shorten the space you are to be dead; 'tis all to
no purpose; you shall be every whit as long in the condition you so much
fear, as if you had died at nurse:

"'*Licet quot vis vivendo vincere secla,*
Mors aeterna tamen nihilominus illa manebit.'

[*"Live triumphing over as many ages as you will, death still will*
remain eternal."--Lucretius, iii. 1103]

"*And yet I will place you in such a condition as you shall have no reason*
to be displeased.

"'*In vera nescis nullum fore morte alium te,*
Qui possit vivus tibi to lugere peremptum,
Stansque jacentem.'

[*"Know you not that, when dead, there can be no other living self to*
lament you dead, standing on your grave."--Idem., ibid., 898.]

"Nor shall you so much as wish for the life you are so concerned about:

> "'Nec sibi enim quisquam tum se vitamque requirit.
> ....
> "'Nec desiderium nostri nos afficit ullum.'

"Death is less to be feared than nothing, if there could be anything less than nothing.

> "'Multo . . . mortem minus ad nos esse putandium,
> Si minus esse potest, quam quod nihil esse videmus.'

"Neither can it any way concern you, whether you are living or dead: living, by reason that you are still in being; dead, because you are no more. Moreover, no one dies before his hour: the time you leave behind was no more yours than that was lapsed and gone before you came into the world; nor does it any more concern you.

> "'Respice enim, quam nil ad nos anteacta vetustas
> Temporis aeterni fuerit.'

> ["Consider how as nothing to us is the old age of times past."
> ⹁Lucretius iii. 985]

Wherever your life ends, it is all there. The utility of living consists not in the length of days, but in the use of time; a man may have lived long, and yet lived but a little. Make use of time while it is present with you. It depends upon your will, and not upon the number of days, to have a sufficient length of life. Is it possible you can imagine never to arrive at the place towards which you are continually going? and yet there is no journey but hath its end. And, if company will make it more pleasant or more easy to you, does not all the world go the self-same way?

> "'Omnia te, vita perfuncta, sequentur.'

> *["All things, then, life over, must follow thee."*
> *~Lucretius, iii. 981.]*

"*Does not all the world dance the same brawl that you do? Is there anything that does not grow old, as well as you? A thousand men, a thousand animals, a thousand other creatures, die at the same moment that you die:*

> "'*Nam nox nulla diem, neque noctem aurora sequuta est,*
>   *Quae non audierit mistos vagitibus aegris*
>   *Ploratus, mortis comites et funeris atri.'*

> *["No night has followed day, no day has followed night, in which there has not been heard sobs and sorrowing cries, the companions of death and funerals."~Lucretius, v. 579.]*

"*To what end should you endeavour to draw back, if there be no possibility to evade it? you have seen examples enough of those who have been well pleased to die, as thereby delivered from heavy miseries; but have you ever found any who have been dissatisfied with dying? It must, therefore, needs be very foolish to condemn a thing you have neither experimented in your own person, nor by that of any other. Why dost thou complain of me and of destiny? Do we do thee any wrong? Is it for thee to govern us, or for us to govern thee? Though, peradventure, thy age may not be accomplished, yet thy life is: a man of low stature is as much a man as a giant; neither men nor their lives are measured by the ell. Chiron refused to be immortal, when he was acquainted with the conditions under which he was to enjoy it, by the god of time itself and its duration, his father Saturn. Do but seriously consider how much more insupportable and painful an immortal life would be to man than what I have already given him. If you had not death, you would eternally curse me for having deprived you of it; I have mixed a little bitterness with it, to the end, that seeing of what convenience it is, you might not too greedily and indiscreetly seek and embrace it: and that you might be so established in this moderation, as neither to nauseate life, nor have any antipathy for dying, which I have decreed you shall once do, I have tempered the one and the other betwixt pleasure and pain. It was I that taught Thales, the most eminent of your sages, that to live and to die were indifferent; which made him, very wisely, answer him, 'Why then he did not die?' 'Because,' said he, 'it is indifferent.'--[Diogenes Laertius, i. 35.]--Water, earth, air, and fire, and the other parts of this creation of mine, are no more instruments of thy life than they are of thy death. Why dost thou fear thy last day? it contributes no more to thy dissolution, than every one of the rest: the last step is not the cause of lassitude: it does not confess it. Every day travels towards death; the last only arrives at it." These are the good lessons our mother Nature teaches.*

I have often considered with myself whence it should proceed, that in war the image of death, whether we look upon it in ourselves or in others, should, without comparison, appear less dreadful than at home in our own houses (for if it were not so, it would be an army of doctors and whining milksops), and that being still in all places the same, there should be, notwithstanding, much more assurance in peasants and the meaner sort of people, than in others of better quality. I believe, in truth, that it is those terrible ceremonies and preparations wherewith we set it out, that more terrify us than the thing itself; a new, quite contrary way of living; the cries of mothers, wives, and children; the visits of astounded and afflicted friends; the attendance of pale and blubbering servants; a dark room, set round with burning tapers; our beds environed with physicians and divines; in sum, nothing but ghostliness and horror round about us; we seem dead and buried already. Children are afraid even of those they are best acquainted with, when disguised in a visor; and so 'tis with us; the visor must be removed as well from things as from persons, that being taken away, we shall find nothing underneath but the very same death that a mean servant or a poor chambermaid died a day or two ago, without any manner of apprehension. Happy is the death that deprives us of leisure for preparing such ceremonials.

CHAPTER XX

OF THE FORCE OF IMAGINATION

"Fortis imaginatio generat casum," say the schoolmen.

["A strong imagination begets the event itself."--Axiom. Scholast.]

I am one of those who are most sensible of the power of imagination: every one is jostled by it, but some are overthrown by it. It has a very piercing impression upon me; and I make it my business to avoid, wanting force to resist it. I could live by the sole help of healthful and jolly company: the very sight of another's pain materially pains me, and I often usurp the sensations of another person. A perpetual cough in another tickles my lungs and throat. I more unwillingly visit the sick in whom by love and duty I am interested, than those I care not for, to whom I less look. I take possession of the disease I am concerned at, and take it to myself. I do not at all wonder that fancy should give fevers and sometimes kill such as allow it too much scope, and are too willing to entertain it. Simon Thomas was a great physician of his time: I remember, that happening one day at Toulouse to meet him at a rich old fellow's house, who was troubled with weak lungs, and discoursing with the patient about the method of his cure, he told him, that one thing which would be very conducive to it, was to give me such occasion to be pleased with his company, that I might come often to see him, by which means, and by fixing his eyes upon the freshness of my complexion, and his imagination upon the sprightliness and vigour that glowed in my youth, and possessing all his senses with the flourishing age wherein I then was, his habit of body might, peradventure, be amended; but he forgot to say that mine, at the same time, might be made worse. Gallus Vibius so much bent his mind to find out the essence and motions of madness, that, in the end, he himself went out of his wits, and to such a degree, that he could never after recover his judgment, and might brag that he was become a fool by too much wisdom. Some there are who through fear anticipate the hangman; and there was the man, whose eyes being unbound to have his pardon read to him, was found stark dead upon the scaffold, by the stroke of imagination. We start, tremble, turn pale, and blush, as we are variously moved by imagination; and, being a-bed, feel our bodies agitated with its power to that degree, as even sometimes to expiring. And boiling youth, when fast asleep, grows so warm with fancy, as in a dream to satisfy amorous desires:--

> *"Ut, quasi transactis saepe omnibu rebu, profundant*
> *Fluminis ingentes, fluctus, vestemque cruentent."*

Although it be no new thing to see horns grown in a night on the forehead of one that had none when he went to bed, notwithstanding, what befell Cippus, King of Italy, is memorable; who having one day been a very delighted spectator of a bullfight, and having all the night dreamed that he had horns on his head, did, by the force of imagination, really cause them to grow there. Passion gave to the son of Croesus the voice which nature had denied him. And Antiochus fell into a fever, inflamed with the beauty of Stratonice, too deeply imprinted in his soul. Pliny pretends to have seen Lucius Cossitius, who from a woman was turned into a man upon her very wedding-day. Pontanus and others report the like metamorphosis to have happened in these latter days in Italy. And, through the vehement desire of him and his mother:

> *"Volta puer solvit, quae foemina voverat, Iphis."*

Myself passing by Vitry le Francois, saw a man the Bishop of Soissons had, in confirmation, called Germain, whom all the inhabitants of the place had known to be a girl till two-and-twenty years of age, called Mary. He was, at the time of my being there, very full of beard, old, and not married. He told us, that by straining himself in a leap his male organs came out; and the girls of that place have, to this day, a song, wherein they advise one another not to take too great strides, for fear of being turned into men, as Mary Germain was. It is no wonder if this sort of accident frequently happen; for if imagination have any power in such things, it is so continually and vigorously bent upon this subject, that to the end it may not so often relapse into the same thought and violence of desire, it were better, once for all, to give these young wenches the things they long for.

Some attribute the scars of King Dagobert and of St. Francis to the force of imagination. It is said, that by it bodies wi ll sometimes be removed from their places; and Celsus tells us of a priest whose soul would be ravished into such an ecstasy that the body would, for a long time, remain without sense or respiration. St. Augustine makes mention of another, who, upon the hearing of any lamentable or doleful cries, would presently fall into a swoon, and be so far out of himself, that it was in vain to call, bawl in his ears, pinch or burn him, till he voluntarily came to himself; and then he would say, that he had heard voices as it were afar off, and did feel when they pinched and burned him; and, to prove that this was no obstinate dissimulation in defiance of his sense of feeling, it was manifest, that all the while he had neither pulse nor breathing.

'Tis very probable, that visions, enchantments, and all extraordinary effects of that nature, derive their credit principally from the power of imagination, working and making its chiefest impression upon vulgar and more easy souls, whose belief is so strangely imposed upon, as to think they see what they do not see.

I am not satisfied whether those pleasant ligatures--[Les nouements d'aiguillettes, as they were called, knots tied by some one, at a wedding, on a strip of leather, cotton, or silk, and which, especially when passed through the wedding-ring, were supposed to have the magical effect of preventing a consummation of the marriage until they were untied. See Louandre, La Sorcellerie, 1853, p. 73. The same superstition and appliance existed in England.]--with which this age of ours is so occupied, that there is almost no other talk, are not mere voluntary impressions of apprehension and fear; for I know, by experience, in the case of a particular friend of mine, one for whom I can be as responsible as for myself, and a man that cannot possibly fall *under any manner of suspicion of insufficiency, and as little of being enchanted, who having heard a companion of his make a relation of an unusual frigidity that surprised him at a very unseasonable time; being afterwards himself engaged upon the same account, the horror of the former story on a sudden so strangely possessed his imagination, that he ran the same fortune the other had done; and from that time forward, the scurvy remembrance of his disaster running in his mind and tyrannising over him, he was subject to relapse into the same misfortune. He found some remedy, however, for this fancy in another fancy, by himself frankly confessing and declaring beforehand to the party with whom he was to have to do, this subjection of his, by which means, the agitation of his soul was, in some sort, appeased; and knowing that, now, some such misbehaviour was expected from him, the restraint upon his faculties grew less. And afterwards, at such times as he was in no such apprehension, when setting about the act (his thoughts being then disengaged and free, and his body in its true and natural estate) he was at leisure to cause the part to be handled and communicated to the knowledge of the other party, he was totally freed from that vexatious infirmity. After a man has once done a woman right, he is never after in danger of misbehaving himself with that person, unless upon the account of some excusable weakness. Neither is this disaster to be feared, but in adventures, where the soul is overextended with desire or respect, and, especially, where the opportunity is of an unforeseen and pressing nature; in those cases, there is no means for a man to defend himself from such a surprise, as shall put him altogether out of sorts. I have known some, who have secured themselves from this mischance, by coming half sated elsewhere, purposely to abate the ardour of the fury, and others, who, being grown old, find themselves less impotent by being less able; and one, who found an advantage in being assured by a friend of his, that he had a counter-charm of enchantments that would secure him from this disgrace. The story itself is not, much amiss, and therefore you shall have it.*

A Count of a very great family, and with whom I was very intimate, being married to a fair lady, who had formerly been courted by one who was at the wedding, all his friends were in very great fear; but especially an old lady his kinswoman, who had the ordering of the solemnity, and in whose house it was kept, suspecting his rival would offer foul play by these sorceries. Which fear she communicated to me. I bade her rely upon me: I had, by chance, about me a certain flat plate of gold, whereon were graven some celestial figures, supposed good against sunstroke or pains in the head, being applied to the suture: where, that it might the better remain firm, it was sewed to a ribbon to be tied under the chin; a foppery cousin-german to this of which I am speaking. Jaques Pelletier, who lived in my house, had presented this to me for a singular rarity. I had a fancy to make some use of this knack, and therefore privately told the Count, that he might possibly run the same fortune other bridegrooms had sometimes done, especially some one being in the house, who, no doubt, would be glad to do him such a courtesy: but let him boldly go to bed. For I would do him the office of a friend, and, if need were, would not spare a miracle it was in my power to do, provided he would engage to me, upon his honour, to keep it to himself; and only, when they came to bring him his caudle,--[A custom in France to bring the bridegroom a caudle in the middle of the night on his wedding-night]-- if matters had not gone well with him, to give me such a sign, and leave the rest to me. Now he had had his ears so battered, and his mind so prepossessed with the eternal tattle of this business, that when he came to't, he did really find himself tied with the trouble of his imagination, and, accordingly, at the time appointed, gave me the sign. Whereupon, I whispered him in the ear, that he should rise, under pretence of putting us out of the room, and after a jesting manner pull my nightgown from my shoulders--we were of much about the same height-- throw it over his own, and there keep it till he had performed what I had appointed him to do, which was, that when we were all gone out of the chamber, he should withdraw to make water, should three times repeat such and such words, and as often do such and such actions; that at every of the three times, he should tie the ribbon I put into his hand about his middle, and be sure to place the medal that was fastened to it, the figures in such a posture, exactly upon his reins, which being done, and having the last of the three times so well girt and fast tied the ribbon that it could neither untie nor slip from its place, let him confidently return to his business, and withal not forget to spread my gown upon the bed, so that it might be sure to cover them both. These ape's tricks are the main of the effect, our fancy being so far seduced as to believe that such strange means must, of necessity, proceed from some abstruse science: their very inanity gives them weight and reverence. And, certain it is, that my figures approved themselves more venereal than solar, more active than prohibitive. 'Twas a sudden whimsey, mixed with a little curiosity, that made me do a thing so contrary to my nature; for I am an enemy to all subtle and counterfeit actions, and abominate all manner of trickery, though it be for sport, and to an advantage; for though the action may not be vicious in itself, its mode is vicious.

Amasis, King of Egypt, having married Laodice, a very beautiful Greek virgin, though noted for his abilities elsewhere, found himself quite another man with his wife, and could by no means enjoy her; at which he was so enraged, that he threatened to kill her, suspecting her to be a witch. As 'tis usual in things that consist in fancy, she put him upon devotion, and having accordingly made his vows to Venus, he found himself divinely restored the very first night after his oblations and sacrifices. Now women are to blame to entertain us with that disdainful, coy, and angry countenance, which extinguishes our vigour, as it kindles our desire; which made the daughter-in-law of Pythagoras--[Theano, the lady in question was the wife, not the daughter-in-law of Pythagoras.]-- say, "That the woman who goes to bed to a man, must put off her modesty with her petticoat, and put it on again with the same." The soul of the assailant, being disturbed with many several alarms, readily loses the power of performance; and whoever the imagination has once put this trick upon, and confounded with the shame of it (and she never does it but at the first acquaintance, by reason men are then more ardent and eager, and also, at this first account a man gives of himself, he is much more timorous of miscarrying), having made an ill beginning, he enters into such fever and despite at the accident, as are apt to remain and continue with him upon following occasions.

Married people, having all their time before them, ought never to compel or so much as to offer at the feat, if they do not find themselves quite ready: and it is less unseemly to fail of handselling the nuptial sheets, when a man perceives himself full of agitation and trembling, and to await another opportunity at more private and more composed leisure, than to make himself perpetually miserable, for having misbehaved himself and been baffled at the first assault. Till possession be taken, a man that knows himself subject to this infirmity, should leisurely and by degrees make several little trials and light offers, without obstinately attempting at once, to Force an absolute conquest over his own mutinous and indisposed faculties. Such as know their members to be naturally obedient, need take no other care but only to counterplot their fantasies.

The indocile liberty of this member is very remarkable, so importunately unruly in its tumidity and impatience, when we do not require it, and so unseasonably disobedient, when we stand most in need of it: so imperiously contesting in authority with the will, and with so much haughty obstinacy denying all solicitation, both of hand and mind. And yet, though his rebellion is so universally complained of, and that proof is thence deduced to condemn him, if he had, nevertheless, feed me to plead his cause, I should peradventure, bring the rest of his fellow-members into suspicion of complotting this mischief against him, out of pure envy at the importance and pleasure especial to his employment; and to have, by confederacy, armed the whole world against him, by malevolently charging him alone, with their common offence. For let any one consider, whether there is any one part of our bodies that does not often refuse to perform its office at the precept of the will, and that does not often exercise its function in defiance of her command. They have every one of them passions of their own, that rouse and awaken, stupefy and benumb them, without our leave or consent. How often do the involuntary motions of the countenance discover our inward thoughts, and betray our most private secrets to the bystanders. The same cause that animates this member, does also, without our knowledge, animate the lungs, pulse, and heart, the sight of a pleasing object imperceptibly diffusing a flame through all our parts, with a feverish motion. Is there nothing but these veins and muscles that swell and flag without the consent, not only of the will, but even of our knowledge also? We do not command our hairs to stand on end, nor our skin to shiver either with fear or desire; the hands often convey themselves to parts to which we do not direct them; the tongue will be interdict, and the voice congealed, when we know not how to help it. When we have nothing to eat, and would willingly forbid it, the appetite does not, for all that, forbear to stir up the parts that are subject to it, no more nor less than the other appetite we were speaking of, and in like manner, as unseasonably leaves us, when it thinks fit. The vessels that serve to discharge the belly have their own proper dilatations and compressions, without and beyond our concurrence, as well as those which are destined to purge the reins; and that which, to justify the prerogative of the will, St. Augustine urges, of having seen a man who could command his rear to discharge as often together as he pleased, Vives, his commentator, yet further fortifies with another example in his time,--of one that could break wind in tune; but these cases do not suppose any more pure obedience in that part; for is anything commonly more tumultuary or indiscreet? To which let me add, that I myself knew one so rude and ungoverned, as for forty years together made his master vent with one continued and unintermitted outbursting, and 'tis like will do so till he die of it. And I could heartily wish, that I only knew by reading, how often a man's belly, by the denial of one single puff, brings him to the very door of an exceeding painful death; and that the emperor,--[The Emperor Claudius, who, however, according to Suetonius (Vita, c. 32), only intended to authorise this singular privilege by an edict.]--who gave liberty to let fly in all places, had, at the same time, given us power to do it. But for our will, in whose behalf we prefer this accusation, with how much greater probability may we reproach herself with mutiny and sedition, for her irregularity and disobedience? Does she always will what we would have her to do? Does she not often will what we forbid her to will, and that to our manifest prejudice? Does she suffer herself, more than any of the rest, to be governed and directed by the results of our reason? To conclude, I should move, in the behalf of the gentleman, my client, it might be considered, that in this fact, his cause being inseparably and indistinctly conjoined with an accessory, yet he only is called in question, and that by arguments and accusations, which cannot be charged upon the other; whose business, indeed, it is sometimes inopportunely to invite, but never to refuse, and invite, moreover, after a tacit and quiet manner; and therefore is the malice and injustice of his accusers most manifestly apparent. But be it how it will, protesting against the proceedings of the advocates and judges, nature will, in the meantime, proceed after her own way, who had done but well, had she endowed this member with some particular privilege; the author of the sole immortal work of mortals; a divine work, according to Socrates; and love, the desire of immortality, and himself an immortal demon.

Some one, perhaps, by such an effect of imagination may have had the good luck to leave behind him here, the scrofula, which his companion who has come after, has carried with him into Spain. And 'tis for this reason you may see why men in such cases require a mind prepared for the thing that is to be done. Why do the physicians possess, before hand, their patients' credulity with so many false promises of cure, if not to the end, that the effect of imagination may supply the imposture of their decoctions? They know very well, that a great master of their trade has given it under his hand, that he has known some with whom the very sight of physic would work. All which conceits come now into my head, by the remembrance of a story was told me by a domestic apothecary of my father's, a blunt Swiss, a nation not much addicted to vanity and lying, of a merchant he had long known at Toulouse, who being a valetudinary, and much afflicted with the stone, had often occasion to take clysters, of which he caused several sorts to be prescribed him by the physicians, acccording to the accidents of his disease; which, being brought him, and none of the usual forms, as feeling if it were not too hot, and the like, being omitted, he lay down, the syringe advanced, and all ceremonies performed, injection alone excepted; after which, the apothecary being gone, and the patient accommodated as if he had really received a clyster, he found the same operation and effect that those do who have taken one indeed; and if at any time the physician did not find the operation sufficient, he would usually give him two or three more doses, after the same manner. And the fellow swore, that to save charges (for he paid as if he had really taken them) this sick man's wife, having sometimes made trial of warm water only, the effect discovered the cheat, and finding these would do no good, was fain to return to the old way.

A woman fancying she had swallowed a pin in a piece of bread, cried and lamented as though she had an intolerable pain in her throat, where she thought she felt it stick; but an ingenious fellow that was brought to her, seeing no outward tumour nor alteration, supposing it to be only a conceit taken at some crust of bread that had hurt her as it went down, caused her to vomit, and, unseen, threw a crooked pin into the basin, which the woman no sooner saw, but believing she had cast it up, she presently found herself eased of her pain. I myself knew a gentleman, who having treated a large company at his house, three or four days after bragged in jest (for there was no such thing), that he had made them eat of a baked cat; at which, a young gentlewoman, who had been at the feast, took such a horror, that falling into a violent vomiting and fever, there was no possible means to save her. Even brute beasts are subject to the force of imagination as well as we; witness dogs, who die of grief for the loss of their masters; and bark and tremble and start in their sleep; so horses will kick and whinny in their sleep.

Now all this may be attributed to the close affinity and relation betwixt the soul and the body intercommunicating their fortunes; but 'tis quite another thing when the imagination works not only upon one's own particular body, but upon that of others also. And as an infected body communicates its malady to those that approach or live near it, as we see in the plague, the smallpox, and sore eyes, that run through whole families and cities:—

> *"Dum spectant oculi laesos, laeduntur et ipsi;*
> *Multaque corporibus transitione nocent."*

["When we look at people with sore eyes, our own eyes become sore. Many things are hurtful to our bodies by transition."
—Ovid, De Rem. Amor., 615.]

—so the imagination, being vehemently agitated, darts out infection capable of offending the foreign object. The ancients had an opinion of certain women of Scythia, that being animated and enraged against any one, they killed him only with their looks. Tortoises and ostriches

hatch their eggs with only looking on them, which infers that their eyes have in them some ejaculative virtue. And the eyes of witches are said to be assailant and hurtful:--

"*Nescio quis teneros oculus mihi fascinat agnos.*"

[*"Some eye, I know not whose is bewitching my tender lambs."*
--Virgil, Eclog., iii. 103.]

Magicians are no very good authority with me. But we experimentally see that women impart the marks of their fancy to the children they carry in the womb; witness her that was brought to bed of a Moor; and there was presented to Charles the Emperor and King of Bohemia, a girl from about Pisa, all over rough and covered with hair, whom her mother said to be so conceived by reason of a picture of St. John the Baptist, that hung within the curtains of her bed.

It is the same with beasts; witness Jacob's sheep, and the hares and partridges that the snow turns white upon the mountains. There was at my house, a little while ago, a cat seen watching a bird upon the top of a tree: these, for some time, mutually fixing their eyes one upon another, the bird at last let herself fall dead into the cat's claws, either dazzled by the force of its own imagination, or drawn by some attractive power of the cat. Such as are addicted to the pleasures of the field, have, I make no question, heard the story of the falconer, who having earnestly fixed his eyes upon a kite in the air; laid a wager that he would bring her down with the sole power of his sight, and did so, as it was said; for the tales I borrow I charge upon the consciences of those from whom I have them. The discourses are my own, and found themselves upon the proofs of reason, not of experience; to which every one has liberty to add his own examples; and who has none, let him not forbear, the number and varieties of accidents considered, to believe that there are plenty of them; if I do not apply them well, let some other do it for me. And, also, in the subject of which I treat, our manners and motions, testimonies and instances; how fabulous soever, provided they are possible, serve as well as the true; whether they have really happened or *no, at Rome or Paris, to John or Peter, 'tis still within the verge of human capacity, which serves me to good use. I see, and make my advantage of it, as well in shadow as in substance; and amongst the various readings thereof in history, I cull out the most rare and memorable to fit my own turn. There are authors whose only end and design it is to give an account of things that have happened; mine, if I could arrive unto it, should be to deliver of what may happen. There is a just liberty allowed in the schools, of supposing similitudes, when they have none at hand. I do not, however, make any use of that privilege, and as to that matter, in superstitious religion, surpass all historical authority. In the examples which I here bring in, of what I have heard, read, done, or said, I have forbidden myself to dare to alter even the most light and indifferent circumstances; my conscience does not falsify one tittle; what my ignorance may do, I cannot say.*

And this it is that makes me sometimes doubt in my own mind, whether a divine, or a philosopher, and such men of exact and tender prudence and conscience, are fit to write history: for how can they stake their reputation upon a popular faith? how be responsible for the opinions of men they do not know? and with what assurance deliver their conjectures for current pay? Of actions performed before their own eyes, wherein several persons were actors, they would be unwilling to give evidence upon oath before a judge; and there is no man, so familiarly known to them, for whose intentions they would become absolute caution. For my part, I think it less hazardous to write of things past, than present, by how much the writer is only to give an account of things every one knows he must of necessity borrow upon trust.

I am solicited to write the affairs of my own time by some, who fancy I look upon them with an eye less blinded with passion than another, and have a clearer insight into them by reason of the free access fortune has given me to the heads of various factions; but they do not consider, that to purchase the glory of Sallust, I would not give myself the trouble, sworn enemy as I am to obligation, assiduity, or perseverance: that there is nothing so contrary to my style, as a continued narrative, I so often interrupt and cut myself short in my writing for want of breath; I have neither composition nor explanation worth anything, and am ignorant, beyond a child, of the phrases and even the very words proper to express the most common things; and for that reason it is, that I have undertaken to say only what I can say, and have accommodated my subject to my strength. Should I take one to be my guide, peradventure I should not be able to keep pace with him; and in the freedom of my liberty might deliver judgments, which upon better thoughts, and according to reason, would be illegitimate and punishable. Plutarch would say of what he has delivered to us, that it is the work of others: that his examples are all and everywhere exactly true: that they are useful to posterity, and are presented with a lustre that will light us the way to virtue, is his own work. It is not of so dangerous consequence, as in a medicinal drug, whether an old story be so or so.

CHAPTER XXI

THAT THE PROFIT OF ONE MAN
IS THE DAMAGE OF ANOTHER

Demades the Athenian--[Seneca, De Beneficiis, vi. 38, whence nearly the whole of this chapter is taken.]--condemned one of his city, whose trade it was to sell the necessaries for funeral ceremonies, upon pretence that he demanded unreasonable profit, and that that profit could not accrue to him, but by the death of a great number of people. A judgment that appears to be ill grounded, forasmuch as no profit whatever can possibly be made but at the expense of another, and that by the same rule he should condemn all gain of what kind soever. The merchant only thrives by the debauchery of youth, the husband man by the dearness of grain, the architect by the ruin of buildings, lawyers and officers of justice by the suits and contentions of men: nay, even the honour and office of divines are derived from our death and vices. A physician takes no pleasure in the health even of his friends, says the ancient Greek comic writer, nor a soldier in the peace of his country, and so of the rest. And, which is yet worse, let every one but dive into his own bosom, and he will find his private wishes spring and his secret hopes grow up at another's expense. Upon which consideration it comes into my head, that nature does not in this swerve from her general polity; for physicians hold, that the birth, nourishment, and increase of every thing is the dissolution and corruption of another:

> *"Nam quodcumque suis mutatum finibus exit,*
> *Continuo hoc mors est illius, quod fuit ante."*

> *["For, whatever from its own confines passes changed, this is at once the death of that which before it was."--Lucretius, ii. 752.]*

CHAPTER XXII

OF CUSTOM, AND THAT WE SHOULD NOT
EASILY CHANGE A LAW RECEIVED

He seems to me to have had a right and true apprehension of the power of custom, who first invented the story of a country-woman who, having accustomed herself to play with and carry a young calf in her arms, and daily continuing to do so as it grew up, obtained this by custom, that, when grown to be a great ox, she was still able to bear it. For, in truth, custom is a violent and treacherous schoolmistress. She, by little and little, slily and unperceived, slips in the foot of her authority, but having by this gentle and humble beginning, with the benefit of time, fixed and established it, she then unmasks a furious and tyrannic countenance, against which we have no more the courage or the power so much as to lift up our eyes. We see her, at every turn, forcing and violating the rules of nature:

"Usus efficacissimus rerum omnium magister."

*["Custom is the best master of all things."
~Pliny, Nat. Hist.,xxvi. 2.]*

I refer to her Plato's cave in his Republic, and the physicians, who so often submit the reasons of their art to her authority; as the story of that king, who by custom brought his stomach to that pass, as to live by poison, and the maid that Albertus reports to have lived upon spiders. In that new world of the Indies, there were found great nations, and in very differing climates, who were of the same diet, made provision of them, and fed them for their tables; as also, they did grasshoppers, mice, lizards, and bats; and in a time of scarcity of such delicacies, a toad was sold for six crowns, all which they cook, and dish up with

several sauces. There were also others found, to whom our diet, and the
flesh we eat, were venomous and mortal:

> "Consuetudinis magna vis est: pernoctant venatores in nive:
> in montibus uri se patiuntur: pugiles, caestibus contusi,
> ne ingemiscunt quidem."

> ["The power of custom is very great: huntsmen will lie out all
> night in the snow, or suffer themselves to be burned up by the sun
> on the mountains; boxers, hurt by the caestus, never utter a
> groan."--Cicero, Tusc., ii. 17]

These strange examples will not appear so strange if we consider what we
have ordinary experience of, how much custom stupefies our senses. We
need not go to what is reported of the people about the cataracts of the
Nile; and what philosophers believe of the music of the spheres, that the
bodies of those circles being solid and smooth, and coming to touch and
rub upon one another, cannot fail of creating a marvellous harmony, the
changes and cadences of which cause the revolutions and dances of the
stars; but that the hearing sense of all creatures here below, being
universally, like that of the Egyptians, deafened, and stupefied with the
continual noise, cannot, how great soever, perceive it--[This passage is
taken from Cicero, "Dream of Scipio"; see his De Republica, vi. II. The
Egyptians were said to be stunned by the noise of the Cataracts.]--
Smiths, millers, pewterers, forgemen, and armourers could never be able
to live in the perpetual noise of their own trades, did it strike their
ears with the same violence that it does ours.

My perfumed doublet gratifies my own scent at first; but after I have
worn it three days together, 'tis only pleasing to the bystanders. This
is yet more strange, that custom, notwithstanding long intermissions and
intervals, should yet have the power to unite and establish the effect of
its impressions upon our senses, as is manifest in such as live near unto
steeples and the frequent noise of the bells. I myself lie at home in a
tower, where every morning and evening a very great bell rings out the
Ave Maria: the noise shakes my very tower, and at first seemed

insupportable to me; but I am so used to it, that I hear it without any manner of offence, and often without awaking at it.

Plato--[Diogenes Laertius, iii. 38. But he whom Plato censured was not a boy playing at nuts, but a man throwing dice.]--reprehending a boy for playing at nuts, "Thou reprovest me," says the boy, "for a very little thing." "Custom," replied Plato, "is no little thing." I find that our greatest vices derive their first propensity from our most tender infancy, and that our principal education depends upon the nurse. Mothers are mightily pleased to see a child writhe off the neck of a chicken, or to please itself with hurting a dog or a cat; and such wise fathers there are in the world, who look upon it as a notable mark of a martial spirit, when they hear a son miscall, or see him domineer over a poor peasant, or a lackey, that dares not reply, nor turn again; and a great sign of wit, when they see him cheat and overreach his playfellow by some malicious treachery and deceit. Yet these are the true seeds and roots of cruelty, tyranny, and treason; they bud and put out there, and afterwards shoot up vigorously, and grow to prodigious bulk, cultivated by custom. And it is a very dangerous mistake to excuse these vile inclinations upon the tenderness of their age, and the triviality of the subject: first, it is nature that speaks, whose declaration is then more sincere, and inward thoughts more undisguised, as it is more weak and young; secondly, the deformity of cozenage does not consist nor depend upon the difference betwixt crowns and pins; but I rather hold it more just to conclude thus: why should he not cozen in crowns since he does it in pins, than as they do, who say they only play for pins, they would not do it if it were for money? Children should carefully be instructed to abhor vices for their own contexture; and the natural deformity of those vices ought so to be represented to them, that they may not only avoid them in their actions, but especially so to abominate them in their hearts, that the very thought should be hateful to them, with what mask soever they may be disguised.

I know very well, for what concerns myself, that from having been brought up in my childhood to a plain and straightforward way of dealing, and from having had an aversion to all manner of juggling and foul play in my childish sports and recreations (and, indeed, it is to be noted, that the plays of children are not performed in play, but are to be judged in them as their most serious actions), there is no game so small wherein from my own bosom naturally, and without study or endeavour, I have not an extreme aversion from deceit. I shuffle and cut and make as much clatter with the cards, and keep as strict account for farthings, as it were for double pistoles; when winning or losing against my wife and daughter, 'tis indifferent to me, as when I play in good earnest with others, for round sums. At all times, and in all places, my own eyes are sufficient to look to my fingers; I am not so narrowly watched by any other, neither is there any I have more respect to.

I saw the other day, at my own house, a little fellow, a native of Nantes, born without arms, who has so well taught his feet to perform the services his hands should have done him, that truly these have half forgotten their natural office; and, indeed, the fellow calls them his hands; with them he cuts anything, charges and discharges a pistol, threads a needle, sews, writes, puts off his hat, combs his head, plays at cards and dice, and all this with as much dexterity as any other could do who had more, and more proper limbs to assist him. The money I gave him--for he gains his living by shewing these feats--he took in his foot, as we do in our hand. I have seen another who, being yet a boy, flourished a two-handed sword, and, if I may so say, handled a halberd with the mere motions of his neck and shoulders for want of hands; tossed them into the air, and caught them again, darted a dagger, and cracked a whip as well as any coachman in France.

But the effects of custom are much more manifest in the strange impressions she imprints in our minds, where she meets with less resistance. What has she not the power to impose upon our judgments and beliefs? Is there any so fantastic opinion (omitting the gross impostures of religions, with which we see so many great nations, and so many understanding men, so strangely besotted; for this being beyond the reach of human reason, any error is more excusable in such as are not endued, through the divine bounty, with an extraordinary illumination from above), but, of other opinions, are there any so extravagant, that she has not planted and established for laws in those parts of the world upon which she has been pleased to exercise her power? And therefore that ancient exclamation was exceeding just:

> *"Non pudet physicum, id est speculatorem venatoremque naturae,*
> *ab animis consuetudine imbutis petere testimonium veritatis?"*

> *["Is it not a shame for a natural philosopher, that is, for an observer and hunter of nature, to seek testimony of the truth from minds prepossessed by custom?"--Cicero, De Natura Deor., i. 30.]*

I do believe, that no so absurd or ridiculous fancy can enter into human imagination, that does not meet with some example of public practice, and that, consequently, our reason does not ground and back up. There are people, amongst whom it is the fashion to turn their backs upon him they salute, and never look upon the man they intend to honour. There is a place, where, whenever the king spits, the greatest ladies of his court put out their hands to receive it; and another nation, where the most eminent persons about him stoop to take up his ordure in a linen cloth. Let us here steal room to insert a story.

A French gentleman was always wont to blow his nose with his fingers (a thing very much against our fashion), and he justifying himself for so doing, and he was a man famous for pleasant repartees, he asked me, what privilege this filthy excrement had, that we must carry about us a fine handkerchief to receive it, and, which was more, afterwards to lap it carefully up, and carry it all day about in our pockets, which, he said, could not but be much more nauseous and offensive, than to see it thrown away, as we did all other evacuations. I found that what he said was not altogether without reason, and by being frequently in his company, that slovenly action of his was at last grown familiar to me; which nevertheless we make a face at, when we hear it reported of another country. Miracles appear to be so, according to our ignorance of nature, and not according to the essence of nature the continually being accustomed to anything, blinds the eye of our judgment. Barbarians are no more a wonder to us, than we are to them; nor with any more reason, as

*every one would confess, if after having travelled over those remote
examples, men could settle themselves to reflect upon, and rightly to
confer them, with their own. Human reason is a tincture almost equally
infused into all our opinions and manners, of what form soever they are;
infinite in matter, infinite in diversity. But I return to my subject.*

*There are peoples, where, his wife and children excepted, no one speaks
to the king but through a tube. In one and the same nation, the virgins
discover those parts that modesty should persuade them to hide, and the
married women carefully cover and conceal them. To which, this custom,
in another place, has some relation, where chastity, but in marriage, is
of no esteem, for unmarried women may prostitute themselves to as many as
they please, and being got with child, may lawfully take physic, in the
sight of every one, to destroy their fruit. And, in another place, if a
tradesman marry, all of the same condition, who are invited to the
wedding, lie with the bride before him; and the greater number of them
there is, the greater is her honour, and the opinion of her ability and
strength: if an officer marry, 'tis the same, the same with a labourer,
or one of mean condition; but then it belongs to the lord of the place to
perform that office; and yet a severe loyalty during marriage is
afterward strictly enjoined. There are places where brothels of young
men are kept for the pleasure of women; where the wives go to war as well
as the husbands, and not only share in the dangers of battle, but,
moreover, in the honours of command. Others, where they wear rings not
only through their noses, lips, cheeks, and on their toes, but also
weighty gimmals of gold thrust through their paps and buttocks; where, in
eating, they wipe their fingers upon their thighs, genitories, and the
soles of their feet: where children are excluded, and brothers and
nephews only inherit; and elsewhere, nephews only, saving in the
succession of the prince: where, for the regulation of community in goods
and estates, observed in the country, certain sovereign magistrates have
committed to them the universal charge and overseeing of the agriculture,
and distribution of the fruits, according to the necessity of every one
where they lament the death of children, and feast at the decease of old
men: where they lie ten or twelve in a bed, men and their wives together:
where women, whose husbands come to violent ends, may marry again, and*

*others not: where the condition of women is looked upon with such
contempt, that they kill all the native females, and buy wives of their
neighbours to supply their use; where husbands may repudiate their wives,
without showing any cause, but wives cannot part from their husbands, for
what cause soever; where husbands may sell their wives in case of
sterility; where they boil the bodies of their dead, and afterward pound
them to a pulp, which they mix with their wine, and drink it; where the
most coveted sepulture is to be eaten by dogs, and elsewhere by birds;
where they believe the souls of the blessed live in all manner of
liberty, in delightful fields, furnished with all sorts of delicacies,
and that it is these souls, repeating the words we utter, which we call
Echo; where they fight in the water, and shoot their arrows with the most
mortal aim, swimming; where, for a sign of subjection, they lift up their
shoulders, and hang down their heads; where they put off their shoes when
they enter the king's palace; where the eunuchs, who take charge of the
sacred women, have, moreover, their lips and noses cut off, that they may
not be loved; where the priests put out their own eyes, to be better
acquainted with their demons, and the better to receive their oracles;
where every one makes to himself a deity of what he likes best; the
hunter of a lion or a fox, the fisher of some fish; idols of every human
action or passion; in which place, the sun, the moon, and the earth are
the 'principal deities, and the form of taking an oath is, to touch the
earth, looking up to heaven; where both flesh and fish is eaten raw;
where the greatest oath they take is, to swear by the name of some dead
person of reputation, laying their hand upon his tomb; where the
newyear's gift the king sends every year to the princes, his vassals, is
fire, which being brought, all the old fire is put out, and the
neighbouring people are bound to fetch of the new, every one for
themselves, upon pain of high treason; where, when the king, to betake
himself wholly to devotion, retires from his administration (which often
falls out), his next successor is obliged to do the same, and the right
of the kingdom devolves to the third in succession: where they vary the
form of government, according to the seeming necessity of affairs: depose
the king when they think good, substituting certain elders to govern in
his stead, and sometimes transferring it into the hands of the
commonality: where men and women are both circumcised and also baptized:*

where the soldier, who in one or several engagements, has been so fortunate as to present seven of the enemies' heads to the king, is made noble: where they live in that rare and unsociable opinion of the mortality of the soul: where the women are delivered without pain or fear: where the women wear copper leggings upon both legs, and if a louse bite them, are bound in magnanimity to bite them again, and dare not marry, till first they have made their king a tender of their virginity, if he please to accept it: where the ordinary way of salutation is by putting a finger down to the earth, and then pointing it up toward heaven: where men carry burdens upon their heads, and women on their shoulders; where the women make water standing, and the men squatting: where they send their blood in token of friendship, and offer incense to the men they would honour, like gods: where, not only to the fourth, but in any other remote degree, kindred are not permitted to marry: where the children are four years at nurse, and often twelve; in which place, also, it is accounted mortal to give the child suck the first day after it is born: where the correction of the male children is peculiarly designed to the fathers, and to the mothers of the girls; the punishment being to hang them by the heels in the smoke: where they circumcise the women: where they eat all sorts of herbs, without other scruple than of the badness of the smell: where all things are open the finest houses, furnished in the richest manner, without doors, windows, trunks, or chests to lock, a thief being there punished double what they are in other places: where they crack lice with their teeth like monkeys, and abhor to see them killed with one's nails: where in all their lives they neither cut their hair nor pare their nails; and, in another place, pare those of the right hand only, letting the left grow for ornament and bravery: where they suffer the hair on the right side to grow as long as it will, and shave the other; and in the neighbouring provinces, some let their hair grow long before, and some behind, shaving close the rest: where parents let out their children, and husbands their wives, to their guests to hire: where a man may get his own mother with child, and fathers make use of their own daughters or sons, without scandal: where, at their solemn feasts, they interchangeably lend their children to one another, without any consideration of nearness of blood. In one place, men feed upon human flesh; in another, 'tis reputed a pious office for a man to kill his father at a certain age; elsewhere, the fathers dispose of their children, whilst yet in their mothers' wombs, some to be preserved and carefully brought up, and others to be abandoned or made away. Elsewhere the old husbands lend their wives to young men; and in another place they are in common without offence; in one place particularly, the women take it for a mark of honour to have as many gay fringed tassels at the bottom of their garment, as they have lain with several men. Moreover, has not custom made a republic of women separately by themselves? has it not put arms into their hands, and made them raise armies and fight battles? And does she not, by her own precept, instruct the most ignorant vulgar, and make them perfect in things which all the philosophy in the world could never beat into the heads of the wisest men? For we know entire nations, where death was not only despised, but entertained with the greatest triumph; where children of seven years old suffered themselves to be whipped to death, without changing countenance; where riches were in such contempt, that the meanest citizen would not have deigned to stoop to take up a purse of crowns. And we know regions, very fruitful in all manner of provisions, where, notwithstanding, the most ordinary diet, and that they are most pleased with, is only bread, cresses, and water. Did not custom, moreover, work that miracle in Chios that, in seven hundred years, it was never known that ever maid or wife committed any act to the prejudice of her honour?

To conclude; there is nothing, in my opinion, that she does not, or may not do; and therefore, with very good reason it is that Pindar calls her the ruler of the world. He that was seen to beat his father, and reproved for so doing, made answer, that it was the custom of their family; that, in like manner, his father had beaten his grandfather, his grandfather his great-grandfather, "And this," says he, pointing to his son, "when he comes to my age, shall beat me." And the father, whom the son dragged and hauled along the streets, commanded him to stop at a certain door, for he himself, he said, had dragged his father no farther, that being the utmost limit of the hereditary outrage the sons used to practise upon the fathers in their family. It is as much by custom as infirmity, says Aristotle, that women tear their hair, bite their nails, and eat coals and earth, and more by custom than nature that men abuse themselves with one another.

The laws of conscience, which we pretend to be derived from nature, proceed from custom; every one, having an inward veneration for the opinions and manners approved and received amongst his own people, cannot, without very great reluctance, depart from them, nor apply himself to them without applause. In times past, when those of Crete would curse any one, they prayed the gods to engage him in some ill custom. But the principal effect of its power is, so to seize and ensnare us, that it is hardly in us to disengage ourselves from its gripe, or so to come to ourselves, as to consider of and to weigh the things it enjoins. To say the truth, by reason that we suck it in with our milk, and that the face of the world presents itself in this posture to our first sight, it seems as if we were born upon condition to follow on this track; and the common fancies that we find in repute everywhere about us, and infused into our minds with the seed of our fathers, appear to be the most universal and genuine; from whence it comes to pass, that whatever is off the hinges of custom, is believed to be also off the hinges of reason; how unreasonably for the most part, God knows.

If, as we who study ourselves have learned to do, every one who hears a good sentence, would immediately consider how it does in any way touch his own private concern, every one would find, that it was not so much a good saying, as a severe lash to the ordinary stupidity of his own judgment: but men receive the precepts and admonitions of truth, as directed to the common sort, and never to themselves; and instead of applying them to their own manners, do only very ignorantly and unprofitably commit them to memory. But let us return to the empire of custom.

Such people as have been bred up to liberty, and subject to no other dominion but the authority of their own will, look upon all other form of government as monstrous and contrary to nature. Those who are inured to monarchy do the same; and what opportunity soever fortune presents them with to change, even then, when with the greatest difficulties they have

disengaged themselves from one master, that was troublesome and grievous
to them, they presently run, with the same difficulties, to create
another; being unable to take into hatred subjection itself.

'Tis by the mediation of custom, that every one is content with the place
where he is planted by nature; and the Highlanders of Scotland no more
pant after Touraine; than the Scythians after Thessaly. Darius asking
certain Greeks what they would take to assume the custom of the Indians,
of eating the dead bodies of their fathers (for that was their use,
believing they could not give them a better nor more noble sepulture than
to bury them in their own bodies), they made answer, that nothing in the
world should hire them to do it; but having also tried to persuade the
Indians to leave their custom, and, after the Greek manner, to burn the
bodies of their fathers, they conceived a still greater horror at the
motion.--[Herodotus, iii. 38.]--Every one does the same, for use veils
from us the true aspect of things.

> "Nil adeo magnum, nec tam mirabile quidquam
> Principio, quod non minuant mirarier omnes Paullatim."

> ["There is nothing at first so grand, so admirable, which by degrees
> people do not regard with less admiration."--Lucretius, ii. 1027]

Taking upon me once to justify something in use amongst us, and that was
received with absolute authority for a great many leagues round about us,
and not content, as men commonly do, to establish it only by force of law
and example, but inquiring still further into its origin, I found the
foundation so weak, that I who made it my business to confirm others, was
very near being dissatisfied myself. 'Tis by this receipt that Plato
--[Laws, viii. 6.]--undertakes to cure the unnatural and preposterous
loves of his time, as one which he esteems of sovereign virtue, namely,
that the public opinion condemns them; that the poets, and all other
sorts of writers, relate horrible stories of them; a recipe, by virtue of
which the most beautiful daughters no more allure their fathers' lust;
nor brothers, of the finest shape and fashion, their sisters' desire; the
very fables of Thyestes, OEdipus, and Macareus, having with the harmony

*of their song, infused this wholesome opinion and belief into the tender
brains of children. Chastity is, in truth, a great and shining virtue,
and of which the utility is sufficiently known; but to treat of it, and
to set it off in its true value, according to nature, is as hard as 'tis
easy to do so according to custom, laws, and precepts. The fundamental
and universal reasons are of very obscure and difficult research, and our
masters either lightly pass them over, or not daring so much as to touch
them, precipitate themselves into the liberty and protection of custom,
there puffing themselves out and triumphing to their heart's content:
such as will not suffer themselves to be withdrawn from this original
source, do yet commit a greater error, and subject themselves to wild
opinions; witness Chrysippus,--[Sextus Empiricus, Pyyrhon. Hypotyp., i.
14.]--who, in so many of his writings, has strewed the little account he
made of incestuous conjunctions, committed with how near relations
soever.*

*Whoever would disengage himself from this violent prejudice of custom,
would find several things received with absolute and undoubting opinion,
that have no other support than the hoary head and rivelled face of
ancient usage. But the mask taken off, and things being referred to the
decision of truth and reason, he will find his judgment as it were
altogether overthrown, and yet restored to a much more sure estate. For
example, I shall ask him, what can be more strange than to see a people
obliged to obey laws they never understood; bound in all their domestic
affairs, as marriages, donations, wills, sales, and purchases, to rules
they cannot possibly know, being neither written nor published in their
own language, and of which they are of necessity to purchase both the
interpretation and the use? Not according to the ingenious opinion of
Isocrates,--[Discourse to Nicocles.]--who counselled his king to make
the traffics and negotiations of his subjects, free, frank, and of profit
to them, and their quarrels and disputes burdensome, and laden with heavy
impositions and penalties; but, by a prodigious opinion, to make sale of
reason itself, and to give to laws a course of merchandise. I think
myself obliged to fortune that, as our historians report, it was a Gascon
gentleman, a countryman of mine, who first opposed Charlemagne, when he
attempted to impose upon us Latin and imperial laws.*

What can be more savage, than to see a nation where, by lawful custom, the office of a judge is bought and sold, where judgments are paid for with ready money, and where justice may legitimately be denied to him that has not wherewithal to pay; a merchandise in so great repute, as in a government to create a fourth estate of wrangling lawyers, to add to the three ancient ones of the church, nobility, and people; which fourth estate, having the laws in their own hands, and sovereign power over men's lives and fortunes, makes another body separate from nobility: whence it comes to pass, that there are double laws, those of honour and those of justice, in many things altogether opposite one to another; the nobles as rigorously condemning a lie taken, as the other do a lie revenged: by the law of arms, he shall be degraded from all nobility and honour who puts up with an affront; and by the civil law, he who vindicates his reputation by revenge incurs a capital punishment: he who applies himself to the law for reparation of an offence done to his honour, disgraces himself; and he who does not, is censured and punished by the law. Yet of these two so different things, both of them referring to one head, the one has the charge of peace, the other of war; those have the profit, these the honour; those the wisdom, these the virtue; those the word, these the action; those justice, these valour; those reason, these force; those the long robe, these the short;--divided betwixt them.

For what concerns indifferent things, as clothes, who is there seeking to bring them back to their true use, which is the body's service and convenience, and upon which their original grace and fitness depend; for the most fantastic, in my opinion, that can be imagined, I will instance amongst others, our flat caps, that long tail of velvet that hangs down from our women's heads, with its party-coloured trappings; and that vain and futile model of a member we cannot in modesty so much as name, which, nevertheless, we make show and parade of in public. These considerations, notwithstanding, will not prevail upon any understanding man to decline the common mode; but, on the contrary, methinks, all singular and particular fashions are rather marks of folly and vain affectation than of sound reason, and that a wise man, within, ought to withdraw and retire his soul from the crowd, and there keep it at liberty and in power to judge freely of things; but as to externals, absolutely to follow and conform himself to the fashion of the time. Public society has nothing to do with our thoughts, but the rest, as our actions, our labours, our fortunes, and our lives, we are to lend and abandon them to its service and to the common opinion, as did that good and great Socrates who refused to preserve his life by a disobedience to the magistrate, though a very wicked and unjust one for it is the rule of rules, the general law of laws, that every one observe those of the place wherein he lives.

> *["It is good to obey the laws of one's country."*
> *--Excerpta ex Trag. Gyaecis, Grotio interp., 1626, p. 937.]*

And now to another point. It is a very great doubt, whether any so manifest benefit can accrue from the alteration of a law received, let it be what it will, as there is danger and inconvenience in altering it; forasmuch as government is a structure composed of divers parts and members joined and united together, with so strict connection, that it is impossible to stir so much as one brick or stone, but the whole body will be sensible of it. The legislator of the Thurians--[Charondas; Diod. Sic., xii. 24.]--ordained, that whosoever would go about either to abolish an old law, or to establish a new, should present himself with a halter about his neck to the people, to the end, that if the innovation he would introduce should not be approved by every one, he might immediately be hanged; and he of the Lacedaemonians employed his life to obtain from his citizens a faithful promise that none of his laws should be violated.--[Lycurgus; Plutarch, in Vita, c. 22.]--The Ephoros who so rudely cut the two strings that Phrynis had added to music never stood to examine whether that addition made better harmony, or that by its means the instrument was more full and complete; it was enough for him to condemn the invention, that it was a novelty, and an alteration of the old fashion. Which also is the meaning of the old rusty sword carried before the magistracy of Marseilles.

For my own part, I have a great aversion from a novelty, what face or what pretence soever it may carry along with it, and have reason, having been an eyewitness of the great evils it has produced. For those which for so many years have lain so heavy upon us, it is not wholly accountable; but one may say, with colour enough, that it has accidentally produced and begotten the mischiefs and ruin that have since happened, both without and against it; it, principally, we are to accuse for these disorders:

"Heu! patior telis vulnera facta meis."

["Alas! The wounds were made by my own weapons."
⁓Ovid, Ep. Phyll. Demophoonti, vers. 48.]

They who give the first shock to a state, are almost naturally the first overwhelmed in its ruin the fruits of public commotion are seldom enjoyed by him who was the first motor; he beats and disturbs the water for another's net. The unity and contexture of this monarchy, of this grand edifice, having been ripped and torn in her old age, by this thing called innovation, has since laid open a rent, and given sufficient admittance to such injuries: the royal majesty with greater difficulty declines from the summit to the middle, then it falls and tumbles headlong from the middle to the bottom. But if the inventors do the greater mischief, the imitators are more vicious to follow examples of which they have felt and punished both the horror and the offence. And if there can be any degree of honour in ill-doing, these last must yield to the others the glory of contriving, and the courage of making the first attempt. All sorts of new disorders easily draw, from this primitive and ever-flowing fountain, examples and precedents to trouble and discompose our government: we read in our very laws, made for the remedy of this first evil, the beginning and pretences of all sorts of wicked enterprises; and that befalls us, which Thucydides said of the civil wars of his time, that, in favour of public vices, they gave them new and more plausible names for their excuse, sweetening and disguising their true titles; which must be done, forsooth, to reform our conscience and belief:

"*Honesta oratio est;*"

["*Fine words truly.*"--Ter. And., i. I, 114.]

but the best pretence for innovation is of very dangerous consequence:

"*Aden nihil motum ex antiquo probabile est.*"

["*We are ever wrong in changing ancient ways.*"--Livy, xxxiv. 54]

And freely to speak my thoughts, it argues a strange self-love and great
presumption to be so fond of one's own opinions, that a public peace must
be overthrown to establish them, and to introduce so many inevitable
mischiefs, and so dreadful a corruption of manners, as a civil war and
the mutations of state consequent to it, always bring in their train, and
to introduce them, in a thing of so high concern, into the bowels of
one's own country. Can there be worse husbandry than to set up so many
certain and knowing vices against errors that are only contested and
disputable? And are there any worse sorts of vices than those committed
against a man's own conscience, and the natural light of his own reason?
The Senate, upon the dispute betwixt it and the people about the
administration of their religion, was bold enough to return this evasion
for current pay:

"*Ad deos id magis, quam ad se, pertinere: ipsos visuros,
ne sacra sua polluantur;*"

["*Those things belong to the gods to determine than to them; let the
gods, therefore, take care that their sacred mysteries were not
profaned.*"--Livy, x. 6.]

according to what the oracle answered to those of Delphos who, fearing to
be invaded by the Persians in the Median war, inquired of Apollo, how
they should dispose of the holy treasure of his temple; whether they
should hide, or remove it to some other place? He returned them answer,
that they should stir nothing from thence, and only take care of

themselves, for he was sufficient to look to what belonged to him.
[Herodotus, viii. 36.].

The Christian religion has all the marks of the utmost utility and
justice: but none more manifest than the severe injunction it lays
indifferently upon all to yield absolute obedience to the civil
magistrate, and to maintain and defend the laws. Of which, what a
wonderful example has the divine wisdom left us, that, to establish the
salvation of mankind, and to conduct His glorious victory over death and
sin, would do it after no other way, but at the mercy of our ordinary
forms of justice subjecting the progress and issue of so high and so
salutiferous an effect, to the blindness and injustice of our customs
and observances; sacrificing the innocent blood of so many of His elect,
and so long a loss of so many years, to the maturing of this inestimable
fruit? There is a vast difference betwixt the case of one who follows
the forms and laws of his country, and of another who will undertake to
regulate and change them; of whom the first pleads simplicity, obedience,
and example for his excuse, who, whatever he shall do, it cannot be
imputed to malice; 'tis at the worst but misfortune:

> *"Quis est enim, quem non moveat clarissimis monumentis*
> *testata consignataque antiquitas?"*

> *["For who is there that antiquity, attested and confirmed by the*
> *fairest monuments, cannot move?"—Cicero, De Divin., i. 40.]*

besides what Isocrates says, that defect is nearer allied to moderation
than excess: the other is a much more ruffling gamester; for whosoever
shall take upon him to choose and alter, usurps the authority of judging,
and should look well about him, and make it his business to discern
clearly the defect of what he would abolish, and the virtue of what he is
about to introduce.

This so vulgar consideration is that which settled me in my station, and
kept even my most extravagant and ungoverned youth under the rein, so as
not to burden my shoulders with so great a weight, as to render myself

*responsible for a science of that importance, and in this to dare, what
in my better and more mature judgment, I durst not do in the most easy
and indifferent things I had been instructed in, and wherein the temerity
of judging is of no consequence at all; it seeming to me very unjust to
go about to subject public and established customs and institutions, to
the weakness and instability of a private and particular fancy (for
private reason has but a private jurisdiction), and to attempt that upon
the divine, which no government will endure a man should do, upon the
civil laws; with which, though human reason has much more commerce than
with the other, yet are they sovereignly judged by their own proper
judges, and the extreme sufficiency serves only to expound and set forth
the law and custom received, and neither to wrest it, nor to introduce
anything, of innovation. If, sometimes, the divine providence has gone
beyond the rules to which it has necessarily bound and obliged us men,
it is not to give us any dispensation to do the same; those are
masterstrokes of the divine hand, which we are not to imitate, but to
admire, and extraordinary examples, marks of express and particular
purposes, of the nature of miracles, presented before us for
manifestations of its almightiness, equally above both our rules and
force, which it would be folly and impiety to attempt to represent and
imitate; and that we ought not to follow, but to contemplate with the
greatest reverence: acts of His personage, and not for us. Cotta very
opportunely declares:*

> *"Quum de religione agitur, Ti. Coruncanium, P. Scipionem,
> P. Scaevolam, pontifices maximos, non Zenonem, aut Cleanthem,
> aut Chrysippum, sequor."*

> *["When matter of religion is in question, I follow the high priests
> T. Coruncanius, P. Scipio, P. Scaevola, and not Zeno, Cleanthes, or
> Chrysippus."--Cicero, De Natura Deor., iii. 2.]*

*God knows, in the present quarrel of our civil war, where there are a
hundred articles to dash out and to put in, great and very considerable,
how many there are who can truly boast, they have exactly and perfectly
weighed and understood the grounds and reasons of the one and the other*

party; 'tis a number, if they make any number, that would be able to give us very little disturbance. But what becomes of all the rest, under what ensigns do they march, in what quarter do they lie? Theirs have the same effect with other weak and ill-applied medicines; they have only set the humours they would purge more violently in work, stirred and exasperated by the conflict, and left them still behind. The potion was too weak to purge, but strong enough to weaken us; so that it does not work, but we keep it still in our bodies, and reap nothing from the operation but intestine gripes and dolours.

So it is, nevertheless, that Fortune still reserving her authority in defiance of whatever we are able to do or say, sometimes presents us with a necessity so urgent, that 'tis requisite the laws should a little yield and give way; and when one opposes the increase of an innovation that thus intrudes itself by violence, to keep a man's self in so doing, in all places and in all things within bounds and rules against those who have the power, and to whom all things are lawful that may in any way serve to advance their design, who have no other law nor rule but what serves best to their own purpose, 'tis a dangerous obligation and an intolerable inequality:

> "Aditum nocendi perfido praestat fides,"

> ["Putting faith in a treacherous person, opens the door to
> harm."--Seneca, OEdip., act iii., verse 686.]

forasmuch as the ordinary discipline of a healthful state does not provide against these extraordinary accidents; it presupposes a body that supports itself in its principal members and offices, and a common consent to its obedience and observation. A legitimate proceeding is cold, heavy, and constrained, and not fit to make head against a headstrong and unbridled proceeding. 'Tis known to be to this day cast in the dish of those two great men, Octavius and Cato, in the two civil wars of Sylla and Caesar, that they would rather suffer their country to undergo the last extremities, than relieve their fellow-citizens at the expense of its laws, or be guilty of any innovation; for in truth, in *these last necessities, where there is no other remedy, it would, peradventure, be more discreetly done, to stoop and yield a little to receive the blow, than, by opposing without possibility of doing good, to give occasion to violence to trample all under foot; and better to make the laws do what they can, when they cannot do what they would. After this manner did he--[Agesilaus.]--who suspended them for four-and-twenty hours, and he who, for once shifted a day in the calendar, and that other--[Alexander the Great.]--who of the month of June made a second of May. The Lacedaemonians themselves, who were so religious observers of the laws of their country, being straitened by one of their own edicts, by which it was expressly forbidden to choose the same man twice to be admiral; and on the other side, their affairs necessarily requiring, that Lysander should again take upon him that command, they made one Aratus admiral; 'tis true, but withal, Lysander went general of the navy; and, by the same subtlety, one of their ambassadors being sent to the Athenians to obtain the revocation of some decree, and Pericles remonstrating to him, that it was forbidden to take away the tablet wherein a law had once been engrossed, he advised him to turn it only, that being not forbidden; and Plutarch commends Philopoemen, that being born to command, he knew how to do it, not only according to the laws, but also to overrule even the laws themselves, when the public necessity so required.*

CHAPTER XXIII

VARIOUS EVENTS
FROM THE SAME COUNSEL

Jacques Amiot, grand almoner of France, one day related to me this story, much to the honour of a prince of ours (and ours he was upon several very good accounts, though originally of foreign extraction),--[The Duc de Guise, surnamed Le Balafre.]--that in the time of our first commotions, at the siege of Rouen,--[In 1562]--this prince, having been advertised by the queen-mother of a conspiracy against his life, and in her letters particular notice being given him of the person who was to execute the business (who was a gentleman of Anjou or of Maine, and who to this effect ordinarily frequented this prince's house), discovered not a syllable of this intelligence to any one whatever; but going the next day to the St. Catherine's Mount,--[An eminence outside Rouen overlooking the Seine. D.W.]--from which our battery played against the town (for it was during the time of the siege), and having in company with him the said lord almoner, and another bishop, he saw this gentleman, who had been denoted to him, and presently sent for him; to whom, being come before him, seeing him already pale and trembling with the conscience of his guilt, he thus said, "Monsieur," such an one, "you guess what I have to say to you; your countenance discovers it; 'tis in vain to disguise your practice, for I am so well informed of your business, that it will but make worse for you, to go about to conceal or deny it: you know very well such and such passages" (which were the most secret circumstances of his conspiracy), "and therefore be sure, as you tender your own life, to confess to me the whole truth of the design." The poor man seeing himself thus trapped and convicted (for the whole business had been discovered to the queen by one of the accomplices), was in such a taking, he knew not what to do; but, folding his hands, to beg and sue for mercy, he threw himself at his prince's feet, who taking him up, proceeded to say, "Come, sir; tell me, have I at any time done you offence? or have

I, through private hatred or malice, offended any kinsman or friend of yours? It is not above three weeks that I have known you; what inducement, then, could move you to attempt my death?" To which the gentleman with a trembling voice replied, "That it was no particular grudge he had to his person, but the general interest and concern of his party, and that he had been put upon it by some who had persuaded him it would be a meritorious act, by any means, to extirpate so great and so powerful an enemy of their religion." "Well," said the prince, "I will now let you see, how much more charitable the religion is that I maintain, than that which you profess: yours has counselled you to kill me, without hearing me speak, and without ever having given you any cause of offence; and mine commands me to forgive you, convict as you are, by your own confession, of a design to kill me without reason.--[Imitated by Voltaire. See Nodier, Questions, p. 165.]--Get you gone; let me see you no more; and, if you are wise, choose henceforward honester men for your counsellors in your designs."--[Dampmartin, La Fortune de la Coup, liv. ii., p. 139]

The Emperor Augustus,--[This story is taken from Seneca, De Clementia, i. 9.]--being in Gaul, had certain information of a conspiracy L. Cinna was contriving against him; he therefore resolved to make him an example; and, to that end, sent to summon his friends to meet the next morning in counsel. But the night between he passed in great unquietness of mind, considering that he was about to put to death a young man, of an illustrious family, and nephew to the great Pompey, and this made him break out into several passionate complainings. "What then," said he, "is it possible that I am to live in perpetual anxiety and alarm, and suffer my would-be assassin, meantime, to walk abroad at liberty? Shall he go unpunished, after having conspired against my life, a life that I have hitherto defended in so many civil wars, in so many battles by land and by sea? And after having settled the universal peace of the whole world, shall this man be pardoned, who has conspired not only to murder, but to sacrifice me?"--for the conspiracy was to kill him at sacrifice. After which, remaining for some time silent, he began again, in louder tones, and exclaimed against himself, saying: "Why livest thou, if it be for the good of so many that thou shouldst die? must there be no end of

*thy revenges and cruelties? Is thy life of so great value, that so many
mischiefs must be done to preserve it?" His wife Livia, seeing him in
this perplexity: "Will you take a woman's counsel?" said she. "Do as
the physicians do, who, when the ordinary recipes will do no good, make
trial of the contrary. By severity you have hitherto prevailed nothing;
Lepidus has followed Salvidienus; Murena, Lepidus; Caepio, Murena;
Egnatius, Caepio. Begin now, and try how sweetness and clemency will
succeed. Cinna is convict; forgive him, he will never henceforth have
the heart to hurt thee, and it will be an act to thy glory." Augustus
was well pleased that he had met with an advocate of his own humour;
wherefore, having thanked his wife, and, in the morning, countermanded
his friends he had before summoned to council, he commanded Cinna all
alone to be brought to him; who being accordingly come, and a chair by
his appointment set him, having ordered all the rest out of the room, he
spake to him after this manner: "In the first place, Cinna, I demand of
thee patient audience; do not interrupt me in what I am about to say, and
I will afterwards give thee time and leisure to answer. Thou knowest,
Cinna,--[This passage, borrowed from Seneca, has been paraphrased in
verse by Corneille. See Nodier, Questions de la Literature llgale, 1828,
pp. 7, 160. The monologue of Augustus in this chapter is also from
Seneca. Ibid., 164.]--that having taken thee prisoner in the enemy's
camp, and thou an enemy, not only so become, but born so, I gave thee thy
life, restored to thee all thy goods, and, finally, put thee in so good a
posture, by my bounty, of living well and at thy ease, that the
victorious envied the conquered. The sacerdotal office which thou madest
suit to me for, I conferred upon thee, after having denied it to others,
whose fathers have ever borne arms in my service. After so many
obligations, thou hast undertaken to kill me." At which Cinna crying out
that he was very far from entertaining any so wicked a thought: "Thou
dost not keep thy promise, Cinna," continued Augustus, "that thou wouldst
not interrupt me. Yes, thou hast undertaken to murder me in such a
place, on such a day, in such and such company, and in such a manner."
At which words, seeing Cinna astounded and silent, not upon the account
of his promise so to be, but interdict with the weight of his conscience:
"Why," proceeded Augustus, "to what end wouldst thou do it? Is it to be
emperor? Believe me, the Republic is in very ill condition, if I am the*

*only man betwixt thee and the empire. Thou art not able so much as to
defend thy own house, and but t'other day was baffled in a suit, by the
opposed interest of a mere manumitted slave. What, hast thou neither
means nor power in any other thing, but only to undertake Caesar? I quit
the throne, if there be no other than I to obstruct thy hopes. Canst
thou believe that Paulus, that Fabius, that the Cossii and the Servilii,
and so many noble Romans, not only so in title, but who by their virtue
honour their nobility, would suffer or endure thee?" After this, and a
great deal more that he said to him (for he was two long hours in
speaking), "Now go, Cinna, go thy way: I give thee that life as traitor
and parricide, which I before gave thee in the quality of an enemy. Let
friendship from this time forward begin betwixt us, and let us show
whether I have given, or thou hast received thy life with the better
faith"; and so departed from him. Some time after, he preferred him to
the consular dignity, complaining that he had not the confidence to
demand it; had him ever after for his very great friend, and was, at
last, made by him sole heir to all his estate. Now, from the time of
this accident which befell Augustus in the fortieth year of his age, he
never had any conspiracy or attempt against him, and so reaped the due
reward of this his so generous clemency. But it did not so happen with
our prince, his moderation and mercy not so securing him, but that he
afterwards fell into the toils of the like treason,--[The Duc de Guise
was assassinated in 1563 by Poltrot.]--so vain and futile a thing is
human prudence; throughout all our projects, counsels and precautions,
Fortune will still be mistress of events.*

*We repute physicians fortunate when they hit upon a lucky cure, as if
there was no other art but theirs that could not stand upon its own legs,
and whose foundations are too weak to support itself upon its own basis;
as if no other art stood in need of Fortune's hand to help it. For my
part, I think of physic as much good or ill as any one would have me:
for, thanks be to God, we have no traffic together. I am of a quite
contrary humour to other men, for I always despise it; but when I am
sick, instead of recanting, or entering into composition with it, I
begin, moreover, to hate and fear it, telling them who importune me to
take physic, that at all events they must give me time to recover my*

strength and health, that I may be the better able to support and
encounter the violence and danger of their potions. I let nature work,
supposing her to be sufficiently armed with teeth and claws to defend
herself from the assaults of infirmity, and to uphold that contexture,
the dissolution of which she flies and abhors. I am afraid, lest,
instead of assisting her when close grappled and struggling with disease,
I should assist her adversary, and burden her still more with work to do.

Now, I say, that not in physic only, but in other more certain arts,
fortune has a very great part.

The poetic raptures, the flights of fancy, that ravish and transport the
author out of himself, why should we not attribute them to his good
fortune, since he himself confesses that they exceed his sufficiency and
force, and acknowledges them to proceed from something else than himself,
and that he has them no more in his power than the orators say they have
those extraordinary motions and agitations that sometimes push them
beyond their design. It is the same in painting, where touches shall
sometimes slip from the hand of the painter, so surpassing both his
conception and his art, as to beget his own admiration and astonishment.
But Fortune does yet more evidently manifest the share she has in all
things of this kind, by the graces and elegances we find in them, not
only beyond the intention, but even without the knowledge of the workman:
a competent reader often discovers in other men's writings other
perfections than the author himself either intended or perceived, a
richer sense and more quaint expression.

As to military enterprises, every one sees how great a hand Fortune has
in them. Even in our counsels and deliberations there must, certainly,
be something of chance and good-luck mixed with human prudence; for all
that our wisdom can do alone is no great matter; the more piercing,
quick, and apprehensive it is, the weaker it finds itself, and is by so
much more apt to mistrust itself. I am of Sylla's opinion;--["Who freed
his great deeds from envy by ever attributing them to his good fortune,
and finally by surnaming himself Faustus, the Lucky."--Plutarch, How far a
Man may praise Himself, c. 9.]--and when I closely examine the most

*glorious exploits of war, I perceive, methinks, that those who carry them
on make use of counsel and debate only for custom's sake, and leave the
best part of the enterprise to Fortune, and relying upon her aid,
transgress, at every turn, the bounds of military conduct and the rules
of war. There happen, sometimes, fortuitous alacrities and strange
furies in their deliberations, that for the most part prompt them to
follow the worst grounded counsels, and swell their courage beyond the
limits of reason. Whence it happened that several of the great captains
of old, to justify those rash resolutions, have been fain to tell their
soldiers that they were invited to such attempts by some inspiration,
some sign and prognostic.*

*Wherefore, in this doubt and uncertainty, that the shortsightedness of
human wisdom to see and choose the best (by reason of the difficulties
that the various accidents and circumstances of things bring along with
them) perplexes us withal, the surest way, in my opinion, did no other
consideration invite us to it, is to pitch upon that wherein is the
greatest appearance of honesty and justice; and not, being certain of the
shortest, to keep the straightest and most direct way; as in the two
examples I have just given, there is no question but it was more noble
and generous in him who had received the offence, to pardon it, than to
do otherwise. If the former--[The Duc de Guise.]--miscarried in it, he
is not, nevertheless, to be blamed for his good intention; neither does
any one know if he had proceeded otherwise, whether by that means he had
avoided the end his destiny had appointed for him; and he had, moreover,
lost the glory of so humane an act.*

*You will read in history, of many who have been in such apprehension,
that the most part have taken the course to meet and anticipate
conspiracies against them by punishment and revenge; but I find very few
who have reaped any advantage by this proceeding; witness so many Roman
emperors. Whoever finds himself in this danger, ought not to expect much
either from his vigilance or power; for how hard a thing is it for a man
to secure himself from an enemy, who lies concealed under the countenance
of the most assiduous friend we have, and to discover and know the wills
and inward thoughts of those who are in our personal service. 'Tis to*

much purpose to have a guard of foreigners about one, and to be always fenced about with a pale of armed men; whosoever despises his own life, is always master of that of another man.--[Seneca, Ep., 4.]--And moreover, this continual suspicion, that makes a prince jealous of all the world, must of necessity be a strange torment to him. Therefore it was, that Dion, being advertised that Callippus watched all opportunities to take away his life, had never the heart to inquire more particularly into it, saying, that he had rather die than live in that misery, that he must continually stand upon his guard, not only against his enemies, but his friends also;--[Plutarch, Apothegms.]--which Alexander much more vividly and more roundly manifested in effect, when, having notice by a letter from Parmenio, that Philip, his most beloved physician, was by Darius' money corrupted to poison him, at the same time he gave the letter to Philip to read, drank off the potion he had brought him. Was not this to express a resolution, that if his friends had a mind to despatch him out of the world, he was willing to give them opportunity to do it? This prince is, indeed, the sovereign pattern of hazardous actions; but I do not know whether there be another passage in his life wherein there is so much firm courage as in this, nor so illustrious an image of the beauty and greatness of his mind.

Those who preach to princes so circumspect and vigilant a jealousy and distrust, under colour of security, preach to them ruin and dishonour: nothing noble can be performed without danger. I know a person, naturally of a very great daring and enterprising courage, whose good fortune is continually marred by such persuasions, that he keep himself close surrounded by his friends, that he must not hearken to any reconciliation with his ancient enemies, that he must stand aloof, and not trust his person in hands stronger than his own, what promises or offers soever they may make him, or what advantages soever he may see before him. And I know another, who has unexpectedly advanced his fortunes by following a clear contrary advice.

Courage, the reputation and glory of which men seek with so greedy an appetite, presents itself, when need requires, as magnificently in

cuerpo, as in full armour; in a closet, as in a camp; with arms pendant,
as with arms raised.

This over-circumspect and wary prudence is a mortal enemy to all high and
generous exploits. Scipio, to sound Syphax's intention, leaving his
army, abandoning Spain, not yet secure nor well settled in his new
conquest, could pass over into Africa in two small ships, to commit
himself, in an enemy's country, to the power of a barbarian king, to a
faith untried and unknown, without obligation, without hostage, under the
sole security of the grandeur of his own courage, his good fortune, and
the promise of his high hopes.--[Livy, xxviii. 17.]

>*"Habita fides ipsam plerumque fidem obligat."*

>*["Trust often obliges fidelity."--Livy, xxii. 22.]*

In a life of ambition and glory, it is necessary to hold a stiff rein
upon suspicion: fear and distrust invite and draw on offence. The most
mistrustful of our kings--[Louis XI.]--established his affairs
principally by voluntarily committing his life and liberty into his
enemies' hands, by that action manifesting that he had absolute
confidence in them, to the end they might repose as great an assurance in
him. Caesar only opposed the authority of his countenance and the
haughty sharpness of his rebukes to his mutinous legions in arms against
him:

>*"Stetit aggere fulti*
>*Cespitis, intrepidus vultu: meruitque timeri,*
>*Nil metuens."*

>*["He stood on a mound, his countenance intrepid, and merited to be*
>*feared, he fearing nothing."--Lucan, v. 316.]*

But it is true, withal, that this undaunted assurance is not to be
represented in its simple and entire form, but by such whom the
apprehension of death, and the worst that can happen, does not terrify

and affright; for to represent a pretended resolution with a pale and doubtful countenance and trembling limbs, for the service of an important reconciliation, will effect nothing to purpose. 'Tis an excellent way to gain the heart and will of another, to submit and intrust one's self to him, provided it appear to be freely done, and without the constraint of necessity, and in such a condition, that a man manifestly does it out of a pure and entire confidence in the party, at least, with a countenance clear from any cloud of suspicion. I saw, when I was a boy, a gentleman, who was governor of a great city, upon occasion of a popular commotion and fury, not knowing what other course to take, go out of a place of very great strength and security, and commit himself to the mercy of the seditious rabble, in hopes by that means to appease the tumult before it grew to a more formidable head; but it was ill for him that he did so, for he was there miserably slain. But I am not, nevertheless, of opinion, that he committed so great an error in going out, as men commonly reproach his memory withal, as he did in choosing a gentle and submissive way for the effecting his purpose, and in endeavouring to quiet this storm, rather by obeying than commanding, and by entreaty rather than remonstrance; and I am inclined to believe, that a gracious severity, with a soldierlike way of commanding, full of security and confidence, suitable to the quality of his person, and the dignity of his command, would have succeeded better with him; at least, he had perished with greater decency and, reputation. There is nothing so little to be expected or hoped for from this many-headed monster, in its fury, as humanity and good nature; it is much more capable of reverence and fear. I should also reproach him, that having taken a resolution (in my judgment rather brave than rash) to expose himself, weak and naked, in this tempestuous sea of enraged madmen, he ought to have stuck to his text, and not for an instant to have abandoned the high part he had undertaken; whereas, coming to discover his danger nearer hand, and his nose happening to bleed, he again changed that demiss and fawning countenance he had at first put on, into another of fear and amazement, filling his voice with entreaties and his eyes with tears, and, endeavouring so to withdraw and secure his person, that carriage more inflamed their fury, and soon brought the effects of it upon him.

It was upon a time intended that there should be a general muster of several troops in arms (and that is the most proper occasion of secret revenges, and there is no place where they can be executed with greater safety), and there were public and manifest appearances, that there was no safe coming for some, whose principal and necessary office it was to review them. Whereupon a consultation was held, and several counsels were proposed, as in a case that was very nice and of great difficulty; and moreover of grave consequence. Mine, amongst the rest, was, that they should by all means avoid giving any sign of suspicion, but that the officers who were most in danger should boldly go, and with cheerful and erect countenances ride boldly and confidently through the ranks, and that instead of sparing fire (which the counsels of the major part tended to) they should entreat the captains to command the soldiers to give round and full volleys in honour of the spectators, and not to spare their powder. This was accordingly done, and served so good use, as to please and gratify the suspected troops, and thenceforward to beget a mutual and wholesome confidence and intelligence amongst them.

I look upon Julius Caesar's way of winning men to him as the best and finest that can be put in practice. First, he tried by clemency to make himself beloved even by his very enemies, contenting himself, in detected conspiracies, only publicly to declare, that he was pre-acquainted with them; which being done, he took a noble resolution to await without solicitude or fear, whatever might be the event, wholly resigning himself to the protection of the gods and fortune: for, questionless, in this state he was at the time when he was killed.

A stranger having publicly said, that he could teach Dionysius, the tyrant of Syracuse, an infallible way to find out and discover all the conspiracies his subjects could contrive against him, if he would give him a good sum of money for his pains, Dionysius hearing of it, caused the man to be brought to him, that he might learn an art so necessary to his preservation. The man made answer, that all the art he knew, was, that he should give him a talent, and afterwards boast that he had obtained a singular secret from him. Dionysius liked the invention, and accordingly caused six hundred crowns to be counted out to him.

--[*Plutarch, Apothegms.*]--It was not likely he should give so great a sum to a person unknown, but upon the account of some extraordinary discovery, and the belief of this served to keep his enemies in awe. Princes, however, do wisely to publish the informations they receive of all the practices against their lives, to possess men with an opinion they have so good intelligence that nothing can be plotted against them, but they have present notice of it. The Duke of Athens did a great many foolish things in the establishment of his new tyranny over Florence: but this especially was most notable, that having received the first intimation of the conspiracies the people were hatching against him, from Matteo di Morozzo, one of the conspirators, he presently put him to death, to suppress that rumour, that it might not be thought any of the city disliked his government.

I remember I have formerly read a story--[*In Appian's Civil Wars, book iv.*]--of some Roman of great quality who, flying the tyranny of the Triumvirate, had a thousand times by the subtlety of as many inventions escaped from falling into the hands of those that pursued him. It happened one day that a troop of horse, which was sent out to take him, passed close by a brake where he was squat, and missed very narrowly of spying him: but he considering, at this point, the pains and difficulties wherein he had so long continued to evade the strict and incessant searches that were every day made for him, the little pleasure he could hope for in such a kind of life, and how much better it was for him to die once for all, than to be perpetually at this pass, he started from his seat, called them back, showed them his form,--[*as of a squatting hare.*]--and voluntarily delivered himself up to their cruelty, by that means to free both himself and them from further trouble. To invite a man's enemies to come and cut his throat, seems a resolution a little extravagant and odd; and yet I think he did better to take that course, than to live in continual feverish fear of an accident for which there was no cure. But seeing all the remedies a man can apply to such a disease, are full of unquietness and uncertainty, 'tis better with a manly courage to prepare one's self for the worst that can happen, and to extract some consolation from this, that we are not certain the thing we fear will ever come to pass.

CHAPTER XXIV

OF PEDANTRY

I was often, when a boy, wonderfully concerned to see, in the Italian farces, a pedant always brought in for the fool of the play, and that the title of Magister was in no greater reverence amongst us: for being delivered up to their tuition, what could I do less than be jealous of their honour and reputation? I sought indeed to excuse them by the natural incompatibility betwixt the vulgar sort and men of a finer thread, both in judgment and knowledge, forasmuch as they go a quite contrary way to one another: but in this, the thing I most stumbled at was, that the finest gentlemen were those who most despised them; witness our famous poet Du Bellay--

"Mais je hay par sur tout un scavoir pedantesque."

["Of all things I hate pedantic learning."--Du Bellay]

And 'twas so in former times; for Plutarch says that Greek and Scholar were terms of reproach and contempt amongst the Romans. But since, with the better experience of age, I find they had very great reason so to do, and that--

"Magis magnos clericos non sunt magis magnos sapientes."

["The greatest clerks are not the wisest men." A proverb given in Rabelais' Gargantua, i. 39.]

But whence it should come to pass, that a mind enriched with the knowledge of so many things should not become more quick and sprightly, and that a gross and vulgar understanding should lodge within it, without correcting and improving itself, all the discourses and judgments of the greatest minds the world ever had, I am yet to seek. To admit so many foreign conceptions, so great, and so high fancies, it is necessary (as a young lady, one of the greatest princesses of the kingdom, said to me once, speaking of a certain person) that a man's own brain must be crowded and squeezed together into a less compass, to make room for the others; I should be apt to conclude, that as plants are suffocated and drowned with too much nourishment, and lamps with too much oil, so with too much study and matter is the active part of the understanding which, being embarrassed, and confounded with a great diversity of things, loses the force and power to disengage itself, and by the pressure of this weight, is bowed, subjected, and doubled up. But it is quite otherwise; for our soul stretches and dilates itself proportionably as it fills; and in the examples of elder times, we see, quite contrary, men very proper for public business, great captains, and great statesmen very learned withal.

And, as to the philosophers, a sort of men remote from all public affairs, they have been sometimes also despised by the comic liberty of their times; their opinions and manners making them appear, to men of another sort, ridiculous. Would you make them judges of a lawsuit, of the actions of men? they are ready to take it upon them, and straight begin to examine if there be life, if there be motion, if man be any other than an ox;--["If Montaigne has copied all this from Plato's Theaetetes, p.127, F. as it is plain by all which he has added immediately after, that he has taken it from that dialogue, he has grossly mistaken Plato's sentiment, who says here no more than this, that the philosopher is so ignorant of what his neighbour does, that he scarce knows whether he is a man, or some other animal:--Coste."]--what it is to do and to suffer? what animals law and justice are? Do they speak of the magistrates, or to him, 'tis with a rude, irreverent, and indecent liberty. Do they hear their prince, or a king commended? they make no more of him, than of a shepherd, goatherd, or neatherd: a lazy Coridon, occupied in milking and shearing his herds and flocks, but more rudely and harshly than the herd or shepherd himself. Do you repute any man the greater for being lord of two thousand acres of land? they laugh at such a pitiful pittance, as laying claim themselves to the whole world for

their possession. Do you boast of your nobility, as being descended from
seven rich successive ancestors? they look upon you with an eye of
contempt, as men who have not a right idea of the universal image of
nature, and that do not consider how many predecessors every one of us
has had, rich, poor, kings, slaves, Greeks, and barbarians; and though
you were the fiftieth descendant from Hercules, they look upon it as a
great vanity, so highly to value this, which is only a gift of fortune.
And 'twas so the vulgar sort contemned them, as men ignorant of the most
elementary and ordinary things; as presumptuous and insolent.

But this Platonic picture is far different from that these pedants are
presented by. Those were envied for raising themselves above the common
sort, for despising the ordinary actions and offices of life, for having
assumed a particular and inimitable way of living, and for using a
certain method of high-flight and obsolete language, quite different from
the ordinary way of speaking: but these are contemned as being as much
below the usual form, as incapable of public employment, as leading a
life and conforming themselves to the mean and vile manners of the
vulgar:

"Odi ignava opera, philosopha sententia."

["I hate men who jabber about philosophy, but do nothing."
--Pacuvius, ap Gellium, xiii. 8.]

For what concerns the philosophers, as I have said, if they were in
science, they were yet much greater in action. And, as it is said of the
geometrician of Syracuse,--[Archimedes.]--who having been disturbed from
his contemplation, to put some of his skill in practice for the defence
of his country, that he suddenly set on foot dreadful and prodigious
engines, that wrought effects beyond all human expectation; himself,
notwithstanding, disdaining all his handiwork, and thinking in this he
had played the mere mechanic, and violated the dignity of his art, of
which these performances of his he accounted but trivial experiments and
playthings so they, whenever they have been put upon the proof of action,

have been seen to fly to so high a pitch, as made it very well appear,
their souls were marvellously elevated, and enriched by the knowledge of
things. But some of them, seeing the reins of government in the hands of
incapable men, have avoided all management of political affairs; and he
who demanded of Crates, how long it was necessary to philosophise,
received this answer: "Till our armies are no more commanded by fools."
--[Diogenes Laertius, vi. 92.]--Heraclitus resigned the royalty to his
brother; and, to the Ephesians, who reproached him that he spent his time
in playing with children before the temple: "Is it not better," said he,
"to do so, than to sit at the helm of affairs in your company?" Others
having their imagination advanced above the world and fortune, have
looked upon the tribunals of justice, and even the thrones of kings, as
paltry and contemptible; insomuch, that Empedocles refused the royalty
that the Agrigentines offered to him. Thales, once inveighing in
discourse against the pains and care men put themselves to to become
rich, was answered by one in the company, that he did like the fox, who
found fault with what he could not obtain. Whereupon, he had a mind, for
the jest's sake, to show them to the contrary; and having, for this
occasion, made a muster of all his wits, wholly to employ them in the
service of profit and gain, he set a traffic on foot, which in one year
brought him in so great riches, that the most experienced in that trade
could hardly in their whole lives, with all their industry, have raked so
much together.--[Diogenes Laertius, Life of Thales, i. 26; Cicero, De
Divin., i. 49.]--That which Aristotle reports of some who called both
him and Anaxagoras, and others of their profession, wise but not prudent,
in not applying their study to more profitable things--though I do not
well digest this verbal distinction--that will not, however, serve to
excuse my pedants, for to see the low and necessitous fortune wherewith
they are content, we have rather reason to pronounce that they are
neither wise nor prudent.

But letting this first reason alone, I think it better to say, that this
evil proceeds from their applying themselves the wrong way to the study
of the sciences; and that, after the manner we are instructed, it is no
wonder if neither the scholars nor the masters become, though more
learned, ever the wiser, or more able. In plain truth, the cares and

expense our parents are at in our education, point at nothing, but to
furnish our heads with knowledge; but not a word of judgment and virtue.
Cry out, of one that passes by, to the people: "O, what a learned man!"
and of another, "O, what a good man!"--[Translated from Seneca, Ep.,
88.]--they will not fail to turn their eyes, and address their respect
to the former. There should then be a third crier, "O, the blockheads!"
Men are apt presently to inquire, does such a one understand Greek or
Latin? Is he a poet? or does he write in prose? But whether he be
grown better or more discreet, which are qualities of principal concern,
these are never thought of. We should rather examine, who is better
learned, than who is more learned.

We only labour to stuff the memory, and leave the conscience and the
understanding unfurnished and void. Like birds who fly abroad to forage
for grain, and bring it home in the beak, without tasting it themselves,
to feed their young; so our pedants go picking knowledge here and there,
out of books, and hold it at the tongue's end, only to spit it out and
distribute it abroad. And here I cannot but smile to think how I have
paid myself in showing the foppery of this kind of learning, who myself
am so manifest an example; for, do I not the same thing throughout almost
this whole composition? I go here and there, culling out of several
books the sentences that best please me, not to keep them (for I have no
memory to retain them in), but to transplant them into this; where, to
say the truth, they are no more mine than in their first places. We are,
I conceive, knowing only in present knowledge, and not at all in what is
past, or more than is that which is to come. But the worst on't is,
their scholars and pupils are no better nourished by this kind of
inspiration; and it makes no deeper impression upon them, but passes from
hand to hand, only to make a show to be tolerable company, and to tell
pretty stories, like a counterfeit coin in counters, of no other use or
value, but to reckon with, or to set up at cards:

"Apud alios loqui didicerunt non ipsi secum."

["They have learned to speak from others, not from themselves."
--Cicero, Tusc. Quaes, v. 36.]

"*Non est loquendum, sed gubernandum.*"

[*"Speaking is not so necessary as governing."*--Seneca, Ep., 108.]

Nature, to shew that there is nothing barbarous where she has the sole conduct, oftentimes, in nations where art has the least to do, causes productions of wit, such as may rival the greatest effect of art whatever. In relation to what I am now speaking of, the Gascon proverb, derived from a cornpipe, is very quaint and subtle:

"*Bouha prou bouha, mas a remuda lous dits quem.*"

[*"You may blow till your eyes start out; but if once you offer to stir your fingers, it is all over."*]

We can say, Cicero says thus; these were the manners of Plato; these are the very words of Aristotle: but what do we say ourselves? What do we judge? A parrot would say as much as that.

And this puts me in mind of that rich gentleman of Rome,--[Calvisius Sabinus. Seneca, Ep., 27.]--who had been solicitous, with very great expense, to procure men that were excellent in all sorts of science, whom he had always attending his person, to the end, that when amongst his friends any occasion fell out of speaking of any subject whatsoever, they might supply his place, and be ready to prompt him, one with a sentence of Seneca, another with a verse of Homer, and so forth, every one according to his talent; and he fancied this knowledge to be his own, because it was in the heads of those who lived upon his bounty; as they also do, whose learning consists in having noble libraries. I know one, who, when I question him what he knows, he presently calls for a book to shew me, and dares not venture to tell me so much, as that he has piles in his posteriors, till first he has consulted his dictionary, what piles and what posteriors are.

*We take other men's knowledge and opinions upon trust; which is an idle
and superficial learning. We must make it our own. We are in this very
like him, who having need of fire, went to a neighbour's house to fetch
it, and finding a very good one there, sat down to warm himself without
remembering to carry any with him home.--[Plutarch, How a Man should
Listen.]--What good does it do us to have the stomach full of meat, if
it do not digest, if it be not incorporated with us, if it does not
nourish and support us? Can we imagine that Lucullus, whom letters,
without any manner of experience, made so great a captain, learned to be
so after this perfunctory manner?--[Cicero, Acad., ii. I.]--We suffer
ourselves to lean and rely so strongly upon the arm of another, that we
destroy our own strength and vigour. Would I fortify myself against the
fear of death, it must be at the expense of Seneca: would I extract
consolation for myself or my friend, I borrow it from Cicero. I might
have found it in myself, had I been trained to make use of my own reason.
I do not like this relative and mendicant understanding; for though we
could become learned by other men's learning, a man can never be wise but
by his own wisdom:*

*["I hate the wise man, who in his own concern is not wise."
--Euripides, ap. Cicero, Ep. Fam., xiii. 15.]*

Whence Ennius:

"Nequidquam sapere sapientem, qui ipse sibi prodesse non quiret."

*["That wise man knows nothing, who cannot profit himself by his
wisdom."--Cicero, De Offic., iii. 15.]*

*"Si cupidus, si
Vanus, et Euganea quantumvis mollior agna."*

*["If he be grasping, or a boaster, and something softer than an
Euganean lamb."--Juvenal, Sat., viii. 14.]*

"Non enim paranda nobis solum, sed fruenda sapientia est."

["For wisdom is not only to be acquired, but to be utilised."
--Cicero, De Finib., i. I.]

Dionysius--[It was not Dionysius, but Diogenes the cynic. Diogenes
Laertius, vi. 27.]--laughed at the grammarians, who set themselves to
inquire into the miseries of Ulysses, and were ignorant of their own;
at musicians, who were so exact in tuning their instruments, and never
tuned their manners; at orators, who made it a study to declare what is
justice, but never took care to do it. If the mind be not better
disposed, if the judgment be no better settled, I had much rather my
scholar had spent his time at tennis, for, at least, his body would by
that means be in better exercise and breath. Do but observe him when he
comes back from school, after fifteen or sixteen years that he has been
there; there is nothing so unfit for employment; all you shall find he
has got, is, that his Latin and Greek have only made him a greater
coxcomb than when he went from home. He should bring back his soul
replete with good literature, and he brings it only swelled and puffed up
with vain and empty shreds and patches of learning; and has really
nothing more in him than he had before.--[Plato's Dialogues: Protagoras.]

These pedants of ours, as Plato says of the Sophists, their
cousin-germans, are, of all men, they who most pretend to be useful to
mankind, and who alone, of all men, not only do not better and improve
that which is committed to them, as a carpenter or a mason would do, but
make them much worse, and make us pay them for making them worse, to
boot. If the rule which Protagoras proposed to his pupils were followed
--either that they should give him his own demand, or make affidavit upon
oath in the temple how much they valued the profit they had received
under his tuition, and satisfy him accordingly--my pedagogues would find
themselves sorely gravelled, if they were to be judged by the affidavits
of my experience. My Perigordin patois very pleasantly calls these
pretenders to learning, 'lettre-ferits', as a man should say,
letter-marked--men on whom letters have been stamped by the blow of a
mallet. And, in truth, for the most part, they appear to be deprived even
of common sense; for you see the husbandman and the cobbler go simply and

fairly about their business, speaking only of what they know and understand; whereas these fellows, to make parade and to get opinion, mustering this ridiculous knowledge of theirs, that floats on the superficies of the brain, are perpetually perplexing, and entangling themselves in their own nonsense. They speak fine words sometimes, 'tis true, but let somebody that is wiser apply them. They are wonderfully well acquainted with Galen, but not at all with the disease of the patient; they have already deafened you with a long ribble-row of laws, but understand nothing of the case in hand; they have the theory of all things, let who will put it in practice.

I have sat by, when a friend of mine, in my own house, for sport-sake, has with one of these fellows counterfeited a jargon of Galimatias, patched up of phrases without head or tail, saving that he interlarded here and there some terms that had relation to their dispute, and held the coxcomb in play a whole afternoon together, who all the while thought he had answered pertinently and learnedly to all his objections; and yet this was a man of letters, and reputation, and a fine gentleman of the long robe:

> *"Vos, O patricius sanguis, quos vivere par est*
> *Occipiti caeco, posticae occurrite sannae."*

> *["O you, of patrician blood, to whom it is permitted to live with(out) eyes in the back of your head, beware of grimaces at you from behind."--Persius, Sat., i. 61.]*

Whosoever shall narrowly pry into and thoroughly sift this sort of people, wherewith the world is so pestered, will, as I have done, find, that for the most part, they neither understand others, nor themselves; and that their memories are full enough, but the judgment totally void and empty; some excepted, whose own nature has of itself formed them into better fashion. As I have observed, for example, in Adrian Turnebus, who having never made other profession than that of mere learning only, and in that, in my opinion, he was the greatest man that has been these thousand years, had nothing at all in him of the pedant, but the wearing

*of his gown, and a little exterior fashion, that could not be civilised
to courtier ways, which in themselves are nothing. I hate our people,
who can worse endure an ill-contrived robe than an ill-contrived mind,
and take their measure by the leg a man makes, by his behaviour, and so
much as the very fashion of his boots, what kind of man he is. For
within there was not a more polished soul upon earth. I have often
purposely put him upon arguments quite wide of his profession, wherein I
found he had so clear an insight, so quick an apprehension, so solid a
judgment, that a man would have thought he had never practised any other
thing but arms, and been all his life employed in affairs of State.
These are great and vigorous natures,*

> *"Queis arte benigna
> Et meliore luto finxit praecordia Titan."*

*["Whom benign Titan (Prometheus) has framed of better clay."
--Juvenal, xiv. 34.]*

*that can keep themselves upright in despite of a pedantic education. But
it is not enough that our education does not spoil us; it must, moreover,
alter us for the better.*

*Some of our Parliaments, when they are to admit officers, examine only
their learning; to which some of the others also add the trial of
understanding, by asking their judgment of some case in law; of these the
latter, methinks, proceed with the better method; for although both are
necessary, and that it is very requisite they should be defective in
neither, yet, in truth, knowledge is not so absolutely necessary as
judgment; the last may make shift without the other, but the other never
without this. For as the Greek verse says--*

*["To what use serves learning, if understanding be away."
--Apud Stobaeus, tit. iii., p. 37 (1609).]*

Would to God that, for the good of our judicature, these societies were as well furnished with understanding and conscience as they are with knowledge.

> *"Non vita, sed scolae discimus."*

> *["We do not study for life, but only for the school."*
> *⁓Seneca, Ep., 106.]*

We are not to tie learning to the soul, but to work and incorporate them together: not to tincture it only, but to give it a thorough and perfect dye; which, if it will not take colour, and meliorate its imperfect state, it were without question better to let it alone. 'Tis a dangerous weapon, that will hinder and wound its master, if put into an awkward and unskilful hand:

> *"Ut fuerit melius non didicisse."*

> *["So that it were better not to have learned."*
> *⁓Cicero, Tusc. Quaes., ii. 4.]*

And this, peradventure, is the reason why neither we nor theology require much learning in women; and that Francis, Duke of Brittany, son of John V., one talking with him about his marriage with Isabella the daughter of Scotland, and adding that she was homely bred, and without any manner of learning, made answer, that he liked her the better, and that a woman was wise enough, if she could distinguish her husband's shirt from his doublet. So that it is no so great wonder, as they make of it, that our ancestors had letters in no greater esteem, and that even to this day they are but rarely met with in the principal councils of princes; and if the end and design of acquiring riches, which is the only thing we propose to ourselves, by the means of law, physic, pedantry, and even divinity itself, did not uphold and keep them in credit, you would, with doubt, see them in as pitiful a condition as ever. And what loss would this be, if they neither instruct us to think well nor to do well?

"Postquam docti prodierunt, boni desunt."

*[Seneca, Ep., 95. "Since the 'savans' have made their appearance
among us, the good people have become eclipsed."
~~Rousseau, Discours sur les Lettres.]*

All other knowledge is hurtful to him who has not the science of
goodness.

But the reason I glanced upon but now, may it not also hence proceed,
that, our studies in France having almost no other aim but profit, except
as to those who, by nature born to offices and employments rather of
glory than gain, addict themselves to letters, if at all, only for so
short a time (being taken from their studies before they can come to have
any taste of them, to a profession that has nothing to do with books),
there ordinarily remain no others to apply themselves wholly to learning,
but people of mean condition, who in that only seek the means to live;
and by such people, whose souls are, both by nature and by domestic
education and example, of the basest alloy the fruits of knowledge are
immaturely gathered and ill digested, and delivered to their recipients
quite another thing. For it is not for knowledge to enlighten a soul
that is dark of itself, nor to make a blind man see. Her business is not
to find a man's eyes, but to guide, govern, and direct them, provided he
have sound feet and straight legs to go upon. Knowledge is an excellent
drug, but no drug has virtue enough to preserve itself from corruption
and decay, if the vessel be tainted and impure wherein it is put to keep.
Such a one may have a sight clear enough who looks asquint, and
consequently sees what is good, but does not follow it, and sees
knowledge, but makes no use of it. Plato's principal institution in his
Republic is to fit his citizens with employments suitable to their
nature. Nature can do all, and does all. Cripples are very unfit for
exercises of the body, and lame souls for exercises of the mind.
Degenerate and vulgar souls are unworthy of philosophy. If we see a
shoemaker with his shoes out at the toes, we say, 'tis no wonder; for,
commonly, none go worse shod than they. In like manner, experience often

presents us a physician worse physicked, a divine less reformed, and
(constantly) a scholar of less sufficiency, than other people.

Old Aristo of Chios had reason to say that philosophers did their
auditors harm, forasmuch as most of the souls of those that heard them
were not capable of deriving benefit from instruction, which, if not
applied to good, would certainly be applied to ill:

> ["They proceeded effeminate debauchees from the school of
> Aristippus, cynics from that of Zeno."
> ⸺Cicero, De Natura Deor., iii., 31.]

In that excellent institution that Xenophon attributes to the Persians,
we find that they taught their children virtue, as other nations do
letters. Plato tells us that the eldest son in their royal succession
was thus brought up; after his birth he was delivered, not to women, but
to eunuchs of the greatest authority about their kings for their virtue,
whose charge it was to keep his body healthful and in good plight; and
after he came to seven years of age, to teach him to ride and to go
a-hunting. When he arrived at fourteen he was transferred into the hands
of four, the wisest, the most just, the most temperate, and most valiant
of the nation; of whom the first was to instruct him in religion, the
second to be always upright and sincere, the third to conquer his
appetites and desires, and the fourth to despise all danger.

It is a thing worthy of very great consideration, that in that excellent,
and, in truth, for its perfection, prodigious form of civil regimen set
down by Lycurgus, though so solicitous of the education of children,
as a thing of the greatest concern, and even in the very seat of the
Muses, he should make so little mention of learning; as if that generous
youth, disdaining all other subjection but that of virtue, ought to be
supplied, instead of tutors to read to them arts and sciences, with such
masters as should only instruct them in valour, prudence, and justice;
an example that Plato has followed in his laws. The manner of their
discipline was to propound to them questions in judgment upon men and
their actions; and if they commended or condemned this or that person or

fact, they were to give a reason for so doing; by which means they at
once sharpened their understanding, and learned what was right.
Astyages, in Xenophon, asks Cyrus to give an account of his last lesson;
and thus it was, "A great boy in our school, having a little short
cassock, by force took a longer from another that was not so tall as he,
and gave him his own in exchange: whereupon I, being appointed judge of
the controversy, gave judgment, that I thought it best each should keep
the coat he had, for that they both of them were better fitted with that
of one another than with their own: upon which my master told me, I had
done ill, in that I had only considered the fitness of the garments,
whereas I ought to have considered the justice of the thing, which
required that no one should have anything forcibly taken from him that is
his own." And Cyrus adds that he was whipped for his pains, as we are in
our villages for forgetting the first aorist of ‒‒‒‒‒‒.

> [Cotton's version of this story commences differently, and includes
> a passage which is not in any of the editions of the original before
> me:

> "Mandane, in Xenophon, asking Cyrus how he would do to learn
> justice, and the other virtues amongst the Medes, having left all
> his masters behind him in Persia? He made answer, that he had
> learned those things long since; that his master had often made him
> a judge of the differences amongst his schoolfellows, and had one
> day whipped him for giving a wrong sentence."‒‒W.C.H.]

My pedant must make me a very learned oration, 'in genere demonstrativo',
before he can persuade me that his school is like unto that. They knew
how to go the readiest way to work; and seeing that science, when most
rightly applied and best understood, can do no more but teach us
prudence, moral honesty, and resolution, they thought fit, at first hand,
to initiate their children with the knowledge of effects, and to instruct
them, not by hearsay and rote, but by the experiment of action, in lively
forming and moulding them; not only by words and precepts, but chiefly by
works and examples; to the end it might not be a knowledge in the mind
only, but its complexion and habit: not an acquisition, but a natural

*possession. One asking to this purpose, Agesilaus, what he thought most
proper for boys to learn? "What they ought to do when they come to be
men," said he.--[Plutarch, Apothegms of the Lacedamonians. Rousseau
adopts the expression in his Diswuys sur tes Lettres.]--It is no wonder,
if such an institution produced so admirable effects.*

*They used to go, it is said, to the other cities of Greece, to inquire
out rhetoricians, painters, and musicians; but to Lacedaemon for
legislators, magistrates, and generals of armies; at Athens they learned
to speak well: here to do well; there to disengage themselves from a
sophistical argument, and to unravel the imposture of captious
syllogisms; here to evade the baits and allurements of pleasure, and with
a noble courage and resolution to conquer the menaces of fortune and
death; those cudgelled their brains about words, these made it their
business to inquire into things; there was an eternal babble of the
tongue, here a continual exercise of the soul. And therefore it is
nothing strange if, when Antipater demanded of them fifty children for
hostages, they made answer, quite contrary to what we should do, that
they would rather give him twice as many full-grown men, so much did they
value the loss of their country's education. When Agesilaus courted
Xenophon to send his children to Sparta to be bred, "it is not," said he,
"there to learn logic or rhetoric, but to be instructed in the noblest of
all sciences, namely, the science to obey and to command."--[Plutarch,
Life of Agesilaus, c. 7.]*

*It is very pleasant to see Socrates, after his manner, rallying Hippias,
--[Plato's Dialogues: Hippias Major.]--who recounts to him what a world
of money he has got, especially in certain little villages of Sicily, by
teaching school, and that he made never a penny at Sparta: "What a
sottish and stupid people," said Socrates, "are they, without sense or
understanding, that make no account either of grammar or poetry, and only
busy themselves in studying the genealogies and successions of their
kings, the foundations, rises, and declensions of states, and such tales
of a tub!" After which, having made Hippias from one step to another
acknowledge the excellency of their form of public administration, and*

*the felicity and virtue of their private life, he leaves him to guess at
the conclusion he makes of the inutilities of his pedantic arts.*

*Examples have demonstrated to us that in military affairs, and all others
of the like active nature, the study of sciences more softens and
untempers the courages of men than it in any way fortifies and excites
them. The most potent empire that at this day appears to be in the whole
world is that of the Turks, a people equally inured to the estimation of
arms and the contempt of letters. I find Rome was more valiant before
she grew so learned. The most warlike nations at this time in being are
the most rude and ignorant: the Scythians, the Parthians, Tamerlane,
serve for sufficient proof of this. When the Goths overran Greece, the
only thing that preserved all the libraries from the fire was, that some
one possessed them with an opinion that they were to leave this kind of
furniture entire to the enemy, as being most proper to divert them from
the exercise of arms, and to fix them to a lazy and sedentary life.
When our King Charles VIII., almost without striking a blow, saw himself
possessed of the kingdom of Naples and a considerable part of Tuscany,
the nobles about him attributed this unexpected facility of conquest to
this, that the princes and nobles of Italy, more studied to render
themselves ingenious and learned, than vigorous and warlike.*

CHAPTER XXV

OF THE EDUCATION OF CHILDREN

TO MADAME DIANE DE FOIX, Comtesse de Gurson

*I never yet saw that father, but let his son be never so decrepit or
deformed, would not, notwithstanding, own him: not, nevertheless, if he
were not totally besotted, and blinded with his paternal affection, that
he did not well enough discern his defects; but that with all defaults he
was still his. Just so, I see better than any other, that all I write
here are but the idle reveries of a man that has only nibbled upon the
outward crust of sciences in his nonage, and only retained a general and
formless image of them; who has got a little snatch of everything and
nothing of the whole, 'a la Francoise'. For I know, in general, that
there is such a thing as physic, as jurisprudence: four parts in
mathematics, and, roughly, what all these aim and point at; and,
peradventure, I yet know farther, what sciences in general pretend unto,
in order to the service of our life: but to dive farther than that, and
to have cudgelled my brains in the study of Aristotle, the monarch of all
modern learning, or particularly addicted myself to any one science,
I have never done it; neither is there any one art of which I am able to
draw the first lineaments and dead colour; insomuch that there is not a
boy of the lowest form in a school, that may not pretend to be wiser than
I, who am not able to examine him in his first lesson, which, if I am at
any time forced upon, I am necessitated in my own defence, to ask him,
unaptly enough, some universal questions, such as may serve to try his
natural understanding; a lesson as strange and unknown to him, as his is
to me.*

*I never seriously settled myself to the reading any book of solid
learning but Plutarch and Seneca; and there, like the Danaides, I
eternally fill, and it as constantly runs out; something of which drops*

upon this paper, but little or nothing stays with me. History is my particular game as to matter of reading, or else poetry, for which I have particular kindness and esteem: for, as Cleanthes said, as the voice, forced through the narrow passage of a trumpet, comes out more forcible and shrill: so, methinks, a sentence pressed within the harmony of verse darts out more briskly upon the understanding, and strikes my ear and apprehension with a smarter and more pleasing effect. As to the natural parts I have, of which this is the essay, I find them to bow under the burden; my fancy and judgment do but grope in the dark, tripping and stumbling in the way; and when I have gone as far as I can, I am in no degree satisfied; I discover still a new and greater extent of land before me, with a troubled and imperfect sight and wrapped up in clouds, that I am not able to penetrate. And taking upon me to write indifferently of whatever comes into my head, and therein making use of nothing but my own proper and natural means, if it befall me, as oft-times it does, accidentally to meet in any good author, the same heads and commonplaces upon which I have attempted to write (as I did but just now in Plutarch's "Discourse of the Force of Imagination"), to see myself so weak and so forlorn, so heavy and so flat, in comparison of those better writers, I at once pity or despise myself. Yet do I please myself with this, that my opinions have often the honour and good fortune to jump with theirs, and that I go in the same path, though at a very great distance, and can say, "Ah, that is so." I am farther satisfied to find that I have a quality, which every one is not blessed withal, which is, to discern the vast difference between them and me; and notwithstanding all that, suffer my own inventions, low and feeble as they are, to run on in their career, without mending or plastering up the defects that this comparison has laid open to my own view. And, in plain truth, a man had need of a good strong back to keep pace with these people. The indiscreet scribblers of our times, who, amongst their laborious nothings, insert whole sections and pages out of ancient authors, with a design, by that means, to illustrate their own writings, do quite contrary; for this infinite dissimilitude of ornaments renders the complexion of their own compositions so sallow and deformed, that they lose much more than they get.

The philosophers, Chrysippus and Epicurus, were in this of two quite contrary humours: the first not only in his books mixed passages and sayings of other authors, but entire pieces, and, in one, the whole Medea of Euripides; which gave Apollodorus occasion to say, that should a man pick out of his writings all that was none of his, he would leave him nothing but blank paper: whereas the latter, quite on the contrary, in three hundred volumes that he left behind him, has not so much as one quotation.--[Diogenes Laertius, Lives of Chyysippus, vii. 181, and Epicurus, x. 26.]

I happened the other day upon this piece of fortune; I was reading a French book, where after I had a long time run dreaming over a great many words, so dull, so insipid, so void of all wit or common sense, that indeed they were only French words: after a long and tedious travel, I came at last to meet with a piece that was lofty, rich, and elevated to the very clouds; of which, had I found either the declivity easy or the ascent gradual, there had been some excuse; but it was so perpendicular a precipice, and so wholly cut off from the rest of the work, that by the first six words, I found myself flying into the other world, and thence discovered the vale whence I came so deep and low, that I have never had since the heart to descend into it any more. If I should set out one of my discourses with such rich spoils as these, it would but too evidently manifest the imperfection of my own writing. To reprehend the fault in others that I am guilty of myself, appears to me no more unreasonable, than to condemn, as I often do, those of others in myself: they are to be everywhere reproved, and ought to have no sanctuary allowed them. I know very well how audaciously I myself, at every turn, attempt to equal myself to my thefts, and to make my style go hand in hand with them, not without a temerarious hope of deceiving the eyes of my reader from discerning the difference; but withal it is as much by the benefit of my application, that I hope to do it, as by that of my invention or any force of my own. Besides, I do not offer to contend with the whole body of these champions, nor hand to hand with anyone of them: 'tis only by flights and little light attempts that I engage them; I do not grapple with them, but try their strength only, and never engage so far as I make a show to do. If I could hold them in play, I were a brave fellow; for I never attack them; but where they are most sinewy and strong. To cover a man's self (as I have seen some do) with another man's armour, so as not to discover so much as his fingers' ends; to carry on a design (as it is not hard for a man that has anything of a scholar in him, in an ordinary subject to do) under old inventions patched up here and there with his own trumpery, and then to endeavour to conceal the theft, and to make it pass for his own, is first injustice and meanness of spirit in those who do it, who having nothing in them of their own fit to procure them a reputation, endeavour to do it by attempting to impose things upon the world in their own name, which they have no manner of title to; and next, a ridiculous folly to content themselves with acquiring the ignorant approbation of the vulgar by such a pitiful cheat, at the price at the same time of degrading themselves in the eyes of men of understanding, who turn up their noses at all this borrowed incrustation, yet whose praise alone is worth the having. For my own part, there is nothing I would not sooner do than that, neither have I said so much of others, but to get a better opportunity to explain myself. Nor in this do I glance at the composers of centos, who declare themselves for such; of which sort of writers I have in my time known many very ingenious, and particularly one under the name of Capilupus, besides the ancients. These are really men of wit, and that make it appear they are so, both by that and other ways of writing; as for example, Lipsius, in that learned and laborious contexture of his Politics.

But, be it how it will, and how inconsiderable soever these ineptitudes may be, I will say I never intended to conceal them, no more than my old bald grizzled likeness before them, where the painter has presented you not with a perfect face, but with mine. For these are my own particular opinions and fancies, and I deliver them as only what I myself believe, and not for what is to be believed by others. I have no other end in this writing, but only to discover myself, who, also shall, peradventure, be another thing to-morrow, if I chance to meet any new instruction to change me. I have no authority to be believed, neither do I desire it, being too conscious of my own inerudition to be able to instruct others.

Some one, then, having seen the preceding chapter, the other day told me at my house, that I should a little farther have extended my discourse on the education of children.⁓["Which, how fit I am to do, let my friends flatter me if they please, I have in the meantime no such opinion of my own talent, as to promise myself any very good success from my endeavour." This passage would appear to be an interpolation by Cotton. At all events, I do not find it in the original editions before me, or in Coste.]⁓

Now, madam, if I had any sufficiency in this subject, I could not possibly better employ it, than to present my best instructions to the little man that threatens you shortly with a happy birth (for you are too generous to begin otherwise than with a male); for, having had so great a hand in the treaty of your marriage, I have a certain particular right and interest in the greatness and prosperity of the issue that shall spring from it; beside that, your having had the best of my services so long in possession, sufficiently obliges me to desire the honour and advantage of all wherein you shall be concerned. But, in truth, all I understand as to that particular is only this, that the greatest and most important difficulty of human science is the education of children. For as in agriculture, the husbandry that is to precede planting, as also planting itself, is certain, plain, and well known; but after that which is planted comes to life, there is a great deal more to be done, more art to be used, more care to be taken, and much more difficulty to cultivate and bring it to perfection so it is with men; it is no hard matter to get children; but after they are born, then begins the trouble, solicitude, and care rightly to train, principle, and bring them up. The symptoms of their inclinations in that tender age are so obscure, and the promises so uncertain and fallacious, that it is very hard to establish any solid judgment or conjecture upon them. Look at Cimon, for example, and Themistocles, and a thousand others, who very much deceived the expectation men had of them. Cubs of bears and puppies readily discover their natural inclination; but men, so soon as ever they are grownup, applying themselves to certain habits, engaging themselves in certain opinions, and conforming themselves to particular laws and customs, easily alter, or at least disguise, their true and real disposition; and yet it is hard to force the propension of nature. Whence it comes to pass, that for not having chosen the right course, we often take very great pains, and consume a good part of our time in training up children to things, for which, by their natural constitution, they are totally unfit. In this difficulty, nevertheless, I am clearly of opinion, that they ought to be elemented in the best and most advantageous studies, without taking too much notice of, or being too superstitious in those light prognostics they give of themselves in their tender years, and to which Plato, in his Republic, gives, methinks, too much authority.

Madam, science is a very great ornament, and a thing of marvellous use, especially in persons raised to that degree of fortune in which you are. And, in truth, in persons of mean and low condition, it cannot perform its true and genuine office, being naturally more prompt to assist in the conduct of war, in the government of peoples, in negotiating the leagues and friendships of princes and foreign nations, than in forming a syllogism in logic, in pleading a process in law, or in prescribing a dose of pills in physic. Wherefore, madam, believing you will not omit this so necessary feature in the education of your children, who yourself have tasted its sweetness, and are of a learned extraction (for we yet have the writings of the ancient Counts of Foix, from whom my lord, your husband, and yourself, are both of you descended, and Monsieur de Candale, your uncle, every day obliges the world with others, which will extend the knowledge of this quality in your family for so many succeeding ages), I will, upon this occasion, presume to acquaint your ladyship with one particular fancy of my own, contrary to the common method, which is all I am able to contribute to your service in this affair.

The charge of the tutor you shall provide for your son, upon the choice of whom depends the whole success of his education, has several other great and considerable parts and duties required in so important a trust, besides that of which I am about to speak: these, however, I shall not mention, as being unable to add anything of moment to the common rules: and in this, wherein I take upon me to advise, he may follow it so far only as it shall appear advisable.

For a, boy of quality then, who pretends to letters not upon the account of profit (for so mean an object is unworthy of the grace and favour of the Muses, and moreover, in it a man directs his service to and depends upon others), nor so much for outward ornament, as for his own proper and peculiar use, and to furnish and enrich himself within, having rather a desire to come out an accomplished cavalier than a mere scholar or learned man; for such a one, I say, I would, also, have his friends solicitous to find him out a tutor, who has rather a well-made than a well-filled head;--["'Tete bien faite', an expression created by Montaigne, and which has remained a part of our language."--Servan.]-- seeking, indeed, both the one and the other, but rather of the two to prefer manners and judgment to mere learning, and that this man should exercise his charge after a new method.

'Tis the custom of pedagogues to be eternally thundering in their pupil's ears, as they were pouring into a funnel, whilst the business of the pupil is only to repeat what the others have said: now I would have a tutor to correct this error, and, that at the very first, he should according to the capacity he has to deal with, put it to the test, permitting his pupil himself to taste things, and of himself to discern and choose them, sometimes opening the way to him, and sometimes leaving him to open it for himself; that is, I would not have him alone to invent and speak, but that he should also hear his pupil speak in turn. Socrates, and since him Arcesilaus, made first their scholars speak, and then they spoke to them--[Diogenes Laertius, iv. 36.]

> *"Obest plerumque iis, qui discere volunt,*
> *auctoritas eorum, qui docent."*

["The authority of those who teach, is very often an impediment to those who desire to learn."--Cicero, De Natura Deor., i. 5.]

It is good to make him, like a young horse, trot before him, that he may judge of his going, and how much he is to abate of his own speed, to accommodate himself to the vigour and capacity of the other. For want of

*which due proportion we spoil all; which also to know how to adjust, and
to keep within an exact and due measure, is one of the hardest things I
know, and 'tis the effect of a high and well-tempered soul, to know how
to condescend to such puerile motions and to govern and direct them.
I walk firmer and more secure up hill than down.*

*Such as, according to our common way of teaching, undertake, with one and
the same lesson, and the same measure of direction, to instruct several
boys of differing and unequal capacities, are infinitely mistaken; and
'tis no wonder, if in a whole multitude of scholars, there are not found
above two or three who bring away any good account of their time and
discipline. Let the master not only examine him about the grammatical
construction of the bare words of his lesson, but about the sense and let
him judge of the profit he has made, not by the testimony of his memory,
but by that of his life. Let him make him put what he has learned into a
hundred several forms, and accommodate it to so many several subjects, to
see if he yet rightly comprehends it, and has made it his own, taking
instruction of his progress by the pedagogic institutions of Plato. 'Tis
a sign of crudity and indigestion to disgorge what we eat in the same
condition it was swallowed; the stomach has not performed its office
unless it have altered the form and condition of what was committed to it
to concoct. Our minds work only upon trust, when bound and compelled to
follow the appetite of another's fancy, enslaved and captivated under the
authority of another's instruction; we have been so subjected to the
trammel, that we have no free, nor natural pace of our own; our own
vigour and liberty are extinct and gone:*

> *"Nunquam tutelae suae fiunt."*

> *["They are ever in wardship."--Seneca, Ep., 33.]*

*I was privately carried at Pisa to see a very honest man, but so great an
Aristotelian, that his most usual thesis was: "That the touchstone and
square of all solid imagination, and of all truth, was an absolute
conformity to Aristotle's doctrine; and that all besides was nothing but
inanity and chimera; for that he had seen all, and said all." A position,*

*that for having been a little too injuriously and broadly interpreted,
brought him once and long kept him in great danger of the Inquisition at
Rome.*

*Let him make him examine and thoroughly sift everything he reads, and
lodge nothing in his fancy upon simple authority and upon trust.
Aristotle's principles will then be no more principles to him, than those
of Epicurus and the Stoics: let this diversity of opinions be propounded
to, and laid before him; he will himself choose, if he be able; if not,
he will remain in doubt.*

> *"Che non men the saver, dubbiar m' aggrata."*

> *["I love to doubt, as well as to know."--Dante, Inferno, xi. 93]*

*for, if he embrace the opinions of Xenophon and Plato, by his own reason,
they will no more be theirs, but become his own. Who follows another,
follows nothing, finds nothing, nay, is inquisitive after nothing.*

> *"Non sumus sub rege; sibi quisque se vindicet."*

> *["We are under no king; let each vindicate himself."
> --Seneca, Ep.,33]*

*Let him, at least, know that he knows. It will be necessary that he
imbibe their knowledge, not that he be corrupted with their precepts;
and no matter if he forget where he had his learning, provided he know
how to apply it to his own use. Truth and reason are common to every
one, and are no more his who spake them first, than his who speaks them
after: 'tis no more according to Plato, than according to me, since both
he and I equally see and understand them. Bees cull their several sweets
from this flower and that blossom, here and there where they find them,
but themselves afterwards make the honey, which is all and purely their
own, and no more thyme and marjoram: so the several fragments he borrows
from others, he will transform and shuffle together to compile a work
that shall be absolutely his own; that is to say, his judgment:*

his instruction, labour and study, tend to nothing else but to form that. He is not obliged to discover whence he got the materials that have assisted him, but only to produce what he has himself done with them. Men that live upon pillage and borrowing, expose their purchases and buildings to every one's view: but do not proclaim how they came by the money. We do not see the fees and perquisites of a gentleman of the long robe; but we see the alliances wherewith he fortifies himself and his family, and the titles and honours he has obtained for him and his. No man divulges his revenue; or, at least, which way it comes in but every one publishes his acquisitions. The advantages of our study are to become better and more wise. 'Tis, says Epicharmus, the understanding that sees and hears, 'tis the understanding that improves everything, that orders everything, and that acts, rules, and reigns: all other faculties are blind, and deaf, and without soul. And certainly we render it timorous and servile, in not allowing it the liberty and privilege to do anything of itself. Whoever asked his pupil what he thought of grammar and rhetoric, or of such and such a sentence of Cicero? Our masters stick them, full feathered, in our memories, and there establish them like oracles, of which the letters and syllables are of the substance of the thing. To know by rote, is no knowledge, and signifies no more but only to retain what one has intrusted to our memory. That which a man rightly knows and understands, he is the free disposer of at his own full liberty, without any regard to the author from whence he had it, or fumbling over the leaves of his book. A mere bookish learning is a poor, paltry learning; it may serve for ornament, but there is yet no foundation for any superstructure to be built upon it, according to the opinion of Plato, who says, that constancy, faith, and sincerity, are the true philosophy, and the other sciences, that are directed to other ends; mere adulterate paint. I could wish that Paluel or Pompey, those two noted dancers of my time, could have taught us to cut capers, by only seeing them do it, without stirring from our places, as these men pretend to inform the understanding without ever setting it to work, or that we could learn to ride, handle a pike, touch a lute, or sing without the trouble of practice, as these attempt to make us judge and speak well, without exercising us in judging or speaking. Now in this initiation of our studies in their progress, whatsoever presents itself before us is

book sufficient; a roguish trick of a page, a sottish mistake of a
servant, a jest at the table, are so many new subjects.

And for this reason, conversation with men is of very great use and
travel into foreign countries; not to bring back (as most of our young
monsieurs do) an account only of how many paces Santa Rotonda--[The
Pantheon of Agrippa.]--is in circuit; or of the richness of Signora
Livia's petticoats; or, as some others, how much Nero's face, in a statue
in such an old ruin, is longer and broader than that made for him on some
medal; but to be able chiefly to give an account of the humours, manners,
customs, and laws of those nations where he has been, and that we may
whet and sharpen our wits by rubbing them against those of others. I
would that a boy should be sent abroad very young, and first, so as to
kill two birds with one stone, into those neighbouring nations whose
language is most differing from our own, and to which, if it be not
formed betimes, the tongue will grow too stiff to bend.

And also 'tis the general opinion of all, that a child should not be
brought up in his mother's lap. Mothers are too tender, and their
natural affection is apt to make the most discreet of them all so
overfond, that they can neither find in their hearts to give them due
correction for the faults they may commit, nor suffer them to be inured
to hardships and hazards, as they ought to be. They will not endure to
see them return all dust and sweat from their exercise, to drink cold
drink when they are hot, nor see them mount an unruly horse, nor take a
foil in hand against a rude fencer, or so much as to discharge a carbine.
And yet there is no remedy; whoever will breed a boy to be good for
anything when he comes to be a man, must by no means spare him when
young, and must very often transgress the rules of physic:

> "Vitamque sub dio, et trepidis agat
> In rebus."

["Let him live in open air, and ever in movement about something."
--Horace, Od. ii., 3, 5.]

It is not enough to fortify his soul; you are also to make his sinews strong; for the soul will be oppressed if not assisted by the members, and would have too hard a task to discharge two offices alone. I know very well to my cost, how much mine groans under the burden, from being accommodated with a body so tender and indisposed, as eternally leans and presses upon her; and often in my reading perceive that our masters, in their writings, make examples pass for magnanimity and fortitude of mind, which really are rather toughness of skin and hardness of bones; for I have seen men, women, and children, naturally born of so hard and insensible a constitution of body, that a sound cudgelling has been less to them than a flirt with a finger would have been to me, and that would neither cry out, wince, nor shrink, for a good swinging beating; and when wrestlers counterfeit the philosophers in patience, 'tis rather strength of nerves than stoutness of heart. Now to be inured to undergo labour, is to be accustomed to endure pain:

"Labor callum obducit dolori."

["Labour hardens us against pain."--Cicero, Tusc. Quaes., ii. 15.]

A boy is to be broken in to the toil and roughness of exercise, so as to be trained up to the pain and suffering of dislocations, cholics, cauteries, and even imprisonment and the rack itself; for he may come by misfortune to be reduced to the worst of these, which (as this world goes) is sometimes inflicted on the good as well as the bad. As for proof, in our present civil war whoever draws his sword against the laws, threatens the honestest men with the whip and the halter.

And, moreover, by living at home, the authority of this governor, which ought to be sovereign over the boy he has received into his charge, is often checked and hindered by the presence of parents; to which may also be added, that the respect the whole family pay him, as their master's son, and the knowledge he has of the estate and greatness he is heir to, are, in my opinion, no small inconveniences in these tender years.

And yet, even in this conversing with men I spoke of but now, I have observed this vice, that instead of gathering observations from others, we make it our whole business to lay ourselves open to them, and are more concerned how to expose and set out our own commodities, than how to increase our stock by acquiring new. Silence, therefore, and modesty are very advantageous qualities in conversation. One should, therefore, train up this boy to be sparing and an husband of his knowledge when he has acquired it; and to forbear taking exceptions at or reproving every idle saying or ridiculous story that is said or told in his presence; for it is a very unbecoming rudeness to carp at everything that is not agreeable to our own palate. Let him be satisfied with correcting himself, and not seem to condemn everything in another he would not do himself, nor dispute it as against common customs.

> *"Licet sapere sine pompa, sine invidia."*

> [*"Let us be wise without ostentation, without envy."*
> ‑‑Seneca, Ep., 103.]

Let him avoid these vain and uncivil images of authority, this childish ambition of coveting to appear better bred and more accomplished, than he really will, by such carriage, discover himself to be. And, as if opportunities of interrupting and reprehending were not to be omitted, to desire thence to derive the reputation of something more than ordinary. For as it becomes none but great poets to make use of the poetical licence, so it is intolerable for any but men of great and illustrious souls to assume privilege above the authority of custom:

> *"Si quid Socrates ant Aristippus contra morem et consuetudinem fecerunt, idem sibi ne arbitretur licere: magnis enim illi et divinis bonis hanc licentiam assequebantur."*

> [*"If Socrates and Aristippus have committed any act against manners and custom, let him not think that he is allowed to do the same; for it was by great and divine benefits that they obtained this privilege."*‑‑Cicero, De Offic., i. 41.]

Let him be instructed not to engage in discourse or dispute but with a
champion worthy of him, and, even there, not to make use of all the
little subtleties that may seem pat for his purpose, but only such
arguments as may best serve him. Let him be taught to be curious in the
election and choice of his reasons, to abominate impertinence, and
consequently, to affect brevity; but, above all, let him be lessoned to
acquiesce and submit to truth so soon as ever he shall discover it,
whether in his opponent's argument, or upon better consideration of his
own; for he shall never be preferred to the chair for a mere clatter of
words and syllogisms, and is no further engaged to any argument whatever,
than as he shall in his own judgment approve it: nor yet is arguing a
trade, where the liberty of recantation and getting off upon better
thoughts, are to be sold for ready money:

> "Neque, ut omnia, quæ præscripta et imperata sint,
> defendat, necessitate ulla cogitur."

> ["Neither is their any necessity upon him, that he should defend
> all things that are prescribed and enjoined him."
> ⸺Cicero, Acad., ii. 3.]

If his governor be of my humour, he will form his will to be a very good
and loyal subject to his prince, very affectionate to his person, and
very stout in his quarrel; but withal he will cool in him the desire of
having any other tie to his service than public duty. Besides several
other inconveniences that are inconsistent with the liberty every honest
man ought to have, a man's judgment, being bribed and prepossessed by
these particular obligations, is either blinded and less free to exercise
its function, or is blemished with ingratitude and indiscretion. A man
that is purely a courtier, can neither have power nor will to speak or
think otherwise than favourably and well of a master, who, amongst so
many millions of other subjects, has picked out him with his own hand to
nourish and advance; this favour, and the profit flowing from it, must
needs, and not without some show of reason, corrupt his freedom and
dazzle him; and we commonly see these people speak in another kind of

phrase than is ordinarily spoken by others of the same nation, though what they say in that courtly language is not much to be believed.

Let his conscience and virtue be eminently manifest in his speaking, and have only reason for their guide. Make him understand, that to acknowledge the error he shall discover in his own argument, though only found out by himself, is an effect of judgment and sincerity, which are the principal things he is to seek after; that obstinacy and contention are common qualities, most appearing in mean souls; that to revise and correct himself, to forsake an unjust argument in the height and heat of dispute, are rare, great, and philosophical qualities.

Let him be advised, being in company, to have his eye and ear in every corner; for I find that the places of greatest honour are commonly seized upon by men that have least in them, and that the greatest fortunes are seldom accompanied with the ablest parts. I have been present when, whilst they at the upper end of the chamber have been only commenting the beauty of the arras, or the flavour of the wine, many things that have been very finely said at the lower end of the table have been lost and thrown away. Let him examine every man's talent; a peasant, a bricklayer, a passenger: one may learn something from every one of these in their several capacities, and something will be picked out of their discourse whereof some use may be made at one time or another; nay, even the folly and impertinence of others will contribute to his instruction. By observing the graces and manners of all he sees, he will create to himself an emulation of the good, and a contempt of the bad.

Let an honest curiosity be suggested to his fancy of being inquisitive after everything; whatever there is singular and rare near the place where he is, let him go and see it; a fine house, a noble fountain, an eminent man, the place where a battle has been anciently fought, the passages of Caesar and Charlemagne:

> "Qux tellus sit lenta gelu, quae putris ab aestu,
> Ventus in Italiam quis bene vela ferat."

["What country is bound in frost, what land is friable with heat,
what wind serves fairest for Italy."--Propertius, iv. 3, 39.]

Let him inquire into the manners, revenues, and alliances of princes,
things in themselves very pleasant to learn, and very useful to know.

In this conversing with men, I mean also, and principally, those who only
live in the records of history; he shall, by reading those books,
converse with the great and heroic souls of the best ages. 'Tis an idle
and vain study to those who make it so by doing it after a negligent
manner, but to those who do it with care and observation, 'tis a study of
inestimable fruit and value; and the only study, as Plato reports, that
the Lacedaemonians reserved to themselves. What profit shall he not reap
as to the business of men, by reading the Lives of Plutarch? But,
withal, let my governor remember to what end his instructions are
principally directed, and that he do not so much imprint in his pupil's
memory the date of the ruin of Carthage, as the manners of Hannibal and
Scipio; nor so much where Marcellus died, as why it was unworthy of his
duty that he died there. Let him not teach him so much the narrative
parts of history as to judge them; the reading of them, in my opinion,
is a thing that of all others we apply ourselves unto with the most
differing measure. I have read a hundred things in Livy that another has
not, or not taken notice of at least; and Plutarch has read a hundred
more there than ever I could find, or than, peradventure, that author
ever wrote; to some it is merely a grammar study, to others the very
anatomy of philosophy, by which the most abstruse parts of our human
nature penetrate. There are in Plutarch many long discourses very worthy
to be carefully read and observed, for he is, in my opinion, of all
others the greatest master in that kind of writing; but there are a
thousand others which he has only touched and glanced upon, where he only
points with his finger to direct us which way we may go if we will, and
contents himself sometimes with giving only one brisk hit in the nicest
article of the question, whence we are to grope out the rest. As, for
example, where he says'--[In the Essay on False Shame.]--that the
inhabitants of Asia came to be vassals to one only, for not having been
able to pronounce one syllable, which is No. Which saying of his gave

perhaps matter and occasion to La Boetie to write his "Voluntary Servitude." Only to see him pick out a light action in a man's life, or a mere word that does not seem to amount even to that, is itself a whole discourse. 'Tis to our prejudice that men of understanding should so immoderately affect brevity; no doubt their reputation is the better by it, but in the meantime we are the worse. Plutarch had rather we should applaud his judgment than commend his knowledge, and had rather leave us with an appetite to read more, than glutted with that we have already read. He knew very well, that a man may say too much even upon the best subjects, and that Alexandridas justly reproached him who made very good. but too long speeches to the Ephori, when he said: "O stranger! thou speakest the things thou shouldst speak, but not as thou shouldst speak them."--[Plutarch, Apothegms of the Lacedamonians.]--Such as have lean and spare bodies stuff themselves out with clothes; so they who are defective in matter endeavour to make amends with words.

Human understanding is marvellously enlightened by daily conversation with men, for we are, otherwise, compressed and heaped up in ourselves, and have our sight limited to the length of our own noses. One asking Socrates of what country he was, he did not make answer, of Athens, but of the world;--[Cicero, Tusc. Quaes., v. 37; Plutarch, On Exile, c. 4.]-- he whose imagination was fuller and wider, embraced the whole world for his country, and extended his society and friendship to all mankind; not as we do, who look no further than our feet. When the vines of my village are nipped with the frost, my parish priest presently concludes, that the indignation of God has gone out against all the human race, and that the cannibals have already got the pip. Who is it that, seeing the havoc of these civil wars of ours, does not cry out, that the machine of the world is near dissolution, and that the day of judgment is at hand; without considering, that many worse things have been seen, and that in the meantime, people are very merry in a thousand other parts of the earth for all this? For my part, considering the licence and impunity that always attend such commotions, I wonder they are so moderate, and that there is no more mischief done. To him who feels the hailstones patter about his ears, the whole hemisphere appears to be in storm and tempest; like the ridiculous Savoyard, who said very gravely, that if

that simple king of France could have managed his fortune as he should
have done, he might in time have come to have been steward of the
household to the duke his master: the fellow could not, in his shallow
imagination, conceive that there could be anything greater than a Duke of
Savoy. And, in truth, we are all of us, insensibly, in this error, an
error of a very great weight and very pernicious consequence. But
whoever shall represent to his fancy, as in a picture, that great image
of our mother nature, in her full majesty and lustre, whoever in her face
shall read so general and so constant a variety, whoever shall observe
himself in that figure, and not himself but a whole kingdom, no bigger
than the least touch or prick of a pencil in comparison of the whole,
that man alone is able to value things according to their true estimate
and grandeur.

This great world which some do yet multiply as several species under one
genus, is the mirror wherein we are to behold ourselves, to be able to
know ourselves as we ought to do in the true bias. In short, I would
have this to be the book my young gentleman should study with the most
attention. So many humours, so many sects, so many judgments, opinions,
laws, and customs, teach us to judge aright of our own, and inform our
understanding to discover its imperfection and natural infirmity, which
is no trivial speculation. So many mutations of states and kingdoms, and
so many turns and revolutions of public fortune, will make us wise enough
to make no great wonder of our own. So many great names, so many famous
victories and conquests drowned and swallowed in oblivion, render our
hopes ridiculous of eternising our names by the taking of half-a-score of
light horse, or a henroost, which only derives its memory from its ruin.
The pride and arrogance of so many foreign pomps, the inflated majesty of
so many courts and grandeurs, accustom and fortify our sight without
closing our eyes to behold the lustre of our own; so many trillions of
men, buried before us, encourage us not to fear to go seek such good
company in the other world: and so of the rest Pythagoras was want to
say,--[Cicero, Tusc. Quaes., v. 3.]--that our life resembles the great
and populous assembly of the Olympic games, wherein some exercise the
body, that they may carry away the glory of the prize: others bring
merchandise to sell for profit: there are also some (and those none of

the worst sort) who pursue no other advantage than only to look on, and consider how and why everything is done, and to be spectators of the lives of other men, thereby the better to judge of and regulate their own.

To examples may fitly be applied all the profitable discourses of philosophy, to which all human actions, as to their best rule, ought to be especially directed: a scholar shall be taught to know--

> "Quid fas optare: quid asper
> Utile nummus habet: patrix carisque propinquis
> Quantum elargiri deceat: quern te Deus esse
> Jussit, et humana qua parte locatus es in re;
> Quid sumus, et quidnam victuri gignimur."

["Learn what it is right to wish; what is the true use of coined money; how much it becomes us to give in liberality to our country and our dear relations; whom and what the Deity commanded thee to be; and in what part of the human system thou art placed; what we are ant to what purpose engendered."--Persius, iii. 69]

what it is to know, and what to be ignorant; what ought to be the end and design of study; what valour, temperance, and justice are; the difference betwixt ambition and avarice, servitude and subjection, licence and liberty; by what token a man may know true and solid contentment; how far death, affliction, and disgrace are to be apprehended;

> "Et quo quemque modo fugiatque feratque laborem."

["And how you may shun or sustain every hardship."
--Virgil, AEneid, iii. 459.]

by what secret springs we move, and the reason of our various agitations and irresolutions: for, methinks the first doctrine with which one should season his understanding, ought to be that which regulates his manners and his sense; that teaches him to know himself, and how both well to dig

and well to live. Amongst the liberal sciences, let us begin with that
which makes us free; not that they do not all serve in some measure to
the instruction and use of life, as all other things in some sort also
do; but let us make choice of that which directly and professedly serves
to that end. If we are once able to restrain the offices of human life
within their just and natural limits, we shall find that most of the
sciences in use are of no great use to us, and even in those that are,
that there are many very unnecessary cavities and dilatations which we
had better let alone, and, following Socrates' direction, limit the
course of our studies to those things only where is a true and real
utility:

> "Sapere aude;
> Incipe; Qui recte vivendi prorogat horam,
> Rusticus exspectat, dum defluat amnis; at ille
> Labitur, et labetur in omne volubilis oevum."

["Dare to be wise; begin! he who defers the hour of living well is
like the clown, waiting till the river shall have flowed out: but
the river still flows, and will run on, with constant course, to
ages without end."--Horace, Ep., i. 2.]

'Tis a great foolery to teach our children:

> "Quid moveant Pisces, animosaque signa Leonis,
> Lotus et Hesperia quid Capricornus aqua,"

["What influence Pisces have, or the sign of angry Leo, or
Capricorn, washed by the Hesperian wave."--Propertius, iv. I, 89.]

the knowledge of the stars and the motion of the eighth sphere before
their own:

["What care I about the Pleiades or the stars of Taurus?"
--Anacreon, Ode, xvii. 10.]

Anaximenes writing to Pythagoras, "To what purpose," said he, "should I trouble myself in searching out the secrets of the stars, having death or slavery continually before my eyes?" for the kings of Persia were at that time preparing to invade his country. Every one ought to say thus, "Being assaulted, as I am by ambition, avarice, temerity, superstition, and having within so many other enemies of life, shall I go ponder over the world's changes?"

After having taught him what will make him more wise and good, you may then entertain him with the elements of logic, physics, geometry, rhetoric, and the science which he shall then himself most incline to, his judgment being beforehand formed and fit to choose, he will quickly make his own. The way of instructing him ought to be sometimes by discourse, and sometimes by reading; sometimes his governor shall put the author himself, which he shall think most proper for him, into his hands, and sometimes only the marrow and substance of it; and if himself be not conversant enough in books to turn to all the fine discourses the books contain for his purpose, there may some man of learning be joined to him, that upon every occasion shall supply him with what he stands in need of, to furnish it to his pupil. And who can doubt but that this way of teaching is much more easy and natural than that of Gaza,--[Theodore Gaza, rector of the Academy of Ferrara.]--in which the precepts are so intricate, and so harsh, and the words so vain, lean; and insignificant, that there is no hold to be taken of them, nothing that quickens and elevates the wit and fancy, whereas here the mind has what to feed upon and to digest. This fruit, therefore, is not only without comparison, much more fair and beautiful; but will also be much more early ripe.

'Tis a thousand pities that matters should be at such a pass in this age of ours, that philosophy, even with men of understanding, should be, looked upon as a vain and fantastic name, a thing of no use, no value, either in opinion or effect, of which I think those ergotisms and petty sophistries, by prepossessing the avenues to it, are the cause. And people are much to blame to represent it to children for a thing of so difficult access, and with such a frowning, grim, and formidable aspect. Who is it that has disguised it thus, with this false, pale, and ghostly

countenance? There is nothing more airy, more gay, more frolic, and I
had like to have said, more wanton. She preaches nothing but feasting
and jollity; a melancholic anxious look shows that she does not inhabit
there. Demetrius the grammarian finding in the temple of Delphos a knot
of philosophers set chatting together, said to them,--[Plutarch, Treatise
on Oracles which have ceased]--"Either I am much deceived, or by your
cheerful and pleasant countenances, you are engaged in no, very deep
discourse." To which one of them, Heracleon the Megarean, replied:
"Tis for such as are puzzled about inquiring whether the future tense of
the verb ~~~~~ is spelt with a double A, or that hunt after the
derivation of the comparatives ~~~~~ and ~~~~~, and the superlatives ~~~~
and ~~~~~~, to knit their brows whilst discoursing of their science: but
as to philosophical discourses, they always divert and cheer up those
that entertain them, and never deject them or make them sad."

> "Deprendas animi tormenta latentis in aegro
>   Corpore; deprendas et gaudia; sumit utrumque
>   Inde habitum facies."

["You may discern the torments of mind lurking in a sick body; you
may discern its joys: either expression the face assumes from the
mind."--Juvenal, ix. 18]

The soul that lodges philosophy, ought to be of such a constitution of
health, as to render the body in like manner healthful too; she ought to
make her tranquillity and satisfaction shine so as to appear without, and
her contentment ought to fashion the outward behaviour to her own mould,
and consequently to fortify it with a graceful confidence, an active and
joyous carriage, and a serene and contented countenance. The most
manifest sign of wisdom is a continual cheerfulness; her state is like
that of things in the regions above the moon, always clear and serene.
'Tis Baroco and Baralipton--[Two terms of the ancient scholastic
logic.]--that render their disciples so dirty and ill-favoured, and not
she; they do not so much as know her but by hearsay. What! It is she
that calms and appeases the storms and tempests of the soul, and who
teaches famine and fevers to laugh and sing; and that, not by certain

*imaginary epicycles, but by natural and manifest reasons. She has virtue
for her end, which is not, as the schoolmen say, situate upon the summit
of a perpendicular, rugged, inaccessible precipice: such as have
approached her find her, quite on the contrary, to be seated in a fair,
fruitful, and flourishing plain, whence she easily discovers all things
below; to which place any one may, however, arrive, if he know but the
way, through shady, green, and sweetly-flourishing avenues, by a
pleasant, easy, and smooth descent, like that of the celestial vault.
'Tis for not having frequented this supreme, this beautiful, triumphant,
and amiable, this equally delicious and courageous virtue, this so
professed and implacable enemy to anxiety, sorrow, fear, and constraint,
who, having nature for her guide, has fortune and pleasure for her
companions, that they have gone, according to their own weak imagination,
and created this ridiculous, this sorrowful, querulous, despiteful,
threatening, terrible image of it to themselves and others, and placed it
upon a rock apart, amongst thorns and brambles, and made of it a
hobgoblin to affright people.*

*But the governor that I would have, that is such a one as knows it to be
his duty to possess his pupil with as much or more affection than
reverence to virtue, will be able to inform him, that the poets have
evermore accommodated themselves to the public humour, and make him
sensible, that the gods have planted more toil and sweat in the avenues
of the cabinets of Venus than in those of Minerva. And when he shall
once find him begin to apprehend, and shall represent to him a Bradamante
or an Angelica--[Heroines of Ariosto.]--for a mistress, a natural,
active, generous, and not a viragoish, but a manly beauty, in comparison
of a soft, delicate, artificial simpering, and affected form; the one in
the habit of a heroic youth, wearing a glittering helmet, the other
tricked up in curls and ribbons like a wanton minx; he will then look
upon his own affection as brave and masculine, when he shall choose quite
contrary to that effeminate shepherd of Phrygia.*

*Such a tutor will make a pupil digest this new lesson, that the height
and value of true virtue consists in the facility, utility, and pleasure
of its exercise; so far from difficulty, that boys, as well as men, and*

the innocent as well as the subtle, may make it their own; it is by order, and not by force, that it is to be acquired. Socrates, her first minion, is so averse to all manner of violence, as totally to throw it aside, to slip into the more natural facility of her own progress; 'tis the nursing mother of all human pleasures, who in rendering them just, renders them also pure and permanent; in moderating them, keeps them in breath and appetite; in interdicting those which she herself refuses, whets our desire to those that she allows; and, like a kind and liberal mother, abundantly allows all that nature requires, even to satiety, if not to lassitude: unless we mean to say that the regimen which stops the toper before he has drunk himself drunk, the glutton before he has eaten to a surfeit, and the lecher before he has got the pox, is an enemy to pleasure. If the ordinary fortune fail, she does without it, and forms another, wholly her own, not so fickle and unsteady as the other. She can be rich, be potent and wise, and knows how to lie upon soft perfumed beds: she loves life, beauty, glory, and health; but her proper and peculiar office is to know how to regulate the use of all these good things, and how to lose them without concern: an office much more noble than troublesome, and without which the whole course of life is unnatural, turbulent, and deformed, and there it is indeed, that men may justly represent those monsters upon rocks and precipices.

If this pupil shall happen to be of so contrary a disposition, that he had rather hear a tale of a tub than the true narrative of some noble expedition or some wise and learned discourse; who at the beat of drum, that excites the youthful ardour of his companions, leaves that to follow another that calls to a morris or the bears; who would not wish, and find it more delightful and more excellent, to return all dust and sweat victorious from a battle, than from tennis or from a ball, with the prize of those exercises; I see no other remedy, but that he be bound prentice in some good town to learn to make minced pies, though he were the son of a duke; according to Plato's precept, that children are to be placed out and disposed of, not according to the wealth, qualities, or condition of the father, but according to the faculties and the capacity of their own souls.

Since philosophy is that which instructs us to live, and that infancy has there its lessons as well as other ages, why is it not communicated to children betimes?

> "Udum et molle lutum est; nunc, nunc properandus, et acri
> Fingendus sine fine rota."

> ["The clay is moist and soft: now, now make haste, and form the
> pitcher on the rapid wheel."--Persius, iii. 23.]

They begin to teach us to live when we have almost done living. A hundred students have got the pox before they have come to read Aristotle's lecture on temperance. Cicero said, that though he should live two men's ages, he should never find leisure to study the lyric poets; and I find these sophisters yet more deplorably unprofitable. The boy we would breed has a great deal less time to spare; he owes but the first fifteen or sixteen years of his life to education; the remainder is due to action. Let us, therefore, employ that short time in necessary instruction. Away with the thorny subtleties of dialectics; they are abuses, things by which our lives can never be amended: take the plain philosophical discourses, learn how rightly to choose, and then rightly to apply them; they are more easy to be understood than one of Boccaccio's novels; a child from nurse is much more capable of them, than of learning to read or to write. Philosophy has discourses proper for childhood, as well as for the decrepit age of men.

I am of Plutarch's mind, that Aristotle did not so much trouble his great disciple with the knack of forming syllogisms, or with the elements of geometry; as with infusing into him good precepts concerning valour, prowess, magnanimity, temperance, and the contempt of fear; and with this ammunition, sent him, whilst yet a boy, with no more than thirty thousand foot, four thousand horse, and but forty-two thousand crowns, to subjugate the empire of the whole earth. For the other acts and sciences, he says, Alexander highly indeed commended their excellence and charm, and had them in very great honour and esteem, but not ravished with them to that degree as to be tempted to affect the practice of them

In his own person:

> *"Petite hinc, juvenesque senesque,*
> *Finem ammo certum, miserisque viatica canis."*

["Young men and old men, derive hence a certain end to the mind,
and stores for miserable grey hairs."--Persius, v. 64.]

Epicurus, in the beginning of his letter to Meniceus,--[Diogenes
Laertius, x. 122.]--says, "That neither the youngest should refuse to
philosophise, nor the oldest grow weary of it." Who does otherwise,
seems tacitly to imply, that either the time of living happily is
not yet come, or that it is already past. And yet, a for all that, I
would not have this pupil of ours imprisoned and made a slave to his
book; nor would I have him given up to the morosity and melancholic
humour of a sour ill-natured pedant.

I would not have his spirit cowed and subdued, by applying him to the
rack, and tormenting him, as some do, fourteen or fifteen hours a day,
and so make a pack-horse of him. Neither should I think it good, when,
by reason of a solitary and melancholic complexion, he is discovered to
be overmuch addicted to his book, to nourish that humour in him; for that
renders him unfit for civil conversation, and diverts him from better
employments. And how many have I seen in my time totally brutified by an
immoderate thirst after knowledge? Carneades was so besotted with it,
that he would not find time so much as to comb his head or to pare his
nails. Neither would I have his generous manners spoiled and corrupted
by the incivility and barbarism of those of another. The French wisdom
was anciently turned into proverb: "Early, but of no continuance." And,
in truth, we yet see, that nothing can be more ingenious and pleasing
than the children of France; but they ordinarily deceive the hope and
expectation that have been conceived of them; and grown up to be men,
have nothing extraordinary or worth taking notice of: I have heard men of
good understanding say, these colleges of ours to which we send our young
people (and of which we have but too many) make them such animals as they
are.--[Hobbes said that if he Had been at college as long as other people

*he should have been as great a blockhead as they. W.C.H.] [And Bacon
before Hobbe's time had discussed the "futility" of university teaching.
D.W.]*

*But to our little monsieur, a closet, a garden, the table, his bed,
solitude, and company, morning and evening, all hours shall be the same,
and all places to him a study; for philosophy, who, as the formatrix of
judgment and manners, shall be his principal lesson, has that privilege
to have a hand in everything. The orator Isocrates, being at a feast
entreated to speak of his art, all the company were satisfied with and
commended his answer: "It is not now a time," said he, "to do what I can
do; and that which it is now time to do, I cannot do."--[Plutarch,
Symp., i. I.]--For to make orations and rhetorical disputes in a company
met together to laugh and make good cheer, had been very unreasonable and
improper, and as much might have been said of all the other sciences.
But as to what concerns philosophy, that part of it at least that treats
of man, and of his offices and duties, it has been the common opinion of
all wise men, that, out of respect to the sweetness of her conversation,
she is ever to be admitted in all sports and entertainments. And Plato,
having invited her to his feast, we see after how gentle and obliging a
manner, accommodated both to time and place, she entertained the company,
though in a discourse of the highest and most important nature:*

> *"Aeque pauperibus prodest, locupletibus aeque;
> Et, neglecta, aeque pueris senibusque nocebit."*

> *["It profits poor and rich alike, but, neglected, equally hurts old
> and young."--Horace, Ep., i. 25.]*

*By this method of instruction, my young pupil will be much more and
better employed than his fellows of the college are. But as the steps we
take in walking to and fro in a gallery, though three times as many, do
not tire a man so much as those we employ in a formal journey, so our
lesson, as it were accidentally occurring, without any set obligation of
time or place, and falling naturally into every action, will insensibly
insinuate itself. By which means our very exercises and recreations,*

running, wrestling, music, dancing, hunting, riding, and fencing, will
prove to be a good part of our study. I would have his outward fashion
and mien, and the disposition of his limbs, formed at the same time with
his mind. 'Tis not a soul, 'tis not a body that we are training up, but
a man, and we ought not to divide him. And, as Plato says, we are not to
fashion one without the other, but make them draw together like two
horses harnessed to a coach. By which saying of his, does he not seem to
allow more time for, and to take more care of exercises for the body, and
to hold that the mind, in a good proportion, does her business at the
same time too?

As to the rest, this method of education ought to be carried on with a
severe sweetness, quite contrary to the practice of our pedants, who,
instead of tempting and alluring children to letters by apt and gentle
ways, do in truth present nothing before them but rods and ferules,
horror and cruelty. Away with this violence! away with this compulsion!
than which, I certainly believe nothing more dulls and degenerates a
well-descended nature. If you would have him apprehend shame and
chastisement, do not harden him to them: inure him to heat and cold, to
wind and sun, and to dangers that he ought to despise; wean him from all
effeminacy and delicacy in clothes and lodging, eating and drinking;
accustom him to everything, that he may not be a Sir Paris,
a carpet-knight, but a sinewy, hardy, and vigorous young man. I have
ever from a child to the age wherein I now am, been of this opinion, and
am still constant to it. But amongst other things, the strict
government of most of our colleges has evermore displeased me;
peradventure, they might have erred less perniciously on the indulgent
side. 'Tis a real house of correction of imprisoned youth. They are
made debauched by being punished before they are so. Do but come in
when they are about their lesson, and you shall hear nothing but the
outcries of boys under execution, with the thundering noise of their
pedagogues drunk with fury. A very pretty way this, to tempt these
tender and timorous souls to love their book, with a furious
countenance, and a rod in hand! A cursed and pernicious way of
proceeding! Besides what Quintilian has very well observed, that this
imperious authority is often attended by very dangerous consequences,

and particularly our way of chastising. How much more decent would it
be to see their classes strewed with green leaves and fine flowers, than
with the bloody stumps of birch and willows? Were it left to my
ordering. I should paint the school with the pictures of joy and
gladness; Flora and the Graces, as the philosopher Speusippus did his.
Where their profit is, let them there have their pleasure too. Such
viands as are proper and wholesome for children, should be sweetened
with sugar, and such as are dangerous to them, embittered with gall.
'Tis marvellous to see how solicitous Plato is in his Laws concerning
the gaiety and diversion of the youth of his city, and how much and
often he enlarges upon the races, sports, songs, leaps, and dances: of
which, he says, that antiquity has given the ordering and patronage
particularly to the gods themselves, to Apollo, Minerva, and the Muses.
He insists long upon, and is very particular in, giving innumerable
precepts for exercises; but as to the lettered sciences, says very
little, and only seems particularly to recommend poetry upon the account
of music.

All singularity in our manners and conditions is to be avoided, as
inconsistent with civil society. Who would not be astonished at so
strange a constitution as that of Demophoon, steward to Alexander the
Great, who sweated in the shade and shivered in the sun? I have seen
those who have run from the smell of a mellow apple with greater
precipitation than from a harquebuss-shot; others afraid of a mouse;
others vomit at the sight of cream; others ready to swoon at the making
of a feather bed; Germanicus could neither endure the sight nor the
crowing of a cock. I will not deny, but that there may, peradventure,
be some occult cause and natural aversion in these cases; but, in my
opinion, a man might conquer it, if he took it in time. Precept has in
this wrought so effectually upon me, though not without some pains on my
part, I confess, that beer excepted, my appetite accommodates itself
indifferently to all sorts of diet. Young bodies are supple; one should,
therefore, in that age bend and ply them to all fashions and customs: and
provided a man can contain the appetite and the will within their due
limits, let a young man, in God's name, be rendered fit for all nations
and all companies, even to debauchery and excess, if need be; that is,

where he shall do it out of complacency to the customs of the place.
Let him be able to do everything, but love to do nothing but what is
good. The philosophers themselves do not justify Callisthenes for
forfeiting the favour of his master Alexander the Great, by refusing to
pledge him a cup of wine. Let him laugh, play, wench with his prince:
nay, I would have him, even in his debauches, too hard for the rest of
the company, and to excel his companions in ability and vigour, and that
he may not give over doing it, either through defect of power or
knowledge how to do it, but for want of will.

"Multum interest, utrum peccare ali quis nolit, an nesciat."

["There is a vast difference betwixt forbearing to sin, and not
knowing how to sin."--Seneca, Ep., 90]

I thought I passed a compliment upon a lord, as free from those excesses
as any man in France, by asking him before a great deal of very good
company, how many times in his life he had been drunk in Germany, in the
time of his being there about his Majesty's affairs; which he also took
as it was intended, and made answer, "Three times"; and withal told us
the whole story of his debauches. I know some who, for want of this
faculty, have found a great inconvenience in negotiating with that
nation. I have often with great admiration reflected upon the wonderful
constitution of Alcibiades, who so easily could transform himself to so
various fashions without any prejudice to his health; one while outdoing
the Persian pomp and luxury, and another, the Lacedaemonian austerity and
frugality; as reformed in Sparta, as voluptuous in Ionia:

"Omnis Aristippum decuit color, et status, et res."

["Every complexion of life, and station, and circumstance became
Aristippus."--Horace, Ep., xvii. 23.]

I would have my pupil to be such an one,

"Quem duplici panno patentia velat,

> *Mirabor, vitae via si conversa decebit,*
> *Personamque feret non inconcinnus utramque."*

[*"I should admire him who with patience bearing a patched garment,
bears well a changed fortune, acting both parts equally well."*
--Horace Ep., xvii. 25.]

These are my lessons, and he who puts them in practice shall reap more
advantage than he who has had them read to him only, and so only knows
them. If you see him, you hear him; if you hear him, you see him. God
forbid, says one in Plato, that to philosophise were only to read a great
many books, and to learn the arts.

> *"Hanc amplissimam omnium artium bene vivendi disciplinam,*
> *vita magis quam literis, persequuti sunt."*

[*"They have proceeded to this discipline of living well, which of
all arts is the greatest, by their lives, rather than by their
reading."*--Cicero, Tusc. Quaes., iv. 3.]

Leo, prince of the Phliasians, asking Heraclides Ponticus--[It was not
Heraclides of Pontus who made this answer, but Pythagoras.]--of what art
or science he made profession: "I know," said he, "neither art nor
science, but I am a philosopher." One reproaching Diogenes that, being
ignorant, he should pretend to philosophy; "I therefore," answered he,
"pretend to it with so much the more reason." Hegesias entreated that he
would read a certain book to him: "You are pleasant," said he; "you
choose those figs that are true and natural, and not those that are
painted; why do you not also choose exercises which are naturally true,
rather than those written?"

The lad will not so much get his lesson by heart as he will practise it:
he will repeat it in his actions. We shall discover if there be prudence
in his exercises, if there be sincerity and justice in his deportment, if
there be grace and judgment in his speaking; if there be constancy in his
sickness; if there be modesty in his mirth, temperance in his pleasures,

order in his domestic economy, indifference in palate, whether what he
eats or drinks be flesh or fish, wine or water:

> "Qui disciplinam suam non ostentationem scientiae, sed legem vitae
> putet: quique obtemperet ipse sibi, et decretis pareat."

> ["Who considers his own discipline, not as a vain ostentation of
> science, but as a law and rule of life; and who obeys his own
> decrees, and the laws he has prescribed for himself."
> ⁓Cicero, Tusc. Quaes., ii. 4.]

The conduct of our lives is the true mirror of our doctrine. Zeuxidamus,
to one who asked him, why the Lacedaemonians did not commit their
constitutions of chivalry to writing, and deliver them to their young men
to read, made answer, that it was because they would inure them to
action, and not amuse them with words. With such a one, after fifteen or
sixteen years' study, compare one of our college Latinists, who has
thrown away so much time in nothing but learning to speak. The world is
nothing but babble; and I hardly ever yet saw that man who did not rather
prate too much, than speak too little. And yet half of our age is
embezzled this way: we are kept four or five years to learn words only,
and to tack them together into clauses; as many more to form them into a
long discourse, divided into four or five parts; and other five years, at
least, to learn succinctly to mix and interweave them after a subtle and
intricate manner let us leave all this to those who make a profession of
it.

Going one day to Orleans, I met in that plain on this side Clery, two
pedants who were travelling towards Bordeaux, about fifty paces distant
from one another; and, a good way further behind them, I discovered a
troop of horse, with a gentleman at the head of them, who was the late
Monsieur le Comte de la Rochefoucauld. One of my people inquired of the
foremost of these masters of arts, who that gentleman was that came after
him; he, having not seen the train that followed after, and thinking his
companion was meant, pleasantly answered, "He is not a gentleman; he is a
grammarian; and I am a logician." Now we who, quite contrary, do not

here pretend to breed a grammarian or a logician, but a gentleman, let us leave them to abuse their leisure; our business lies elsewhere. Let but our pupil be well furnished with things, words will follow but too fast; he will pull them after him if they do not voluntarily follow. I have observed some to make excuses, that they cannot express themselves, and pretend to have their fancies full of a great many very fine things, which yet, for want of eloquence, they cannot utter; 'tis a mere shift, and nothing else. Will you know what I think of it? I think they are nothing but shadows of some imperfect images and conceptions that they know not what to make of within, nor consequently bring out; they do not yet themselves understand what they would be at, and if you but observe how they haggle and stammer upon the point of parturition, you will soon conclude, that their labour is not to delivery, but about conception, and that they are but licking their formless embryo. For my part, I hold, and Socrates commands it, that whoever has in his mind a sprightly and clear imagination, he will express it well enough in one kind of tongue or another, and, if he be dumb, by signs--

"Verbaque praevisam rem non invita sequentur;"

["Once a thing is conceived in the mind, the words to express it soon present themselves." ("The words will not reluctantly follow the thing preconceived.")--Horace, De Arte Poetica. v. 311]

And as another as poetically says in his prose:

"Quum res animum occupavere, verbs ambiunt,"

["When things are once in the mind, the words offer themselves readily." ("When things have taken possession of the mind, the words trip.")--Seneca, Controvers., iii. proem.]

and this other.

"Ipsae res verbs rapiunt."

*[“The things themselves force the words to express them.”
--Cicero, De Finib., iii. 5.]*

He knows nothing of ablative, conjunctive, substantive, or grammar, no
more than his lackey, or a fishwife of the Petit Pont; and yet these will
give you a bellyful of talk, if you will hear them, and peradventure
shall trip as little in their language as the best masters of art in
France. He knows no rhetoric, nor how in a preface to bribe the
benevolence of the courteous reader; neither does he care to know it.
Indeed all this fine decoration of painting is easily effaced by the
lustre of a simple and blunt truth; these fine flourishes serve only to
amuse the vulgar, of themselves incapable of more solid and nutritive
diet, as Aper very evidently demonstrates in Tacitus. The ambassadors
of Samos, prepared with a long and elegant oration, came to Cleomenes,
king of Sparta, to incite him to a war against the tyrant Polycrates;
who, after he had heard their harangue with great gravity and patience,
gave them this answer: “As to the exordium, I remember it not, nor
consequently the middle of your speech; and for what concerns your
conclusion, I will not do what you desire:”--[Plutarch, Apothegms of the
Lacedaemonians.]--a very pretty answer this, methinks, and a pack of
learned orators most sweetly gravelled. And what did the other man say?
The Athenians were to choose one of two architects for a very great
building they had designed; of these, the first, a pert affected fellow,
offered his service in a long premeditated discourse upon the subject of
the work in hand, and by his oratory inclined the voices of the people in
his favour; but the other in three words: “O Athenians, what this man
says, I will do.”--[Plutarch, Instructions to Statesmen, c. 4.]--
When Cicero was in the height and heat of an eloquent harangue, many were
struck with admiration; but Cato only laughed, saying, “We have a
pleasant (mirth-making) consul.” Let it go before, or come after, a good
sentence or a thing well said, is always in season; if it neither suit
well with what went before, nor has much coherence with what follows
after, it is good in itself. I am none of those who think that good
rhyme makes a good poem. Let him make short long, and long short if he
will, 'tis no great matter; if there be invention, and that the wit and

judgment have well performed their offices, I will say, here's a good poet, but an ill rhymer.

> *"Emunctae naris, durus componere versus."*

> *["Of delicate humour, but of rugged versification."*
> *--Horace, Sat, iv. 8.]*

Let a man, says Horace, divest his work of all method and measure,

> *"Tempora certa modosque, et, quod prius ordine verbum est,*
> *Posterius facias, praeponens ultima primis*
> *Invenias etiam disjecti membra poetae."*

> *["Take away certain rhythms and measures, and make the word which*
> *was first in order come later, putting that which should be last*
> *first, you will still find the scattered remains of the poet."*
> *--Horace, Sat., i. 4, 58.]*

he will never the more lose himself for that; the very pieces will be fine by themselves. Menander's answer had this meaning, who being reproved by a friend, the time drawing on at which he had promised a comedy, that he had not yet fallen in hand with it; "It is made, and ready," said he, "all but the verses."--[Plutarch, Whether the Athenians more excelled in Arms or in Letters.]--Having contrived the subject, and disposed the scenes in his fancy, he took little care for the rest. Since Ronsard and Du Bellay have given reputation to our French poesy, every little dabbler, for aught I see, swells his words as high, and makes his cadences very near as harmonious as they:

> *"Plus sonat, quam valet."*

> *["More sound than sense"--Seneca, Ep., 40.]*

For the vulgar, there were never so many poetasters as now; but though they find it no hard matter to imitate their rhyme, they yet fall

infinitely short of imitating the rich descriptions of the one, and the
delicate invention of the other of these masters.

But what will become of our young gentleman, if he be attacked with the
sophistic subtlety of some syllogism? "A Westfalia ham makes a man
drink; drink quenches thirst: ergo a Westfalia ham quenches thirst."
Why, let him laugh at it; it will be more discretion to do so, than to go
about to answer it; or let him borrow this pleasant evasion from
Aristippus: "Why should I trouble myself to untie that, which bound as
it is, gives me so much trouble?"--[Diogenes Laertius, ii. 70.]--
One offering at this dialectic juggling against Cleanthes, Chrysippus
took him short, saying, "Reserve these baubles to play with children,
and do not by such fooleries divert the serious thoughts of a man of
years." If these ridiculous subtleties,

> "Contorta et aculeata sophismata,"

as Cicero calls them, are designed to possess him with an untruth, they
are dangerous; but if they signify no more than only to make him laugh,
I do not see why a man need to be fortified against them. There are some
so ridiculous, as to go a mile out of their way to hook in a fine word:

> "Aut qui non verba rebus aptant, sed res extrinsecus
> arcessunt, quibus verba conveniant."

> ["Who do not fit words to the subject, but seek out for things
> quite from the purpose to fit the words."--Quintilian, viii. 3.]

And as another says,

> "Qui, alicujus verbi decore placentis, vocentur ad id,
> quod non proposuerant scribere."

> ["Who by their fondness of some fine sounding word, are tempted to
> something they had no intention to treat of."--Seneca, Ep., 59.]

I for my part rather bring in a fine sentence by head and shoulders to fit my purpose, than divert my designs to hunt after a sentence. On the contrary, words are to serve, and to follow a man's purpose; and let Gascon come in play where French will not do. I would have things so excelling, and so wholly possessing the imagination of him that hears, that he should have something else to do, than to think of words. The way of speaking that I love, is natural and plain, the same in writing as in speaking, and a sinewy and muscular way of expressing a man's self, short and pithy, not so elegant and artificial as prompt and vehement;

"Haec demum sapiet dictio, quæ feriet;"

["That has most weight and wisdom which pierces the ear." ("That utterance indeed will have a taste which shall strike the ear.") --Epitaph on Lucan, in Fabricius, Biblioth. Lat., ii. 10.]

rather hard than wearisome; free from affectation; irregular, incontinuous, and bold; where every piece makes up an entire body; not like a pedant, a preacher, or a pleader, but rather a soldier-like style, as Suetonius calls that of Julius Caesar; and yet I see no reason why he should call it so. I have ever been ready to imitate the negligent garb, which is yet observable amongst the young men of our time, to wear my cloak on one shoulder, my cap on one side, a stocking in disorder, which seems to express a kind of haughty disdain of these exotic ornaments, and a contempt of the artificial; but I find this negligence of much better use in the form of speaking. All affectation, particularly in the French gaiety and freedom, is ungraceful in a courtier, and in a monarchy every gentleman ought to be fashioned according to the court model; for which reason, an easy and natural negligence does well. I no more like a web where the knots and seams are to be seen, than a fine figure, so delicate, that a man may tell all the bones and veins:

"Quae veritati operam dat oratio, incomposita sit et simplex."

["Let the language that is dedicated to truth be plain and unaffected.--Seneca, Ep. 40.]

"Quis accurat loquitur, nisi qui vult putide loqui?"

*["For who studies to speak accurately, that does not at the same
time wish to perplex his auditory?"--Idem, Ep., 75.]*

*That eloquence prejudices the subject it would advance, that wholly
attracts us to itself. And as in our outward habit, 'tis a ridiculous
effeminacy to distinguish ourselves by a particular and unusual garb or
fashion; so in language, to study new phrases, and to affect words that
are not of current use, proceeds from a puerile and scholastic ambition.
May I be bound to speak no other language than what is spoken in the
market-places of Paris! Aristophanes the grammarian was quite out, when
he reprehended Epicurus for his plain way of delivering himself, and the
design of his oratory, which was only perspicuity of speech.
The imitation of words, by its own facility, immediately disperses itself
through a whole people; but the imitation of inventing and fitly applying
those words is of a slower progress. The generality of readers, for
having found a like robe, very mistakingly imagine they have the same
body and inside too, whereas force and sinews are never to be borrowed;
the gloss, and outward ornament, that is, words and elocution, may. Most
of those I converse with, speak the same language I here write; but
whether they think the same thoughts I cannot say. The Athenians, says
Plato, study fulness and elegancy of speaking; the Lacedaemonians affect
brevity, and those of Crete to aim more at the fecundity of conception
than the fertility of speech; and these are the best. Zeno used to say
that he had two sorts of disciples, one that he called cy~~~~~ous,
curious to learn things, and these were his favourites; the other,
aoy~~~ous, that cared for nothing but words. Not that fine speaking is
not a very good and commendable quality; but not so excellent and so
necessary as some would make it; and I am scandalised that our whole life
should be spent in nothing else. I would first understand my own
language, and that of my neighbours, with whom most of my business and
conversation lies.*

No doubt but Greek and Latin are very great ornaments, and of very great use, but we buy them too dear. I will here discover one way, which has been experimented in my own person, by which they are to be had better cheap, and such may make use of it as will. My late father having made the most precise inquiry that any man could possibly make amongst men of the greatest learning and judgment, of an exact method of education, was by them cautioned of this inconvenience then in use, and made to believe, that the tedious time we applied to the learning of the tongues of them who had them for nothing, was the sole cause we could not arrive to the grandeur of soul and perfection of knowledge, of the ancient Greeks and Romans. I do not, however, believe that to be the only cause. So it is, that the expedient my father found out for this was, that in my infancy, and before I began to speak, he committed me to the care of a German, who since died a famous physician in France, totally ignorant of our language, and very fluent and a great critic in Latin. This man, whom he had fetched out of his own country, and whom he entertained with a great salary for this only one end, had me continually with him; he had with him also joined two others, of inferior learning, to attend me, and to relieve him; these spoke to me in no other language but Latin. As to the rest of his household, it was an inviolable rule, that neither himself, nor my mother, nor valet, nor chambermaid, should speak anything in my company, but such Latin words as each one had learned to gabble with me. ⁀[These passages are, the basis of a small volume by the Abbe Mangin: "Education de Montaigne; ou, L'Art d'enseigner le Latin a l'instar des meres latines."]⁀It is not to be imagined how great an advantage this proved to the whole family; my father and my mother by this means learned Latin enough to understand it perfectly well, and to speak it to such a degree as was sufficient for any necessary use; as also those of the servants did who were most frequently with me. In short, we Latined it at such a rate, that it overflowed to all the neighbouring villages, where there yet remain, that have established themselves by custom, several Latin appellations of artisans and their tools. As for what concerns myself, I was above six years of age before I understood either French or Perigordin, any more than Arabic; and without art, book, grammar, or precept, whipping, or the expense of a tear, I had, by that time, learned to speak as pure Latin as my master himself, for I had no

means of mixing it up with any other. If, for example, they were to give
me a theme after the college fashion, they gave it to others in French;
but to me they were to give it in bad Latin, to turn it into that which
was good. And Nicolas Grouchy, who wrote a book De Comitiis Romanorum;
Guillaume Guerente, who wrote a comment upon Aristotle: George Buchanan,
that great Scottish poet: and Marc Antoine Muret (whom both France and
Italy have acknowledged for the best orator of his time), my domestic
tutors, have all of them often told me that I had in my infancy that
language so very fluent and ready, that they were afraid to enter into
discourse with me. And particularly Buchanan, whom I since saw attending
the late Mareschal de Brissac, then told me, that he was about to write a
treatise of education, the example of which he intended to take from
mine; for he was then tutor to that Comte de Brissac who afterward proved
so valiant and so brave a gentleman.

As to Greek, of which I have but a mere smattering, my father also
designed to have it taught me by a device, but a new one, and by way of
sport; tossing our declensions to and fro, after the manner of those who,
by certain games of tables, learn geometry and arithmetic. For he,
amongst other rules, had been advised to make me relish science and duty
by an unforced will, and of my own voluntary motion, and to educate my
soul in all liberty and delight, without any severity or constraint;
which he was an observer of to such a degree, even of superstition, if I
may say so, that some being of opinion that it troubles and disturbs the
brains of children suddenly to wake them in the morning, and to snatch
them violently--and over-hastily from sleep (wherein they are much more
profoundly involved than we), he caused me to be wakened by the sound of
some musical instrument, and was never unprovided of a musician for that
purpose. By this example you may judge of the rest, this alone being
sufficient to recommend both the prudence and the affection of so good a
father, who is not to be blamed if he did not reap fruits answerable to
so exquisite a culture. Of this, two things were the cause: first, a
sterile and improper soil; for, though I was of a strong and healthful
constitution, and of a disposition tolerably sweet and tractable, yet I
was, withal, so heavy, idle, and indisposed, that they could not rouse me
from my sloth, not even to get me out to play. What I saw, I saw clearly

enough, and under this heavy complexion nourished a bold imagination and opinions above my age. I had a slow wit that would go no faster than it was led; a tardy understanding, a languishing invention, and above all, incredible defect of memory; so that, it is no wonder, if from all these nothing considerable could be extracted. Secondly, like those who, impatient of along and steady cure, submit to all sorts of prescriptions and recipes, the good man being extremely timorous of any way failing in a thing he had so wholly set his heart upon, suffered himself at last to be overruled by the common opinions, which always follow their leader as a flight of cranes, and complying with the method of the time, having no more those persons he had brought out of Italy, and who had given him the first model of education, about him, he sent me at six years of age to the College of Guienne, at that time the best and most flourishing in France. And there it was not possible to add anything to the care he had to provide me the most able tutors, with all other circumstances of education, reserving also several particular rules contrary to the college practice; but so it was, that with all these precautions, it was a college still. My Latin immediately grew corrupt, of which also by discontinuance I have since lost all manner of use; so that this new way of education served me to no other end, than only at my first coming to prefer me to the first forms; for at thirteen years old, that I came out of the college, I had run through my whole course (as they call it), and, in truth, without any manner of advantage, that I can honestly brag of, in all this time.

The first taste which I had for books came to me from the pleasure in reading the fables of Ovid's Metamorphoses; for, being about seven or eight years old, I gave up all other diversions to read them, both by reason that this was my own natural language, the easiest book that I was acquainted with, and for the subject, the most accommodated to the capacity of my age: for as for the Lancelot of the Lake, the Amadis of Gaul, the Huon of Bordeaux, and such farragos, by which children are most delighted with, I had never so much as heard their names, no more than I yet know what they contain; so exact was the discipline wherein I was brought up. But this was enough to make me neglect the other lessons that were prescribed me; and here it was infinitely to my advantage, to have to do with an understanding tutor, who very well knew discreetly to connive at this and other truantries of the same nature; for by this means I ran through Virgil's AEneid, and then Terence, and then Plautus, and then some Italian comedies, allured by the sweetness of the subject; whereas had he been so foolish as to have taken me off this diversion, I do really believe, I had brought away nothing from the college but a hatred of books, as almost all our young gentlemen do. But he carried himself very discreetly in that business, seeming to take no notice, and allowing me only such time as I could steal from my other regular studies, which whetted my appetite to devour those books. For the chief things my father expected from their endeavours to whom he had delivered me for education, were affability and good-humour; and, to say the truth, my manners had no other vice but sloth and want of metal. The fear was not that I should do ill, but that I should do nothing; nobody prognosticated that I should be wicked, but only useless; they foresaw idleness, but no malice; and I find it falls out accordingly: The complaints I hear of myself are these: "He is idle, cold in the offices of friendship and relation, and in those of the public, too particular, too disdainful." But the most injurious do not say, "Why has he taken such a thing? Why has he not paid such an one?" but, "Why does he part with nothing? Why does he not give?" And I should take it for a favour that men would expect from me no greater effects of supererogation than these. But they are unjust to exact from me what I do not owe, far more rigorously than they require from others that which they do owe. In condemning me to it, they efface the gratification of the action, and deprive me of the gratitude that would be my due for it; whereas the active well-doing ought to be of so much the greater value from my hands, by how much I have never been passive that way at all. I can the more freely dispose of my fortune the more it is mine, and of myself the more I am my own. Nevertheless, if I were good at setting out my own actions, I could, peradventure, very well repel these reproaches, and could give some to understand, that they are not so much offended, that I do not enough, as that I am able to do a great deal more than I do.

Yet for all this heavy disposition of mine, my mind, when retired into itself, was not altogether without strong movements, solid and clear *judgments about those objects it could comprehend, and could also, without any helps, digest them; but, amongst other things, I do really believe, it had been totally impossible to have made it to submit by violence and force. Shall I here acquaint you with one faculty of my youth? I had great assurance of countenance, and flexibility of voice and gesture, in applying myself to any part I undertook to act: for before--*

"Alter ab undecimo tum me vix ceperat annus,"

["I had just entered my twelfth year."--Virgil, Bucol., 39.]

I played the chief parts in the Latin tragedies of Buchanan, Guerente, and Muret, that were presented in our College of Guienne with great dignity: now Andreas Goveanus, our principal, as in all other parts of his charge, was, without comparison, the best of that employment in France; and I was looked upon as one of the best actors. 'Tis an exercise that I do not disapprove in young people of condition; and I have since seen our princes, after the example of some of the ancients, in person handsomely and commendably perform these exercises; it was even allowed to persons of quality to make a profession of it in Greece.

"Aristoni tragico actori rem aperit: huic et genus et fortuna honesta erant: nec ars, quia nihil tale apud Graecos pudori est, ea deformabat."

["He imparted this matter to Aristo the tragedian; a man of good family and fortune, which neither of them receive any blemish by that profession; nothing of this kind being reputed a disparagement in Greece."--Livy, xxiv. 24.]

Nay, I have always taxed those with impertinence who condemn these entertainments, and with injustice those who refuse to admit such comedians as are worth seeing into our good towns, and grudge the people that public diversion. Well-governed corporations take care to assemble their citizens, not only to the solemn duties of devotion, but also to sports and spectacles. They find society and friendship augmented by it; and besides, can there possibly be allowed a more orderly and regular diversion than what is performed m the sight of every one, and very often in the presence of the supreme magistrate himself? And I, for my part, should think it reasonable, that the prince should sometimes gratify his people at his own expense, out of paternal goodness and affection; and that in populous cities there should be theatres erected for such entertainments, if but to divert them from worse and private actions.

To return to my subject, there is nothing like alluring the appetite and affections; otherwise you make nothing but so many asses laden with books; by dint of the lash, you give them their pocketful of learning to keep; whereas, to do well you should not only lodge it with them, but make them espouse it.

CHAPTER XXVI

THAT IT IS FOLLY TO MEASURE TRUTH AND ERROR
BY OUR OWN CAPACITY

'Tis not, perhaps, without reason, that we attribute facility of belief and easiness of persuasion to simplicity and ignorance: for I fancy I have heard belief compared to the impression of a seal upon the soul, which by how much softer and of less resistance it is, is the more easy to be impressed upon.

> *"Ut necesse est, lancem in Libra, ponderibus impositis, deprimi, sic animum perspicuis cedere."*

> *["As the scale of the balance must give way to the weight that presses it down, so the mind yields to demonstration."*
> *⁃⁃Cicero, Acad., ii. 12.]*

By how much the soul is more empty and without counterpoise, with so much greater facility it yields under the weight of the first persuasion. And this is the reason that children, the common people, women, and sick folks, are most apt to be led by the ears. But then, on the other hand, 'tis a foolish presumption to slight and condemn all things for false that do not appear to us probable; which is the ordinary vice of such as fancy themselves wiser than their neighbours. I was myself once one of those; and if I heard talk of dead folks walking, of prophecies, enchantments, witchcrafts, or any other story I had no mind to believe:

> *"Somnia, terrores magicos, miracula, sagas, Nocturnos lemures, portentaque Thessala,"*

> *["Dreams, magic terrors, marvels, sorceries, Thessalian prodigies."*
> *⁃⁃Horace. Ep. ii. 3, 208.]*

I presently pitied the poor people that were abused by these follies.
Whereas I now find, that I myself was to be pitied as much, at least,
as they; not that experience has taught me anything to alter my former
opinions, though my curiosity has endeavoured that way; but reason has
instructed me, that thus resolutely to condemn anything for false and
impossible, is arrogantly and impiously to circumscribe and limit the
will of God, and the power of our mother nature, within the bounds of my
own capacity, than which no folly can be greater. If we give the names
of monster and miracle to everything our reason cannot comprehend, how
many are continually presented before our eyes? Let us but consider
through what clouds, and as it were groping in the dark, our teachers
lead us to the knowledge of most of the things about us; assuredly we
shall find that it is rather custom than knowledge that takes away their
strangeness--

> "Jam nemo, fessus saturusque videndi,
> Suspicere in coeli dignatur lucida templa;"

[*"Weary of the sight, now no one deigns to look up to heaven's lucid
temples."--Lucretius, ii. 1037. The text has 'statiate videnai']*

and that if those things were now newly presented to us, we should think
them as incredible, if not more, than any others.

> "Si nunc primum mortalibus adsint
> Ex improviso, si sint objecta repente,
> Nil magis his rebus poterat mirabile dici,
> Aute minus ante quod auderent fore credere gentes."

[*Lucretius, ii. 1032. The sense of the passage is in the preceding
sentence.*]

He that had never seen a river, imagined the first he met with to be the
sea; and the greatest things that have fallen within our knowledge, we
conclude the extremes that nature makes of the kind.

> "Scilicet et fluvius qui non est maximus, ei'st
> Qui non ante aliquem majorem vidit; et ingens
> Arbor, homoque videtur, et omnia de genere omni
> Maxima quae vidit quisque, haec ingentia fingit."

["A little river seems to him, who has never seen a larger river, a mighty stream; and so with other things--a tree, a man--anything appears greatest to him that never knew a greater."--Idem, vi. 674.]

> "Consuetudine oculorum assuescunt animi, neque admirantur, neque requirunt rationes earum rerum, quas semper vident."

["Things grow familiar to men's minds by being often seen; so that they neither admire nor are they inquisitive about things they daily see."--Cicero, De Natura Deor., lib. ii. 38.]

The novelty, rather than the greatness of things, tempts us to inquire into their causes. We are to judge with more reverence, and with greater acknowledgment of our own ignorance and infirmity, of the infinite power of nature. How many unlikely things are there testified by people worthy of faith, which, if we cannot persuade ourselves absolutely to believe, we ought at least to leave them in suspense; for, to condemn them as impossible, is by a temerarious presumption to pretend to know the utmost bounds of possibility. Did we rightly understand the difference betwixt the impossible and the unusual, and betwixt that which is contrary to the order and course of nature and contrary to the common opinion of men, in not believing rashly, and on the other hand, in not being too incredulous, we should observe the rule of 'Ne quid nimis' enjoined by Chilo.

When we find in Froissart, that the Comte de Foix knew in Bearn the defeat of John, king of Castile, at Jubera the next day after it happened, and the means by which he tells us he came to do so, we may be allowed to be a little merry at it, as also at what our annals report, that Pope Honorius, the same day that King Philip Augustus died at

Mantes, performed his public obsequies at Rome, and commanded the like
throughout Italy, the testimony of these authors not being, perhaps, of
authority enough to restrain us. But what if Plutarch, besides several
examples that he produces out of antiquity, tells us, he knows of certain
knowledge, that in the time of Domitian, the news of the battle lost by
Antony in Germany was published at Rome, many days' journey from thence,
and dispersed throughout the whole world, the same day it was fought;
and if Caesar was of opinion, that it has often happened, that the report
has preceded the incident, shall we not say, that these simple people
have suffered themselves to be deceived with the vulgar, for not having
been so clear-sighted as we? Is there anything more delicate, more
clear, more sprightly; than Pliny's judgment, when he is pleased to set
it to work? Anything more remote from vanity? Setting aside his
learning, of which I make less account, in which of these excellences do
any of us excel him? And yet there is scarce a young schoolboy that does
not convict him of untruth, and that pretends not to instruct him in the
progress of the works of nature. When we read in Bouchet the miracles of
St. Hilary's relics, away with them: his authority is not sufficient to
deprive us of the liberty of contradicting him; but generally and offhand
to condemn all suchlike stories, seems to me a singular impudence. That
great St. Augustin' testifies to have seen a blind child recover sight
upon the relics of St. Gervasius and St. Protasius at Milan; a woman at
Carthage cured of a cancer, by the sign of the cross made upon her by a
woman newly baptized; Hesperius, a familiar friend of his, to have driven
away the spirits that haunted his house, with a little earth of the
sepulchre of our Lord; which earth, being also transported thence into
the church, a paralytic to have there been suddenly cured by it; a woman
in a procession, having touched St. Stephen's shrine with a nosegay, and
rubbing her eyes with it, to have recovered her sight, lost many years
before; with several other miracles of which he professes himself to have
been an eyewitness: of what shall we excuse him and the two holy bishops,
Aurelius and Maximinus, both of whom he attests to the truth of these
things? Shall it be of ignorance, simplicity, and facility; or of malice
and imposture? Is any man now living so impudent as to think himself
comparable to them in virtue, piety, learning, judgment, or any kind of
perfection?

"*Qui, ut rationem nullam afferrent,*
ipsa auctoritate me frangerent."

[*"Who, though they should adduce no reason, would convince me with
their authority alone."*~~Cicero, Tusc. Quaes, i. 21.*]

'Tis a presumption of great danger and consequence, besides the absurd
temerity it draws after it, to contemn what we do not comprehend. For
after, according to your fine understanding, you have established the
limits of truth and error, and that, afterwards, there appears a
necessity upon you of believing stranger things than those you have
contradicted, you are already obliged to quit your limits. Now, that
which seems to me so much to disorder our consciences in the commotions
we are now in concerning religion, is the Catholics dispensing so much
with their belief. They fancy they appear moderate, and wise, when they
grant to their opponents some of the articles in question; but, besides
that they do not discern what advantage it is to those with whom we
contend, to begin to give ground and to retire, and how much this
animates our enemy to follow his blow: these articles which they select
as things indifferent, are sometimes of very great importance. We are
either wholly and absolutely to submit ourselves to the authority of our
ecclesiastical polity, or totally throw off all obedience to it: 'tis not
for us to determine what and how much obedience we owe to it. And this I
can say, as having myself made trial of it, that having formerly taken
the liberty of my own swing and fancy, and omitted or neglected certain
rules of the discipline of our Church, which seemed to me vain and
strange coming afterwards to discourse of it with learned men, I have
found those same things to be built upon very good and solid ground and
strong foundation; and that nothing but stupidity and ignorance makes us
receive them with less reverence than the rest. Why do we not consider
what contradictions we find in our own judgments; how many things were
yesterday articles of our faith, that to-day appear no other than fables?
Glory and curiosity are the scourges of the soul; the last prompts us to

thrust our noses into everything, the other forbids us to leave anything doubtful and undecided.

CHAPTER XXVII

OF FRIENDSHIP

Having considered the proceedings of a painter that serves me, I had a mind to imitate his way. He chooses the fairest place and middle of any wall, or panel, wherein to draw a picture, which he finishes with his utmost care and art, and the vacuity about it he fills with grotesques, which are odd fantastic figures without any grace but what they derive from their variety, and the extravagance of their shapes. And in truth, what are these things I scribble, other than grotesques and monstrous bodies, made of various parts, without any certain figure, or any other than accidental order, coherence, or proportion?

> *"Desinit in piscem mulier formosa superne."*

> *["A fair woman in her upper form terminates in a fish."*
> *~~Horace, De Arte Poetica, v. 4.]*

In this second part I go hand in hand with my painter; but fall very short of him in the first and the better, my power of handling not being such, that I dare to offer at a rich piece, finely polished, and set off according to art. I have therefore thought fit to borrow one of Estienne de la Boetie, and such a one as shall honour and adorn all the rest of my work~~namely, a discourse that he called 'Voluntary Servitude'; but, since, those who did not know him have properly enough called it "Le contr Un." He wrote in his youth,~~["Not being as yet eighteen years old."~~Edition of 1588.] by way of essay, in honour of liberty against tyrants; and it has since run through the hands of men of great learning and judgment, not without singular and merited commendation; for it is finely written, and as full as anything can possibly be. And yet one may confidently say it is far short of what he was able to do; and if in that more mature age, wherein I had the happiness to know him, he had taken a

design like this of mine, to commit his thoughts to writing, we should
have seen a great many rare things, and such as would have gone very near
to have rivalled the best writings of antiquity: for in natural parts
especially, I know no man comparable to him. But he has left nothing
behind him, save this treatise only (and that too by chance, for I
believe he never saw it after it first went out of his hands), and some
observations upon that edict of January‒‒[1562, which granted to the
Huguenots the public exercise of their religion.]‒‒made famous by our
civil‒wars, which also shall elsewhere, peradventure, find a place.
These were all I could recover of his remains, I to whom with so
affectionate a remembrance, upon his death‒bed, he by his last will
bequeathed his library and papers, the little book of his works only
excepted, which I committed to the press. And this particular obligation
I have to this treatise of his, that it was the occasion of my first
coming acquainted with him; for it was showed to me long before I had the
good fortune to know him; and the first knowledge of his name, proving
the first cause and foundation of a friendship, which we afterwards
improved and maintained, so long as God was pleased to continue us
together, so perfect, inviolate, and entire, that certainly the like is
hardly to be found in story, and amongst the men of this age, there is no
sign nor trace of any such thing in use; so much concurrence is required
to the building of such a one, that 'tis much, if fortune bring it but
once to pass in three ages.

There is nothing to which nature seems so much to have inclined us, as to
society; and Aristotle , says that the good legislators had more respect
to friendship than to justice. Now the most supreme point of its
perfection is this: for, generally, all those that pleasure, profit,
public or private interest create and nourish, are so much the less
beautiful and generous, and so much the less friendships, by how much
they mix another cause, and design, and fruit in friendship, than itself.
Neither do the four ancient kinds, natural, social, hospitable, venereal,
either separately or jointly, make up a true and perfect friendship.

That of children to parents is rather respect: friendship is nourished by
communication, which cannot by reason of the great disparity, be betwixt

these, but would rather perhaps offend the duties of nature; for neither are all the secret thoughts of fathers fit to be communicated to children, lest it beget an indecent familiarity betwixt them; nor can the advices and reproofs, which is one of the principal offices of friendship, be properly performed by the son to the father. There are some countries where 'twas the custom for children to kill their fathers; and others, where the fathers killed their children, to avoid their being an impediment one to another in life; and naturally the expectations of the one depend upon the ruin of the other. There have been great philosophers who have made nothing of this tie of nature, as Aristippus for one, who being pressed home about the affection he owed to his children, as being come out of him, presently fell to spit, saying, that this also came out of him, and that we also breed worms and lice; and that other, that Plutarch endeavoured to reconcile to his brother: "I make never the more account of him," said he, "for coming out of the same hole." This name of brother does indeed carry with it a fine and delectable sound, and for that reason, he and I called one another brothers but the complication of interests, the division of estates, and that the wealth of the one should be the property of the other, strangely relax and weaken the fraternal tie: brothers pursuing their fortune and advancement by the same path, 'tis hardly possible but they must of necessity often jostle and hinder one another. Besides, why is it necessary that the correspondence of manners, parts, and inclinations, which begets the true and perfect friendships, should always meet in these relations? The father and the son may be of quite contrary humours, and so of brothers: he is my son, he is my brother; but he is passionate, ill-natured, or a fool. And moreover, by how much these are friendships that the law and natural obligation impose upon us, so much less is there of our own choice and voluntary freedom; whereas that voluntary liberty of ours has no production more promptly and; properly its own than affection and friendship. Not that I have not in my own person experimented all that can possibly be expected of that kind, having had the best and most indulgent father, even to his extreme old age, that ever was, and who was himself descended from a family for many generations famous and exemplary for brotherly concord:

> "*Et ipse*
> *Notus in fratres animi paterni.*"

[*"And I myself, known for paternal love toward my brothers."*
--Horace, Ode, ii. 2, 6.]

We are not here to bring the love we bear to women, though it be an act of our own choice, into comparison, nor rank it with the others. The fire of this, I confess,

> "*Neque enim est dea nescia nostri*
> *Qux dulcem curis miscet amaritiem,*"

[*"Nor is the goddess unknown to me who mixes a sweet bitterness with my love."*---Catullus, lxviii. 17.]

is more active, more eager, and more sharp: but withal, 'tis more precipitant, fickle, moving, and inconstant; a fever subject to intermissions and paroxysms, that has seized but on one part of us. Whereas in friendship, 'tis a general and universal fire, but temperate and equal, a constant established heat, all gentle and smooth, without poignancy or roughness. Moreover, in love, 'tis no other than frantic desire for that which flies from us:

> "*Come segue la lepre il cacciatore*
> *Al freddo, al caldo, alla montagna, al lito;*
> *Ne piu l'estima poi the presa vede;*
> *E sol dietro a chi fugge affretta il piede*"

[*"As the hunter pursues the hare, in cold and heat, to the mountain, to the shore, nor cares for it farther when he sees it taken, and only delights in chasing that which flees from him."*--Aristo, x. 7.]

so soon as it enters unto the terms of friendship, that is to say, into a concurrence of desires, it vanishes and is gone, fruition destroys it, as having only a fleshly end, and such a one as is subject to satiety.

Friendship, on the contrary, is enjoyed proportionably as it is desired; and only grows up, is nourished and improved by enjoyment, as being of itself spiritual, and the soul growing still more refined by practice. Under this perfect friendship, the other fleeting affections have in my younger years found some place in me, to say nothing of him, who himself so confesses but too much in his verses; so that I had both these passions, but always so, that I could myself well enough distinguish them, and never in any degree of comparison with one another; the first maintaining its flight in so lofty and so brave a place, as with disdain to look down, and see the other flying at a far humbler pitch below.

As concerning marriage, besides that it is a covenant, the entrance into which only is free, but the continuance in it forced and compulsory, having another dependence than that of our own free will, and a bargain commonly contracted to other ends, there almost always happens a thousand intricacies in it to unravel, enough to break the thread and to divert the current of a lively affection: whereas friendship has no manner of business or traffic with aught but itself. Moreover, to say truth, the ordinary talent of women is not such as is sufficient to maintain the conference and communication required to the support of this sacred tie; nor do they appear to be endued with constancy of mind, to sustain the pinch of so hard and durable a knot. And doubtless, if without this, there could be such a free and voluntary familiarity contracted, where not only the souls might have this entire fruition, but the bodies also might share in the alliance, and a man be engaged throughout, the friendship would certainly be more full and perfect; but it is without example that this sex has ever yet arrived at such perfection; and, by the common consent of the ancient schools, it is wholly rejected from it.

That other Grecian licence is justly abhorred by our manners, which also, from having, according to their practice, a so necessary disparity of age and difference of offices betwixt the lovers, answered no more to the perfect union and harmony that we here require than the other:

> *"Quis est enim iste amor amicitiae? cur neque deformem adolescentem quisquam amat, neque formosum senem?"*

["For what is that friendly love? why does no one love a deformed
youth or a comely old man?"--Cicero, Tusc. Quaes., iv. 33.]

Neither will that very picture that the Academy presents of it, as I
conceive, contradict me, when I say, that this first fury inspired by the
son of Venus into the heart of the lover, upon sight of the flower and
prime of a springing and blossoming youth, to which they allow all the
insolent and passionate efforts that an immoderate ardour can produce,
was simply founded upon external beauty, the false image of corporal
generation; for it could not ground this love upon the soul, the sight of
which as yet lay concealed, was but now springing, and not of maturity to
blossom; that this fury, if it seized upon a low spirit, the means by
which it preferred its suit were rich presents, favour in advancement to
dignities, and such trumpery, which they by no means approve; if on a
more generous soul, the pursuit was suitably generous, by philosophical
instructions, precepts to revere religion, to obey the laws, to die for
the good of one's country; by examples of valour, prudence, and justice,
the lover studying to render himself acceptable by the grace and beauty
of the soul, that of his body being long since faded and decayed, hoping
by this mental society to establish a more firm and lasting contract.
When this courtship came to effect in due season (for that which they do
not require in the lover, namely, leisure and discretion in his pursuit,
they strictly require in the person loved, forasmuch as he is to judge of
an internal beauty, of difficult knowledge and abstruse discovery), then
there sprung in the person loved the desire of a spiritual conception;
by the mediation of a spiritual beauty. This was the principal; the
corporeal, an accidental and secondary matter; quite the contrary as to
the lover. For this reason they prefer the person beloved, maintaining
that the gods in like manner preferred him too, and very much blame the
poet Æschylus for having, in the loves of Achilles and Patroclus, given
the lover's part to Achilles, who was in the first and beardless flower
of his adolescence, and the handsomest of all the Greeks. After this
general community, the sovereign, and most worthy part presiding and
governing, and performing its proper offices, they say, that thence great
utility was derived, both by private and public concerns; that it

constituted the force and power of the countries where it prevailed, and the chiefest security of liberty and justice. Of which the healthy loves of Harmodius and Aristogiton are instances. And therefore it is that they called it sacred and divine, and conceive that nothing but the violence of tyrants and the baseness of the common people are inimical to it. Finally, all that can be said in favour of the Academy is, that it was a love which ended in friendship, which well enough agrees with the Stoical definition of love:

> *"Amorem conatum esse amicitiae faciendae*
> *ex pulchritudinis specie."*

> *["Love is a desire of contracting friendship arising from the beauty of the object."--Cicero, Tusc. Quaes., vi. 34.]*

I return to my own more just and true description:

> *"Omnino amicitiae, corroboratis jam confirmatisque,*
> *et ingeniis, et aetatibus, judicandae sunt."*

> *["Those are only to be reputed friendships that are fortified and confirmed by judgement and the length of time."*
> *--Cicero, De Amicit., c. 20.]*

For the rest, what we commonly call friends and friendships, are nothing but acquaintance and familiarities, either occasionally contracted, or upon some design, by means of which there happens some little intercourse betwixt our souls. But in the friendship I speak of, they mix and work themselves into one piece, with so universal a mixture, that there is no more sign of the seam by which they were first conjoined. If a man should importune me to give a reason why I loved him, I find it could no otherwise be expressed, than by making answer: because it was he, because it was I. There is, beyond all that I am able to say, I know not what inexplicable and fated power that brought on this union. We sought one another long before we met, and by the characters we heard of one another, which wrought upon our affections more than, in reason, mere reports should do; I think 'twas by some secret appointment of heaven. We embraced in our names; and at our first meeting, which was accidentally at a great city entertainment, we found ourselves so mutually taken with one another, so acquainted, and so endeared betwixt ourselves, that from thenceforward nothing was so near to us as one another. He wrote an excellent Latin satire, since printed, wherein he excuses the precipitation of our intelligence, so suddenly come to perfection, saying, that destined to have so short a continuance, as begun so late (for we were both full-grown men, and he some years the older), there was no time to lose, nor were we tied to conform to the example of those slow and regular friendships, that require so many precautions of long preliminary conversation: This has no other idea than that of itself, and can only refer to itself: this is no one special consideration, nor two, nor three, nor four, nor a thousand; 'tis I know not what quintessence of all this mixture, which, seizing my whole will, carried it to plunge and lose itself in his, and that having seized his whole will, brought it back with equal concurrence and appetite to plunge and lose itself in mine. I may truly say lose, reserving nothing to ourselves that was either his or mine.--[All this relates to Estienne de la Boetie.]

When Laelius,--[Cicero, De Amicit., c. II.]--in the presence of the Roman consuls, who after thay had sentenced Tiberius Gracchus, prosecuted all those who had had any familiarity with him also; came to ask Caius Blosius, who was his chiefest friend, how much he would have done for him, and that he made answer: "All things."--"How! All things!" said Laelius. "And what if he had commanded you to fire our temples?"--"He would never have commanded me that," replied Blosius.--"But what if he had?" said Laelius.--"I would have obeyed him," said the other. If he was so perfect a friend to Gracchus as the histories report him to have been, there was yet no necessity of offending the consuls by such a bold confession, though he might still have retained the assurance he had of Gracchus' disposition. However, those who accuse this answer as seditious, do not well understand the mystery; nor presuppose, as it was true, that he had Gracchus' will in his sleeve, both by the power of a friend, and the perfect knowledge he had of the man: they were more *friends than citizens, more friends to one another than either enemies or friends to their country, or than friends to ambition and innovation; having absolutely given up themselves to one another, either held absolutely the reins of the other's inclination; and suppose all this guided by virtue, and all this by the conduct of reason, which also without these it had not been possible to do, Blosius' answer was such as it ought to be. If any of their actions flew out of the handle, they were neither (according to my measure of friendship) friends to one another, nor to themselves. As to the rest, this answer carries no worse sound, than mine would do to one that should ask me: "If your will should command you to kill your daughter, would you do it?" and that I should make answer, that I would; for this expresses no consent to such an act, forasmuch as I do not in the least suspect my own will, and as little that of such a friend. 'Tis not in the power of all the eloquence in the world, to dispossess me of the certainty I have of the intentions and resolutions of my friend; nay, no one action of his, what face soever it might bear, could be presented to me, of which I could not presently, and at first sight, find out the moving cause. Our souls had drawn so unanimously together, they had considered each other with so ardent an affection, and with the like affection laid open the very bottom of our hearts to one another's view, that I not only knew his as well as my own; but should certainly in any concern of mine have trusted my interest much more willingly with him, than with myself.*

Let no one, therefore, rank other common friendships with such a one as this. I have had as much experience of these as another, and of the most perfect of their kind: but I do not advise that any should confound the rules of the one and the other, for they would find themselves much deceived. In those other ordinary friendships, you are to walk with bridle in your hand, with prudence and circumspection, for in them the knot is not so sure that a man may not half suspect it will slip. "Love him," said Chilo,--[Aulus Gellius, i. 3.]--"so as if you were one day to hate him; and hate him so as you were one day to love him." This precept, though abominable in the sovereign and perfect friendship I speak of, is nevertheless very sound as to the practice of the ordinary and customary ones, and to which the saying that Aristotle had so frequent in his mouth, "O my friends, there is no friend," may very fitly be applied. In this noble commerce, good offices, presents, and benefits, by which other friendships are supported and maintained, do not deserve so much as to be mentioned; and the reason is the concurrence of our wills; for, as the kindness I have for myself receives no increase, for anything I relieve myself withal in time of need (whatever the Stoics say), and as I do not find myself obliged to myself for any service I do myself: so the union of such friends, being truly perfect, deprives them of all idea of such duties, and makes them loathe and banish from their conversation these words of division and distinction, benefits, obligation, acknowledgment, entreaty, thanks, and the like. All things, wills, thoughts, opinions, goods, wives, children, honours, and lives, being in effect common betwixt them, and that absolute concurrence of affections being no other than one soul in two bodies (according to that very proper definition of Aristotle), they can neither lend nor give anything to one another. This is the reason why the lawgivers, to honour marriage with some resemblance of this divine alliance, interdict all gifts betwixt man and wife; inferring by that, that all should belong to each of them, and that they have nothing to divide or to give to each other.

If, in the friendship of which I speak, one could give to the other, the receiver of the benefit would be the man that obliged his friend; for each of them contending and above all things studying how to be useful to the other, he that administers the occasion is the liberal man, in giving his friend the satisfaction of doing that towards him which above all things he most desires. When the philosopher Diogenes wanted money, he used to say, that he redemanded it of his friends, not that he demanded it. And to let you see the practical working of this, I will here produce an ancient and singular example. Eudamidas, a Corinthian, had two friends, Charixenus a Sicyonian and Areteus a Corinthian; this man coming to die, being poor, and his two friends rich, he made his will after this manner. "I bequeath to Areteus the maintenance of my mother, to support and provide for her in her old age; and to Charixenus I bequeath the care of marrying my daughter, and to give her as good a portion as he is able; and in case one of these chance to die, I hereby substitute the survivor in his place." They who first saw this will made themselves very merry at the contents: but the legatees, being made acquainted with it, accepted it with very great content; and one of them, Charixenus, dying within five days after, and by that means the charge of both duties devolving solely on him, Areteus nurtured the old woman with very great care and tenderness, and of five talents he had in estate, he gave two and a half in marriage with an only daughter he had of his own, and two and a half in marriage with the daughter of Eudamidas, and on one and the same day solemnised both their nuptials.

This example is very full, if one thing were not to be objected, namely the multitude of friends for the perfect friendship I speak of is indivisible; each one gives himself so entirely to his friend, that he has nothing left to distribute to others: on the contrary, is sorry that he is not double, treble, or quadruple, and that he has not many souls and many wills, to confer them all upon this one object. Common friendships will admit of division; one may love the beauty of this person, the good-humour of that, the liberality of a third, the paternal affection of a fourth, the fraternal love of a fifth, and so of the rest: but this friendship that possesses the whole soul, and there rules and sways with an absolute sovereignty, cannot possibly admit of a rival. If two at the same time should call to you for succour, to which of them would you run? Should they require of you contrary offices, how could you serve them both? Should one commit a thing to your silence that it were of importance to the other to know, how would you disengage yourself? A unique and particular friendship dissolves all other obligations whatsoever: the secret I have sworn not to reveal to any other, I may without perjury communicate to him who is not another, but myself. 'Tis miracle enough certainly, for a man to double himself, and those that talk of tripling, talk they know not of what. Nothing is extreme, that has its like; and he who shall suppose, that of two, I love one as much as the other, that they mutually love one another too, and love me as much as I love them, multiplies into a confraternity the most single of units, and whereof, moreover, one alone is the hardest thing in the world to find. The rest of this story suits very well with what I was saying; for Eudamidas, as a bounty and favour, bequeaths to his *friends a legacy of employing themselves in his necessity; he leaves them heirs to this liberality of his, which consists in giving them the opportunity of conferring a benefit upon him; and doubtless, the force of friendship is more eminently apparent in this act of his, than in that of Areteus. In short, these are effects not to be imagined nor comprehended by such as have not experience of them, and which make me infinitely honour and admire the answer of that young soldier to Cyrus, by whom being asked how much he would take for a horse, with which he had won the prize of a race, and whether he would exchange him for a kingdom? "No, truly, sir," said he, "but I would give him with all my heart, to get thereby a true friend, could I find out any man worthy of that alliance." [Xenophon, Cyropadia, viii. 3.] He did not say ill in saying, "could I find": for though one may almost everywhere meet with men sufficiently qualified for a superficial acquaintance, yet in this, where a man is to deal from the very bottom of his heart, without any manner of reservation, it will be requisite that all the wards and springs be truly wrought and perfectly sure.*

In confederations that hold but by one end, we are only to provide against the imperfections that particularly concern that end. It can be of no importance to me of what religion my physician or my lawyer is; this consideration has nothing in common with the offices of friendship which they owe me; and I am of the same indifference in the domestic acquaintance my servants must necessarily contract with me. I never inquire, when I am to take a footman, if he be chaste, but if he be diligent; and am not solicitous if my muleteer be given to gaming, as if he be strong and able; or if my cook be a swearer, if he be a good cook. I do not take upon me to direct what other men should do in the government of their families, there are plenty that meddle enough with that, but only give an account of my method in my own:

"Mihi sic usus est: tibi, ut opus est facto, face."

["This has been my way; as for you, do as you find needful. "Terence, Heaut., i. I., 28.]

*For table-talk, I prefer the pleasant and witty before the learned and
the grave; in bed, beauty before goodness; in common discourse the ablest
speaker, whether or no there be sincerity in the case. And, as he that
was found astride upon a hobby-horse, playing with his children,
entreated the person who had surprised him in that posture to say nothing
of it till himself came to be a father,--[Plutarch, Life of Agesilaus,
c. 9.]--supposing that the fondness that would then possess his own
soul, would render him a fairer judge of such an action; so I, also,
could wish to speak to such as have had experience of what I say: though,
knowing how remote a thing such a friendship is from the common practice,
and how rarely it is to be found, I despair of meeting with any such
judge. For even these discourses left us by antiquity upon this subject,
seem to me flat and poor, in comparison of the sense I have of it, and in
this particular, the effects surpass even the precepts of philosophy.*

"Nil ego contulerim jucundo sanus amico."

*["While I have sense left to me, there will never be anything more
acceptable to me than an agreeable friend."
--Horace, Sat., i. 5, 44.]*

*The ancient Menander declared him to be happy that had had the good
fortune to meet with but the shadow of a friend: and doubtless he had
good reason to say so, especially if he spoke by experience: for in good
earnest, if I compare all the rest of my life, though, thanks be to God,
I have passed my time pleasantly enough, and at my ease, and the loss of
such a friend excepted, free from any grievous affliction, and in great
tranquillity of mind, having been contented with my natural and original
commodities, without being solicitous after others; if I should compare
it all, I say, with the four years I had the happiness to enjoy the sweet
society of this excellent man, 'tis nothing but smoke, an obscure and
tedious night. From the day that I lost him:*

*"Quern semper acerbum,
Semper honoratum (sic, di, voluistis) habebo,"*

["A day for me ever sad, for ever sacred, so have you willed ye
gods."--AEneid, v. 49.]

I have only led a languishing life; and the very pleasures that present
themselves to me, instead of administering anything of consolation,
double my affliction for his loss. We were halves throughout, and to
that degree, that methinks, by outliving him, I defraud him of his part.

> "Nec fas esse ulla me voluptate hic frui
> Decrevi, tantisper dum ille abest meus particeps."

["I have determined that it will never be right for me to enjoy any
pleasure, so long as he, with whom I shared all pleasures is away."
--Terence, Heaut., i. I. 97.]

I was so grown and accustomed to be always his double in all places and
in all things, that methinks I am no more than half of myself:

> "Illam meae si partem anima tulit
> Maturior vis, quid moror altera?
>   Nec carus aeque, nec superstes
>   Integer? Ille dies utramque
> Duxit ruinam."

["If that half of my soul were snatch away from me by an untimely
stroke, why should the other stay? That which remains will not be
equally dear, will not be whole: the same day will involve the
destruction of both."]

or:

["If a superior force has taken that part of my soul, why do I, the
remaining one, linger behind? What is left is not so dear, nor an
entire thing: this day has wrought the destruction of both."
--Horace, Ode, ii. 17, 5.]

There is no action or imagination of mine wherein I do not miss him; as I know that he would have missed me: for as he surpassed me by infinite degrees in virtue and all other accomplishments, so he also did in the duties of friendship:

> "Quis desiderio sit pudor, aut modus
> Tam cari capitis?"

["What shame can there, or measure, in lamenting so dear a friend?" ⁓Horace, Ode, i. 24, I.]

> "O misero frater adempte mihi!
> Omnia tecum una perierunt gaudia nostra,
> Quae tuus in vita dulcis alebat amor.
> Tu mea, tu moriens fregisti commoda, frater;
> Tecum una tota est nostra sepulta anima
> Cujus ego interitu tota de menthe fugavi
> Haec studia, atque omnes delicias animi.
> Alloquar? audiero nunquam tua verba loquentem?
> Nunquam ego te, vita frater amabilior
> Aspiciam posthac; at certe semper amabo;"

["O brother, taken from me miserable! with thee, all our joys have vanished, those joys which, in thy life, thy dear love nourished. Dying, thou, my brother, hast destroyed all my happiness. My whole soul is buried with thee. Through whose death I have banished from my mind these studies, and all the delights of the mind. Shall I address thee? I shall never hear thy voice. Never shall I behold thee hereafter. O brother, dearer to me than life. Nought remains, but assuredly I shall ever love thee."⁓Catullus, lxviii. 20; lxv.]

But let us hear a boy of sixteen speak:

⁓[In Cotton's translation the work referred to is "those Memoirs upon the famous edict of January," of which mention has already been made in the present edition. The edition of 1580, however, and the

Variorum edition of 1872-1900, indicate no particular work; but the edition of 1580 has it "this boy of eighteen years" (which was the age at which La Boetie wrote his "Servitude Volontaire"), speaks of "a boy of sixteen" as occurring only in the common editions, and it would seem tolerably clear that this more important work was, in fact, the production to which Montaigne refers, and that the proper reading of the text should be "sixteen years." What "this boy spoke" is not given by Montaigne, for the reason stated in the next following paragraph.]

"Because I have found that that work has been since brought out, and with a mischievous design, by those who aim at disturbing and changing the condition of our government, without troubling themselves to think whether they are likely to improve it: and because they have mixed up his work with some of their own performance, I have refrained from inserting it here. But that the memory of the author may not be injured, nor suffer with such as could not come near-hand to be acquainted with his principles, I here give them to understand, that it was written by him in his boyhood, and that by way of exercise only, as a common theme that has been hackneyed by a thousand writers. I make no question but that he himself believed what he wrote, being so conscientious that he would not so much as lie in jest: and I moreover know, that could it have been in his own choice, he had rather have been born at Venice, than at Sarlac; and with reason. But he had another maxim sovereignty imprinted in his soul, very religiously to obey and submit to the laws under which he was born. There never was a better citizen, more affectionate to his country; nor a greater enemy to all the commotions and innovations of his time: so that he would much rather have employed his talent to the extinguishing of those civil flames, than have added any fuel to them; he had a mind fashioned to the model of better ages. Now, in exchange of this serious piece, I will present you with another of a more gay and frolic air, from the same hand, and written at the same age."

CHAPTER XXVIII.

NINE AND TWENTY SONNETS
OF ESTIENNE DE LA BOITIE

TO MADAME DE GRAMMONT,
COMTESSE DE GUISSEN

[They scarce contain anything but amorous complaints, expressed in a very rough style, discovering the follies and outrages of a restless passion, overgorged, as it were, with jealousies, fears and suspicions.--Coste.]

[These....contained in the edition of 1588 nine-and-twenty sonnets of La Boetie, accompanied by a dedicatory epistle to Madame de Grammont. The former, which are referred to at the end of Chap. XXVIL, do not really belong to the book, and are of very slight interest at this time; the epistle is transferred to the Correspondence. The sonnets, with the letter, were presumably sent some time after Letters V. et seq. Montaigne seems to have had several copies written out to forward to friends or acquaintances.]

CHAPTER XXIX.

OF MODERATION

As if we had an infectious touch, we, by our manner of handling, corrupt things that in themselves are laudable and good: we may grasp virtue so that it becomes vicious, if we embrace it too stringently and with too violent a desire. Those who say, there is never any excess in virtue, forasmuch as it is not virtue when it once becomes excess, only play upon words:

> *"Insani sapiens nomen ferat, aequus iniqui,*
> *Ultra quam satis est, virtutem si petat ipsam."*

["Let the wise man bear the name of a madman, the just one of an unjust, if he seek wisdom more than is sufficient."
⁓Horace, Ep., i. 6, 15.]

["The wise man is no longer wise, the just man no longer just, if he seek to carry his love for wisdom or virtue beyond that which is necessary."]

This is a subtle consideration of philosophy. A man may both be too much in love with virtue, and be excessive in a just action. Holy Writ agrees with this, Be not wiser than you should, but be soberly wise.⁓[St. Paul, Epistle to the Romans, xii. 3.]⁓I have known a great man,

⁓["It is likely that Montaigne meant Henry III., king of France. The Cardinal d'Ossat, writing to Louise, the queen-dowager, told her, in his frank manner, that he had lived as much or more like a monk than a monarch (Letter XXIII.) And Pope Sextus V., speaking of that prince one day to the Cardinal de Joyeuse, protector of the affairs of France, said to him pleasantly, 'There is nothing that

*your king hath not done, and does not do so still, to be a monk, nor
anything that I have not done, not to be a monk.'"--Coste.]*

prejudice the opinion men had of his devotion, by pretending to be devout
beyond all examples of others of his condition. I love temperate and
moderate natures. An immoderate zeal, even to that which is good, even
though it does not offend, astonishes me, and puts me to study what name
to give it. Neither the mother of Pausanias,

> --["Montaigne would here give us to understand, upon the authority of
> Diodorus Siculus, that Pausanias' mother gave the first hint of the
> punishment that was to be inflicted on her son. 'Pausanias,' says
> this historian, 'perceiving that the ephori, and some other
> Lacedoemonians, aimed at apprehending him, got the start of them,
> and went and took sanctuary m Minerva's temple: and the
> Lacedaemonians, being doubtful whether they ought to take him from
> thence in violation of the franchise there, it is said that his own
> mother came herself to the temple but spoke nothing nor did anything
> more than lay a piece of brick, which she brought with her, on the
> threshold of the temple, which, when she had done, she returned
> home. The Lacedaemonians, taking the hint from the mother, caused
> the gate of the temple to be walled up, and by this means starved
> Pausanias, so that he died with hunger, &c. (lib. xi. cap. 10., of
> Amyot's translation). The name of Pausanias' mother was Alcithea,
> as we are informed by Thucydides' scholiast, who only says that it
> was reported, that when they set about walling up the gates of the
> chapel in which Pausanias had taken refuge, his mother Alcithea laid
> the first stone."--Coste.]

who was the first instructor of her son's process, and threw the first
stone towards his death, nor Posthumius the dictator, who put his son to
death, whom the ardour of youth had successfully pushed upon the enemy a
little more advanced than the rest of his squadron, do appear to me so
much just as strange; and I should neither advise nor like to follow so
savage a virtue, and that costs so dear.

--["Opinions differ as to the truth of this fact. Livy thinks he
has good authority for rejecting it because it does not appear in
history that Posthumious was branded with it, as Titus Manlius was,
about 100 years after his time; for Manlius, having put his son to
death for the like cause, obtained the odious name of Imperiosus,
and since that time Manliana imperia has been used as a term to
signify orders that are too severe; Manliana Imperia, says Livy,
were not only horrible for the time present, but of a bad example to
posterity. And this historian makes no doubt but such commands
would have been actually styled Posthumiana Imperia, if Posthumius
had been the first who set so barbarous an example (Livy, lib. iv.
cap. 29, and lib. viii. cap. 7). But, however, Montaigne has Valer.
Maximus on his side, who says expressly, that Posthumius caused his
son to be put to death, and Diodorus of Sicily (lib. xii. cap.
19)."--Coste.]

The archer that shoots over, misses as much as he that falls short, and
'tis equally troublesome to my sight, to look up at a great light, and
to look down into a dark abyss. Callicles in Plato says, that the
extremity of philosophy is hurtful, and advises not to dive into it
beyond the limits of profit; that, taken moderately, it is pleasant and
useful; but that in the end it renders a man brutish and vicious, a
contemner of religion and the common laws, an enemy to civil
conversation, and all human pleasures, incapable of all public
administration, unfit either to assist others or to relieve himself, and
a fit object for all sorts of injuries and affronts. He says true; for
in its excess, it enslaves our natural freedom, and by an impertinent
subtlety, leads us out of the fair and beaten way that nature has traced
for us.

The love we bear to our wives is very lawful, and yet theology thinks fit
to curb and restrain it. As I remember, I have read in one place of St.
Thomas Aquinas,--[Secunda Secundx, Quaest. 154, art. 9.]--where he
condemns marriages within any of the forbidden degrees, for this reason,
amongst others, that there is some danger, lest the friendship a man
bears to such a woman, should be immoderate; for if the conjugal

*affection be full and perfect betwixt them, as it ought to be, and that
it be over and above surcharged with that of kindred too, there is no
doubt, but such an addition will carry the husband beyond the bounds of
reason.*

*Those sciences that regulate the manners of men, divinity and philosophy,
will have their say in everything; there is no action so private and
secret that can escape their inspection and jurisdiction. They are best
taught who are best able to control and curb their own liberty; women
expose their nudities as much as you will upon the account of pleasure,
though in the necessities of physic they are altogether as shy. I will,
therefore, in their behalf:*

> *--[Coste translates this: "on the part of philosophy and theology,"
> observing that but few wives would think themselves obliged to
> Montaigne for any such lesson to their husbands.]--*

*teach the husbands, that is, such as are too vehement in the exercise of
the matrimonial duty--if such there still be--this lesson, that the very
pleasures they enjoy in the society of their wives are reproachable if
immoderate, and that a licentious and riotous abuse of them is a fault as
reprovable here as in illicit connections. Those immodest and debauched
tricks and postures, that the first ardour suggests to us in this affair,
are not only indecently but detrimentally practised upon our wives. Let
them at least learn impudence from another hand; they are ever ready
enough for our business, and I for my part always went the plain way to
work.*

*Marriage is a solemn and religious tie, and therefore the pleasure we
extract from it should be a sober and serious delight, and mixed with a
certain kind of gravity; it should be a sort of discreet and
conscientious pleasure. And seeing that the chief end of it is
generation, some make a question, whether when men are out of hopes as
when they are superannuated or already with child, it be lawful to
embrace our wives. 'Tis homicide, according to Plato.--[Laws, 8.]--
Certain nations (the Mohammedan, amongst others) abominate all conjunction*

with women with child, others also, with those who are in their courses.
Zenobia would never admit her husband for more than one encounter, after
which she left him to his own swing for the whole time of her conception,
and not till after that would again receive him:--[Trebellius Pollio,
Triginta Tyran., c. 30.]--a brave and generous example of conjugal
continence. It was doubtless from some lascivious poet,--[The lascivious
poet is Homer; see his Iliad, xiv. 294.]--and one that himself was in
great distress for a little of this sport, that Plato borrowed this
story; that Jupiter was one day so hot upon his wife, that not having so
much patience as till she could get to the couch, he threw her upon the
floor, where the vehemence of pleasure made him forget the great and
important resolutions he had but newly taken with the rest of the gods in
his celestial council, and to brag that he had had as good a bout, as
when he got her maidenhead, unknown to their parents.

The kings of Persia were wont to invite their wives to the beginning of
their festivals; but when the wine began to work in good earnest, and
that they were to give the reins to pleasure, they sent them back to
their private apartments, that they might not participate in their
immoderate lust, sending for other women in their stead, with whom they
were not obliged to so great a decorum of respect.--[Plutarch, Precepts
of Marriage, c. 14.]--All pleasures and all sorts of gratifications
are not properly and fitly conferred upon all sorts of persons.
Epaminondas had committed to prison a young man for certain debauches;
for whom Pelopidas mediated, that at his request he might be set at
liberty, which Epaminondas denied to him, but granted it at the first
word to a wench of his, that made the same intercession; saying, that it
was a gratification fit for such a one as she, but not for a captain.
Sophocles being joint praetor with Pericles, seeing accidentally a fine
boy pass by: "O what a charming boy is that!" said he. "That might be
very well," answered Pericles, "for any other than a praetor, who ought
not only to have his hands, but his eyes, too, chaste."--[Cicero, De
Offic., i. 40.] AElius Verus, the emperor, answered his wife, who
reproached him with his love to other women, that he did it upon a
conscientious account, forasmuch as marriage was a name of honour and
dignity, not of wanton and lascivious desire; and our ecclesiastical

history preserves the memory of that woman in great veneration, who parted from her husband because she would not comply with his indecent and inordinate desires. In fine, there is no pleasure so just and lawful, where intemperance and excess are not to be condemned.

But, to speak the truth, is not man a most miserable creature the while? It is scarce, by his natural condition, in his power to taste one pleasure pure and entire; and yet must he be contriving doctrines and precepts to curtail that little he has; he is not yet wretched enough, unless by art and study he augment his own misery:

"Fortunae miseras auximus arte vias."

["We artificially augment the wretchedness of fortune."
~Properitius, lib. iii. 7, 44.]

Human wisdom makes as ill use of her talent, when she exercises it in rescinding from the number and sweetness of those pleasures that are naturally our due, as she employs it favourably and well in artificially disguising and tricking out the ills of life, to alleviate the sense of them. Had I ruled the roast, I should have taken another and more natural course, which, to say the truth, is both commodious and holy, and should, peradventure, have been able to have limited it too; notwithstanding that both our spiritual and corporal physicians, as by compact betwixt themselves, can find no other way to cure, nor other remedy for the infirmities of the body and the soul, than by misery and pain. To this end, watchings, fastings, hair-shirts, remote and solitary banishments, perpetual imprisonments, whips and other afflictions, have been introduced amongst men: but so, that they should carry a sting with them, and be real afflictions indeed; and not fall out as it once did to one Gallio, who having been sent an exile into the isle of Lesbos, news was not long after brought to Rome, that he there lived as merry as the day was long; and that what had been enjoined him for a penance, turned to his pleasure and satisfaction: whereupon the Senate thought fit to recall him home to his wife and family, and confine him to his own house, to accommodate their punishment to his feeling and apprehension. For to

him whom fasting would make more healthful and more sprightly, and to him
to whose palate fish were more acceptable than flesh, the prescription of
these would have no curative effect; no more than in the other sort of
physic, where drugs have no effect upon him who swallows them with
appetite and pleasure: the bitterness of the potion and the abhorrence of
the patient are necessary circumstances to the operation. The nature
that would eat rhubarb like buttered turnips, would frustrate the use and
virtue of it; it must be something to trouble and disturb the stomach,
that must purge and cure it; and here the common rule, that things are
cured by their contraries, fails; for in this one ill is cured by
another.

This belief a little resembles that other so ancient one, of thinking to
gratify the gods and nature by massacre and murder: an opinion
universally once received in all religions. And still, in these later
times wherein our fathers lived, Amurath at the taking of the Isthmus,
immolated six hundred young Greeks to his father's soul, in the nature of
a propitiatory sacrifice for his sins. And in those new countries
discovered in this age of ours, which are pure and virgin yet, in
comparison of ours, this practice is in some measure everywhere received:
all their idols reek with human blood, not without various examples of
horrid cruelty: some they burn alive, and take, half broiled, off the
coals to tear out their hearts and entrails; some, even women, they flay
alive, and with their bloody skins clothe and disguise others. Neither
are we without great examples of constancy and resolution in this affair
the poor souls that are to be sacrificed, old men, women, and children,
themselves going about some days before to beg alms for the offering of
their sacrifice, presenting themselves to the slaughter, singing and
dancing with the spectators.

The ambassadors of the king of Mexico, setting out to Fernando Cortez the
power and greatness of their master, after having told him, that he had
thirty vassals, of whom each was able to raise an hundred thousand
fighting men, and that he kept his court in the fairest and best
fortified city under the sun, added at last, that he was obliged yearly
to offer to the gods fifty thousand men. And it is affirmed, that he

maintained a continual war, with some potent neighbouring nations, not only to keep the young men in exercise, but principally to have wherewithal to furnish his sacrifices with his prisoners of war. At a certain town in another place, for the welcome of the said Cortez, they sacrificed fifty men at once. I will tell you this one tale more, and I have done; some of these people being beaten by him, sent to acknowledge him, and to treat with him of a peace, whose messengers carried him three sorts of gifts, which they presented in these terms: "Behold, lord, here are five slaves: if thou art a furious god that feedeth upon flesh and blood, eat these, and we will bring thee more; if thou art an affable god, behold here incense and feathers; but if thou art a man, take these fowls and these fruits that we have brought thee."

CHAPTER XXX

OF CANNIBALS

When King Pyrrhus invaded Italy, having viewed and considered the order of the army the Romans sent out to meet him; "I know not," said he, "what kind of barbarians" (for so the Greeks called all other nations) "these may be; but the disposition of this army that I see has nothing of barbarism in it."--[Plutarch, Life of Pyrrhus, c. 8.]--As much said the Greeks of that which Flaminius brought into their country; and Philip, beholding from an eminence the order and distribution of the Roman camp formed in his kingdom by Publius Sulpicius Galba, spake to the same effect. By which it appears how cautious men ought to be of taking things upon trust from vulgar opinion, and that we are to judge by the eye of reason, and not from common report.

I long had a man in my house that lived ten or twelve years in the New World, discovered in these latter days, and in that part of it where Villegaignon landed,--[At Brazil, in 1557.]--which he called Antarctic France. This discovery of so vast a country seems to be of very great consideration. I cannot be sure, that hereafter there may not be another, so many wiser men than we having been deceived in this. I am afraid our eyes are bigger than our bellies, and that we have more curiosity than capacity; for we grasp at all, but catch nothing but wind.

Plato brings in Solon,--[In Timaeus.]--telling a story that he had heard from the priests of Sais in Egypt, that of old, and before the Deluge, there was a great island called Atlantis, situate directly at the mouth of the straits of Gibraltar, which contained more countries than both Africa and Asia put together; and that the kings of that country, who not only possessed that Isle, but extended their dominion so far into the continent that they had a country of Africa as far as Egypt, and extending in Europe to Tuscany, attempted to encroach even upon Asia, and to subjugate all the nations that border upon the Mediterranean Sea, as far as the Black Sea; and to that effect overran all Spain, the Gauls, and Italy, so far as to penetrate into Greece, where the Athenians stopped them: but that some time after, both the Athenians, and they and their island, were swallowed by the Flood.

It is very likely that this extreme irruption and inundation of water made wonderful changes and alterations in the habitations of the earth, as 'tis said that the sea then divided Sicily from Italy⸗

> "Haec loca, vi quondam et vasta convulsa ruina,
> Dissiluisse ferunt, quum protenus utraque tellus
> Una foret"

["These lands, they say, formerly with violence and vast desolation convulsed, burst asunder, where erewhile were."⸗AEneid, iii. 414.]

Cyprus from Syria, the isle of Negropont from the continent of Beeotia, and elsewhere united lands that were separate before, by filling up the channel betwixt them with sand and mud:

> "Sterilisque diu palus, aptaque remis,
> Vicinas urbes alit, et grave sentit aratrum."

["That which was once a sterile marsh, and bore vessels on its bosom, now feeds neighbouring cities, and admits the plough." ⸗Horace, De Arte Poetica, v. 65.]

But there is no great appearance that this isle was this New World so lately discovered: for that almost touched upon Spain, and it were an incredible effect of an inundation, to have tumbled back so prodigious a mass, above twelve hundred leagues: besides that our modern navigators have already almost discovered it to be no island, but terra firma, and continent with the East Indies on the one side, and with the lands under the two poles on the other side; or, if it be separate from them, it is by so narrow a strait and channel, that it none the more deserves the name of an island for that.

It should seem, that in this great body, there are two sorts of motions, the one natural and the other febrific, as there are in ours. When I consider the impression that our river of Dordogne has made in my time on the right bank of its descent, and that in twenty years it has gained so much, and undermined the foundations of so many houses, I perceive it to be an extraordinary agitation: for had it always followed this course, or were hereafter to do it, the aspect of the world would be totally changed. But rivers alter their course, sometimes beating against the one side, and sometimes the other, and some times quietly keeping the channel. I do not speak of sudden inundations, the causes of which everybody understands. In Medoc, by the seashore, the Sieur d'Arsac, my brother, sees an estate he had there, buried under the sands which the sea vomits before it: where the tops of some houses are yet to be seen, and where his rents and domains are converted into pitiful barren pasturage. The inhabitants of this place affirm, that of late years the sea has driven so vehemently upon them, that they have lost above four leagues of land. These sands are her harbingers: and we now see great heaps of moving sand, that march half a league before her, and occupy the land.

The other testimony from antiquity, to which some would apply this discovery of the New World, is in Aristotle; at least, if that little book of Unheard of Miracles be his--[one of the spurious publications brought out under his name--D.W.]. He there tells us, that certain Carthaginians, having crossed the Atlantic Sea without the Straits of Gibraltar, and sailed a very long time, discovered at last a great and fruitful island, all covered over with wood, and watered with several broad and deep rivers, far remote from all terra firma; and that they, and others after them, allured by the goodness and fertility of the soil, went thither with their wives and children, and began to plant a colony. But the senate of Carthage perceiving their people by little and little to diminish, issued out an express prohibition, that none, upon pain of death, should transport themselves thither; and also drove out these new

inhabitants; fearing, 'tis said, lest' in process of time they should so
multiply as to supplant themselves and ruin their state. But this
relation of Aristotle no more agrees with our new-found lands than the
other.

This man that I had was a plain ignorant fellow, and therefore the more
likely to tell truth: for your better-bred sort of men are much more
curious in their observation, 'tis true, and discover a great deal more;
but then they gloss upon it, and to give the greater weight to what they
deliver, and allure your belief, they cannot forbear a little to alter
the story; they never represent things to you simply as they are, but
rather as they appeared to them, or as they would have them appear to
you, and to gain the reputation of men of judgment, and the better to
induce your faith, are willing to help out the business with something
more than is really true, of their own invention. Now in this case, we
should either have a man of irreproachable veracity, or so simple that he
has not wherewithal to contrive, and to give a colour of truth to false
relations, and who can have no ends in forging an untruth. Such a one
was mine; and besides, he has at divers times brought to me several
seamen and merchants who at the same time went the same voyage. I shall
therefore content myself with his information, without inquiring what the
cosmographers say to the business. We should have topographers to trace
out to us the particular places where they have been; but for having had
this advantage over us, to have seen the Holy Land, they would have the
privilege, forsooth, to tell us stories of all the other parts of the
world beside. I would have every one write what he knows, and as much as
he knows, but no more; and that not in this only but in all other
subjects; for such a person may have some particular knowledge and
experience of the nature of such a river, or such a fountain, who, as to
other things, knows no more than what everybody does, and yet to give a
currency to his little pittance of learning, will undertake to write the
whole body of physics: a vice from which great inconveniences derive
their original.

Now, to return to my subject, I find that there is nothing barbarous and
savage in this nation, by anything that I can gather, excepting, that

*every one gives the title of barbarism to everything that is not in use
in his own country. As, indeed, we have no other level of truth and
reason than the example and idea of the opinions and customs of the place
wherein we live: there is always the perfect religion, there the perfect
government, there the most exact and accomplished usage of all things.
They are savages at the same rate that we say fruits are wild, which
nature produces of herself and by her own ordinary progress; whereas, in
truth, we ought rather to call those wild whose natures we have changed
by our artifice and diverted from the common order. In those, the
genuine, most useful, and natural virtues and properties are vigorous and
sprightly, which we have helped to degenerate in these, by accommodating
them to the pleasure of our own corrupted palate. And yet for all this,
our taste confesses a flavour and delicacy excellent even to emulation of
the best of ours, in several fruits wherein those countries abound
without art or culture. Neither is it reasonable that art should gain
the pre-eminence of our great and powerful mother nature. We have so
surcharged her with the additional ornaments and graces we have added to
the beauty and riches of her own works by our inventions, that we have
almost smothered her; yet in other places, where she shines in her own
purity and proper lustre, she marvellously baffles and disgraces all our
vain and frivolous attempts:*

> *"Et veniunt hederae sponte sua melius;*
> *Surgit et in solis formosior arbutus antris;*
> *Et volucres nulls dulcius arte canunt."*

*["The ivy grows best spontaneously, the arbutus best in shady caves;
and the wild notes of birds are sweeter than art can teach.
--"Propertius, i. 2, 10.]*

*Our utmost endeavours cannot arrive at so much as to imitate the nest of
the least of birds, its contexture, beauty, and convenience: not so much
as the web of a poor spider.*

All things, says Plato,--[Laws, 10.]--are produced either by nature, by fortune, or by art; the greatest and most beautiful by the one or the other of the former, the least and the most imperfect by the last.

These nations then seem to me to be so far barbarous, as having received but very little form and fashion from art and human invention, and consequently to be not much remote from their original simplicity. The laws of nature, however, govern them still, not as yet much vitiated with any mixture of ours: but 'tis in such purity, that I am sometimes troubled we were not sooner acquainted with these people, and that they were not discovered in those better times, when there were men much more able to judge of them than we are. I am sorry that Lycurgus and Plato had no knowledge of them; for to my apprehension, what we now see in those nations, does not only surpass all the pictures with which the poets have adorned the golden age, and all their inventions in feigning a happy state of man, but, moreover, the fancy and even the wish and desire of philosophy itself; so native and so pure a simplicity, as we by experience see to be in them, could never enter into their imagination, nor could they ever believe that human society could have been maintained with so little artifice and human patchwork. I should tell Plato that it is a nation wherein there is no manner of traffic, no knowledge of letters, no science of numbers, no name of magistrate or political superiority; no use of service, riches or poverty, no contracts, no successions, no dividends, no properties, no employments, but those of leisure, no respect of kindred, but common, no clothing, no agriculture, no metal, no use of corn or wine; the very words that signify lying, treachery, dissimulation, avarice, envy, detraction, pardon, never heard of.

--[This is the famous passage which Shakespeare, through Florio's version, 1603, or ed. 1613, p. 102, has employed in the "Tempest," ii. 1.]

How much would he find his imaginary Republic short of his perfection?

"Viri a diis recentes."

["Men fresh from the gods." ̶ Seneca, Ep., 90.]

"Hos natura modos primum dedit."

*["These were the manners first taught by nature."
 ̶ Virgil, Georgics, ii. 20.]*

*As to the rest, they live in a country very pleasant and temperate, so
that, as my witnesses inform me, 'tis rare to hear of a sick person, and
they moreover assure me, that they never saw any of the natives, either
paralytic, bleareyed, toothless, or crooked with age. The situation of
their country is along the sea-shore, enclosed on the other side towards
the land, with great and high mountains, having about a hundred leagues
in breadth between. They have great store of fish and flesh, that have
no resemblance to those of ours: which they eat without any other
cookery, than plain boiling, roasting, and broiling. The first that rode
a horse thither, though in several other voyages he had contracted an
acquaintance and familiarity with them, put them into so terrible a
fright, with his centaur appearance, that they killed him with their
arrows before they could come to discover who he was. Their buildings
are very long, and of capacity to hold two or three hundred people, made
of the barks of tall trees, reared with one end upon the ground, and
leaning to and supporting one another at the top, like some of our barns,
of which the covering hangs down to the very ground, and serves for the
side walls. They have wood so hard, that they cut with it, and make their
swords of it, and their grills of it to broil their meat. Their beds are
of cotton, hung swinging from the roof, like our seamen's hammocks, every
man his own, for the wives lie apart from their husbands. They rise with
the sun, and so soon as they are up, eat for all day, for they have no
more meals but that; they do not then drink, as Suidas reports of some
other people of the East that never drunk at their meals; but drink very
often all day after, and sometimes to a rousing pitch. Their drink is
made of a certain root, and is of the colour of our claret, and they
never drink it but lukewarm. It will not keep above two or three days;
it has a somewhat sharp, brisk taste, is nothing heady, but very*

comfortable to the stomach; laxative to strangers, but a very pleasant beverage to such as are accustomed to it. They make use, instead of bread, of a certain white compound, like coriander seeds; I have tasted of it; the taste is sweet and a little flat. The whole day is spent in dancing. Their young men go a-hunting after wild beasts with bows and arrows; one part of their women are employed in preparing their drink the while, which is their chief employment. One of their old men, in the morning before they fall to eating, preaches to the whole family, walking from the one end of the house to the other, and several times repeating the same sentence, till he has finished the round, for their houses are at least a hundred yards long. Valour towards their enemies and love towards their wives, are the two heads of his discourse, never failing in the close, to put them in mind, that 'tis their wives who provide them their drink warm and well seasoned. The fashion of their beds, ropes, swords, and of the wooden bracelets they tie about their wrists, when they go to fight, and of the great canes, bored hollow at one end, by the sound of which they keep the cadence of their dances, are to be seen in several places, and amongst others, at my house. They shave all over, and much more neatly than we, without other razor than one of wood or stone. They believe in the immortality of the soul, and that those who have merited well of the gods are lodged in that part of heaven where the sun rises, and the accursed in the west.

They have I know not what kind of priests and prophets, who very rarely present themselves to the people, having their abode in the mountains. At their arrival, there is a great feast, and solemn assembly of many villages: each house, as I have described, makes a village, and they are about a French league distant from one another. This prophet declaims to them in public, exhorting them to virtue and their duty: but all their ethics are comprised in these two articles, resolution in war, and affection to their wives. He also prophesies to them events to come, and the issues they are to expect from their enterprises, and prompts them to or diverts them from war: but let him look to't; for if he fail in his divination, and anything happen otherwise than he has foretold, he is cut into a thousand pieces, if he be caught, and condemned for a false

*prophet: for that reason, if any of them has been mistaken, he is no more
heard of.*

*Divination is a gift of God, and therefore to abuse it, ought to be a
punishable imposture. Amongst the Scythians, where their diviners failed
in the promised effect, they were laid, bound hand and foot, upon carts
loaded with firs and bavins, and drawn by oxen, on which they were burned
to death.--[Herodotus, iv. 69.]--Such as only meddle with things
subject to the conduct of human capacity, are excusable in doing the best
they can: but those other fellows that come to delude us with assurances
of an extraordinary faculty, beyond our understanding, ought they not to
be punished, when they do not make good the effect of their promise, and
for the temerity of their imposture?*

*They have continual war with the nations that live further within the
mainland, beyond their mountains, to which they go naked, and without
other arms than their bows and wooden swords, fashioned at one end like
the head of our javelins. The obstinacy of their battles is wonderful,
and they never end without great effusion of blood: for as to running
away, they know not what it is. Every one for a trophy brings home the
head of an enemy he has killed, which he fixes over the door of his
house. After having a long time treated their prisoners very well, and
given them all the regales they can think of, he to whom the prisoner
belongs, invites a great assembly of his friends. They being come, he
ties a rope to one of the arms of the prisoner, of which, at a distance,
out of his reach, he holds the one end himself, and gives to the friend
he loves best the other arm to hold after the same manner; which being
done, they two, in the presence of all the assembly, despatch him with
their swords. After that, they roast him, eat him amongst them, and send
some chops to their absent friends. They do not do this, as some think,
for nourishment, as the Scythians anciently did, but as a representation
of an extreme revenge; as will appear by this: that having observed the
Portuguese, who were in league with their enemies, to inflict another
sort of death upon any of them they took prisoners, which was to set them
up to the girdle in the earth, to shoot at the remaining part till it was
stuck full of arrows, and then to hang them, they thought those people of*

the other world (as being men who had sown the knowledge of a great many vices amongst their neighbours, and who were much greater masters in all sorts of mischief than they) did not exercise this sort of revenge without a meaning, and that it must needs be more painful than theirs, they began to leave their old way, and to follow this. I am not sorry that we should here take notice of the barbarous horror of so cruel an action, but that, seeing so clearly into their faults, we should be so blind to our own. I conceive there is more barbarity in eating a man alive, than when he is dead; in tearing a body limb from limb by racks and torments, that is yet in perfect sense; in roasting it by degrees; in causing it to be bitten and worried by dogs and swine (as we have not only read, but lately seen, not amongst inveterate and mortal enemies, but among neighbours and fellow-citizens, and, which is worse, under colour of piety and religion), than to roast and eat him after he is dead.

Chrysippus and Zeno, the two heads of the Stoic sect, were of opinion that there was no hurt in making use of our dead carcasses, in what way soever for our necessity, and in feeding upon them too;--[Diogenes Laertius, vii. 188.]--as our own ancestors, who being besieged by Caesar in the city Alexia, resolved to sustain the famine of the siege with the bodies of their old men, women, and other persons who were incapable of bearing arms.

> "Vascones, ut fama est, alimentis talibus usi
> Produxere animas."

> ["'Tis said the Gascons with such meats appeased their hunger."
> --Juvenal, Sat., xv. 93.]

And the physicians make no bones of employing it to all sorts of use, either to apply it outwardly; or to give it inwardly for the health of the patient. But there never was any opinion so irregular, as to excuse treachery, disloyalty, tyranny, and cruelty, which are our familiar vices. We may then call these people barbarous, in respect to the rules of reason: but not in respect to ourselves, who in all sorts of barbarity exceed them. Their wars are throughout noble and generous, and carry as much excuse and fair pretence, as that human malady is capable of; having with them no other foundation than the sole jealousy of valour. Their disputes are not for the conquest of new lands, for these they already possess are so fruitful by nature, as to supply them without labour or concern, with all things necessary, in such abundance that they have no need to enlarge their borders. And they are, moreover, happy in this, that they only covet so much as their natural necessities require: all beyond that is superfluous to them: men of the same age call one another generally brothers, those who are younger, children; and the old men are fathers to all. These leave to their heirs in common the full possession of goods, without any manner of division, or other title than what nature bestows upon her creatures, in bringing them into the world. If their neighbours pass over the mountains to assault them, and obtain a victory, all the victors gain by it is glory only, and the advantage of having proved themselves the better in valour and virtue: for they never meddle with the goods of the conquered, but presently return into their own country, where they have no want of anything necessary, nor of this greatest of all goods, to know happily how to enjoy their condition and to be content. And those in turn do the same; they demand of their prisoners no other ransom, than acknowledgment that they are overcome: but there is not one found in an age, who will not rather choose to die than make such a confession, or either by word or look recede from the entire grandeur of an invincible courage. There is not a man amongst them who had not rather be killed and eaten, than so much as to open his mouth to entreat he may not. They use them with all liberality and freedom, to the end their lives may be so much the dearer to them; but frequently entertain them with menaces of their approaching death, of the torments they are to suffer, of the preparations making in order to it, of the mangling their limbs, and of the feast that is to be made, where their carcass is to be the only dish. All which they do, to no other end, but only to extort some gentle or submissive word from them, or to frighten them so as to make them run away, to obtain this advantage that they were terrified, and that their constancy was shaken; and indeed, if rightly taken, it is in this point only that a true victory consists:

> *"Victoria nulla est,*
> *Quam quae confessor animo quoque subjugat hostes."*

["No victory is complete, which the conquered do not admit to be
so.¬¬"Claudius, De Sexto Consulatu Honorii, v. 248.]

The Hungarians, a very warlike people, never pretend further than to
reduce the enemy to their discretion; for having forced this confession
from them, they let them go without injury or ransom, excepting, at the
most, to make them engage their word never to bear arms against them
again. We have sufficient advantages over our enemies that are borrowed
and not truly our own; it is the quality of a porter, and no effect of
virtue, to have stronger arms and legs; it is a dead and corporeal
quality to set in array; 'tis a turn of fortune to make our enemy
stumble, or to dazzle him with the light of the sun; 'tis a trick of
science and art, and that may happen in a mean base fellow, to be a good
fencer. The estimate and value of a man consist in the heart and in the
will: there his true honour lies. Valour is stability, not of legs and
arms, but of the courage and the soul; it does not lie in the goodness of
our horse or our arms but in our own. He that falls obstinate in his
courage¬¬

> *"Si succiderit, de genu pugnat"*

["If his legs fail him, he fights on his knees."
¬¬Seneca, De Providentia, c. 2.]

¬¬he who, for any danger of imminent death, abates nothing of his
assurance; who, dying, yet darts at his enemy a fierce and disdainful
look, is overcome not by us, but by fortune; he is killed, not conquered;
the most valiant are sometimes the most unfortunate. There are defeats
more triumphant than victories. Never could those four sister victories,
the fairest the sun ever be held, of Salamis, Plataea, Mycale, and
Sicily, venture to oppose all their united glories, to the single glory
of the discomfiture of King Leonidas and his men, at the pass of
Thermopylae. Who ever ran with a more glorious desire and greater

ambition, to the winning, than Captain Iscolas to the certain loss of a battle?--[Diodorus Siculus, xv. 64.]--Who could have found out a more subtle invention to secure his safety, than he did to assure his destruction? He was set to defend a certain pass of Peloponnesus against the Arcadians, which, considering the nature of the place and the inequality of forces, finding it utterly impossible for him to do, and seeing that all who were presented to the enemy, must certainly be left upon the place; and on the other side, reputing it unworthy of his own virtue and magnanimity and of the Lacedaemonian name to fail in any part of his duty, he chose a mean betwixt these two extremes after this manner; the youngest and most active of his men, he preserved for the service and defence of their country, and sent them back; and with the rest, whose loss would be of less consideration, he resolved to make good the pass, and with the death of them, to make the enemy buy their entry as dear as possibly he could; as it fell out, for being presently environed on all sides by the Arcadians, after having made a great slaughter of the enemy, he and his were all cut in pieces. Is there any trophy dedicated to the conquerors which was not much more due to these who were overcome? The part that true conquering is to play, lies in the encounter, not in the coming off; and the honour of valour consists in fighting, not in subduing.

But to return to my story: these prisoners are so far from discovering the least weakness, for all the terrors that can be represented to them, that, on the contrary, during the two or three months they are kept, they always appear with a cheerful countenance; importune their masters to make haste to bring them to the test, defy, rail at them, and reproach them with cowardice, and the number of battles they have lost against those of their country. I have a song made by one of these prisoners, wherein he bids them "come all, and dine upon him, and welcome, for they shall withal eat their own fathers and grandfathers, whose flesh has served to feed and nourish him. These muscles," says he, "this flesh and these veins, are your own: poor silly souls as you are, you little think that the substance of your ancestors' limbs is here yet; notice what you eat, and you will find in it the taste of your own flesh:" in which song there is to be observed an invention that nothing relishes of the

barbarian. Those that paint these people dying after this manner,
represent the prisoner spitting in the faces of his executioners and
making wry mouths at them. And 'tis most certain, that to the very last
gasp, they never cease to brave and defy them both in word and gesture.
In plain truth, these men are very savage in comparison of us; of
necessity, they must either be absolutely so or else we are savages; for
there is a vast difference betwixt their manners and ours.

polygamy

The men there have several wives, and so much the greater number, by how
much they have the greater reputation for valour. And it is one very
remarkable feature in their marriages, that the same jealousy our wives
have to hinder and divert us from the friendship and familiarity of other
women, those employ to promote their husbands' desires, and to procure
them many spouses; for being above all things solicitous of their
husbands' honour, 'tis their chiefest care to seek out, and to bring in
the most companions they can, forasmuch as it is a testimony of the
husband's virtue. Most of our ladies will cry out, that 'tis monstrous;
whereas in truth it is not so, but a truly matrimonial virtue, and of the
highest form. In the Bible, Sarah, with Leah and Rachel, the two wives
of Jacob, gave the most beautiful of their handmaids to their husbands;
Livia preferred the passions of Augustus to her own interest;
[Suetonius, Life of Augustus, c. 71.] and the wife of King Deiotarus,
Stratonice, did not only give up a fair young maid that served her to her
husband's embraces, but moreover carefully brought up the children he had
by her, and assisted them in the succession to their father's crown.

And that it may not be supposed, that all this is done by a simple and
servile obligation to their common practice, or by any authoritative
impression of their ancient custom, without judgment or reasoning, and
from having a soul so stupid that it cannot contrive what else to do, I
must here give you some touches of their sufficiency in point of
understanding. Besides what I repeated to you before, which was one of
their songs of war, I have another, a love-song, that begins thus:

"Stay, adder, stay, that by thy pattern my sister may draw the
fashion and work of a rich ribbon, that I may present to my beloved,

*by which means thy beauty and the excellent order of thy scales
shall for ever be preferred before all other serpents."*

*Wherein the first couplet, "Stay, adder," &c., makes the burden of the
song. Now I have conversed enough with poetry to judge thus much that
not only there is nothing barbarous in this invention, but, moreover,
that it is perfectly Anacreontic. To which it may be added, that their
language is soft, of a pleasing accent, and something bordering upon the
Greek termination.*

*Three of these people, not foreseeing how dear their knowledge of the
corruptions of this part of the world will one day cost their happiness
and repose, and that the effect of this commerce will be their ruin, as I
presuppose it is in a very fair way (miserable men to suffer themselves
to be deluded with desire of novelty and to have left the serenity of
their own heaven to come so far to gaze at ours!), were at Rouen at the
time that the late King Charles IX. was there. The king himself talked
to them a good while, and they were made to see our fashions, our pomp,
and the form of a great city. After which, some one asked their opinion,
and would know of them, what of all the things they had seen, they found
most to be admired? To which they made answer, three things, of which I
have forgotten the third, and am troubled at it, but two I yet remember.
They said, that in the first place they thought it very strange that so
many tall men, wearing beards, strong, and well armed, who were about the
king ('tis like they meant the Swiss of the guard), should submit to obey
a child, and that they did not rather choose out one amongst themselves
to command. Secondly (they have a way of speaking in their language to
call men the half of one another), that they had observed that there were
amongst us men full and crammed with all manner of commodities, whilst,
in the meantime, their halves were begging at their doors, lean and
half-starved with hunger and poverty; and they thought it strange that
these necessitous halves were able to suffer so great an inequality and
injustice, and that they did not take the others by the throats, or set
fire to their houses.*

I talked to one of them a great while together, but I had so ill an interpreter, and one who was so perplexed by his own ignorance to apprehend my meaning, that I could get nothing out of him of any moment: Asking him what advantage he reaped from the superiority he had amongst his own people (for he was a captain, and our mariners called him king), he told me, to march at the head of them to war. Demanding of him further how many men he had to follow him, he showed me a space of ground, to signify as many as could march in such a compass, which might be four or five thousand men; and putting the question to him whether or no his authority expired with the war, he told me this remained: that when he went to visit the villages of his dependence, they planed him paths through the thick of their woods, by which he might pass at his ease. All this does not sound very ill, and the last was not at all amiss, for they wear no breeches.

most vulnerable position

CHAPTER XXXI

THAT A MAN IS SOBERLY TO JUDGE
OF THE DIVINE ORDINANCES

*The true field and subject of imposture are things unknown, forasmuch as,
in the first place, their very strangeness lends them credit, and
moreover, by not being subjected to our ordinary reasons, they deprive us
of the means to question and dispute them: For which reason, says Plato,
--[In Critias.]--it is much more easy to satisfy the hearers, when
speaking of the nature of the gods than of the nature of men, because the
ignorance of the auditory affords a fair and large career and all manner
of liberty in the handling of abstruse things. Thence it comes to pass,
that nothing is so firmly believed, as what we least know; nor any people
so confident, as those who entertain us with fables, such as your
alchemists, judicial astrologers, fortune-tellers, and physicians,*

> *"Id genus omne."*

> *["All that sort of people."--Horace, Sat., i. 2, 2.]*

*To which I would willingly, if I durst, join a pack of people that take
upon them to interpret and control the designs of God Himself, pretending
to find out the cause of every accident, and to pry into the secrets of
the divine will, there to discover the incomprehensible motive, of His
works; and although the variety, and the continual discordance of events,
throw them from corner to corner, and toss them from east to west, yet do
they still persist in their vain inquisition, and with the same pencil to
paint black and white.*

*In a nation of the Indies, there is this commendable custom, that when
anything befalls them amiss in any encounter or battle, they publicly ask
pardon of the sun, who is their god, as having committed an unjust*

action, always imputing their good or evil fortune to the divine justice, and to that submitting their own judgment and reason. 'Tis enough for a Christian to believe that all things come from God, to receive them with acknowledgment of His divine and inscrutable wisdom, and also thankfully to accept and receive them, with what face soever they may present themselves. But I do not approve of what I see in use, that is, to seek to affirm and support our religion by the prosperity of our enterprises. Our belief has other foundation enough, without going about to authorise it by events: for the people being accustomed to such plausible arguments as these and so proper to their taste, it is to be feared, lest when they fail of success they should also stagger in their faith: as in the war wherein we are now engaged upon the account of religion, those who had the better in the business of Rochelabeille,--[May 1569.]--making great brags of that success as an infallible approbation of their cause, when they came afterwards to excuse their misfortunes of Moncontour and Jarnac, by saying they were fatherly scourges and corrections that they had not a people wholly at their mercy, they make it manifestly enough appear, what it is to take two sorts of grist out of the same sack, and with the same mouth to blow hot and cold. It were better to possess the vulgar with the solid and real foundations of truth. 'Twas a fine naval battle that was gained under the command of Don John of Austria a few months since--[That of Lepanto, October 7, 1571.]--against the Turks; but it has also pleased God at other times to let us see as great victories at our own expense. In fine, 'tis a hard matter to reduce divine things to our balance, without waste and losing a great deal of the weight. And who would take upon him to give a reason that Arius and his Pope Leo, the principal heads of the Arian heresy, should die, at several times, of so like and strange deaths (for being withdrawn from the disputation by a griping in the bowels, they both of them suddenly gave up the ghost upon the stool), and would aggravate this divine vengeance by the circumstances of the place, might as well add the death of Heliogabalus, who was also slain in a house of office. And, indeed, Irenaeus was involved in the same fortune. God, being pleased to show us, that the good have something else to hope for and the wicked something else to fear, than the fortunes or misfortunes of this world, manages and applies these according to His own occult will and pleasure,

and deprives us of the means foolishly to make thereof our own profit.
And those people abuse themselves who will pretend to dive into these
mysteries by the strength of human reason. They never give one hit that
they do not receive two for it; of which St. Augustine makes out a great
proof upon his adversaries. 'Tis a conflict that is more decided by
strength of memory than by the force of reason. We are to content
ourselves with the light it pleases the sun to communicate to us, by
virtue of his rays; and who will lift up his eyes to take in a greater,
let him not think it strange, if for the reward of his presumption, he
there lose his sight.

> "Quis hominum potest scire consilium Dei?
> Aut quis poterit cogitare quid velit Dominus?"

["Who of men can know the counsel of God? or who can think what the
will of the Lord is."--Book of Wisdom, ix. 13.]

CHAPTER XXXII

THAT WE ARE TO AVOID PLEASURES,
EVEN AT THE EXPENSE OF LIFE

I had long ago observed most of the opinions of the ancients to concur in this, that it is high time to die when there is more ill than good in living, and that to preserve life to our own torment and inconvenience is contrary to the very rules of nature, as these old laws instruct us.

> *["Either tranquil life, or happy death. It is well to die when life is wearisome. It is better to die than to live miserable."*
> *⸺Stobaeus, Serm. xx.]*

But to push this contempt of death so far as to employ it to the removing our thoughts from the honours, riches, dignities, and other favours and goods, as we call them, of fortune, as if reason were not sufficient to persuade us to avoid them, without adding this new injunction, I had never seen it either commanded or practised, till this passage of Seneca fell into my hands; who advising Lucilius, a man of great power and authority about the emperor, to alter his voluptuous and magnificent way of living, and to retire himself from this worldly vanity and ambition, to some solitary, quiet, and philosophical life, and the other alleging some difficulties: "I am of opinion," says he, "either that thou leave that life of thine, or life itself; I would, indeed, advise thee to the gentle way, and to untie, rather than to break, the knot thou hast indiscreetly knit, provided, that if it be not otherwise to be untied, thou resolutely break it. There is no man so great a coward, that had not rather once fall than to be always falling." I should have found this counsel conformable enough to the Stoical roughness: but it appears the more strange, for being borrowed from Epicurus, who writes the same thing upon the like occasion to Idomeneus. And I think I have observed something like it, but with Christian moderation, amongst our own people.

St. Hilary, Bishop of Poictiers, that famous enemy of the Arian heresy, being in Syria, had intelligence thither sent him, that Abra, his only daughter, whom he left at home under the eye and tuition of her mother, was sought in marriage by the greatest noblemen of the country, as being a virgin virtuously brought up, fair, rich, and in the flower of her age; whereupon he wrote to her (as appears upon record), that she should remove her affection from all the pleasures and advantages proposed to her; for that he had in his travels found out a much greater and more worthy fortune for her, a husband of much greater power and magnificence, who would present her with robes and jewels of inestimable value; wherein his design was to dispossess her of the appetite and use of worldly delights, to join her wholly to God; but the nearest and most certain way to this, being, as he conceived, the death of his daughter; he never ceased, by vows, prayers, and orisons, to beg of the Almighty, that He would please to call her out of this world, and to take her to Himself; as accordingly it came to pass; for soon after his return, she died, at which he expressed a singular joy. This seems to outdo the other, forasmuch as he applies himself to this means at the outset, which they only take subsidiarily; and, besides, it was towards his only daughter. But I will not omit the latter end of this story, though it be for my purpose; St. Hilary's wife, having understood from him how the death of their daughter was brought about by his desire and design, and how much happier she was to be removed out of this world than to have stayed in it, conceived so vivid an apprehension of the eternal and heavenly beatitude, that she begged of her husband, with the extremest importunity, to do as much for her; and God, at their joint request, shortly after calling her to Him, it was a death embraced with singular and mutual content.

CHAPTER XXXIII

THAT FORTUNE IS OFTENTIMES OBSERVED
TO ACT BY THE RULE OF REASON

The inconstancy and various motions of Fortune

*[The term Fortune, so often employed by Montaigne, and in passages
where he might have used Providence, was censured by the doctors who
examined his Essays when he was at Rome in 1581. See his Travels,
i. 35 and 76.]*

*may reasonably make us expect she should present us with all sorts of
faces. Can there be a more express act of justice than this? The Duc de
Valentinois,--[Caesar Borgia.]--having resolved to poison Adrian,
Cardinal of Corneto, with whom Pope Alexander VI., his father and
himself, were to sup in the Vatican, he sent before a bottle of poisoned
wine, and withal, strict order to the butler to keep it very safe.
The Pope being come before his son, and calling for drink, the butler
supposing this wine had not been so strictly recommended to his care,
but only upon the account of its excellency, presented it forthwith to
the Pope, and the duke himself coming in presently after, and being
confident they had not meddled with his bottle, took also his cup; so
that the father died immediately upon the spot--[Other historians assign
the Pope several days of misery prior to death. D.W.]--, and the son,
after having been long tormented with sickness, was reserved to another
and a worse fortune.*

*Sometimes she seems to play upon us, just in the nick of an affair;
Monsieur d'Estrees, at that time ensign to Monsieur de Vendome, and
Monsieur de Licques, lieutenant in the company of the Duc d'Ascot, being
both pretenders to the Sieur de Fougueselles' sister, though of several
parties (as it oft falls out amongst frontier neighbours), the Sieur de*

Licques carried her; but on the same day he was married, and which was worse, before he went to bed to his wife, the bridegroom having a mind to break a lance in honour of his new bride, went out to skirmish near St. Omer, where the Sieur d'Estrees proving the stronger, took him prisoner, and the more to illustrate his victory, the lady was fain--

> *"Conjugis ante coacta novi dimittere collum,*
> *Quam veniens una atque altera rursus hyems*
> *Noctibus in longis avidum saturasset amorem,"*

> *["Compelled to abstain from embracing her new spouse in her arms before two winters pass in succession, during their long nights had satiated her eager love."--Catullus, lxviii. 81.]*

--to request him of courtesy, to deliver up his prisoner to her, as he accordingly did, the gentlemen of France never denying anything to ladies.

Does she not seem to be an artist here? Constantine, son of Helena, founded the empire of Constantinople, and so many ages after, Constantine, the son of Helen, put an end to it. Sometimes she is pleased to emulate our miracles we are told, that King Clovis besieging Angouleme, the walls fell down of themselves by divine favour and Bouchet has it from some author, that King Robert having sat down before a city, and being stolen away from the siege to go keep the feast of St. Aignan at Orleans, as he was in devotion at a certain part of the Mass, the walls of the beleaguered city, without any manner of violence, fell down with a sudden ruin. But she did quite contrary in our Milan wars; for, le Capitaine Rense laying siege for us to the city Arona, and having carried a mine under a great part of the wall, the mine being sprung, the wall was lifted from its base, but dropped down again nevertheless, whole and entire, and so exactly upon its foundation, that the besieged suffered no inconvenience by that attempt.

Sometimes she plays the physician. Jason of Pheres being given over by the physicians, by reason of an imposthume in his breast, having a mind to rid himself of his pain, by death at least, threw himself in a battle desperately into the thickest of the enemy, where he was so fortunately wounded quite through the body, that the imposthume broke, and he was perfectly cured. Did she not also excel the painter Protogenes in his art? who having finished the picture of a dog quite tired and out of breath, in all the other parts excellently well to his own liking, but not being able to express, as he would, the slaver and foam that should come out of its mouth, vexed and angry at his work, he took his sponge, which by cleaning his pencils had imbibed several sorts of colours, and threw it in a rage against the picture, with an intent utterly to deface it; when fortune guiding the sponge to hit just upon the mouth of the dog, it there performed what all his art was not able to do. Does she not sometimes direct our counsels and correct them? Isabel, Queen of England, having to sail from Zealand into her own kingdom,--[in 1326]-- with an army, in favour of her son against her husband, had been lost, had she come into the port she intended, being there laid wait for by the enemy; but fortune, against her will, threw her into another haven, where she landed in safety. And that man of old who, throwing a stone at a dog, hit and killed his mother-in-law, had he not reason to pronounce this verse:

["Fortune has more judgement than we."--Menander]

Icetes had contracted with two soldiers to kill Timoleon at Adrana in Sicily.--[Plutarch, Life of Timoleon, c. 7.]--They took their time to do it when he was assisting at a sacrifice, and thrusting into the crowd, as they were making signs to one another, that now was a fit time to do their business, in steps a third, who, with a sword takes one of them full drive over the pate, lays him dead upon the place and runs away, which the others see, and concluding himself discovered and lost, runs to the altar and begs for mercy, promising to discover the whole truth, which as he was doing, and laying open the full conspiracy, behold the third man, who being apprehended, was, as a murderer, thrust and hauled by the people through the press, towards Timoleon, and the other most eminent persons of the assembly, before whom being brought, he cries out for pardon, pleading that he had justly slain his father's murderer;

which he, also, proving upon the spot, by sufficient witnesses, whom his good fortune very opportunely supplied him withal, that his father was really killed in the city of Leontini, by that very man on whom he had taken his revenge, he was presently awarded ten Attic minae, for having had the good fortune, by designing to revenge the death of his father, to preserve the life of the common father of Sicily. Fortune, truly, in her conduct surpasses all the rules of human prudence.

But to conclude: is there not a direct application of her favour, bounty, and piety manifestly discovered in this action? Ignatius the father and Ignatius the son being proscribed by the triumvirs of Rome, resolved upon this generous act of mutual kindness, to fall by the hands of one another, and by that means to frustrate and defeat the cruelty of the tyrants; and accordingly with their swords drawn, ran full drive upon one another, where fortune so guided the points, that they made two equally mortal wounds, affording withal so much honour to so brave a friendship, as to leave them just strength enough to draw out their bloody swords, that they might have liberty to embrace one another in this dying condition, with so close and hearty an embrace, that the executioner cut off both their heads at once, leaving the bodies still fast linked together in this noble bond, and their wounds joined mouth to mouth, affectionately sucking in the last blood and remainder of the lives of each other.

CHAPTER XXXIV

OF ONE DEFECT IN OUR GOVERNMENT

My late father, a man that had no other advantages than experience and his own natural parts, was nevertheless of a very clear judgment, formerly told me that he once had thoughts of endeavouring to introduce this practice; that there might be in every city a certain place assigned to which such as stood in need of anything might repair, and have their business entered by an officer appointed for that purpose. As for example: I want a chapman to buy my pearls; I want one that has pearls to sell; such a one wants company to go to Paris; such a one seeks a servant of such a quality; such a one a master; such a one such an artificer; some inquiring for one thing, some for another, every one according to what he wants. And doubtless, these mutual advertisements would be of no contemptible advantage to the public correspondence and intelligence: for there are evermore conditions that hunt after one another, and for want of knowing one another's occasions leave men in very great necessity.

I have heard, to the great shame of the age we live in, that in our very sight two most excellent men for learning died so poor that they had scarce bread to put in their mouths: Lilius Gregorius Giraldus in Italy and Sebastianus Castalio in Germany: and I believe there are a thousand men would have invited them into their families, with very advantageous conditions, or have relieved them where they were, had they known their wants. The world is not so generally corrupted, but that I know a man that would heartily wish the estate his ancestors have left him might be employed, so long as it shall please fortune to give him leave to enjoy it, to secure rare and remarkable persons of any kind, whom misfortune sometimes persecutes to the last degree, from the dangers of necessity; and at least place them in such a condition that they must be very hard to please, if they are not contented.

My father in his domestic economy had this rule (which I know how to commend, but by no means to imitate), namely, that besides the day-book or memorial of household affairs, where the small accounts, payments, and disbursements, which do not require a secretary's hand, were entered, and which a steward always had in custody, he ordered him whom he employed to write for him, to keep a journal, and in it to set down all the remarkable occurrences, and daily memorials of the history of his house: very pleasant to look over, when time begins to wear things out of memory, and very useful sometimes to put us out of doubt when such a thing was begun, when ended; what visitors came, and when they went; our travels, absences, marriages, and deaths; the reception of good or ill news; the change of principal servants, and the like. An ancient custom, which I think it would not be amiss for every one to revive in his own house; and I find I did very foolishly in neglecting it.

CHAPTER XXXV

OF THE CUSTOM OF WEARING CLOTHES

*Whatever I shall say upon this subject, I am of necessity to invade some
of the bounds of custom, so careful has she been to shut up all the
avenues. I was disputing with myself in this shivering season, whether
the fashion of going naked in those nations lately discovered is imposed
upon them by the hot temperature of the air, as we say of the Indians and
Moors, or whether it be the original fashion of mankind. Men of
understanding, forasmuch as all things under the sun, as the Holy Writ
declares, are subject to the same laws, were wont in such considerations
as these, where we are to distinguish the natural laws from those which
have been imposed by man's invention, to have recourse to the general
polity of the world, where there can be nothing counterfeit. Now, all
other creatures being sufficiently furnished with all things necessary
for the support of their being--[Montaigne's expression is, "with needle
and thread."--W.C.H.]--it is not to be imagined that we only are brought
into the world in a defective and indigent condition, and in such a state
as cannot subsist without external aid. Therefore it is that I believe,
that as plants, trees, and animals, and all things that have life, are
seen to be by nature sufficiently clothed and covered, to defend them
from the injuries of weather:*

> *"Proptereaque fere res omnes ant corio sunt,
> Aut seta, ant conchis, ant callo, ant cortice tectae,"*

> *["And that for this reason nearly all things are clothed with skin,
> or hair, or shells, or bark, or some such thing."
> --Lucretius, iv. 936.]*

*so were we: but as those who by artificial light put out that of day, so
we by borrowed forms and fashions have destroyed our own. And 'tis plain*

enough to be seen, that 'tis custom only which renders that impossible that otherwise is nothing so; for of those nations who have no manner of knowledge of clothing, some are situated under the same temperature that we are, and some in much colder climates. And besides, our most tender parts are always exposed to the air, as the eyes, mouth, nose, and ears; and our country labourers, like our ancestors in former times, go with their breasts and bellies open. Had we been born with a necessity upon us of wearing petticoats and breeches, there is no doubt but nature would have fortified those parts she intended should be exposed to the fury of the seasons with a thicker skin, as she has done the finger-ends and the soles of the feet. And why should this seem hard to believe? I observe much greater distance betwixt my habit and that of one of our country boors, than betwixt his and that of a man who has no other covering but his skin. How many men, especially in Turkey, go naked upon the account of devotion? Some one asked a beggar, whom he saw in his shirt in the depth of winter, as brisk and frolic as he who goes muffled up to the ears in furs, how he was able to endure to go so? "Why, sir," he answered, "you go with your face bare: I am all face." The Italians have a story of the Duke of Florence's fool, whom his master asking how, being so thinly clad, he was able to support the cold, when he himself, warmly wrapped up as he was, was hardly able to do it? "Why," replied the fool, "use my receipt to put on all your clothes you have at once, and you'll feel no more cold than I." King Massinissa, to an extreme old age, could never be prevailed upon to go with his head covered, how cold, stormy, or rainy soever the weather might be; which also is reported of the Emperor Severus. Herodotus tells us, that in the battles fought betwixt the Egyptians and the Persians, it was observed both by himself and by others, that of those who were left dead upon the field, the heads of the Egyptians were without comparison harder than those of the Persians, by reason that the last had gone with their heads always covered from their infancy, first with biggins, and then with turbans, and the others always shaved and bare. King Agesilaus continued to a decrepit age to wear always the same clothes in winter that he did in summer. Caesar, says Suetonius, marched always at the head of his army, for the most part on foot, with his head bare, whether it was rain or sunshine, and as much is said of Hannibal:

> "*Tum vertice nudo,*
> *Excipere insanos imbres, coelique ruinam.*"

[*"Bareheaded he marched in snow, exposed to pouring rain and the
utmost rigour of the weather."*--Silius Italicus, i. 250.]

A Venetian who has long lived in Pegu, and has lately returned thence,
writes that the men and women of that kingdom, though they cover all
their other parts, go always barefoot and ride so too; and Plato very
earnestly advises for the health of the whole body, to give the head and
the feet no other clothing than what nature has bestowed. He whom the
Poles have elected for their king,--[Stephen Bathory]--since ours came
thence, who is, indeed, one of the greatest princes of this age, never
wears any gloves, and in winter or whatever weather can come, never wears
other cap abroad than that he wears at home. Whereas I cannot endure to
go unbuttoned or untied; my neighbouring labourers would think themselves
in chains, if they were so braced. Varro is of opinion, that when it was
ordained we should be bare in the presence of the gods and before the
magistrate, it was so ordered rather upon the score of health, and to
inure us to the injuries of weather, than upon the account of reverence;
and since we are now talking of cold, and Frenchmen used to wear variety
of colours (not I myself, for I seldom wear other than black or white, in
imitation of my father), let us add another story out of Le Capitaine
Martin du Bellay, who affirms, that in the march to Luxembourg he saw so
great frost, that the munition-wine was cut with hatchets and wedges, and
delivered out to the soldiers by weight, and that they carried it away in
baskets: and Ovid,

> "*Nudaque consistunt, formam servantia testae,*
> *Vina; nec hausta meri, sed data frusta, bibunt.*"

[*"The wine when out of the cask retains the form of the cask;
and is given out not in cups, but in bits."*
--Ovid, Trist., iii. 10, 23.]

At the mouth of Lake Maeotis the frosts are so very sharp, that in the very same place where Mithridates' lieutenant had fought the enemy dryfoot and given them a notable defeat, the summer following he obtained over them a naval victory. The Romans fought at a very great disadvantage, in the engagement they had with the Carthaginians near Piacenza, by reason that they went to the charge with their blood congealed and their limbs numbed with cold, whereas Hannibal had caused great fires to be dispersed quite through his camp to warm his soldiers, and oil to be distributed amongst them, to the end that anointing themselves, they might render their nerves more supple and active, and fortify the pores against the violence of the air and freezing wind, which raged in that season.

The retreat the Greeks made from Babylon into their own country is famous for the difficulties and calamities they had to overcome; of which this was one, that being encountered in the mountains of Armenia with a horrible storm of snow, they lost all knowledge of the country and of the ways, and being driven up, were a day and a night without eating or drinking; most of their cattle died, many of themselves were starved to death, several struck blind with the force of the hail and the glare of the snow, many of them maimed in their fingers and toes, and many stiff and motionless with the extremity of the cold, who had yet their understanding entire.

Alexander saw a nation, where they bury their fruit-trees in winter to protect them from being destroyed by the frost, and we also may see the same.

But, so far as clothes go, the King of Mexico changed four times a day his apparel, and never put it on again, employing that he left off in his continual liberalities and rewards; and neither pot, dish, nor other utensil of his kitchen or table was ever served twice.

CHAPTER XXXVI

OF CATO THE YOUNGER

*["I am not possessed with this common errour, to judge of others
according to what I am my selfe. I am easie to beleeve things
differing from my selfe. Though I be engaged to one forme, I do not
tie the world unto it, as every man doth. And I beleeve and
conceive a thousand manners of life, contrary to the common sorte."
~Florio, ed. 1613, p. 113.]*

*I am not guilty of the common error of judging another by myself. I
easily believe that in another's humour which is contrary to my own; and
though I find myself engaged to one certain form, I do not oblige others
to it, as many do; but believe and apprehend a thousand ways of living;
and, contrary to most men, more easily admit of difference than
uniformity amongst us. I as frankly as any one would have me, discharge
a man from my humours and principles, and consider him according to his
own particular model. Though I am not continent myself, I nevertheless
sincerely approve the continence of the Feuillans and Capuchins, and
highly commend their way of living. I insinuate myself by imagination
into their place, and love and honour them the more for being other than
I am. I very much desire that we may be judged every man by himself, and
would not be drawn into the consequence of common examples. My own
weakness nothing alters the esteem I ought to have for the force and
vigour of those who deserve it:*

"Sunt qui nihil suadent, quam quod se imitari posse confidunt."

*["There are who persuade nothing but what they believe they can
imitate themselves."~Cicero, De Orator., c. 7.]*

Crawling upon the slime of the earth, I do not for all that cease to

– 272 –

observe up in the clouds the inimitable height of some heroic souls.
'Tis a great deal for me to have my judgment regular and just, if the
effects cannot be so, and to maintain this sovereign part, at least, free
from corruption; 'tis something to have my will right and good where my
legs fail me. This age wherein we live, in our part of the world at
least, is grown so stupid, that not only the exercise, but the very
imagination of virtue is defective, and seems to be no other but college
jargon:

> "Virtutem verba putant, ut
> Lucum ligna:"

["They think words virtue, as they think mere wood a sacred grove."
⸌Horace, Ep., i. 6, 31.]

> "Quam vereri deberent, etiam si percipere non possent."

["Which they ought to reverence, though they cannot comprehend."
⸌Cicero, Tusc. Quas., v. 2.]

'Tis a gewgaw to hang in a cabinet or at the end of the tongue, as on the
tip of the ear, for ornament only. There are no longer virtuous actions
extant; those actions that carry a show of virtue have yet nothing of its
essence; by reason that profit, glory, fear, custom, and other suchlike
foreign causes, put us on the way to produce them. Our justice also,
valour, courtesy, may be called so too, in respect to others and
according to the face they appear with to the public; but in the doer it
can by no means be virtue, because there is another end proposed, another
moving cause. Now virtue owns nothing to be hers, but what is done by
herself and for herself alone.

In that great battle of Plataea, that the Greeks under the command of
Pausanias gained against Mardonius and the Persians, the conquerors,
according to their custom, coming to divide amongst them the glory of the
exploit, attributed to the Spartan nation the pre⸍eminence of valour in
the engagement. The Spartans, great judges of virtue, when they came to

determine to what particular man of their nation the honour was due of
having the best behaved himself upon this occasion, found that
Aristodemus had of all others hazarded his person with the greatest
bravery; but did not, however, allow him any prize, by reason that his
virtue had been incited by a desire to clear his reputation from the
reproach of his miscarriage at the business of Thermopylae, and to die
bravely to wipe off that former blemish.

Our judgments are yet sick, and obey the humour of our depraved manners.
I observe most of the wits of these times pretend to ingenuity, by
endeavouring to blemish and darken the glory of the bravest and most
generous actions of former ages, putting one vile interpretation or
another upon them, and forging and supposing vain causes and motives for
the noble things they did: a mighty subtlety indeed! Give me the
greatest and most unblemished action that ever the day beheld, and I will
contrive a hundred plausible drifts and ends to obscure it. God knows,
whoever will stretch them out to the full, what diversity of images our
internal wills suffer under. They do not so maliciously play the
censurers, as they do it ignorantly and rudely in all their detractions.

The same pains and licence that others take to blemish and bespatter
these illustrious names, I would willingly undergo to lend them a
shoulder to raise them higher. These rare forms, that are culled out by
the consent of the wisest men of all ages, for the world's example,
I should not stick to augment in honour, as far as my invention would
permit, in all the circumstances of favourable interpretation; and we may
well believe that the force of our invention is infinitely short of their
merit. 'Tis the duty of good men to portray virtue as beautiful as they
can, and there would be nothing wrong should our passion a little
transport us in favour of so sacred a form. What these people do, on the
contrary, they either do out of malice, or by the vice of confining their
belief to their own capacity; or, which I am more inclined to think, for
not having their sight strong, clear, and elevated enough to conceive the
splendour of virtue in her native purity: as Plutarch complains, that in
his time some attributed the cause of the younger Cato's death to his
fear of Caesar, at which he seems very angry, and with good reason; and

by this a man may guess how much more he would have been offended with those who have attributed it to ambition. Senseless people! He would rather have performed a noble, just, and generous action, and to have had ignominy for his reward, than for glory. That man was in truth a pattern that nature chose out to show to what height human virtue and constancy could arrive.

But I am not capable of handling so rich an argument, and shall therefore only set five Latin poets together, contending in the praise of Cato; and, incidentally, for their own too. Now, a well-educated child will judge the two first, in comparison of the others, a little flat and languid; the third more vigorous, but overthrown by the extravagance of his own force; he will then think that there will be room for one or two gradations of invention to come to the fourth, and, mounting to the pitch of that, he will lift up his hands in admiration; coming to the last, the first by some space' (but a space that he will swear is not to be filled up by any human wit), he will be astounded, he will not know where he is.

And here is a wonder: we have far more poets than judges and interpreters of poetry; it is easier to write it than to understand it. There is, indeed, a certain low and moderate sort of poetry, that a man may well enough judge by certain rules of art; but the true, supreme, and divine poesy is above all rules and reason. And whoever discerns the beauty of it with the most assured and most steady sight, sees no more than the quick reflection of a flash of lightning: it does not exercise, but ravishes and overwhelms our judgment. The fury that possesses him who is able to penetrate into it wounds yet a third man by hearing him repeat it; like a loadstone that not only attracts the needle, but also infuses into it the virtue to attract others. And it is more evidently manifest in our theatres, that the sacred inspiration of the Muses, having first stirred up the poet to anger, sorrow, hatred, and out of himself, to whatever they will, does moreover by the poet possess the actor, and by the actor consecutively all the spectators. So much do our passions hang and depend upon one another.

*Poetry has ever had that power over me from a child to transpierce and
transport me; but this vivid sentiment that is natural to me has been
variously handled by variety of forms, not so much higher or lower (for
they were ever the highest of every kind), as differing in colour.
First, a gay and sprightly fluency; afterwards, a lofty and penetrating
subtlety; and lastly, a mature and constant vigour. Their names will
better express them: Ovid, Lucan, Virgil.*

But our poets are beginning their career:

> *"Sit Cato, dum vivit, sane vel Caesare major,"*

> *["Let Cato, whilst he live, be greater than Caesar."
> ⸺Martial, vi. 32]*

says one.

> *"Et invictum, devicta morte, Catonem,"*

> *["And Cato invincible, death being overcome."
> ⸺Manilius, Astron., iv. 87.]*

*says the second. And the third, speaking of the civil wars betwixt
Caesar and Pompey,*

> *"Victrix causa diis placuit, set victa Catoni."*

> *["The victorious cause blessed the gods, the defeated one Cato.
> ⸺"Lucan, i. 128.]*

And the fourth, upon the praises of Caesar:

> *"Et cuncta terrarum subacta,
> Praeter atrocem animum Catonis."*

[*"And conquered all but the indomitable mind of Cato."*
--Horace, Od., ii. 1, 23.]

*And the master of the choir, after having set forth all the great names
of the greatest Romans, ends thus:*

"His dantem jura Catonem."

[*"Cato giving laws to all the rest."--AEneid, viii. 670.*]

CHAPTER XXXVII

THAT WE LAUGH AND CRY
FOR THE SAME THING

When we read in history that Antigonus was very much displeased with his
son for presenting him the head of King Pyrrhus his enemy, but newly
slain fighting against him, and that seeing it, he wept; and that Rene,
Duke of Lorraine, also lamented the death of Charles, Duke of Burgundy,
whom he had himself defeated, and appeared in mourning at his funeral;
and that in the battle of D'Auray (which Count Montfort obtained over
Charles de Blois, his competitor for the duchy of Brittany), the
conqueror meeting the dead body of his enemy, was very much afflicted at
his death, we must not presently cry out:

> *"E cosi avven, the l'animo ciascuna*
> *Sua passion sotto 'l contrario manto,*
> *Ricopre, con la vista or'chiara, or'bruna."*

> *["And thus it happens that the mind of each veils its passion under*
> *a different appearance, and beneath a smiling visage, gay beneath a*
> *sombre air."--Petrarch.]*

When Pompey's head was presented to Caesar, the histories tell us that he
turned away his face, as from a sad and unpleasing object. There had
been so long an intelligence and society betwixt them in the management
of the public affairs, so great a community of fortunes, so many mutual
offices, and so near an alliance, that this countenance of his ought not
to suffer under any misinterpretation, or to be suspected for either
false or counterfeit, as this other seems to believe:

> *"Tutumque putavit*

Jam bonus esse socer; lacrymae non sponte cadentes,
Effudit, gemitusque expressit pectore laeto;"

[*"And now he thought it safe to play the kind father-in-law,*
shedding forced tears, and from a joyful breast discharging sighs
and groans."--Lucan, ix. 1037.]

for though it be true that the greatest part of our actions are no other
than visor and disguise, and that it may sometimes be true that

"*Haeredis fletus sub persona rises est,*"

[*"The heir's tears behind the mask are smiles."*
--Publius Syrus, apud Gellium, xvii. 14.]

yet, in judging of these accidents, we are to consider how much our souls
are oftentimes agitated with divers passions. And as they say that in
our bodies there is a congregation of divers humours, of which that is
the sovereign which, according to the complexion we are of, is commonly
most predominant in us: so, though the soul have in it divers motions to
give it agitation, yet must there of necessity be one to overrule all the
rest, though not with so necessary and absolute a dominion but that
through the flexibility and inconstancy of the soul, those of less
authority may upon occasion reassume their place and make a little sally
in turn. Thence it is, that we see not only children, who innocently
obey and follow nature, often laugh and cry at the same thing, but not
one of us can boast, what journey soever he may have in hand that he has
the most set his heart upon, but when he comes to part with his family
and friends, he will find something that troubles him within; and though
he refrain his tears yet he puts foot in the stirrup with a sad and
cloudy countenance. And what gentle flame soever may warm the heart of
modest and wellborn virgins, yet are they fain to be forced from about
their mothers' necks to be put to bed to their husbands, whatever this
boon companion is pleased to say:

"Estne novis nuptis odio Venus? anne parentum
Frustrantur falsis gaudia lachrymulis,
Ubertim thalami quasi intra limina fundunt?
Non, ita me divi, vera gemunt, juverint."

["Is Venus really so alarming to the new-made bride, or does she
honestly oppose her parent's rejoicing the tears she so abundantly
sheds on entering the nuptial chamber? No, by the Gods, these are
no true tears."--Catullus, lxvi. 15.]

["Is Venus really so repugnant to newly-married maids? Do they meet
the smiles of parents with feigned tears? They weep copiously
within the very threshold of the nuptial chamber. No, so the gods
help me, they do not truly grieve."--Catullus, lxvi. 15.]--
[A more literal translation. D.W.]

Neither is it strange to lament a person dead whom a man would by no
means should be alive. When I rattle my man, I do it with all the mettle
I have, and load him with no feigned, but downright real curses; but the
heat being over, if he should stand in need of me, I should be very ready
to do him good: for I instantly turn the leaf. When I call him calf and
coxcomb, I do not pretend to entail those titles upon him for ever;
neither do I think I give myself the lie in calling him an honest fellow
presently after. No one quality engrosses us purely and universally.
Were it not the sign of a fool to talk to one's self, there would hardly
be a day or hour wherein I might not be heard to grumble and mutter to
myself and against myself, "Confound the fool!" and yet I do not think
that to be my definition. Who for seeing me one while cold and presently
very fond towards my wife, believes the one or the other to be
counterfeited, is an ass. Nero, taking leave of his mother whom he was
sending to be drowned, was nevertheless sensible of some emotion at this
farewell, and was struck with horror and pity. 'Tis said, that the light
of the sun is not one continuous thing, but that he darts new rays so
thick one upon another that we cannot perceive the intermission:

> "*Largus enim liquidi fons luminis, aetherius sol,*
> *Irrigat assidue coelum candore recenti,*
> *Suppeditatque novo confestim lumine lumen.*"

> [*"So the wide fountain of liquid light, the ethereal sun, steadily*
> *fertilises the heavens with new heat, and supplies a continuous*
> *store of fresh light."--Lucretius, v. 282.*]

Just so the soul variously and imperceptibly darts out her passions.

Artabanus coming by surprise once upon his nephew Xerxes, chid him for the sudden alteration of his countenance. He was considering the immeasurable greatness of his forces passing over the Hellespont for the Grecian expedition: he was first seized with a palpitation of joy, to see so many millions of men under his command, and this appeared in the gaiety of his looks: but his thoughts at the same instant suggesting to him that of so many lives, within a century at most, there would not be one left, he presently knit his brows and grew sad, even to tears.

We have resolutely pursued the revenge of an injury received, and been sensible of a singular contentment for the victory; but we shall weep notwithstanding. 'Tis not for the victory, though, that we shall weep: there is nothing altered in that but the soul looks upon things with another eye and represents them to itself with another kind of face; for everything has many faces and several aspects.

Relations, old acquaintances, and friendships, possess our imaginations and make them tender for the time, according to their condition; but the turn is so quick, that 'tis gone in a moment:

> "*Nil adeo fieri celeri ratione videtur,*
> *Quam si mens fieri proponit, et inchoat ipsa,*
> *Ocius ergo animus, quam res se perciet ulla,*
> *Ante oculos quorum in promptu natura videtur;*"

> [*"Nothing therefore seems to be done in so swift a manner than if the mind proposes it to be done, and itself begins. It is more active than anything which we see in nature."--Lucretius, iii. 183.*]

and therefore, if we would make one continued thing of all this succession of passions, we deceive ourselves. When Timoleon laments the murder he had committed upon so mature and generous deliberation, he does not lament the liberty restored to his country, he does not lament the tyrant; but he laments his brother: one part of his duty is performed; let us give him leave to perform the other.

CHAPTER XXXVIII

OF SOLITUDE

Let us pretermit that long comparison betwixt the active and the solitary life; and as for the fine sayings with which ambition and avarice palliate their vices, that we are not born for ourselves but for the public,--[This is the eulogium passed by Lucan on Cato of Utica, ii. 383.]--let us boldly appeal to those who are in public affairs; let them lay their hands upon their hearts, and then say whether, on the contrary, they do not rather aspire to titles and offices and that tumult of the world to make their private advantage at the public expense. The corrupt ways by which in this our time they arrive at the height to which their ambitions aspire, manifestly enough declares that their ends cannot be very good. Let us tell ambition that it is she herself who gives us a taste of solitude; for what does she so much avoid as society? What does she so much seek as elbowroom? A man many do well or ill everywhere; but if what Bias says be true, that the greatest part is the worse part, or what the Preacher says: there is not one good of a thousand:

> "Rari quippe boni: numero vix sunt totidem quot
> Thebarum portae, vel divitis ostia Nili,"

> ["Good men forsooth are scarce: there are hardly as many as there
> are gates of Thebes or mouths of the rich Nile."
> --Juvenal, Sat., xiii. 26.]

the contagion is very dangerous in the crowd. A man must either imitate the vicious or hate them both are dangerous things, either to resemble them because they are many or to hate many because they are unresembling to ourselves. Merchants who go to sea are in the right when they are cautious that those who embark with them in the same bottom be neither dissolute blasphemers nor vicious other ways, looking upon such society as unfortunate. And therefore it was that Bias pleasantly said to some, who being with him in a dangerous storm implored the assistance of the gods: "Peace, speak softly," said he, "that they may not know you are here in my company."--[Diogenes Laertius]--And of more pressing example, Albuquerque, viceroy in the Indies for Emmanuel, king of Portugal, in an extreme peril of shipwreck, took a young boy upon his shoulders, for this only end that, in the society of their common danger his innocence might serve to protect him, and to recommend him to the divine favour, that they might get safe to shore. 'Tis not that a wise man may not live everywhere content, and be alone in the very crowd of a palace; but if it be left to his own choice, the schoolman will tell you that he should fly the very sight of the crowd: he will endure it if need be; but if it be referred to him, he will choose to be alone. He cannot think himself sufficiently rid of vice, if he must yet contend with it in other men. Charondas punished those as evil men who were convicted of keeping ill company. There is nothing so unsociable and sociable as man, the one by his vice, the other by his nature. And Antisthenes, in my opinion, did not give him a satisfactory answer, who reproached him with frequenting ill company, by saying that the physicians lived well enough amongst the sick, for if they contribute to the health of the sick, no doubt but by the contagion, continual sight of, and familiarity with diseases, they must of necessity impair their own.

Now the end, I take it, is all one, to live at more leisure and at one's ease: but men do not always take the right way. They often think they have totally taken leave of all business, when they have only exchanged one employment for another: there is little less trouble in governing a private family than a whole kingdom. Wherever the mind is perplexed, it is in an entire disorder, and domestic employments are not less troublesome for being less important. Moreover, for having shaken off the court and the exchange, we have not taken leave of the principal vexations of life:

> "Ratio et prudentia curas,
> Non locus effusi late maris arbiter, aufert;"

*["Reason and prudence, not a place with a commanding view of the
great ocean, banish care."--Horace, Ep., i. 2.]*

ambition, avarice, irresolution, fear, and inordinate desires, do not
leave us because we forsake our native country:

"Et
Post equitem sedet atra cura;"

*["Black care sits behind the horse man."
--Horace, Od., iii. 1, 40].*

they often follow us even to cloisters and philosophical schools; nor
deserts, nor caves, hair-shirts, nor fasts, can disengage us from them:

"Haeret lateri lethalis arundo."

["The fatal shaft adheres to the side."--AEneid, iv. 73.]

One telling Socrates that such a one was nothing improved by his travels:
"I very well believe it," said he, "for he took himself along with him"

"Quid terras alio calentes
Sole mutamus? patriae quis exsul
Se quoque fugit?"

*["Why do we seek climates warmed by another sun? Who is the man
that by fleeing from his country, can also flee from himself?"
--Horace, Od., ii. 16, 18.]*

If a man do not first discharge both himself and his mind of the burden
with which he finds himself oppressed, motion will but make it press the
harder and sit the heavier, as the lading of a ship is of less
encumbrance when fast and bestowed in a settled posture. You do a sick
man more harm than good in removing him from place to place; you fix and
establish the disease by motion, as stakes sink deeper and more firmly

into the earth by being moved up and down in the place where they are designed to stand. Therefore, it is not enough to get remote from the public; 'tis not enough to shift the soil only; a man must flee from the popular conditions that have taken possession of his soul, he must sequester and come again to himself:

> "Rupi jam vincula, dicas
> Nam luctata canis nodum arripit; attamen illi,
> Quum fugit, a collo trahitur pars longa catenae."

[*"You say, perhaps, you have broken your chains: the dog who after long efforts has broken his chain, still in his flight drags a heavy portion of it after him."--Persius, Sat., v. 158.*]

We still carry our fetters along with us. 'Tis not an absolute liberty; we yet cast back a look upon what we have left behind us; the fancy is still full of it:

> "Nisi purgatum est pectus, quae praelia nobis
> Atque pericula tunc ingratis insinuandum?
> Quantae connscindunt hominem cupedinis acres
> Sollicitum curae? quantique perinde timores?
> Quidve superbia, spurcitia, ac petulantia, quantas
> Efficiunt clades? quid luxus desidiesque?"

[*"But unless the mind is purified, what internal combats and dangers must we incur in spite of all our efforts! How many bitter anxieties, how many terrors, follow upon unregulated passion! What destruction befalls us from pride, lust, petulant anger! What evils arise from luxury and sloth!"--Lucretius, v. 4.*]

Our disease lies in the mind, which cannot escape from itself;

> "In culpa est animus, qui se non effugit unquam,"
> --Horace, Ep., i. 14, 13.

and therefore is to be called home and confined within itself: that is
the true solitude, and that may be enjoyed even in populous cities and
the courts of kings, though more commodiously apart.

Now, since we will attempt to live alone, and to waive all manner of
conversation amongst them, let us so order it that our content may depend
wholly upon ourselves; let us dissolve all obligations that ally us to
others; let us obtain this from ourselves, that we may live alone in good
earnest, and live at our ease too.

Stilpo having escaped from the burning of his town, where he lost wife,
children, and goods, Demetrius Poliorcetes seeing him, in so great a ruin
of his country, appear with an undisturbed countenance, asked him if he
had received no loss? To which he made answer, No; and that, thank God,
nothing was lost of his.--[Seneca, Ep. 7.]--This also was the meaning of
the philosopher Antisthenes, when he pleasantly said, that "men should
furnish themselves with such things as would float, and might with the
owner escape the storm";--[Diogenes Laertius, vi. 6.] and certainly a
wise man never loses anything if he have himself. When the city of Nola
was ruined by the barbarians, Paulinus, who was bishop of that place,
having there lost all he had, himself a prisoner, prayed after this
manner: "O Lord, defend me from being sensible of this loss; for Thou
knowest they have yet touched nothing of that which is mine."--[St.
Augustin, De Civit. Dei, i. 10.]--The riches that made him rich and the
goods that made him good, were still kept entire. This it is to make
choice of treasures that can secure themselves from plunder and violence,
and to hide them in such a place into which no one can enter and that is
not to be betrayed by any but ourselves. Wives, children, and goods must
be had, and especially health, by him that can get it; but we are not so
to set our hearts upon them that our happiness must have its dependence
upon them; we must reserve a backshop, wholly our own and entirely free,
wherein to settle our true liberty, our principal solitude and retreat.
And in this we must for the most part entertain ourselves with ourselves,
and so privately that no exotic knowledge or communication be admitted
there; there to laugh and to talk, as if without wife, children, goods,
train, or attendance, to the end that when it shall so fall out that we

must lose any or all of these, it may be no new thing to be without them. We have a mind pliable in itself, that will be company; that has wherewithal to attack and to defend, to receive and to give: let us not then fear in this solitude to languish under an uncomfortable vacuity.

> *"In solis sis tibi turba locis."*

> [*"In solitude, be company for thyself."*--Tibullus, vi. 13. 12.]

Virtue is satisfied with herself, without discipline, without words, without effects. In our ordinary actions there is not one of a thousand that concerns ourselves. He that thou seest scrambling up the ruins of that wall, furious and transported, against whom so many harquebuss-shots are levelled; and that other all over scars, pale, and fainting with hunger, and yet resolved rather to die than to open the gates to him; dost thou think that these men are there upon their own account? No; peradventure in the behalf of one whom they never saw and who never concerns himself for their pains and danger, but lies wallowing the while in sloth and pleasure: this other slavering, blear-eyed, slovenly fellow, that thou seest come out of his study after midnight, dost thou think he has been tumbling over books to learn how to become a better man, wiser, and more content? No such matter; he will there end his days, but he will teach posterity the measure of Plautus' verses and the true orthography of a Latin word. Who is it that does not voluntarily exchange his health, his repose, and his very life for reputation and glory, the most useless, frivolous, and false coin that passes current amongst us? Our own death does not sufficiently terrify and trouble us; let us, moreover, charge ourselves with those of our wives, children, and family: our own affairs do not afford us anxiety enough; let us undertake those of our neighbours and friends, still more to break our brains and torment us:

> *"Vah! quemquamne hominem in animum instituere, aut*
> *Parare, quod sit carius, quam ipse est sibi?"*

["Ah! can any man conceive in his mind or realise what is dearer than he is to himself?"--Terence, Adelph., i. I, 13.]

Solitude seems to me to wear the best favour in such as have already employed their most active and flourishing age in the world's service, after the example of Thales. We have lived enough for others; let us at least live out the small remnant of life for ourselves; let us now call in our thoughts and intentions to ourselves, and to our own ease and repose. 'Tis no light thing to make a sure retreat; it will be enough for us to do without mixing other enterprises. Since God gives us leisure to order our removal, let us make ready, truss our baggage, take leave betimes of the company, and disentangle ourselves from those violent importunities that engage us elsewhere and separate us from ourselves.

We must break the knot of our obligations, how strong soever, and hereafter love this or that, but espouse nothing but ourselves: that is to say, let the remainder be our own, but not so joined and so close as not to be forced away without flaying us or tearing out part of our whole. The greatest thing in the world is for a man to know that he is his own. 'Tis time to wean ourselves from society when we can no longer add anything to it; he who is not in a condition to lend must forbid himself to borrow. Our forces begin to fail us; let us call them in and concentrate them in and for ourselves. He that can cast off within himself and resolve the offices of friendship and company, let him do it. In this decay of nature which renders him useless, burdensome, and importunate to others, let him take care not to be useless, burdensome, and importunate to himself. Let him soothe and caress himself, and above all things be sure to govern himself with reverence to his reason and conscience to that degree as to be ashamed to make a false step in their presence:

"*Rarum est enim, ut satis se quisque vereatur.*"

["For 'tis rarely seen that men have respect and reverence enough for themselves."--Quintilian, x. 7.]

Socrates says that boys are to cause themselves to be instructed, men to exercise themselves in well-doing, and old men to retire from all civil and military employments, living at their own discretion, without the obligation to any office. There are some complexions more proper for these precepts of retirement than others. Such as are of a soft and dull apprehension, and of a tender will and affection, not readily to be subdued or employed, whereof I am one, both by natural condition and by reflection, will sooner incline to this advice than active and busy souls, which embrace: all, engage in all, are hot upon everything, which offer, present, and give themselves up to every occasion. We are to use these accidental and extraneous commodities, so far as they are pleasant to us, but by no means to lay our principal foundation there; 'tis no true one; neither nature nor reason allows it so to be. Why therefore should we, contrary to their laws, enslave our own contentment to the power of another? To anticipate also the accidents of fortune, to deprive ourselves of the conveniences we have in our own power, as several have done upon the account of devotion, and some philosophers by reasoning; to be one's own servant, to lie hard, to put out our own eyes, to throw our wealth into the river, to go in search of grief; these, by the misery of this life, aiming at bliss in another; those by laying themselves low to avoid the danger of falling: all such are acts of an excessive virtue. The stoutest and most resolute natures render even their seclusion glorious and exemplary:

> "Tuta et parvula laudo,
> Quum res deficiunt, satis inter vilia fortis
> Verum, ubi quid melius contingit et unctius, idem
> Hos sapere et solos aio bene vivere, quorum
> Conspicitur nitidis fundata pecunia villis."

["When means are deficient, I laud a safe and humble condition, content with little: but when things grow better and more easy, I all the same say that you alone are wise and live well, whose invested money is visible in beautiful villas."
--Horace, Ep., i. 15, 42.]

A great deal less would serve my turn well enough. 'Tis enough for me, under fortune's favour, to prepare myself for her disgrace, and, being at my ease, to represent to myself, as far as my imagination can stretch, the ill to come; as we do at jousts and tiltings, where we counterfeit war in the greatest calm of peace. I do not think Arcesilaus the philosopher the less temperate and virtuous for knowing that he made use of gold and silver vessels, when the condition of his fortune allowed him so to do; I have indeed a better opinion of him than if he had denied himself what he used with liberality and moderation. I see the utmost limits of natural necessity: and considering a poor man begging at my door, ofttimes more jocund and more healthy than I myself am, I put myself into his place, and attempt to dress my mind after his mode; and running, in like manner, over other examples, though I fancy death, poverty, contempt, and sickness treading on my heels, I easily resolve not to be affrighted, forasmuch as a less than I takes them with so much patience; and am not willing to believe that a less understanding can do more than a greater, or that the effects of precept cannot arrive to as great a height as those of custom. And knowing of how uncertain duration these accidental conveniences are, I never forget, in the height of all my enjoyments, to make it my chiefest prayer to Almighty God, that He will please to render me content with myself and the condition wherein I am. I see young men very gay and frolic, who nevertheless keep a mass of pills in their trunk at home, to take when they've got a cold, which they fear so much the less, because they think they have remedy at hand. Every one should do in like manner, and, moreover, if they find themselves subject to some more violent disease, should furnish themselves with such medicines as may numb and stupefy the part.

The employment a man should choose for such a life ought neither to be a laborious nor an unpleasing one; otherwise 'tis to no purpose at all to be retired. And this depends upon every one's liking and humour. Mine has no manner of complacency for husbandry, and such as love it ought to apply themselves to it with moderation:

> *["Endeavour to make circumstances subject to me,*
> *and not me subject to circumstances."*
> *⸺Horace, Ep., i. i, 19.]*

Husbandry is otherwise a very servile employment, as Sallust calls it; though some parts of it are more excusable than the rest, as the care of gardens, which Xenophon attributes to Cyrus; and a mean may be found out betwixt the sordid and low application, so full of perpetual solicitude, which is seen in men who make it their entire business and study, and the stupid and extreme negligence, letting all things go at random which we see in others

> *"Democriti pecus edit agellos*
> *Cultaque, dum peregre est animus sine corpore velox."*

> *["Democritus' cattle eat his corn and spoil his fields, whilst his*
> *soaring mind ranges abroad without the body."*
> *⸺Horace, Ep., i, 12, 12.]*

But let us hear what advice the younger Pliny gives his friend Caninius Rufus upon the subject of solitude: "I advise thee, in the full and plentiful retirement wherein thou art, to leave to thy hinds the care of thy husbandry, and to addict thyself to the study of letters, to extract from thence something that may be entirely and absolutely thine own." By which he means reputation; like Cicero, who says that he would employ his solitude and retirement from public affairs to acquire by his writings an immortal life.

> *"Usque adeone*
> *Scire tuum, nihil est, nisi to scire hoc, sciat alter?"*

> *["Is all that thy learning nothing, unless another knows*
> *that thou knowest?"⸺Persius, Sat., i. 23.]*

It appears to be reason, when a man talks of retiring from the world, that he should look quite out of [for] himself. These do it but by halves: they design well enough for themselves when they shall be no more in it; but still they pretend to extract the fruits of that design from the world, when absent from it, by a ridiculous contradiction.

The imagination of those who seek solitude upon the account of devotion, filling their hopes and courage with certainty of divine promises in the other life, is much more rationally founded. They propose to themselves God, an infinite object in goodness and power; the soul has there wherewithal, at full liberty, to satiate her desires: afflictions and sufferings turn to their advantage, being undergone for the acquisition of eternal health and joy; death is to be wished and longed for, where it is the passage to so perfect a condition; the asperity of the rules they impose upon themselves is immediately softened by custom, and all their carnal appetites baffled and subdued, by refusing to humour and feed them, these being only supported by use and exercise. This sole end of another happily immortal life is that which really merits that we should abandon the pleasures and conveniences of this; and he who can really and constantly inflame his soul with the ardour of this vivid faith and hope, erects for himself in solitude a more voluptuous and delicious life than any other sort of existence.

Neither the end, then, nor the means of this advice pleases me, for we often fall out of the frying-pan into the fire.--[or: we always relapse ill from fever into fever.]--This book-employment is as painful as any other, and as great an enemy to health, which ought to be the first thing considered; neither ought a man to be allured with the pleasure of it, which is the same that destroys the frugal, the avaricious, the voluptuous, and the ambitious man.

["This plodding occupation of bookes is as painfull as any other, and as great an enemie vnto health, which ought principally to be considered. And a man should not suffer him selfe to be inveagled by the pleasure he takes in them."--Florio, edit. 1613, p. 122.]

The sages give us caution enough to beware the treachery of our desires, and to distinguish true and entire pleasures from such as are mixed and complicated with greater pain. For the most of our pleasures, say they, wheedle and caress only to strangle us, like those thieves the Egyptians called Philistae; if the headache should come before drunkenness, we should have a care of drinking too much; but pleasure, to deceive us, marches before and conceals her train. Books are pleasant, but if, by being over-studious, we impair our health and spoil our goodhumour, the best pieces we have, let us give it over; I, for my part, am one of those who think, that no fruit derived from them can recompense so great a loss. As men who have long felt themselves weakened by indisposition, give themselves up at last to the mercy of medicine and submit to certain rules of living, which they are for the future never to transgress; so he who retires, weary of and disgusted with the common way of living, ought to model this new one he enters into by the rules of reason, and to institute and establish it by premeditation and reflection. He ought to have taken leave of all sorts of labour, what advantage soever it may promise, and generally to have shaken off all those passions which disturb the tranquillity of body and soul, and then choose the way that best suits with his own humour:

> "Unusquisque sua noverit ire via."

In husbandry, study, hunting, and all other exercises, men are to proceed to the utmost limits of pleasure, but must take heed of engaging further, where trouble begins to mix with it. We are to reserve so much employment only as is necessary to keep us in breath and to defend us from the inconveniences that the other extreme of a dull and stupid laziness brings along with it. There are sterile knotty sciences, chiefly hammered out for the crowd; let such be left to them who are engaged in the world's service. I for my part care for no other books, but either such as are pleasant and easy, to amuse me, or those that comfort and instruct me how to regulate my life and death:

> "Tacitum sylvas inter reptare salubres,
> Curantem, quidquid dignum sapienti bonoque est."

["Silently meditating in the healthy groves, whatever is worthy of a wise and good man."--Horace, Ep., i. 4, 4.]

Wiser men, having great force and vigour of soul, may propose to themselves a rest wholly spiritual but for me, who have a very ordinary soul, it is very necessary to support myself with bodily conveniences; and age having of late deprived me of those pleasures that were more acceptable to me, I instruct and whet my appetite to those that remain, more suitable to this other reason. We ought to hold with all our force, both of hands and teeth, the use of the pleasures of life that our years, one after another, snatch away from us:

> *"Carpamus dulcia; nostrum est,*
> *Quod vivis; cinis, et manes, et fabula fies."*

["Let us pluck life's sweets, 'tis for them we live: by and by we shall be ashes, a ghost, a mere subject of talk."
--Persius, Sat., v. 151.]

Now, as to the end that Pliny and Cicero propose to us of glory, 'tis infinitely wide of my account. Ambition is of all others the most contrary humour to solitude; glory and repose are things that cannot possibly inhabit in one and the same place. For so much as I understand, these have only their arms and legs disengaged from the crowd; their soul and intention remain confined behind more than ever:

> *"Tun', vetule, auriculis alienis colligis escas?"*

["Dost thou, then, old man, collect food for others' ears?"
--Persius, Sat., i. 22.]

they have only retired to take a better leap, and by a stronger motion to give a brisker charge into the crowd. Will you see how they shoot short? Let us put into the counterpoise the advice of two philosophers, of two very different sects, writing, the one to Idomeneus, the other to Lucilius, their friends, to retire into solitude from worldly honours and affairs. "You have," say they, "hitherto lived swimming and floating; come now and die in the harbour: you have given the first part of your life to the light, give what remains to the shade. It is impossible to give over business, if you do not also quit the fruit; therefore disengage yourselves from all concern of name and glory; 'tis to be feared the lustre of your former actions will give you but too much light, and follow you into your most private retreat. Quit with other pleasures that which proceeds from the approbation of another man: and as to your knowledge and parts, never concern yourselves; they will not lose their effect if yourselves be the better for them. Remember him, who being asked why he took so much pains in an art that could come to the knowledge of but few persons? 'A few are enough for me,' replied he; 'I have enough with one; I have enough with never an one.'--[Seneca, Ep., 7.]--He said true; you and a companion are theatre enough to one another, or you to yourself. Let the people be to you one, and be you one to the whole people. 'Tis an unworthy ambition to think to derive glory from a man's sloth and privacy: you are to do like the beasts of chase, who efface the track at the entrance into their den. You are no more to concern yourself how the world talks of you, but how you are to talk to yourself. Retire yourself into yourself, but first prepare yourself there to receive yourself: it were a folly to trust yourself in your own hands, if you cannot govern yourself. A man may miscarry alone as well as in company. Till you have rendered yourself one before whom you dare not trip, and till you have a bashfulness and respect for yourself,

"Obversentur species honestae animo;"

["Let honest things be ever present to the mind"
--Cicero, Tusc. Quaes., ii. 22.]

present continually to your imagination Cato, Phocion, and Aristides, in whose presence the fools themselves will hide their faults, and make them controllers of all your intentions; should these deviate from virtue, your respect to those will set you right; they will keep you in this way to be contented with yourself; to borrow nothing of any other but *yourself; to stay and fix your soul in certain and limited thoughts, wherein she may please herself, and having understood the true and real goods, which men the more enjoy the more they understand, to rest satisfied, without desire of prolongation of life or name." This is the precept of the true and natural philosophy, not of a boasting and prating philosophy, such as that of the two former.*

CHAPTER XXXIX

A CONSIDERATION UPON CICERO

One word more by way of comparison betwixt these two. There are to be gathered out of the writings of Cicero and the younger Pliny (but little, in my opinion, resembling his uncle in his humours) infinite testimonies of a beyond measure ambitious nature; and amongst others, this for one, that they both, in the sight of all the world, solicit the historians of their time not to forget them in their memoirs; and fortune, as if in spite, has made the vanity of those requests live upon record down to this age of ours, while she has long since consigned the histories themselves to oblivion. But this exceeds all meanness of spirit in persons of such a quality as they were, to think to derive any great renown from babbling and prating; even to the publishing of their private letters to their friends, and so withal, that though some of them were never sent, the opportunity being lost, they nevertheless presented them to the light, with this worthy excuse that they were unwilling to lose their labours and lucubrations. Was it not very well becoming two consuls of Rome, sovereign magistrates of the republic that commanded the world, to spend their leisure in contriving quaint and elegant missives, thence to gain the reputation of being versed in their own mother-tongues? What could a pitiful schoolmaster have done worse, whose trade it was thereby to get his living? If the acts of Xenophon and Caesar had not far transcended their eloquence, I scarce believe they would ever have taken the pains to have written them; they made it their business to recommend not their speaking, but their doing. And could the perfection of eloquence have added a lustre suitable to a great personage, certainly Scipio and Laelius had never resigned the honour of their comedies, with all the luxuriances and elegances of the Latin tongue, to an African slave; for that the work was theirs, its beauty and excellence sufficiently declare; Terence himself confesses as much, and I should take it ill from any one that would dispossess me of that belief.

'Tis a kind of mockery and offence to extol a man for qualities misbecoming his condition, though otherwise commendable in themselves, but such as ought not, however, to be his chief talent; as if a man should commend a king for being a good painter, a good architect, a good marksman, or a good runner at the ring: commendations that add no honour, unless mentioned altogether and in the train of those that are properly applicable to him, namely, justice and the science of governing and conducting his people both in peace and war. At this rate, agriculture was an honour to Cyrus, and eloquence and the knowledge of letters to Charlemagne. I have in my time known some, who by writing acquired both their titles and fortune, disown their apprenticeship, corrupt their style, and affect ignorance in so vulgar a quality (which also our nation holds to be rarely seen in very learned hands), and to seek a reputation by better qualities. Demosthenes' companions in the embassy to Philip, extolling that prince as handsome, eloquent, and a stout drinker, Demosthenes said that those were commendations more proper for a woman, an advocate, or a sponge, than for a king':

> "Imperet bellante prior, jacentem
> Lenis in hostem."

["In the fight, overthrow your enemy, but be merciful to him when fallen."¬"Horace, Carm. Saec., v. 51.]

'Tis not his profession to know either how to hunt or to dance well;

> "Orabunt causas alii, coelique meatus
> Describent radio, et fulgentia sidera dicent;
> Hic regere imperio populos sciat."

["Let others plead at the bar, or describe the spheres, and point out the glittering stars; let this man learn to rule the nations."
¬AEneid, vi. 849.]

Plutarch says, moreover, that to appear so excellent in these less necessary qualities is to produce witness against a man's self, that he has spent his time and applied his study ill, which ought to have been employed in the acquisition of more necessary and more useful things. So that Philip, king of Macedon, having heard that great Alexander his son sing once at a feast to the wonder of the best musicians there: "Art thou not ashamed," said he to him, "to sing so well?" And to the same Philip a musician, with whom he was disputing about some things concerning his art: "Heaven forbid, sir," said he, "that so great a misfortune should ever befall you as to understand these things better than I." A king should be able to answer as Iphicrates did the orator, who pressed upon him in his invective after this manner: "And what art thou that thou bravest it at this rate? art thou a man at arms, art thou an archer, art thou a pikeman?"~~"I am none of all this; but I know how to command all these." And Antisthenes took it for an argument of little value in Ismenias that he was commended for playing excellently well upon a flute.

I know very well, that when I hear any one dwell upon the language of my essays, I had rather a great deal he would say nothing: 'tis not so much to elevate the style as to depress the sense, and so much the more offensively as they do it obliquely; and yet I am much deceived if many other writers deliver more worth noting as to the matter, and, how well or ill soever, if any other writer has sown things much more materials or at all events more downright, upon his paper than myself. To bring the more in, I only muster up the heads; should I annex the sequel, I should trebly multiply the volume. And how many stories have I scattered up and down in this book that I only touch upon, which, should any one more curiously search into, they would find matter enough to produce infinite essays. Neither those stories nor my quotations always serve simply for example, authority, or ornament; I do not only regard them for the use I make of them: they carry sometimes besides what I apply them to, the seed of a more rich and a bolder matter, and sometimes, collaterally, a more delicate sound both to myself who will say no more about it in this place, and to others who shall be of my humour.

But returning to the speaking virtue: I find no great choice betwixt not knowing to speak anything but ill, and not knowing to speak anything but well.

> *"Non est ornamentum virile concinnitas."*

> [*"A carefully arranged dress is no manly ornament."*
> ⁓*Seneca, Ep., 115.*]

The sages tell us that, as to what concerns knowledge, 'tis nothing but philosophy; and as to what concerns effects, nothing but virtue, which is generally proper to all degrees and to all orders.

There is something like this in these two other philosophers, for they also promise eternity to the letters they write to their friends; but 'tis after another manner, and by accommodating themselves, for a good end, to the vanity of another; for they write to them that if the concern of making themselves known to future ages, and the thirst of glory, do yet detain them in the management of public affairs, and make them fear the solitude and retirement to which they would persuade them, let them never trouble themselves more about it, forasmuch as they shall have credit enough with posterity to ensure them that were there nothing else but the letters thus written to them, those letters will render their names as known and famous as their own public actions could do. And besides this difference, these are not idle and empty letters, that contain nothing but a fine jingle of well-chosen words and delicate couched phrases, but rather replete and abounding with grand discourses of reason, by which a man may render himself not more eloquent, but more wise, and that instruct us not to speak, but to do well. Away with that eloquence that enchants us with itself, and not with actual things! unless you will allow that of Cicero to be of so supreme a perfection as to form a complete body of itself.

I shall farther add one story we read of him to this purpose, wherein his nature will much more manifestly be laid open to us. He was to make an oration in public, and found himself a little straitened for time to make

*himself ready at his ease; when Eros, one of his slaves, brought him word
that the audience was deferred till the next day, at which he was so
ravished with joy that he enfranchised him for the good news.*

*Upon this subject of letters, I will add this more to what has been
already said, that it is a kind of writing wherein my friends think I can
do something; and I am willing to confess I should rather have chosen to
publish my whimsies that way than any other, had I had to whom to write;
but I wanted such a settled intercourse, as I once had, to attract me to
it, to raise my fancy, and to support me. For to traffic with the wind,
as some others have done, and to forge vain names to direct my letters
to, in a serious subject, I could never do it but in a dream, being a
sworn enemy to all manner of falsification. I should have been more
diligent and more confident had I had a judicious and indulgent friend
whom to address, than thus to expose myself to the various judgments of a
whole people, and I am deceived if I had not succeeded better. I have
naturally a humorous and familiar style; but it is a style of my own, not
proper for public business, but, like the language I speak, too compact,
irregular, abrupt, and singular; and as to letters of ceremony that have
no other substance than a fine contexture of courteous words, I am wholly
to seek. I have neither faculty nor relish for those tedious tenders of
service and affection; I believe little in them from others, and I should
not forgive myself should I say to others more than I myself believe.
'Tis, doubtless, very remote from the present practice; for there never
was so abject and servile prostitution of offers: life, soul, devotion,
adoration, vassal, slave, and I cannot tell what, as now; all which
expressions are so commonly and so indifferently posted to and fro by
every one and to every one, that when they would profess a greater and
more respectful inclination upon more just occasions, they have not
wherewithal to express it. I mortally hate all air of flattery, which is
the cause that I naturally fall into a shy, rough, and crude way of
speaking, that, to such as do not know me, may seem a little to relish of
disdain. I honour those most to whom I show the least honour, and where
my soul moves with the greatest cheerfulness, I easily forget the
ceremonies of look and gesture, and offer myself faintly and bluntly to
them to whom I am the most devoted: methinks they should read it in my*

heart, and that the expression of my words does but injure the love I
have conceived within. To welcome, take leave, give thanks, accost,
offer my service, and such verbal formalities as the ceremonious laws of
our modern civility enjoin, I know no man so stupidly unprovided of
language as myself; and I have never been employed in writing letters of
favour and recommendation, that he, in whose behalf it was written, did
not think my mediation cold and imperfect. The Italians are great
printers of letters; I do believe I have at least an hundred several
volumes of them; of all which those of Annibale Caro seem to me to be the
best. If all the paper I have scribbled to the ladies at the time when
my hand was really prompted by my passion, were now in being, there
might, peradventure, be found a page worthy to be communicated to our
young inamoratos, that are besotted with that fury. I always write my
letters post-haste--so precipitately, that though I write intolerably
ill, I rather choose to do it myself, than to employ another; for I can
find none able to follow me: and I never transcribe any. I have
accustomed the great ones who know me to endure my blots and dashes, and
upon paper without fold or margin. Those that cost me the most pains,
are the worst; when I once begin to draw it in by head and shoulders,
'tis a sign that I am not there. I fall too without premeditation or
design; the first word begets the second, and so to the end of the
chapter. The letters of this age consist more in fine edges and prefaces
than in matter. Just as I had rather write two letters than close and
fold up one, and always assign that employment to some other, so, when
the real business of my letter is dispatched, I would with all my heart
transfer it to another hand to add those long harangues, offers, and
prayers, that we place at the bottom, and should be glad that some new
custom would discharge us of that trouble; as also of superscribing them
with a long legend of qualities and titles, which for fear of mistakes,
I have often not written at all, and especially to men of the long robe
and finance; there are so many new offices, such a dispensation and
ordering of titles of honour, that 'tis hard to set them forth aright
yet, being so dearly bought, they are neither to be altered nor forgotten
without offence. I find it equally in bad taste to encumber the fronts
and inscriptions of the books we commit to the press with such.

CHAPTER XL

THAT THE RELISH FOR GOOD AND EVIL DEPENDS
IN GREAT MEASURE UPON THE OPINION
WE HAVE OF THEM

*Men (says an ancient Greek sentence)--[Manual of Epictetus, c. 10.]--
are tormented with the opinions they have of things and not by the things
themselves. It were a great victory obtained for the relief of our
miserable human condition, could this proposition be established for
certain and true throughout. For if evils have no admission into us but
by the judgment we ourselves make of them, it should seem that it is,
then, in our own power to despise them or to turn them to good. If
things surrender themselves to our mercy, why do we not convert and
accommodate them to our advantage? If what we call evil and torment is
neither evil nor torment of itself, but only that our fancy gives it that
quality, it is in us to change it, and it being in our own choice, if
there be no constraint upon us, we must certainly be very strange fools
to take arms for that side which is most offensive to us, and to give
sickness, want, and contempt a bitter and nauseous taste, if it be in our
power to give them a pleasant relish, and if, fortune simply providing
the matter, 'tis for us to give it the form. Now, that what we call evil
is not so of itself, or at least to that degree that we make it, and that
it depends upon us to give it another taste and complexion (for all comes
to one), let us examine how that can be maintained.*

*If the original being of those things we fear had power to lodge itself
in us by its own authority, it would then lodge itself alike, and in like
manner, in all; for men are all of the same kind, and saving in greater
and less proportions, are all provided with the same utensils and
instruments to conceive and to judge; but the diversity of opinions we
have of those things clearly evidences that they only enter us by*

composition; one person, peradventure, admits them in their true being, but a thousand others give them a new and contrary being in them. We hold death, poverty, and pain for our principal enemies; now, this death, which some repute the most dreadful of all dreadful things, who does not know that others call it the only secure harbour from the storms and tempests of life, the sovereign good of nature, the sole support of liberty, and the common and prompt remedy of all evils? And as the one expect it with fear and trembling, the others support it with greater ease than life. That one complains of its facility:

> "Mors! utinam pavidos vitae subducere nolles.
> Sed virtus to sola daret!"

> ["O death! wouldst that thou might spare the coward, but that
> valour alone should pay thee tribute."--Lucan, iv. 580.]

Now, let us leave these boastful courages. Theodorus answered Lysimachus, who threatened to kill him, "Thou wilt do a brave feat," said he, "to attain the force of a cantharides." The majority of philosophers are observed to have either purposely anticipated, or hastened and assisted their own death. How many ordinary people do we see led to execution, and that not to a simple death, but mixed with shame and sometimes with grievous torments, appear with such assurance, whether through firm courage or natural simplicity, that a man can discover no change from their ordinary condition; settling their domestic affairs, commending themselves to their friends, singing, preaching, and addressing the people, nay, sometimes sallying into jests, and drinking to their companions, quite as well as Socrates?

One that they were leading to the gallows told them they must not take him through such a street, lest a merchant who lived there should arrest him by the way for an old debt. Another told the hangman he must not touch his neck for fear of making him laugh, he was so ticklish. Another answered his confessor, who promised him he should that day sup with our Lord, "Do you go then," said he, "in my room [place]; for I for my part keep fast to-day." Another having called for drink, and the hangman

*having drunk first, said he would not drink after him, for fear of
catching some evil disease. Everybody has heard the tale of the Picard,
to whom, being upon the ladder, they presented a common wench, telling
him (as our law does some times permit) that if he would marry her they
would save his life; he, having a while considered her and perceiving
that she halted: "Come, tie up, tie up," said he, "she limps." And they
tell another story of the same kind of a fellow in Denmark, who being
condemned to lose his head, and the like condition being proposed to him
upon the scaffold, refused it, by reason the girl they offered him had
hollow cheeks and too sharp a nose. A servant at Toulouse being accused
of heresy, for the sum of his belief referred himself to that of his
master, a young student, prisoner with him, choosing rather to die than
suffer himself to be persuaded that his master could err. We read that
of the inhabitants of Arras, when Louis XI. took that city, a great many
let themselves be hanged rather than they would say, "God save the King."
And amongst that mean-souled race of men, the buffoons, there have been
some who would not leave their fooling at the very moment of death. One
that the hang man was turning off the ladder cried: "Launch the galley,"
an ordinary saying of his. Another, whom at the point of death his
friends had laid upon a bed of straw before the fire, the physician
asking him where his pain lay: "Betwixt the bench and the fire," said he,
and the priest, to give him extreme unction, groping for his feet which
his pain had made him pull up to him: "You will find them," said he, "at
the end of my legs." To one who being present exhorted him to recommend
himself to God: "Why, who goes thither?" said he; and the other
replying: "It will presently be yourself, if it be His good pleasure."
"Shall I be sure to be there by to-morrow night?" said he. "Do, but
recommend yourself to Him," said the other, "and you will soon be there."
"I were best then," said he, "to carry my recommendations myself."*

*In the kingdom of Narsingah to this day the wives of their priests are
buried alive with the bodies of their husbands; all other wives are burnt
at their husbands' funerals, which they not only firmly but cheerfully
undergo. At the death of their king, his wives and concubines, his
favourites, all his officers, and domestic servants, who make up a whole
people, present themselves so gaily to the fire where his body is burnt,*

*that they seem to take it for a singular honour to accompany their master
in death. During our late wars of Milan, where there happened so many
takings and retakings of towns, the people, impatient of so many changes
of fortune, took such a resolution to die, that I have heard my father
say he there saw a list taken of five-and-twenty masters of families who
made themselves away in one week's time: an incident somewhat resembling
that of the Xanthians, who being besieged by Brutus, fell--men, women,
and children--into such a furious appetite of dying, that nothing can be
done to evade death which they did not to avoid life; insomuch that
Brutus had much difficulty in saving a very small number.--["Only fifty
were saved."--Plutarch, Life of Brutus, c. 8.]*

*Every opinion is of force enough to cause itself to be espoused at the
expense of life. The first article of that valiant oath that Greece took
and observed in the Median war, was that every one should sooner exchange
life for death, than their own laws for those of Persia. What a world of
people do we see in the wars betwixt the Turks and the Greeks, rather
embrace a cruel death than uncircumcise themselves to admit of baptism?
An example of which no sort of religion is incapable.*

*The kings of Castile having banished the Jews out of their dominions,
John, King of Portugal, in consideration of eight crowns a head, sold
them a retreat into his for a certain limited time, upon condition that
the time fixed coming to expire they should begone, and he to furnish
them with shipping to transport them into Africa. The day comes, which
once lapsed they were given to understand that such as were afterward
found in the kingdom should remain slaves; vessels were very slenderly
provided; and those who embarked in them were rudely and villainously
used by the passengers, who, besides other indignities, kept them
cruising upon the sea, one while forwards and another backwards, till
they had spent all their provisions, and were constrained to buy of them
at so dear a rate and so long withal, that they set them not on shore
till they were all stripped to the very shirts. The news of this inhuman
usage being brought to those who remained behind, the greater part of
them resolved upon slavery and some made a show of changing religion.
Emmanuel, the successor of John, being come to the crown, first set them*

at liberty, and afterwards altering his mind, ordered them to depart his country, assigning three ports for their passage. He hoped, says Bishop Osorius, no contemptible Latin historian of these later times, that the favour of the liberty he had given them having failed of converting them to Christianity, yet the difficulty of committing themselves to the mercy of the mariners and of abandoning a country they were now habituated to and were grown very rich in, to go and expose themselves in strange and unknown regions, would certainly do it. But finding himself deceived in his expectation, and that they were all resolved upon the voyage, he cut off two of the three ports he had promised them, to the end that the length and incommodity of the passage might reduce some, or that he might have opportunity, by crowding them all into one place, the more conveniently to execute what he had designed, which was to force all the children under fourteen years of age from the arms of their fathers and mothers, to transport them from their sight and conversation, into a place where they might be instructed and brought up in our religion. He says that this produced a most horrid spectacle the natural affection betwixt the parents and their children, and moreover their zeal to their ancient belief, contending against this violent decree, fathers and mothers were commonly seen making themselves away, and by a yet much more rigorous example, precipitating out of love and compassion their young children into wells and pits, to avoid the severity of this law. As to the remainder of them, the time that had been prefixed being expired, for want of means to transport them they again returned into slavery. Some also turned Christians, upon whose faith, as also that of their posterity, even to this day, which is a hundred years since, few Portuguese can yet rely; though custom and length of time are much more powerful counsellors in such changes than all other constraints whatever. In the town of Castelnaudari, fifty heretic Albigeois at one time suffered themselves to be burned alive in one fire rather than they would renounce their opinions.

"Quoties non modo ductores nostri, sed universi etiam exercitus, ad non dubiam mortem concurrerunt?"

["How often have not only our leaders, but whole armies, run to a certain and manifest death."--Cicero, Tusc. Quaes., i. 37.]

I have seen an intimate friend of mine run headlong upon death with a real affection, and that was rooted in his heart by divers plausible arguments which he would never permit me to dispossess him of, and upon the first honourable occasion that offered itself to him, precipitate himself into it, without any manner of visible reason, with an obstinate and ardent desire of dying. We have several examples in our own times of persons, even young children, who for fear of some little inconvenience have despatched themselves. And what shall we not fear, says one of the ancients--[Seneca, Ep., 70.]--to this purpose, if we dread that which cowardice itself has chosen for its refuge?

Should I here produce a long catalogue of those, of all sexes and conditions and sects, even in the most happy ages, who have either with great constancy looked death in the face, or voluntarily sought it, and sought it not only to avoid the evils of this life, but some purely to avoid the satiety of living, and others for the hope of a better condition elsewhere, I should never have done. Nay, the number is so infinite that in truth I should have a better bargain on't to reckon up those who have feared it. This one therefore shall serve for all: Pyrrho the philosopher being one day in a boat in a very great tempest, shewed to those he saw the most affrighted about him, and encouraged them, by the example of a hog that was there, nothing at all concerned at the storm. Shall we then dare to say that this advantage of reason, of which we so much boast, and upon the account of which we think ourselves masters and emperors over the rest of all creation, was given us for a torment? To what end serves the knowledge of things if it renders us more unmanly? if we thereby lose the tranquillity and repose we should enjoy without it? and if it put us into a worse condition than Pyrrho's hog? Shall we employ the understanding that was conferred upon us for our greatest good to our own ruin; setting ourselves against the design of nature and the universal order of things, which intend that every one should make use of the faculties, members, and means he has to his own best advantage?

But it may, peradventure, be objected against me: Your rule is true
enough as to what concerns death; but what will you say of indigence?
What will you, moreover, say of pain, which Aristippus, Hieronimus, and
most of the sages have reputed the worst of evils; and those who have
denied it by word of mouth have, however, confessed it in effect?
Posidonius being extremely tormented with a sharp and painful disease,
Pompeius came to visit him, excusing himself that he had taken so
unseasonable a time to come to hear him discourse of philosophy.
"The gods forbid," said Posidonius to him, "that pain should ever have
the power to hinder me from talking," and thereupon fell immediately upon
a discourse of the contempt of pain: but, in the meantime, his own
infirmity was playing his part, and plagued him to purpose; to which he
cried out, "Thou mayest work thy will, pain, and torment me with all the
power thou hast, but thou shalt never make me say that thou art an evil."
This story that they make such a clutter withal, what has it to do,
I fain would know, with the contempt of pain? He only fights it with
words, and in the meantime, if the shootings and dolours he felt did not
move him, why did he interrupt his discourse? Why did he fancy he did so
great a thing in forbearing to confess it an evil? All does not here
consist in the imagination; our fancies may work upon other things: but
here is the certain science that is playing its part, of which our senses
themselves are judges:

"Qui nisi sunt veri, ratio quoque falsa sit omnis."

["Which, if they be not true, all reasoning may also be false.
✍"Lucretius, iv. 486.]

Shall we persuade our skins that the jerks of a whip agreeably tickle us,
or our taste that a potion of aloes is vin de Graves? Pyrrho's hog is
here in the same predicament with us; he is not afraid of death, 'tis
true, but if you beat him he will cry out to some purpose. Shall we
force the general law of nature, which in every living creature under
heaven is seen to tremble under pain? The very trees seem to groan under

*the blows they receive. Death is only felt by reason, forasmuch as it is
the motion of an instant;*

> *"Aut fuit, aut veniet; nihil est praesentis in illa."*

> *["Death has been, or will come: there is nothing of the present in
> it."--Estienne de la Boetie, Satires.]*

> *"Morsque minus poenae, quam mora mortis, habet;"*

> *["The delay of death is more painful than death itself."
> --Ovid, Ep. Ariadne to Theseus, v. 42.]*

*a thousand beasts, a thousand men, are sooner dead than threatened. That
also which we principally pretend to fear in death is pain, its ordinary
forerunner: yet, if we may believe a holy father:*

> *"Malam mortem non facit, nisi quod sequitur mortem."*

> *["That which follows death makes death bad."
> --St. Augustin, De Civit. Dei, i. ii.]*

*And I should yet say, more probably, that neither that which goes before
nor that which follows after is at all of the appurtenances of death.*

*We excuse ourselves falsely: and I find by experience that it is rather
the impatience of the imagination of death that makes us impatient of
pain, and that we find it doubly grievous as it threatens us with death.
But reason accusing our cowardice for fearing a thing so sudden, so
inevitable, and so insensible, we take the other as the more excusable
pretence. All ills that carry no other danger along with them but simply
the evils themselves, we treat as things of no danger: the toothache or
the gout, painful as they are, yet being not reputed mortal, who reckons
them in the catalogue of diseases?*

But let us presuppose that in death we principally regard the pain; as also there is nothing to be feared in poverty but the miseries it brings along with it of thirst, hunger, cold, heat, watching, and the other inconveniences it makes us suffer, still we have nothing to do with anything but pain. I will grant, and very willingly, that it is the worst incident of our being (for I am the man upon earth who the most hates and avoids it, considering that hitherto, I thank God, I have had so little traffic with it), but still it is in us, if not to annihilate, at least to lessen it by patience; and though the body and the reason should mutiny, to maintain the soul, nevertheless, in good condition. Were it not so, who had ever given reputation to virtue; valour, force, magnanimity, and resolution? where were their parts to be played if there were no pain to be defied?

> *"Avida est periculi virtus."*

> [*"Courage is greedy of danger."*--Seneca, De Providentia, c. 4]

Were there no lying upon the hard ground, no enduring, armed at all points, the meridional heats, no feeding upon the flesh of horses and asses, no seeing a man's self hacked and hewed to pieces, no suffering a bullet to be pulled out from amongst the shattered bones, no sewing up, cauterising and searching of wounds, by what means were the advantage we covet to have over the vulgar to be acquired? 'Tis far from flying evil and pain, what the sages say, that of actions equally good, a man should most covet to perform that wherein there is greater labour and pain.

> *"Non est enim hilaritate, nec lascivia, nec risu, aut joco comite levitatis, sed saepe etiam tristes firmitate et constantia sunt beati."*

> [*"For men are not only happy by mirth and wantonness, by laughter and jesting, the companion of levity, but ofttimes the serious sort reap felicity from their firmness and constancy."* --Cicero, De Finib. ii. 10.]

And for this reason it has ever been impossible to persuade our forefathers but that the victories obtained by dint of force and the hazard of war were not more honourable than those performed in great security by stratagem or practice:

> *"Laetius est, quoties magno sibi constat honestum."*

> *["A good deed is all the more a satisfaction by how much the more it has cost us"--Lucan, ix. 404.]*

Besides, this ought to be our comfort, that naturally, if the pain be violent, 'tis but short; and if long, nothing violent:

> *"Si gravis, brevis;*
> *Si longus, levis."*

Thou wilt not feel it long if thou feelest it too much; it will either put an end to itself or to thee; it comes to the same thing; if thou canst not support it, it will export thee:

> *["Remember that the greatest pains are terminated by death; that slighter pains have long intermissions of repose, and that we are masters of the more moderate sort: so that, if they be tolerable, we bear them; if not, we can go out of life, as from a theatre, when it does not please us"--Cicero, De Finib. i. 15.]*

That which makes us suffer pain with so much impatience is the not being accustomed to repose our chiefest contentment in the soul; that we do not enough rely upon her who is the sole and sovereign mistress of our condition. The body, saving in the greater or less proportion, has but one and the same bent and bias; whereas the soul is variable into all sorts of forms; and subject to herself and to her own empire, all things whatsoever, both the senses of the body and all other accidents: and therefore it is that we ought to study her, to inquire into her, and to rouse up all her powerful faculties. There is neither reason, force, nor prescription that can anything prevail against her inclination and choice. Of so many thousands of biases that she has at her disposal, let us give her one proper to our repose and conversation, and then we shall not only be sheltered and secured from all manner of injury and offence, but moreover gratified and obliged, if she will, with evils and offences. She makes her profit indifferently of all things; error, dreams, serve her to good use, as loyal matter to lodge us in safety and contentment. 'Tis plain enough to be seen that 'tis the sharpness of our mind that gives the edge to our pains and pleasures: beasts that have no such thing, leave to their bodies their own free and natural sentiments, and consequently in every kind very near the same, as appears by the resembling application of their motions. If we would not disturb in our members the jurisdiction that appertains to them in this, 'tis to be believed it would be the better for us, and that nature has given them a just and moderate temper both to pleasure and pain; neither can it fail of being just, being equal and common. But seeing we have enfranchised ourselves from her rules to give ourselves up to the rambling liberty of our own fancies, let us at least help to incline them to the most agreeable side. Plato fears our too vehemently engaging ourselves with pain and pleasure, forasmuch as these too much knit and ally the soul to the body; whereas I rather, quite contrary, by reason it too much separates and disunites them. As an enemy is made more fierce by our flight, so pain grows proud to see us truckle under her. She will surrender upon much better terms to them who make head against her: a man must oppose and stoutly set himself against her. In retiring and giving ground, we invite and pull upon ourselves the ruin that threatens us. As the body is more firm in an encounter, the more stiffly and obstinately it applies itself to it, so is it with the soul.

But let us come to examples, which are the proper game of folks of such feeble force as myself; where we shall find that it is with pain as with stones, that receive a brighter or a duller lustre according to the foil they are set in, and that it has no more room in us than we are pleased to allow it:

"*Tantum doluerunt, quantum doloribus se inseruerunt.*"

[*"They suffered so much the more, by how much more they gave way to suffering."*--St. Augustin, De Civit. Dei, i. 10.]

We are more sensible of one little touch of a surgeon's lancet than of twenty wounds with a sword in the heat of fight. The pains of childbearing, said by the physicians and by God himself to be great, and which we pass through with so many ceremonies--there are whole nations that make nothing of them. I set aside the Lacedaemonian women, but what else do you find in the Swiss among our foot-soldiers, if not that, as they trot after their husbands, you see them to-day carry the child at their necks that they carried yesterday in their bellies? The counterfeit Egyptians we have amongst us go themselves to wash theirs, so soon as they come into the world, and bathe in the first river they meet. Besides so many wenches as daily drop their children by stealth, as they conceived them, that fair and noble wife of Sabinus, a patrician of Rome, for another's interest, endured alone, without help, without crying out, or so much as a groan, the bearing of twins.--[Plutarch, On Love, c. 34.]--A poor simple boy of Lacedaemon having stolen a fox (for they more fear the shame of stupidity in stealing than we do the punishment of the knavery), and having got it under his coat, rather endured the tearing out of his bowels than he would discover his theft. And another offering incense at a sacrifice, suffered himself to be burned to the bone by a coal that fell into his sleeve, rather than disturb the ceremony. And there have been a great number, for a sole trial of virtue, following their institutions, who have at seven years old endured to be whipped to death without changing their countenance. And Cicero has seen them fight in parties, with fists, feet, and teeth, till they have fainted and sunk down, rather than confess themselves overcome:

[*"Custom could never conquer nature; she is ever invincible; but we have infected the mind with shadows, delights, negligence, sloth; we have grown effeminate through opinions and corrupt morality."* --Cicero, Tusc. Quaes., v. 27.]

Every one knows the story of Scaevola, that having slipped into the enemy's camp to kill their general, and having missed his blow, to repair his fault, by a more strange invention and to deliver his country, he boldly confessed to Porsenna, who was the king he had a purpose to kill, not only his design, but moreover added that there were then in the camp a great number of Romans, his accomplices in the enterprise, as good men as he; and to show what a one he himself was, having caused a pan of burning coals to be brought, he saw and endured his arm to broil and roast, till the king himself, conceiving horror at the sight, commanded the pan to be taken away. What would you say of him that would not vouchsafe to respite his reading in a book whilst he was under incision? And of the other that persisted to mock and laugh in contempt of the pains inflicted upon him; so that the provoked cruelty of the executioners that had him in handling, and all the inventions of tortures redoubled upon him, one after another, spent in vain, gave him the bucklers? But he was a philosopher. But what! a gladiator of Caesar's endured, laughing all the while, his wounds to be searched, lanced, and laid open:

["What ordinary gladiator ever groaned? Which of them ever changed countenance? Which of them not only stood or fell indecorously? Which, when he had fallen and was commanded to receive the stroke of the sword, contracted his neck."--Cicero, Tusc. Quaes., ii. 17.]

Let us bring in the women too. Who has not heard at Paris of her that caused her face to be flayed only for the fresher complexion of a new skin? There are who have drawn good and sound teeth to make their voices more soft and sweet, or to place the other teeth in better order. How many examples of the contempt of pain have we in that sex? What can they not do, what do they fear to do, for never so little hope of an addition to their beauty?

> *"Vallere queis cura est albos a stirpe capillos,*
> *Et faciem, dempta pelle, referre novam."*

["Who carefully pluck out their grey hairs by the roots, and renew
their faces by peeling off the old skin."--Tibullus, i. 8, 45.]

I have seen some of them swallow sand, ashes, and do their utmost to
destroy their stomachs to get pale complexions. To make a fine Spanish
body, what racks will they not endure of girding and bracing, till they
have notches in their sides cut into the very quick, and sometimes to
death?

It is an ordinary thing with several nations at this day to wound
themselves in good earnest to gain credit to what they profess; of which
our king, relates notable examples of what he has seen in Poland and done
towards himself.--[Henry III.]--But besides this, which I know to have
been imitated by some in France, when I came from that famous assembly of
the Estates at Blois, I had a little before seen a maid in Picardy, who
to manifest the ardour of her promises, as also her constancy, give
herself, with a bodkin she wore in her hair, four or five good lusty
stabs in the arm, till the blood gushed out to some purpose. The Turks
give themselves great scars in honour of their mistresses, and to the end
they may the longer remain, they presently clap fire to the wound, where
they hold it an incredible time to stop the blood and form the cicatrice;
people that have been eyewitnesses of it have both written and sworn it
to me. But for ten aspers--[A Turkish coin worth about a penny]--there
are there every day fellows to be found that will give themselves a good
deep slash in the arms or thighs. I am willing, however, to have the
testimonies nearest to us when we have most need of them; for Christendom
furnishes us with enough. After the example of our blessed Guide there
have been many who have crucified themselves. We learn by testimony very
worthy of belief, that King St. Louis wore a hair-shirt till in his old
age his confessor gave him a dispensation to leave it off; and that every
Friday he caused his shoulders to be drubbed by his priest with five
small chains of iron which were always carried about amongst his night
accoutrements for that purpose.

William, our last Duke of Guienne, the father of that Eleanor who
transmitted that duchy to the houses of France and England, continually

for the last ten or twelve years of his life wore a suit of armour under
a religious habit by way of penance. Foulke, Count of Anjou, went as far
as Jerusalem, there to cause himself to be whipped by two of his
servants, with a rope about his neck, before the sepulchre of our Lord.
But do we not, moreover, every Good Friday, in various places, see great
numbers of men and women beat and whip themselves till they lacerate and
cut the flesh to the very bones? I have often seen it, and 'tis without
any enchantment; and it was said there were some amongst them (for they
go disguised) who for money undertook by this means to save harmless the
religion of others, by a contempt of pain, so much the greater, as the
incentives of devotion are more effectual than those of avarice.
Q. Maximus buried his son when he was a consul, and M. Cato his when
praetor elect, and L. Paulus both his, within a few days one after
another, with such a countenance as expressed no manner of grief. I said
once merrily of a certain person, that he had disappointed the divine
justice; for the violent death of three grown-up children of his being
one day sent him, for a severe scourge, as it is to be supposed, he was
so far from being afflicted at the accident, that he rather took it for a
particular grace and favour of heaven. I do not follow these monstrous
humours, though I lost two or three at nurse, if not without grief, at
least without repining, and yet there is hardly any accident that pierces
nearer to the quick. I see a great many other occasions of sorrow, that
should they happen to me I should hardly feel; and have despised some,
when they have befallen me, to which the world has given so terrible a
figure that I should blush to boast of my constancy:

> *"Ex quo intelligitur, non in natura, sed in opinione,*
> *esse aegritudinem."*

> *["By which one may understand that grief is not in nature, but in*
> *opinion."—Cicero, Tusc. Quaes., iii. 28.]*

Opinion is a powerful party, bold, and without measure. Who ever so
greedily hunted after security and repose as Alexander and Caesar did
after disturbance and difficulties? Teres, the father of Sitalces, was
wont to say that "when he had no wars, he fancied there was no difference

*betwixt him and his groom." Cato the consul, to secure some cities of
Spain from revolt, only interdicting the inhabitants from wearing arms, a
great many killed themselves:*

> *"Ferox gens, nullam vitam rati sine armis esse."*

> *["A fierce people, who thought there was no life without war."
> ~Livy, xxxiv. 17.]*

*How many do we know who have forsaken the calm and sweetness of a quiet
life at home amongst their acquaintance, to seek out the horror of
unhabitable deserts; and having precipitated themselves into so abject a
condition as to become the scorn and contempt of the world, have hugged
themselves with the conceit, even to affectation. Cardinal Borromeo, who
died lately at Milan, amidst all the jollity that the air of Italy, his
youth, birth, and great riches, invited him to, kept himself in so
austere a way of living, that the same robe he wore in summer served him
for winter too; he had only straw for his bed, and his hours of leisure
from affairs he continually spent in study upon his knees, having a
little bread and a glass of water set by his book, which was all the
provision of his repast, and all the time he spent in eating.*

*I know some who consentingly have acquired both profit and advancement
from cuckoldom, of which the bare name only affrights so many people.*

*If the sight be not the most necessary of all our senses, 'tis at least
the most pleasant; but the most pleasant and most useful of all our
members seem to be those of generation; and yet a great many have
conceived a mortal hatred against them only for this, that they were too
pleasant, and have deprived themselves of them only for their value:
as much thought he of his eyes that put them out. The generality and
more solid sort of men look upon abundance of children as a great
blessing; I, and some others, think it as great a benefit to be without
them. And when you ask Thales why he does not marry, he tells you,
because he has no mind to leave any posterity behind him.*

That our opinion gives the value to things is very manifest in the great number of those which we do, not so much prizing them, as ourselves, and never considering either their virtues or their use, but only how dear they cost us, as though that were a part of their substance; and we only repute for value in them, not what they bring to us, but what we add to them. By which I understand that we are great economisers of our expense: as it weighs, it serves for so much as it weighs. Our opinion will never suffer it to want of its value: the price gives value to the diamond; difficulty to virtue; suffering to devotion; and griping to physic. A certain person, to be poor, threw his crowns into the same sea to which so many come, in all parts of the world, to fish for riches. Epicurus says that to be rich is no relief, but only an alteration, of affairs. In truth, it is not want, but rather abundance, that creates avarice. I will deliver my own experience concerning this affair.

I have since my emergence from childhood lived in three sorts of conditions. The first, which continued for some twenty years, I passed over without any other means but what were casual and depending upon the allowance and assistance of others, without stint, but without certain revenue. I then spent my money so much the more cheerfully, and with so much the less care how it went, as it wholly depended upon my overconfidence of fortune. I never lived more at my ease; I never had the repulse of finding the purse of any of my friends shut against me, having enjoined myself this necessity above all other necessities whatever, by no means to fail of payment at the appointed time, which also they have a thousand times respited, seeing how careful I was to satisfy them; so that I practised at once a thrifty, and withal a kind of alluring, honesty. I naturally feel a kind of pleasure in paying, as if I eased my shoulders of a troublesome weight and freed myself from an image of slavery; as also that I find a ravishing kind of satisfaction in pleasing another and doing a just action. I except payments where the trouble of bargaining and reckoning is required; and in such cases; where I can meet with nobody to ease me of that charge, I delay them, how scandalously and injuriously soever, all I possibly can, for fear of the wranglings for which both my humour and way of speaking are so totally improper and unfit. There is nothing I hate so much as driving a bargain; 'tis a mere traffic of cozenage and impudence, where, after an hour's cheapening and hesitating, both parties abandon their word and oath for five sols' abatement. Yet I always borrowed at great disadvantage; for, wanting the confidence to speak to the person myself, I committed my request to the persuasion of a letter, which usually is no very successful advocate, and is of very great advantage to him who has a mind to deny. I, in those days, more jocundly and freely referred the conduct of my affairs to the stars, than I have since done to my own providence and judgment. Most good managers look upon it as a horrible thing to live always thus in uncertainty, and do not consider, in the first place, that the greatest part of the world live so: how many worthy men have wholly abandoned their own certainties, and yet daily do it, to the winds, to trust to the inconstant favour of princes and of fortune? Caesar ran above a million of gold, more than he was worth, in debt to become Caesar; and how many merchants have begun their traffic by the sale of their farms, which they sent into the Indies,

"Tot per impotentia freta."

["Through so many ungovernable seas."--Catullus, iv. 18.]

In so great a siccity of devotion as we see in these days, we have a thousand and a thousand colleges that pass it over commodiously enough, expecting every day their dinner from the liberality of Heaven. Secondly, they do not take notice that this certitude upon which they so much rely is not much less uncertain and hazardous than hazard itself. I see misery as near beyond two thousand crowns a year as if it stood close by me; for besides that it is in the power of chance to make a hundred breaches to poverty through the greatest strength of our riches --there being very often no mean betwixt the highest and the lowest fortune:

"Fortuna vitrea est: turn, quum splendet, frangitur,"

["Fortune is glass: in its greatest brightness it breaks." --Ex Mim. P. Syrus.]

and to turn all our barricadoes and bulwarks topsy-turvy, I find that, by divers causes, indigence is as frequently seen to inhabit with those who have estates as with those that have none; and that, peradventure, it is then far less grievous when alone than when accompanied with riches. These flow more from good management than from revenue;

"Faber est suae quisque fortunae"

["Every one is the maker of his own fortune."
--Sallust, De Repub. Ord., i. I.]

and an uneasy, necessitous, busy, rich man seems to me more miserable than he that is simply poor.

"In divitiis mopes, quod genus egestatis gravissimum est."

["Poor in the midst of riches, which is the sorest kind of poverty."
--Seneca, Ep., 74.]

The greatest and most wealthy princes are by poverty and want driven to the most extreme necessity; for can there be any more extreme than to become tyrants and unjust usurpers of their subjects' goods and estates?

My second condition of life was to have money of my own, wherein I so ordered the matter that I had soon laid up a very notable sum out of a mean fortune, considering with myself that that only was to be reputed having which a man reserves from his ordinary expense, and that a man cannot absolutely rely upon revenue he hopes to receive, how clear soever the hope may be. For what, said I, if I should be surprised by such or such an accident? And after such-like vain and vicious imaginations, would very learnedly, by this hoarding of money, provide against all inconveniences; and could, moreover, answer such as objected to me that the number of these was too infinite, that if I could not lay up for all, I could, however, do it at least for some and for many. Yet was not this done without a great deal of solicitude and anxiety of mind; I kept it

*very close, and though I dare talk so boldly of myself, never spoke of my
money, but falsely, as others do, who being rich, pretend to be poor, and
being poor, pretend to be rich, dispensing their consciences from ever
telling sincerely what they have: a ridiculous and shameful prudence.
Was I going a journey? Methought I was never enough provided: and the
more I loaded myself with money, the more also was I loaded with fear,
one while of the danger of the roads, another of the fidelity of him who
had the charge of my baggage, of whom, as some others that I know, I was
never sufficiently secure if I had him not always in my eye. If I
chanced to leave my cash-box behind me, O, what strange suspicions and
anxiety of mind did I enter into, and, which was worse, without daring to
acquaint anybody with it. My mind was eternally taken up with such
things as these, so that, all things considered, there is more trouble in
keeping money than in getting it. And if I did not altogether so much as
I say, or was not really so scandalously solicitous of my money as I have
made myself out to be, yet it cost me something at least to restrain
myself from being so. I reaped little or no advantage by what I had, and
my expenses seemed nothing less to me for having the more to spend; for,
as Bion said, the hairy men are as angry as the bald to be pulled; and
after you are once accustomed to it and have once set your heart upon
your heap, it is no more at your service; you cannot find in your heart
to break it: 'tis a building that you will fancy must of necessity all
tumble down to ruin if you stir but the least pebble; necessity must
first take you by the throat before you can prevail upon yourself to
touch it; and I would sooner have pawned anything I had, or sold a horse,
and with much less constraint upon myself, than have made the least
breach in that beloved purse I had so carefully laid by. But the danger
was that a man cannot easily prescribe certain limits to this desire
(they are hard to find in things that a man conceives to be good), and to
stint this good husbandry so that it may not degenerate into avarice: men
still are intent upon adding to the heap and increasing the stock from
sum to sum, till at last they vilely deprive themselves of the enjoyment
of their own proper goods, and throw all into reserve, without making any
use of them at all. According to this rule, they are the richest people
in the world who are set to guard the walls and gates of a wealthy city.
All moneyed men I conclude to be covetous. Plato places corporal or*

human goods in this order: health, beauty, strength, riches; and riches, says he, are not blind, but very clear-sighted, when illuminated by prudence. Dionysius the son did a very handsome act upon this subject; he was informed that one of the Syracusans had hid a treasure in the earth, and thereupon sent to the man to bring it to him, which he accordingly did, privately reserving a small part of it only to himself, with which he went to another city, where being cured of his appetite of hoarding, he began to live at a more liberal rate; which Dionysius hearing, caused the rest of his treasure to be restored to him, saying, that since he had learned to use it, he very willingly returned it back to him.

I continued some years in this hoarding humour, when I know not what good demon fortunately put me out of it, as he did the Syracusan, and made me throw abroad all my reserve at random, the pleasure of a certain journey I took at very great expense having made me spurn this fond love of money underfoot; by which means I am now fallen into a third way of living (I speak what I think of it), doubtless much more pleasant and regular, which is, that I live at the height of my revenue; sometimes the one, sometimes the other may perhaps exceed, but 'tis very little and but rarely that they differ. I live from hand to mouth, and content myself in having sufficient for my present and ordinary expense; for as to extraordinary occasions, all the laying up in the world would never suffice. And 'tis the greatest folly imaginable to expect that fortune should ever sufficiently arm us against herself; 'tis with our own arms that we are to fight her; accidental ones will betray us in the pinch of the business. If I lay up, 'tis for some near and contemplated purpose; not to purchase lands, of which I have no need, but to purchase pleasure:

"Non esse cupidum, pecunia est; non esse emacem, vertigal est."

["Not to be covetous, is money; not to be acquisitive, is revenue." ⸺Cicero, Paradox., vi. 3.]

I neither am in any great apprehension of wanting, nor in desire of any more:

"Divinarum fructus est in copia; copiam declarat satietas."

["The fruit of riches is in abundance; satiety declares abundance."
⸺Idem, ibid., vi. 2.]

And I am very well pleased that this reformation in me has fallen out in an age naturally inclined to avarice, and that I see myself cleared of a folly so common to old men, and the most ridiculous of all human follies.

Feraulez, a man that had run through both fortunes, and found that the increase of substance was no increase of appetite either to eating or drinking, sleeping or the enjoyment of his wife, and who on the other side felt the care of his economics lie heavy upon his shoulders, as it does on mine, was resolved to please a poor young man, his faithful friend, who panted after riches, and made him a gift of all his, which were excessively great, and, moreover, of all he was in the daily way of getting by the liberality of Cyrus, his good master, and by the war; conditionally that he should take care handsomely to maintain and plentifully to entertain him as his guest and friend; which being accordingly done, they afterwards lived very happily together, both of them equally content with the change of their condition. 'Tis an example that I could imitate with all my heart; and I very much approve the fortune of the aged prelate whom I see to have so absolutely stripped himself of his purse, his revenue, and care of his expense, committing them one while to one trusty servant, and another while to another, that he has spun out a long succession of years, as ignorant, by this means, of his domestic affairs as a mere stranger.

The confidence in another man's virtue is no light evidence of a man's own, and God willingly favours such a confidence. As to what concerns him of whom I am speaking, I see nowhere a better governed house, more nobly and constantly maintained than his. Happy to have regulated his affairs to so just a proportion that his estate is sufficient to do it without his care or trouble, and without any hindrance, either in the *spending or laying it up, to his other more quiet employments, and more suitable both to his place and liking.*

Plenty, then, and indigence depend upon the opinion every one has of them; and riches no more than glory or health have other beauty or pleasure than he lends them by whom they are possessed.

Every one is well or ill at ease, according as he so finds himself; not he whom the world believes, but he who believes himself to be so, is content; and in this alone belief gives itself being and reality. Fortune does us neither good nor hurt; she only presents us the matter and the seed, which our soul, more powerful than she, turns and applies as she best pleases; the sole cause and sovereign mistress of her own happy or unhappy condition. All external accessions receive taste and colour from the internal constitution, as clothes warm us, not with their heat, but our own, which they are fit to cover and nourish; he who would shield therewith a cold body, would do the same service for the cold, for so snow and ice are preserved. And, certes, after the same manner that study is a torment to an idle man, abstinence from wine to a drunkard, frugality to the spendthrift, and exercise to a lazy, tender-bred fellow, so it is of all the rest. The things are not so painful and difficult of themselves, but our weakness or cowardice makes them so. To judge of great, and high matters requires a suitable soul; otherwise we attribute the vice to them which is really our own. A straight oar seems crooked in the water it does not only import that we see the thing, but how and after what manner we see it.

After all this, why, amongst so many discourses that by so many arguments persuade men to despise death and to endure pain, can we not find out one that helps us? And of so many sorts of imaginations as have so prevailed upon others as to persuade them to do so, why does not every one apply some one to himself, the most suitable to his own humour? If he cannot digest a strong-working decoction to eradicate the evil, let him at least take a lenitive to ease it:

*["It is an effeminate and flimsy opinion, nor more so in pain than
in pleasure, in which, while we are at our ease, we cannot bear
without a cry the sting of a bee. The whole business is to commend
thyself."--Cicero, Tusc. Quaes., ii. 22.]*

*As to the rest, a man does not transgress philosophy by permitting the
acrimony of pains and human frailty to prevail so much above measure; for
they constrain her to go back to her unanswerable replies: "If it be ill
to live in necessity, at least there is no necessity upon a man to live
in necessity": "No man continues ill long but by his own fault." He who
has neither the courage to die nor the heart to live, who will neither
resist nor fly, what can we do with him?*

CHAPTER XLI

NOT TO COMMUNICATE A MAN'S HONOUR

Of all the follies of the world, that which is most universally received is the solicitude of reputation and glory; which we are fond of to that degree as to abandon riches, peace, life, and health, which are effectual and substantial goods, to pursue this vain phantom and empty word, that has neither body nor hold to be taken of it:

> *La fama, ch'invaghisce a un dolce suono*
> *Gli superbi mortali, et par si bella,*
> *E un eco, un sogno, anzi d'un sogno un'ombra,*
> *Ch'ad ogni vento si dilegua a sgombra."*

> *["Fame, which with alluring sound charms proud mortals, and appears so fair, is but an echo, a dream, nay, the shadow of a dream, which at every breath vanishes and dissolves."*
> *⁓Tasso, Gerus., xiv. 63.]*

And of all the irrational humours of men, it should seem that the philosophers themselves are among the last and the most reluctant to disengage themselves from this: 'tis the most restive and obstinate of all:

> *"Quia etiam bene proficientes animos tentare non cessat."*

> *["Because it ceases not to assail even well-directed minds"*
> *⁓St. Augustin, De Civit. Dei, v. 14.]*

There is not any one of which reason so clearly accuses the vanity; but it is so deeply rooted in us that I dare not determine whether any one ever clearly discharged himself from it or no. After you have said all and believed all has been said to its prejudice, it produces so intestine an inclination in opposition to your best arguments that you have little power to resist it; for, as Cicero says, even those who most controvert it, would yet that the books they write about it should visit the light under their own names, and seek to derive glory from seeming to despise it. All other things are communicable and fall into commerce: we lend our goods and stake our lives for the necessity and service of our friends; but to communicate a man's honour, and to robe another with a man's own glory, is very rarely seen.

And yet we have some examples of that kind. Catulus Luctatius in the Cimbrian war, having done all that in him lay to make his flying soldiers face about upon the enemy, ran himself at last away with the rest, and counterfeited the coward, to the end his men might rather seem to follow their captain than to fly from the enemy; which was to abandon his own reputation in order to cover the shame of others. When Charles V. came into Provence in the year 1537, 'tis said that Antonio de Leva, seeing the emperor positively resolved upon this expedition, and believing it would redound very much to his honour, did, nevertheless, very stiffly oppose it in the council, to the end that the entire glory of that resolution should be attributed to his master, and that it might be said his own wisdom and foresight had been such as that, contrary to the opinion of all, he had brought about so great an enterprise; which was to do him honour at his own expense. The Thracian ambassadors coming to comfort Archileonida, the mother of Brasidas, upon the death of her son, and commending him to that height as to say he had not left his like behind him, she rejected this private and particular commendation to attribute it to the public: "Tell me not that," said she; "I know the city of Sparta has many citizens both greater and of greater worth than he." In the battle of Crecy, the Prince of Wales, being then very young, had the vanguard committed to him: the main stress of the battle happened to be in that place, which made the lords who were with him, finding themselves overmatched, send to King Edward to advance to their relief. He inquired of the condition his son was in, and being answered that he was alive and on horseback: "I should, then, do him wrong," said the king, "now to go and deprive him of the honour of winning this battle he has so long and so bravely sustained; what hazard soever he runs, that shall be entirely his own"; and, accordingly, would neither go nor send, knowing that if he went, it would be said all had been lost without his succour, and that the honour of the victory would be wholly attributed to him.

> "Semper enim quod postremum adjectum est,
> id rem totam videtur traxisse."

[*"For always that which is last added, seems to have accomplished the whole affair."--Livy, xxvii. 45.*]

Many at Rome thought, and would usually say, that the greatest of Scipio's acts were in part due to Laelius, whose constant practice it was still to advance and support Scipio's grandeur and renown, without any care of his own. And Theopompus, king of Sparta, to him who told him the republic could not miscarry since he knew so well how to command, "'Tis rather," answered he, "because the people know so well how to obey." As women succeeding to peerages had, notwithstanding their sex, the privilege to attend and give their votes in the trials that appertained to the jurisdiction of peers; so the ecclesiastical peers, notwithstanding their profession, were obliged to attend our kings in their wars, not only with their friends and servants, but in their own persons. As the Bishop of Beauvais did, who being with Philip Augustus at the battle of Bouvines, had a notable share in that action; but he did not think it fit for him to participate in the fruit and glory of that violent and bloody trade. He with his own hand reduced several of the enemy that day to his mercy, whom he delivered to the first gentleman he met either to kill or receive them to quarter, referring the whole execution to this other hand; and he did this with regard to William, Earl of Salisbury, whom he gave up to Messire Jehan de Nesle. With a like subtlety of conscience to that I have just named, he would kill but not wound, and for that reason ever fought with a mace. And a certain person of my time, being reproached by the king that he had laid hands on a priest, stiffly and positively denied he had done any such thing: the meaning of which was, he had cudgelled and kicked him.

CHAPTER XLII

OF THE INEQUALITY AMOUNGST US

Plutarch says somewhere that he does not find so great a difference betwixt beast and beast as he does betwixt man and man; which he says in reference to the internal qualities and perfections of the soul. And, in truth, I find so vast a distance betwixt Epaminondas, according to my judgment of him, and some that I know, who are yet men of good sense, that I could willingly enhance upon Plutarch, and say that there is more difference betwixt such and such a man than there is betwixt such a man and such a beast:

> *["Ah! how much may one man surpass another!"*
> *--Terence, Eunuchus, ii. 2.]*

and that there are as many and innumerable degrees of mind as there are cubits betwixt this and heaven. But as touching the estimate of men, 'tis strange that, ourselves excepted, no other creature is esteemed beyond its proper qualities; we commend a horse for his strength and sureness of foot,

> *"Volucrem*
> *Sic laudamus equum, facili cui plurima palma*
> *Fervet, et exsultat rauco victoria circo,"*

> *["So we praise the swift horse, for whose easy mastery many a hand glows in applause, and victory exults in the hoarse circus.*
> *--"Juvenal, viii. 57.]*

and not for his rich caparison; a greyhound for his speed of heels, not for his fine collar; a hawk for her wing, not for her gesses and bells. Why, in like manner, do we not value a man for what is properly his own?

*He has a great train, a beautiful palace, so much credit, so many
thousand pounds a year: all these are about him, but not in him. You
will not buy a pig in a poke: if you cheapen a horse, you will see him
stripped of his housing-cloths, you will see him naked and open to your
eye; or if he be clothed, as they anciently were wont to present them to
princes to sell, 'tis only on the less important parts, that you may not
so much consider the beauty of his colour or the breadth of his crupper,
as principally to examine his legs, eyes, and feet, which are the members
of greatest use:*

> *"Regibus hic mos est: ubi equos mercantur, opertos*
> *Inspiciunt; ne, si facies, ut saepe, decora*
> *Molli fulta pede est, emptorem inducat hiantem"*

> *["This is the custom of kings: when they buy horses, they have open
> inspection, lest, if a fair head, as often chances, is supported by
> a weak foot, it should tempt the gaping purchaser."*
> *--Horace, Sat., i. 2, 86.]*

*why, in giving your estimate of a man, do you prize him wrapped and
muffled up in clothes? He then discovers nothing to you but such parts
as are not in the least his own, and conceals those by which alone one
may rightly judge of his value. 'Tis the price of the blade that you
inquire into, not of the scabbard: you would not peradventure bid a
farthing for him, if you saw him stripped. You are to judge him by
himself and not by what he wears; and, as one of the ancients very
pleasantly said: "Do you know why you repute him tall? You reckon withal
the height of his pattens."--[Seneca, Ep. 76.]--The pedestal is no part
of the statue. Measure him without his stilts; let him lay aside his
revenues and his titles; let him present himself in his shirt. Then
examine if his body be sound and sprightly, active and disposed to
perform its functions. What soul has he? Is she beautiful, capable, and
happily provided of all her faculties? Is she rich of what is her own,
or of what she has borrowed? Has fortune no hand in the affair? Can
she, without winking, stand the lightning of swords? is she indifferent
whether her life expire by the mouth or through the throat? Is she*

settled, even and content? This is what is to be examined, and by that you are to judge of the vast differences betwixt man and man. Is he:

> *"Sapiens, sibique imperiosus,*
> *Quern neque pauperies, neque mors, neque vincula terrent;*
> *Responsare cupidinibus, contemnere honores*
> *Fortis; et in seipso totus teres atque rotundus,*
> *Externi ne quid valeat per laeve morari;*
> *In quem manca ruit semper fortuna?"*

> *["The wise man, self-governed, whom neither poverty, nor death,*
> *nor chains affright: who has the strength to resist his appetites*
> *and to contemn honours: who is wholly self-contained: whom no*
> *external objects affect: whom fortune assails in vain."*
> *--Horace, Sat., ii. 7,]*

such a man is five hundred cubits above kingdoms and duchies; he is an absolute monarch in and to himself:

> *"Sapiens, . . . Pol! ipse fingit fortunam sibi;"*

> *["The wise man is the master of his own fortune,"*
> *--Plautus, Trin., ii. 2, 84.]*

what remains for him to covet or desire?

> *"Nonne videmus,*
> *Nil aliud sibi naturam latrare, nisi ut, quoi*
> *Corpore sejunctus dolor absit, mente fruatur,*
> *Jucundo sensu, cura semotu' metuque?"*

> *["Do we not see that human nature asks no more for itself than*
> *that, free from bodily pain, it may exercise its mind agreeably,*
> *exempt from care and fear."--Lucretius, ii. 16.]*

Compare with such a one the common rabble of mankind, stupid and mean-spirited, servile, instable, and continually floating with the tempest of various passions, that tosses and tumbles them to and fro, and all depending upon others, and you will find a greater distance than betwixt heaven and earth; and yet the blindness of common usage is such that we make little or no account of it; whereas if we consider a peasant and a king, a nobleman and a vassal, a magistrate and a private man, a rich man and a poor, there appears a vast disparity, though they differ no more, as a man may say, than in their breeches.

In Thrace the king was distinguished from his people after a very pleasant and especial manner; he had a religion by himself, a god all his own, and which his subjects were not to presume to adore, which was Mercury, whilst, on the other hand, he disdained to have anything to do with theirs, Mars, Bacchus, and Diana. And yet they are no other than pictures that make no essential dissimilitude; for as you see actors in a play representing the person of a duke or an emperor upon the stage, and immediately after return to their true and original condition of valets and porters, so the emperor, whose pomp and lustre so dazzle you in public:

> "Scilicet grandes viridi cum luce smaragdi
> Auto includuntur, teriturque thalassina vestis
> Assidue, et Veneris sudorem exercita potat;"

[*"Because he wears great emeralds richly set in gold, darting green lustre; and the sea-blue silken robe, worn with pressure, and moist with illicit love (and absorbs the sweat of Venus)."*
--Lucretius, iv. 1123.]

do but peep behind the curtain, and you will see no thing more than an ordinary man, and peradventure more contemptible than the meanest of his subjects:

"Ille beatus introrsum est, istius bracteata felicitas est;"

["The one is happy in himself; the happiness of the other is counterfeit."~Seneca, Ep., 115.]

cowardice, irresolution, ambition, spite, and envy agitate him as much as another:

> *"Non enim gazae, neque consularis*
> *Submovet lictor miseros tumultus*
> *Mentis, et curas laqueata circum*
> *Tecta volantes."*

["For not treasures, nor the consular lictor, can remove the miserable tumults of the mind, nor cares that fly about panelled ceilings."~Horace, Od., ii. 16, 9.]

Care and fear attack him even in the centre of his battalions:

> *"Re veraque metus hominum curaeque sequaces*
> *Nec metuunt sonitus armorum, nee fera tela;*
> *Audacterque inter reges, rerumque potentes*
> *Versantur, neque fulgorem reverentur ab auro."*

["And in truth the fears and haunting cares of men fear not the clash of arms nor points of darts, and mingle boldly with great kings and men in authority, nor respect the glitter of gold."
~Lucretius, ii. 47.]

Do fevers, gout, and apoplexies spare him any more than one of us? When old age hangs heavy upon his shoulders, can the yeomen of his guard ease him of the burden? When he is astounded with the apprehension of death, can the gentlemen of his bedchamber comfort and assure him? When jealousy or any other caprice swims in his brain, can our compliments and ceremonies restore him to his good-humour? The canopy embroidered with pearl and gold he lies under has no virtue against a violent fit of the colic:

> "Nec calidae citius decedunt corpore febres
> Textilibus si in picturis, ostroque rubenti
> Jactaris, quam si plebeia in veste cubandum est."

["Nor do burning fevers quit you sooner if you are stretched on a couch of rich tapestry and in a vest of purple dye, than if you be in a coarse blanket."--Idem, ii. 34.]

The flatterers of Alexander the Great possessed him that he was the son of Jupiter; but being one day wounded, and observing the blood stream from his wound: "What say you now, my masters," said he, "is not this blood of a crimson colour and purely human? This is not of the complexion of that which Homer makes to issue from the wounded gods." The poet Hermodorus had written a poem in honour of Antigonus, wherein he called him the son of the sun: "He who has the emptying of my close-stool," said Antigonus, "knows to the contrary." He is but a man at best, and if he be deformed or ill-qualified from his birth, the empire of the universe cannot set him to rights:

> "Puellae
> Hunc rapiant; quidquid calcaverit hic, rosa fiat,"

["Let girls carry him off; wherever he steps let there spring up a rose!"--Persius, Sat., ii. 38.]

what of all that, if he be a fool? even pleasure and good fortune are not relished without vigour and understanding:

> "Haec perinde sunt, ut ilius animus; qui ea possidet
> Qui uti scit, ei bona; illi, qui non uritur recte, mala."

["Things are, as is the mind of their possessor; who knows how to
use them, to him they are good; to him who abuses them, ill."
--Terence, Heart., i. 3, 21.]

Whatever the benefits of fortune are, they yet require a palate to relish
them. 'Tis fruition, and not possession, that renders us happy:

["'Tis not lands, or a heap of brass and gold, that has removed
fevers from the ailing body of the owner, or cares from his mind.
The possessor must be healthy, if he thinks to make good use of his
realised wealth. To him who is covetous or timorous his house and
estate are as a picture to a blind man, or a fomentation to a
gouty."--Horace, Ep., i. 2, 47.]

He is a sot, his taste is palled and flat; he no more enjoys what he has
than one that has a cold relishes the flavour of canary, or than a horse
is sensible of his rich caparison. Plato is in the right when he tells
us that health, beauty, vigour, and riches, and all the other things
called goods, are equally evil to the unjust as good to the just, and the
evil on the contrary the same. And therefore where the body and the mind
are in disorder, to what use serve these external conveniences:
considering that the least prick with a pin, or the least passion of the
soul, is sufficient to deprive one of the pleasure of being sole monarch
of the world. At the first twitch of the gout it signifies much to be
called Sir and Your Majesty!

"Totus et argento conflatus, totus et auro;"

["Wholly made up of silver and gold."--Tibullus, i. 2, 70.]

does he not forget his palaces and girandeurs? If he be angry, can his
being a prince keep him from looking red and looking pale, and grinding
his teeth like a madman? Now, if he be a man of parts and of right
nature, royalty adds very little to his happiness;

"*Si ventri bene, si lateri est, pedibusque tuffs, nil
Divitix poterunt regales addere majus;*"

["*If it is well with thy belly, thy side and thy feet, regal wealth
will be able to add nothing.*"--Horace, Ep., i. 12, 5.]

he discerns 'tis nothing but counterfeit and gullery. Nay, perhaps he
would be of King Seleucus' opinion, that he who knew the weight of a
sceptre would not stoop to pick it up, if he saw it lying before him, so
great and painful are the duties incumbent upon a good king.--[Plutarch,
If a Sage should Meddle with Affairs of Stale, c. 12.]--Assuredly it can
be no easy task to rule others, when we find it so hard a matter to
govern ourselves; and as to dominion, that seems so charming, the frailty
of human judgment and the difficulty of choice in things that are new and
doubtful considered, I am very much of opinion that it is far more easy
and pleasant to follow than to lead; and that it is a great settlement
and satisfaction of mind to have only one path to walk in, and to have
none to answer for but a man's self;

"*Ut satius multo jam sit parere quietum,
Quam regere imperio res velle.*"

["'*Tis much better quietly to obey than wish to rule.*"
--Lucretius, V, 1126.]

To which we may add that saying of Cyrus, that no man was fit to rule but
he who in his own worth was of greater value than those he was to govern;
but King Hiero in Xenophon says further, that in the fruition even of
pleasure itself they are in a worse condition than private men; forasmuch
as the opportunities and facility they have of commanding those things at
will takes off from the delight that ordinary folks enjoy:

"*Pinguis amor, nimiumque patens, in taedia nobis
Vertitur, et, stomacho dulcis ut esca, nocet.*"

*["Love in excess and too palpable turns to weariness, and, like
sweetmeats to the stomach, is injurious."--Ovid, Amoy., ii. 19, 25.]*

Can we think that the singing boys of the choir take any great delight in
music? the satiety rather renders it troublesome and tedious to them.
Feasts, balls, masquerades and tiltings delight such as but rarely see,
and desire to see, them; but having been frequently at such
entertainments, the relish of them grows flat and insipid. Nor do women
so much delight those who make a common practice of the sport. He who
will not give himself leisure to be thirsty can never find the true
pleasure of drinking. Farces and tumbling tricks are pleasant to the
spectators, but a wearisome toil to those by whom they are performed.
And that this is so, we see that princes divert themselves sometimes in
disguising their quality, awhile to depose themselves, and to stoop to
the poor and ordinary way of living of the meanest of their people.

> *"Plerumque gratae divitibus vices
> Mundaeque parvo sub lare pauperum
> Coenae, sine aulaeis et ostro,
> Soliicitam explicuere frontem."*

*["The rich are often pleased with variety; and the plain supper in a
poor cottage, without tapestry and purple, has relaxed the anxious
brow."--Horace, Od., iii. 29, 13.]*

Nothing is so distasteful and clogging as abundance. What appetite would
not be baffled to see three hundred women at its mercy, as the grand
signor has in his seraglio? And, of his ancestors what fruition or taste
of sport did he reserve to himself, who never went hawking without seven
thousand falconers? And besides all this, I fancy that this lustre of
grandeur brings with it no little disturbance and uneasiness upon the
enjoyment of the most tempting pleasures; the great are too conspicuous
and lie too open to every one's view. Neither do I know to what end a
man should more require of them to conceal their errors, since what is
only reputed indiscretion in us, the people in them brand with the names
of tyranny and contempt of the laws, and, besides their proclivity to

vice, are apt to hold that it is a heightening of pleasure to them, to insult over and to trample upon public observances. Plato, indeed, in his Goygias, defines a tyrant to be one who in a city has licence to do whatever his own will leads him to do; and by reason of this impunity, the display and publication of their vices do ofttimes more mischief than the vice itself. Every one fears to be pried into and overlooked; but princes are so, even to their very gestures, looks and thoughts, the people conceiving they have right and title to be judges of them besides that the blemishes of the great naturally appear greater by reason of the eminence and lustre of the place where they are seated, and that a mole or a wart appears greater in them than a wide gash in others. And this is the reason why the poets feign the amours of Jupiter to be performed in the disguises of so many borrowed shapes, and that amongst the many amorous practices they lay to his charge, there is only one, as I remember, where he appears in his own majesty and grandeur.

But let us return to Hiero, who further complains of the inconveniences he found in his royalty, in that he could not look abroad and travel the world at liberty, being as it were a prisoner in the bounds and limits of his own dominion, and that in all his actions he was evermore surrounded with an importunate crowd. And in truth, to see our kings sit all alone at table, environed with so many people prating about them, and so many strangers staring upon them, as they always are, I have often been moved rather to pity than to envy their condition. King Alfonso was wont to say, that in this asses were in a better condition than kings, their masters permitting them to feed at their own ease and pleasure, a favour that kings cannot obtain of their servants. And it has never come into my fancy that it could be of any great benefit to the life of a man of sense to have twenty people prating about him when he is at stool; or that the services of a man of ten thousand livres a year, or that has taken Casale or defended Siena, should be either more commodious or more acceptable to him, than those of a good groom of the chamber who understands his place. The advantages of sovereignty are in a manner but imaginary: every degree of fortune has in it some image of principality. Caesar calls all the lords of France, having free franchise within their own demesnes, roitelets or petty kings; and in truth, the name of sire excepted, they go pretty far towards kingship; for do but look into the provinces remote from court, as Brittany for example; take notice of the train, the vassals, the officers, the employments, service, ceremony, and state of a lord who lives retired from court in his own house, amongst his own tenants and servants; and observe withal the flight of his imagination; there is nothing more royal; he hears talk of his master once a year, as of a king of Persia, without taking any further recognition of him, than by some remote kindred his secretary keeps in some register. And, to speak the truth, our laws are easy enough, so easy that a gentleman of France scarce feels the weight of sovereignty pinch his shoulders above twice in his life. Real and effectual subjection only concerns such amongst us as voluntarily thrust their necks under the yoke, and who design to get wealth and honours by such services: for a man that loves his own fireside, and can govern his house without falling by the ears with his neighbours or engaging in suits of law, is as free as a Duke of Venice.

"Paucos servitus, plures servitutem tenent."

["Servitude enchains few, but many enchain themselves to servitude."--Seneca, Ep., 22.]

But that which Hiero is most concerned at is, that he finds himself stripped of all friendship, deprived of all mutual society, wherein the true and most perfect fruition of human life consists. For what testimony of affection and goodwill can I extract from him that owes me, whether he will or no, all that he is able to do? Can I form any assurance of his real respect to me, from his humble way of speaking and submissive behaviour, when these are ceremonies it is not in his choice to deny? The honour we receive from those that fear us is not honour; those respects are due to royalty and not to me:

"Maximum hoc regni bonum est
Quod facta domini cogitur populus sui
Quam ferre, tam laudare."

[*"'Tis the greatest benefit of a kingdom that the people is forced
to commend, as well as to bear the acts of the ruler."
~Seneca, Thyestes, ii. i, 30.*]

*Do I not see that the wicked and the good king, he that is hated and he
that is beloved, have the one as much reverence paid him as the other?
My predecessor was, and my successor shall be, served with the same
ceremony and state. If my subjects do me no harm, 'tis no evidence of
any good affection; why should I look upon it as such, seeing it is not
in their power to do it if they would? No one follows me or obeys my
commands upon the account of any friendship, betwixt him and me; there
can be no contracting of friendship where there is so little relation and
correspondence: my own height has put me out of the familiarity of and
intelligence with men; there is too great disparity and disproportion
betwixt us. They follow me either upon the account of decency and
custom; or rather my fortune, than me, to increase their own. All they
say to me or do for me is but outward paint, appearance, their liberty
being on all parts restrained by the great power and authority I have
over them. I see nothing about me but what is dissembled and disguised.*

*The Emperor Julian being one day applauded by his courtiers for his exact
justice: "I should be proud of these praises," said he, "did they come
from persons that durst condemn or disapprove the contrary, in case I
should do it." All the real advantages of princes are common to them
with men of meaner condition ('tis for the gods to mount winged horses
and feed upon ambrosia): they have no other sleep, nor other appetite
than we; the steel they arm themselves withal is of no better temper than
that we also use; their crowns neither defend them from the rain nor the
sun.*

*Diocletian, who wore a crown so fortunate and revered, resigned it to
retire to the felicity of a private life; and some time after the
necessity of public affairs requiring that he should reassume his charge,
he made answer to those who came to court him to it: "You would not
offer," said he, "to persuade me to this, had you seen the fine order of*

the trees I have planted in my orchard, and the fair melons I have sown in my garden."

In Anacharsis' opinion, the happiest state of government would be where, all other things being equal, precedence should be measured out by the virtues, and repulses by the vices of men.

When King Pyrrhus prepared for his expedition into Italy, his wise counsellor Cyneas, to make him sensible of the vanity of his ambition: "Well, sir," said he, "to what end do you make all this mighty preparation?"--"To make myself master of Italy," replied the king. "And what after that is done?" said Cyneas. "I will pass over into Gaul and Spain," said the other. "And what then?"--"I will then go to subdue Africa; and lastly, when I have brought the whole world to my subjection, I will sit down and rest content at my own ease."

"For God sake, sir," replied Cyneas, "tell me what hinders that you may not, if you please, be now in the condition you speak of? Why do you not now at this instant settle yourself in the state you seem to aim at, and spare all the labour and hazard you interpose?"

> "Nimirum, quia non cognovit, quæ esset habendi
> Finis, et omnino quoad crescat vera voluptas."

> ["Forsooth because he does not know what should be the limit of acquisition, and altogether how far real pleasure should increase."
> --Lucretius, v. 1431]

I will conclude with an old versicle, that I think very apt to the purpose:

> "Mores cuique sui fingunt fortunam."

> ["Every man frames his own fortune."
> --Cornelius Nepos, Life of Atticus]

CHAPTER XLIII

OF SUMPTUARY LAWS

The way by which our laws attempt to regulate idle and vain expenses in meat and clothes, seems to be quite contrary to the end designed. The true way would be to beget in men a contempt of silks and gold, as vain, frivolous, and useless; whereas we augment to them the honours, and enhance the value of such things, which, sure, is a very improper way to create a disgust. For to enact that none but princes shall eat turbot, shall wear velvet or gold lace, and interdict these things to the people, what is it but to bring them into a greater esteem, and to set every one more agog to eat and wear them? Let kings leave off these ensigns of grandeur; they have others enough besides; those excesses are more excusable in any other than a prince. We may learn by the example of several nations better ways of exterior distinction of quality (which, truly, I conceive to be very requisite in a state) enough, without fostering to this purpose such corruption and manifest inconvenience. 'Tis strange how suddenly and with how much ease custom in these indifferent things establishes itself and becomes authority. We had scarce worn cloth a year, in compliance with the court, for the mourning of Henry II., but that silks were already grown into such contempt with every one, that a man so clad was presently concluded a citizen: silks were divided betwixt the physicians and surgeons, and though all other people almost went in the same habit, there was, notwithstanding, in one thing or other, sufficient distinction of the several conditions of men. How suddenly do greasy chamois and linen doublets become the fashion in our armies, whilst all neatness and richness of habit fall into contempt? Let kings but lead the dance and begin to leave off this expense, and in a month the business will be done throughout the kingdom, without edict or ordinance; we shall all follow. It should be rather proclaimed, on the contrary, that no one should wear scarlet or goldsmiths' work but courtesans and tumblers.

Zeleucus by the like invention reclaimed the corrupted manners of the Locrians. His laws were, that no free woman should be allowed any more than one maid to follow her, unless she was drunk: nor was to stir out of the city by night, wear jewels of gold about her, or go in an embroidered robe, unless she was a professed and public prostitute; that, bravos excepted, no man was to wear a gold ring, nor be seen in one of those effeminate robes woven in the city of Miletus. By which infamous exceptions he discreetly diverted his citizens from superfluities and pernicious pleasures, and it was a project of great utility to attract then by honour and ambition to their duty and obedience.

Our kings can do what they please in such external reformations; their own inclination stands in this case for a law:

"Quicquid principes faciunt, praecipere videntur."

*["What princes themselves do, they seem to prescribe."
--Quintil., Declam., 3.]*

Whatever is done at court passes for a rule through the rest of France. Let the courtiers fall out with these abominable breeches, that discover so much of those parts should be concealed; these great bellied doublets, that make us look like I know not what, and are so unfit to admit of arms; these long effeminate locks of hair; this foolish custom of kissing what we present to our equals, and our hands in saluting them, a ceremony in former times only due to princes. Let them not permit that a gentleman shall appear in place of respect without his sword, unbuttoned and untrussed, as though he came from the house of office; and that, contrary to the custom of our forefathers and the particular privilege of the nobles of this kingdom, we stand a long time bare to them in what place soever, and the same to a hundred others, so many tiercelets and quartelets of kings we have got nowadays and other like vicious innovations: they will see them all presently vanish and cried down. These are, 'tis true, but superficial errors; but they are of ill augury, and enough to inform us that the whole fabric is crazy and tottering, when we see the roughcast of our walls to cleave and split.

Plato in his Laws esteems nothing of more pestiferous consequence to his city than to give young men the liberty of introducing any change in their habits, gestures, dances, songs, and exercises, from one form to another; shifting from this to that, hunting after novelties, and applauding the inventors; by which means manners are corrupted and the old institutions come to be nauseated and despised. In all things, saving only in those that are evil, a change is to be feared; even the change of seasons, winds, viands, and humours. And no laws are in their true credit, but such to which God has given so long a continuance that no one knows their beginning, or that there ever was any other.

CHAPTER XLIV

OF SLEEP

Reason directs that we should always go the same way, but not always at the same pace. And, consequently, though a wise man ought not so much to give the reins to human passions as to let him deviate from the right path, he may, notwithstanding, without prejudice to his duty, leave it to them to hasten or to slacken his speed, and not fix himself like a motionless and insensible Colossus. Could virtue itself put on flesh and blood, I believe the pulse would beat faster going on to assault than in going to dinner: that is to say, there is a necessity she should heat and be moved upon this account. I have taken notice, as of an extraordinary thing, of some great men, who in the highest enterprises and most important affairs have kept themselves in so settled and serene a calm, as not at all to break their sleep. Alexander the Great, on the day assigned for that furious battle betwixt him and Darius, slept so profoundly and so long in the morning, that Parmenio was forced to enter his chamber, and coming to his bedside, to call him several times by his name, the time to go to fight compelling him so to do. The Emperor Otho, having put on a resolution to kill himself that night, after having settled his domestic affairs, divided his money amongst his servants, and set a good edge upon a sword he had made choice of for the purpose, and now staying only to be satisfied whether all his friends had retired in safety, he fell into so sound a sleep that the gentlemen of his chamber heard him snore. The death of this emperor has in it circumstances paralleling that of the great Cato, and particularly this just related for Cato being ready to despatch himself, whilst he only stayed his hand in expectation of the return of a messenger he had sent to bring him news whether the senators he had sent away were put out from the Port of Utica, he fell into so sound a sleep, that they heard him snore in the next room; and the man, whom he had sent to the port, having awakened him to let him know that the tempestuous weather had hindered the senators

from putting to sea, he despatched away another messenger, and composing
again himself in the bed, settled to sleep, and slept till by the return
of the last messenger he had certain intelligence they were gone. We may
here further compare him with Alexander in the great and dangerous storm
that threatened him by the sedition of the tribune Metellus, who,
attempting to publish a decree for the calling in of Pompey with his army
into the city at the time of Catiline's conspiracy, was only and that
stoutly opposed by Cato, so that very sharp language and bitter menaces
passed betwixt them in the senate about that affair; but it was the next
day, in the forenoon, that the controversy was to be decided, where
Metellus, besides the favour of the people and of Caesar--at that time of
Pompey's faction--was to appear accompanied with a rabble of slaves and
gladiators; and Cato only fortified with his own courage and constancy;
so that his relations, domestics, and many virtuous people of his friends
were in great apprehensions for him; and to that degree, that some there
were who passed over the whole night without sleep, eating, or drinking,
for the danger they saw him running into; his wife and sisters did
nothing but weep and torment themselves in his house; whereas, he, on the
contrary, comforted every one, and after having supped after his usual
manner, went to bed, and slept profoundly till morning, when one of his
fellow-tribunes roused him to go to the encounter. The knowledge we have
of the greatness of this man's courage by the rest of his life, may
warrant us certainly to judge that his indifference proceeded from a soul
so much elevated above such accidents, that he disdained to let it take
any more hold of his fancy than any ordinary incident.

In the naval engagement that Augustus won of Sextus Pompeius in Sicily,
just as they were to begin the fight, he was so fast asleep that his
friends were compelled to wake him to give the signal of battle: and this
was it that gave Mark Antony afterwards occasion to reproach him that he
had not the courage so much as with open eyes to behold the order of his
own squadrons, and not to have dared to present himself before the
soldiers, till first Agrippa had brought him news of the victory
obtained. But as to the young Marius, who did much worse (for the day of
his last battle against Sylla, after he had marshalled his army and given
the word and signal of battle, he laid him down under the shade of a tree

to repose himself, and fell so fast asleep that the rout and flight of
his men could hardly waken him, he having seen nothing of the fight), he
is said to have been at that time so extremely spent and worn out with
labour and want of sleep, that nature could hold out no longer. Now,
upon what has been said, the physicians may determine whether sleep be so
necessary that our lives depend upon it: for we read that King Perseus of
Macedon, being prisoner at Rome, was killed by being kept from sleep; but
Pliny instances such as have lived long without sleep. Herodotus speaks
of nations where the men sleep and wake by half-years, and they who write
the life of the sage Epimenides affirm that he slept seven-and-fifty
years together.

CHAPTER XLV

OF THE BATTLE OF DREUX

*[December 19, 1562, in which the Catholics, under the command of the
Duc de Guise and the Constable de Montmorenci, defeated the
Protestants, commanded by the Prince de Conde. See Sismondi, Hist.
des Francais, vol. xviii., p. 354.]*

*Our battle of Dreux is remarkable for several extraordinary incidents;
but such as have no great kindness for M. de Guise, nor much favour his
reputation, are willing to have him thought to blame, and that his making
a halt and delaying time with the forces he commanded, whilst the
Constable, who was general of the army, was racked through and through
with the enemy's artillery, his battalion routed, and himself taken
prisoner, is not to be excused; and that he had much better have run the
hazard of charging the enemy in flank, than staying for the advantage of
falling in upon the rear, to suffer so great and so important a loss.
But, besides what the event demonstrated, he who will consider it without
passion or prejudice will easily be induced to confess that the aim and
design, not of a captain only, but of every private soldier, ought to
regard the victory in general, and that no particular occurrences, how
nearly soever they may concern his own interest, should divert him from
that pursuit. Philopoemen, in an encounter with Machanidas, having sent
before a good strong party of his archers and slingers to begin the
skirmish, and these being routed and hotly pursued by the enemy, who,
pushing on the fortune of their arms, and in that pursuit passing by the
battalion where Philopoemen was, though his soldiers were impatient to
fall on, he did not think fit to stir from his post nor to present
himself to the enemy to relieve his men, but having suffered these to be
chased and cut in pieces before his face, charged in upon the enemy's
foot when he saw them left unprotected by the horse, and notwithstanding
that they were Lacedaemonians, yet taking them in the nick, when thinking*

themselves secure of the victory, they began to disorder their ranks; he did this business with great facility, and then put himself in pursuit of Machanidas. Which case is very like that of Monsieur de Guise.

In that bloody battle betwixt Agesilaus and the Boeotians, which Xenophon, who was present at it, reports to be the sharpest that he had ever seen, Agesilaus waived the advantage that fortune presented him, to let the Boeotian battalions pass by and then to charge them in the rear, how certain soever he might make himself of the victory, judging it would rather be an effect of conduct than valour, to proceed that way; and therefore, to show his prowess, rather chose with a marvellous ardour of courage to charge them in the front; but he was well beaten and well wounded for his pains, and constrained at last to disengage himself, and to take the course he had at first neglected; opening his battalion to give way to this torrent of Boeotians, and they being passed by, taking notice that they marched in disorder, like men who thought themselves out of danger, he pursued and charged them in flank; yet could not so prevail as to bring it to so general a rout but that they leisurely retreated, still facing about upon him till they had retired to safety.

CHAPTER XLVI

OF NAMES

What variety of herbs soever are shuffed together in the dish, yet the whole mass is swallowed up under one name of a sallet. In like manner, under the consideration of names, I will make a hodge-podge of divers articles.

Every nation has certain names, that, I know not why, are taken in no good sense, as with us, John, William, Benedict. In the genealogy of princes, also, there seem to be certain names fatally affected, as the Ptolemies of Egypt, the Henries in England, the Charleses in France, the Baldwins in Flanders, and the Williams of our ancient Aquitaine, from whence, 'tis said, the name of Guyenne has its derivation; which would seem far fetched were there not as crude derivations in Plato himself.

Item, 'tis a frivolous thing in itself, but nevertheless worthy to be recorded for the strangeness of it, that is written by an eyewitness, that Henry, Duke of Normandy, son of Henry II., king of England, making a great feast in France, the concourse of nobility and gentry was so great, that being, for sport's sake, divided into troops, according to their names, in the first troop, which consisted of Williams, there were found an hundred and ten knights sitting at the table of that name, without reckoning the ordinary gentlemen and servants.

It is as pleasant to distinguish the tables by the names of the guests as it was in the Emperor Geta to distinguish the several courses of his meat by the first letters of the meats themselves; so that those that began with B were served up together, as brawn, beef, bream, bustards, becca-ficos; and so of the others. Item, there is a saying that it is a good thing to have a good name, that is to say, credit and a good repute; but besides this, it is really convenient to have a well-sounding name,

*such as is easy of pronunciation and easy to be remembered, by reason
that kings and other great persons do by that means the more easily know
and the more hardly forget us; and indeed of our own servants we more
frequently call and employ those whose names are most ready upon the
tongue. I myself have seen Henry II., when he could not for his heart
hit of a gentleman's name of our country of Gascony, and moreover was
fain to call one of the queen's maids of honour by the general name of
her race, her own family name being so difficult to pronounce or
remember; and Socrates thinks it worthy a father's care to give fine
names to his children.*

*Item, 'tis said that the foundation of Notre Dame la Grande at Poitiers
took its original from hence that a debauched young fellow formerly
living in that place, having got to him a wench, and, at her first coming
in, asking her name, and being answered that it was Mary, he felt himself
so suddenly pierced through with the awe of religion and the reverence to
that sacred name of the Blessed Virgin, that he not only immediately sent
the girl away, but became a reformed man and so continued the remainder
of his life; and that, in consideration of this miracle, there was
erected upon the place where this young man's house stood, first a chapel
dedicated to our Lady and afterwards the church that we now see standing
there. This vocal and auricular reproof wrought upon the conscience, and
that right into the soul; this that follows, insinuated itself merely by
the senses. Pythagoras being in company with some wild young fellows,
and perceiving that, heated with the feast, they comploted to go violate
an honest house, commanded the singing wench to alter her wanton airs;
and by a solemn, grave, and spondaic music, gently enchanted and laid
asleep their ardour.*

*Item, will not posterity say that our modern reformation has been
wonderfully delicate and exact, in having not only combated errors and
vices, and filled the world with devotion, humility, obedience, peace,
and all sorts of virtue; but in having proceeded so far as to quarrel
with our ancient baptismal names of Charles, Louis, Francis, to fill the
world with Methuselahs, Ezekiels, and Malachis, names of a more spiritual
sound? A gentleman, a neighbour of mine, a great admirer of antiquity,*

and who was always extolling the excellences of former times in comparison with this present age of ours, did not, amongst the rest, forget to dwell upon the lofty and magnificent sound of the gentleman's names of those days, Don Grumedan, Quedregan, Agesilan, which, but to hear named he conceived to denote other kind of men than Pierre, Guillot, and Michel.

Item, I am mightily pleased with Jacques Amyot for leaving, throughout a whole French oration, the Latin names entire, without varying and garbling them to give them a French cadence. It seemed a little harsh and rough at first; but already custom, by the authority of his Plutarch, has overcome that novelty. I have often wished that such as write histories in Latin would leave our names as they find them and as they are; for in making Vaudemont into Vallemontanus, and metamorphosing names to make them suit better with the Greek or Latin, we know not where we are, and with the persons of the men lose the benefit of the story.

To conclude, 'tis a scurvy custom and of very ill consequence that we have in our kingdom of France to call every one by the name of his manor or seigneury; 'tis the thing in the world that the most prejudices and confounds families and descents. A younger brother of a good family, having a manor left him by his father, by the name of which he has been known and honoured, cannot handsomely leave it; ten years after his decease it falls into the hand of a stranger, who does the same: do but judge whereabouts we shall be concerning the knowledge of these men. We need look no further for examples than our own royal family, where every partition creates a new surname, whilst, in the meantime, the original of the family is totally lost. There is so great liberty taken in these mutations, that I have not in my time seen any one advanced by fortune to any extraordinary condition who has not presently had genealogical titles added to him, new and unknown to his father, and who has not been inoculated into some illustrious stem by good luck; and the obscurest families are the most apt for falsification. How many gentlemen have we in France who by their own account are of royal extraction? more, I think, than who will confess they are not. Was it not a pleasant passage of a friend of mine? There were, several gentlemen assembled together *about the dispute of one seigneur with another; which other had, in truth, some preeminence of titles and alliances above the ordinary gentry. Upon the debate of this prerogative, every one, to make himself equal to him, alleged, this one extraction, that another; this, the near resemblance of name, that, of arms; another, an old worm-eaten patent; the very least of them was great-grandchild to some foreign king. When they came to sit down, to dinner, my friend, instead of taking his place amongst them, retiring with most profound conges, entreated the company to excuse him for having hitherto lived with them at the saucy rate of a companion; but being now better informed of their quality, he would begin to pay them the respect due to their birth and grandeur, and that it would ill become him to sit down among so many princes--ending this farce with a thousand reproaches: "Let us, in God's name, satisfy ourselves with what our fathers were contented with, with what we are. We are great enough, if we rightly understand how to maintain it. Let us not disown the fortune and condition of our ancestors, and let us lay aside these ridiculous pretences, that can never be wanting to any one that has the impudence to allege them."*

Arms have no more security than surnames. I bear azure powdered with trefoils or, with a lion's paw of the same armed gules in fesse. What privilege has this to continue particularly in my house? A son-in-law will transport it into another family, or some paltry purchaser will make them his first arms. There is nothing wherein there is more change and confusion.

But this consideration leads me, perforce, into another subject. Let us pry a little narrowly into, and, in God's name, examine upon what foundation we erect this glory and reputation for which the world is turned topsy-turvy: wherein do we place this renown that we hunt after with so much pains? It is, in the end, Peter or William that carries it, takes it into his possession, and whom it only concerns. O what a valiant faculty is hope, that in a mortal subject, and in a moment, makes nothing of usurping infinity, immensity, eternity, and of supplying its master's indigence, at its pleasure, with all things he can imagine or desire! Nature has given us this passion for a pretty toy to play withal. And this Peter or William, what is it but a sound, when all is done? or three or four dashes with a pen, so easy to be varied that I would fain know to whom is to be attributed the glory of so many victories, to Guesquin, to Glesquin, or to Gueaquin? and yet there would be something of greater moment in the case than in Lucian, that Sigma should serve Tau with a process; for

> "Non levia aut ludicra petuntur
> Praemia;"

["They aim at no slight or jocular rewards."--AEneid, xii. 764.]

the chase is there in very good earnest: the question is, which of these letters is to be rewarded for so many sieges, battles, wounds, imprisonments, and services done to the crown of France by this famous constable? Nicholas Denisot--[Painter and poet, born at Le Mans,1515.]-- never concerned himself further than the letters of his name, of which he has altered the whole contexture to build up by anagram the Count d'Alsinois, whom he has handsomely endowed with the glory of his poetry and painting. The historian Suetonius was satisfied with only the meaning of his name, which made him cashier his father's surname, Lenis, to leave Tranquillus successor to the reputation of his writings. Who would believe that Captain Bayard should have no honour but what he derives from the deeds of Peter Terrail; and that Antonio Iscalin should suffer himself to his face to be robbed of the honour of so many navigations and commands at sea and land by Captain Paulin and the Baron de la Garde? Secondly, these are dashes of the pen common to a thousand people. How many are there, in every family, of the same name and surname? and how many more in several families, ages, and countries? History tells us of three of the name of Socrates, of five Platos, of eight Aristotles, of seven Xenophons, of twenty Demetrii, and of twenty Theodores; and how many more she was not acquainted with we may imagine. Who hinders my groom from calling himself Pompey the Great? But after all, what virtue, what authority, or what secret springs are there that fix upon my deceased groom, or the other Pompey, who had his head cut off

in Egypt, this glorious renown, and these so much honoured flourishes of
the pen, so as to be of any advantage to them?

"Id cinerem et manes credis curare sepultos?"

["Do you believe the dead regard such things?"--AEneid, iv. 34.]

What sense have the two companions in greatest esteem amongst me,
Epaminondas, of this fine verse that has been so many ages current in his
praise,

"Consiliis nostris laus est attrita Laconum;"

["The glory of the Spartans is extinguished by my plans.
--"Cicero, Tusc. Quaes., v. 17.]

or Africanus, of this other,

"A sole exoriente supra Maeotis Paludes
Nemo est qui factis me aequiparare queat."

["From where the sun rises over the Palus Maeotis, to where it sets,
there is no one whose acts can compare with mine"--Idem, ibid.]

Survivors indeed tickle themselves with these fine phrases, and by them
incited to jealousy and desire, inconsiderately and according to their
own fancy, attribute to the dead this their own feeling, vainly
flattering themselves that they shall one day in turn be capable of the
same character. However:

"Ad haec se
Romanus Graiusque, et Barbaras induperator
Erexit; caucus discriminis atque laboris
Inde habuit: tanto major famae sitis est, quam
Virtutis."

*["For these the Roman, the Greek, and the Barbarian commander hath aroused himself; he has incurred thence causes of danger and toil: so much greater is the thirst for fame than for virtue."
⁓Juvenal, x. 137.]*

CHAPTER XLVII

OF THE UNCERTAINTY OF OUR JUDGMENT

Well says this verse:

[*"There is everywhere much liberty of speech."--Iliad, xx. 249.*]

For example:

[*"Hannibal conquered, but knew not how to make the best use of his victorious venture."--Petrarch, Son., 83.*]

Such as would improve this argument, and condemn the oversight of our leaders in not pushing home the victory at Moncontour, or accuse the King of Spain of not knowing how to make the best use of the advantage he had against us at St. Quentin, may conclude these oversights to proceed from a soul already drunk with success, or from a spirit which, being full and overgorged with this beginning of good fortune, had lost the appetite of adding to it, already having enough to do to digest what it had taken in: he has his arms full, and can embrace no more: unworthy of the benefit fortune has conferred upon him and the advantage she had put into his hands: for what utility does he reap from it, if, notwithstanding, he give his enemy respite to rally and make head against him? What hope is there that he will dare at another time to attack an enemy reunited and recomposed, and armed anew with anger and revenge, who did not dare to pursue them when routed and unmanned by fear?

"Dum fortuna calet, dum conficit omnia terror."

[*"Whilst fortune is fresh, and terror finishes all."
--Lucan, vii. 734.*]

But withal, what better opportunity can he expect than that he has lost? 'Tis not here, as in fencing, where the most hits gain the prize; for so long as the enemy is on foot, the game is new to begin, and that is not to be called a victory that puts not an end to the war. In the encounter where Caesar had the worst, near the city of Oricum, he reproached Pompey's soldiers that he had been lost had their general known how to overcome; and afterwards clawed him in a very different fashion when it came to his turn.

But why may not a man also argue, on the contrary, that it is the effect of a precipitous and insatiate spirit not to know how to bound and restrain its coveting; that it is to abuse the favours of God to exceed the measure He has prescribed them: and that again to throw a man's self into danger after a victory obtained is again to expose himself to the mercy of fortune: that it is one of the greatest discretions in the rule of war not to drive an enemy to despair? Sylla and Marius in the social war, having defeated the Marsians, seeing yet a body of reserve that, prompted by despair, was coming on like enraged brutes to dash in upon them, thought it not convenient to stand their charge. Had not Monsieur de Foix's ardour transported him so furiously to pursue the remains of the victory of Ravenna, he had not obscured it by his own death. And yet the recent memory of his example served to preserve Monsieur d'Anguien from the same misfortune at the battle of Serisoles. 'Tis dangerous to attack a man you have deprived of all means to escape but by his arms, for necessity teaches violent resolutions:

"Gravissimi sunt morsus irritatae necessitatis."

["Irritated necessity bites deepest."--Portius Latro., Declam.]

"Vincitur haud gratis, jugulo qui provocat hostem."

["He is not readily beaten who provokes the enemy by shewing his throat."--or: "He who presents himself to his foe, sells his life dear."--Lucan, iv. 275.]

*This was it that made Pharax withhold the King of Lacedaemon, who had won
a battle against the Mantineans, from going to charge a thousand Argians,
who had escaped in an entire body from the defeat, but rather let them
steal off at liberty that he might not encounter valour whetted and
enraged by mischance. Clodomir, king of Aquitaine, after his victory
pursuing Gondemar, king of Burgundy, beaten and making off as fast as he
could for safety, compelled him to face about and make head, wherein his
obstinacy deprived him of the fruit of his conquest, for he there lost
his life.*

*In like manner, if a man were to choose whether he would have his
soldiers richly and sumptuously accoutred or armed only for the necessity
of the matter in hand, this argument would step in to favour the first,
of which opinion was Sertorius, Philopœmen, Brutus, Caesar, and others,
that it is to a soldier an enflaming of courage and a spur himself in
brave attire; and withal a motive to be more obstinate in fight, having
his arms, which are in a manner his estate and whole inheritance to
defend; which is the reason, says Xenophon, why those of Asia carried
their wives and concubines, with their choicest jewels and greatest
wealth, along with them to the wars. But then these arguments would be
as ready to stand up for the other side; that a general ought rather to
lessen in his men their solicitude of preserving themselves than to
increase it; that by such means they will be in a double fear of
hazarding their persons, as it will be a double temptation to the enemy
to fight with greater resolution where so great booty and so rich spoils
are to be obtained; and this very thing has been observed in former
times, notably to encourage the Romans against the Samnites. Antiochus,
shewing Hannibal the army he had raised, wonderfully splendid and rich in
all sorts of equipage, asked him if the Romans would be satisfied with
that army? "Satisfied," replied the other, "yes, doubtless, were their
avarice never so great." Lycurgus not only forbad his soldiers all
manner of bravery in their equipage, but, moreover, to strip their
conquered enemies, because he would, as he said, that poverty and
frugality should shine with the rest of the battle.*

At sieges and elsewhere, where occasion draws us near to the enemy, we willingly suffer our men to brave, rate, and affront him with all sorts of injurious language; and not without some colour of reason: for it is of no little consequence to take from them all hopes of mercy and composition, by representing to them that there is no fair quarter to be expected from an enemy they have incensed to that degree, nor other remedy remaining but in victory. And yet Vitellius found himself deceived in this way of proceeding; for having to do with Otho, weaker in the valour of his soldiers, long unaccustomed to war and effeminated with the delights of the city, he so nettled them at last with injurious language, reproaching them with cowardice and regret for the mistresses and entertainments they had left behind at Rome, that by this means he inspired them with such resolution as no exhortation had had the power to have done, and himself made them fall upon him, with whom their own captains before could by no means prevail. And, indeed, when they are injuries that touch to the quick, it may very well fall out that he who went but unwillingly to work in the behalf of his prince will fall to't with another sort of mettle when the quarrel is his own.

Considering of how great importance is the preservation of the general of an army, and that the universal aim of an enemy is levelled directly at the head, upon which all the others depend, the course seems to admit of no dispute, which we know has been taken by so many great captains, of changing their habit and disguising their persons upon the point of going to engage. Nevertheless, the inconvenience a man by so doing runs into is not less than that he thinks to avoid; for the captain, by this means being concealed from the knowledge of his own men, the courage they should derive from his presence and example happens by degrees to cool and to decay; and not seeing the wonted marks and ensigns of their leader, they presently conclude him either dead, or that, despairing of the business, he is gone to shift for himself. And experience shows us that both these ways have been successful and otherwise. What befell Pyrrhus in the battle he fought against the Consul Levinus in Italy will serve us to both purposes; for though by shrouding his person under the armour of Megacles and making him wear his own, he undoubtedly preserved his own life, yet, by that very means, he was withal very near running into the other mischief of losing the battle. Alexander, Caesar, and Lucullus loved to make themselves known in a battle by rich accoutrements and armour of a particular lustre and colour: Agis, Agesilaus, and that great Gilippus, on the contrary, used to fight obscurely armed, and without any imperial attendance or distinction.

Amongst other oversights Pompey is charged withal at the battle of Pharsalia, he is condemned for making his army stand still to receive the enemy's charge; by "reason that" (I shall here steal Plutarch's own words, which are better than mine) "he by so doing deprived himself of the violent impression the motion of running adds to the first shock of arms, and hindered that clashing of the combatants against one another which is wont to give them greater impetuosity and fury; especially when they come to rush in with their utmost vigour, their courages increasing by the shouts and the career; 'tis to render the soldiers' ardour, as a man may say, more reserved and cold." This is what he says. But if Caesar had come by the worse, why might it not as well have been urged by another, that, on the contrary, the strongest and most steady posture of fighting is that wherein a man stands planted firm without motion; and that they who are steady upon the march, closing up, and reserving their force within themselves for the push of the business, have a great advantage against those who are disordered, and who have already spent half their breath in running on precipitately to the charge? Besides that an army is a body made up of so many individual members, it is impossible for it to move in this fury with so exact a motion as not to break the order of battle, and that the best of them are not engaged before their fellows can come on to help them. In that unnatural battle betwixt the two Persian brothers, the Lacedaemonian Clearchus, who commanded the Greeks of Cyrus' party, led them on softly and without precipitation to the charge; but, coming within fifty paces, hurried them on full speed, hoping in so short a career both to keep their order and to husband their breath, and at the same time to give the advantage of impetuosity and impression both to their persons and their missile arms. Others have regulated this question as to their armies thus if your enemy come full drive upon you, stand firm to receive him; if he stand to receive you, run full drive upon him.

In the expedition of the Emperor Charles V. into Provence, King Francis was put to choose either to go meet him in Italy or to await him in his own dominions; wherein, though he very well considered of how great advantage it was to preserve his own territory entire and clear from the troubles of war, to the end that, being unexhausted of its stores, it might continually supply men and money at need; that the necessity of war requires at every turn to spoil and lay waste the country before us, which cannot very well be done upon one's own; to which may be added, that the country people do not so easily digest such a havoc by those of their own party as from an enemy, so that seditions and commotions might by such means be kindled amongst us; that the licence of pillage and plunder (which are not to be tolerated at home) is a great ease and refreshment against the fatigues and sufferings of war; and that he who has no other prospect of gain than his bare pay will hardly be kept from running home, being but two steps from his wife and his own house; that he who lays the cloth is ever at the charge of the feast; that there is more alacrity in assaulting than defending; and that the shock of a battle's loss in our own bowels is so violent as to endanger the disjointing of the whole body, there being no passion so contagious as that of fear, that is so easily believed, or that so suddenly diffuses itself; and that the cities that should hear the rattle of this tempest at their gates, that should take in their captains and soldiers yet trembling and out of breath, would be in danger in this heat and hurry to precipitate themselves upon some untoward resolution: notwithstanding all this, so it was that he chose to recall the forces he had beyond the mountains and to suffer the enemy to come to him. For he might, on the other hand, imagine that, being at home and amongst his friends, he could not fail of plenty of all manner of conveniences; the rivers and passes he had at his devotion would bring him in both provisions and money in all security, and without the trouble of convoy; that he should find his subjects by so much the more affectionate to him, by how much their danger was more near and pressing; that having so many cities and barriers to secure him, it would be in his power to give the law of battle at his own opportunity and advantage; and that, if it pleased him to delay the time, under cover and at his ease he might see his enemy

*founder and defeat himself with the difficulties he was certain to
encounter, being engaged in a hostile country, where before, behind, and
on every side war would be made upon him; no means to refresh himself or
to enlarge his quarters, should diseases infest them, or to lodge his
wounded men in safety; no money, no victuals, but at the point of the
lance; no leisure to repose and take breath; no knowledge of the ways or
country to secure him from ambushes and surprises; and in case of losing
a battle, no possible means of saving the remains. Neither is there want
of example in both these cases.*

*Scipio thought it much better to go and attack his enemy's territories in
Africa than to stay at home to defend his own and to fight him in Italy,
and it succeeded well with him. But, on the contrary, Hannibal in the
same war ruined himself by abandoning the conquest of a foreign country
to go and defend his own. The Athenians having left the enemy in their
own dominions to go over into Sicily, were not favoured by fortune in
their design; but Agathocles, king of Syracuse, found her favourable to
him when he went over into Africa and left the war at home.*

*By which examples we are wont to conclude, and with some reason, that
events, especially in war, for the most part depend upon fortune, who
will not be governed by nor submit unto human reasons and prudence,
according to the poet:*

> *"Et male consultis pretium est: prudentia fallit*
> *Nec fortune probat causas, sequiturque merentes,*
> *Sed vaga per cunctos nullo discrimine fertur.*
> *Scilicet est aliud, quod nos cogatque regatque*
> *Majus, et in proprias ducat mortalia leges."*

*["And there is value in ill counsel: prudence deceives: nor does
fortune inquire into causes, nor aid the most deserving, but turns
hither and thither without discrimination. Indeed there is a
greater power which directs and rules us, and brings mortal affairs
under its own laws."--Manilius, iv. 95.]*

But, to take the thing right, it should seem that our counsels and deliberations depend as much upon fortune as anything else we do, and that she engages also our arguments in her uncertainty and confusion. "We argue rashly and adventurously," says Timaeus in Plato, "by reason that, as well as ourselves, our discourses have great participation in the temerity of chance."

CHAPTER XLVIII

OF WAR HORSES, OR DESTRIERS

I here have become a grammarian, I who never learned any language but by rote, and who do not yet know adjective, conjunction, or ablative. I think I have read that the Romans had a sort of horses by them called 'funales' or 'dextrarios', which were either led horses, or horses laid on at several stages to be taken fresh upon occasion, and thence it is that we call our horses of service 'destriers'; and our romances commonly use the phrase of 'adestrer' for 'accompagner', to accompany. They also called those that were trained in such sort, that running full speed, side by side, without bridle or saddle, the Roman gentlemen, armed at all pieces, would shift and throw themselves from one to the other, 'desultorios equos'. The Numidian men-at-arms had always a led horse in one hand, besides that they rode upon, to change in the heat of battle:

> *"Quibus, desultorum in modum, binos trahentibus equos, inter acerrimam saepe pugnam, in recentem equum, ex fesso, armatis transultare mos erat: tanta velocitas ipsis, tamque docile equorum genus."*

> *["To whom it was a custom, leading along two horses, often in the hottest fight, to leap armed from a tired horse to a fresh one; so active were the men, and the horses so docile."--Livy, xxiii. 29.]*

There are many horses trained to help their riders so as to run upon any one, that appears with a drawn sword, to fall both with mouth and heels upon any that front or oppose them: but it often happens that they do more harm to their friends than to their enemies; and, moreover, you cannot loose them from their hold, to reduce them again into order, when they are once engaged and grappled, by which means you remain at the mercy of their quarrel. It happened very ill to Artybius, general of the

Persian army, fighting, man to man, with Onesilus, king of Salamis, to be mounted upon a horse trained after this manner, it being the occasion of his death, the squire of Onesilus cleaving the horse down with a scythe betwixt the shoulders as it was reared up upon his master. And what the Italians report, that in the battle of Fornova, the horse of Charles VIII., with kicks and plunges, disengaged his master from the enemy that pressed upon him, without which he had been slain, sounds like a very great chance, if it be true.

[In the narrative which Philip de Commines has given of this battle, in which he himself was present (lib. viii. ch. 6), he tells us of wonderful performances by the horse on which the king was mounted. The name of the horse was Savoy, and it was the most beautiful horse he had ever seen. During the battle the king was personally attacked, when he had nobody near him but a valet de chambre, a little fellow, and not well armed. "The king," says Commines, "had the best horse under him in the world, and therefore he stood his ground bravely, till a number of his men, not a great way from him, arrived at the critical minute."]

The Mamalukes make their boast that they have the most ready horses of any cavalry in the world; that by nature and custom they were taught to know and distinguish the enemy, and to fall foul upon them with mouth and heels, according to a word or sign given; as also to gather up with their teeth darts and lances scattered upon the field, and present them to their riders, on the word of command. 'T is said, both of Caesar and Pompey, that amongst their other excellent qualities they were both very good horsemen, and particularly of Caesar, that in his youth, being mounted on the bare back, without saddle or bridle, he could make the horse run, stop, and turn, and perform all its airs, with his hands behind him. As nature designed to make of this person, and of Alexander, two miracles of military art, so one would say she had done her utmost to arm them after an extraordinary manner for every one knows that Alexander's horse, Bucephalus, had a head inclining to the shape of a bull; that he would suffer himself to be mounted and governed by none but his master, and that he was so honoured after his death as to have a city erected to his name. Caesar had also one which had forefeet like those of a man, his hoofs being divided in the form of fingers, which likewise was not to be ridden, by any but Caesar himself, who, after his death, dedicated his statue to the goddess Venus.

I do not willingly alight when I am once on horseback, for it is the place where, whether well or sick, I find myself most at ease. Plato recommends it for health, as also Pliny says it is good for the stomach and the joints. Let us go further into this matter since here we are.

We read in Xenophon a law forbidding any one who was master of a horse to travel on foot. Trogus Pompeius and Justin say that the Parthians were wont to perform all offices and ceremonies, not only in war but also all affairs whether public or private, make bargains, confer, entertain, take the air, and all on horseback; and that the greatest distinction betwixt freemen and slaves amongst them was that the one rode on horseback and the other went on foot, an institution of which King Cyrus was the founder.

There are several examples in the Roman history (and Suetonius more particularly observes it of Caesar) of captains who, on pressing occasions, commanded their cavalry to alight, both by that means to take from them all hopes of flight, as also for the advantage they hoped in this sort of fight.

"Quo haud dubie superat Romanus,"

["Wherein the Roman does questionless excel."--Livy, ix. 22.]

says Livy. And so the first thing they did to prevent the mutinies and insurrections of nations of late conquest was to take from them their arms and horses, and therefore it is that we so often meet in Caesar:

"Arma proferri, jumenta produci, obsides dari jubet."

[*"He commanded the arms to be produced, the horses brought out, hostages to be given."--De Bello Gall., vii. II.*]

The Grand Signior to this day suffers not a Christian or a Jew to keep a horse of his own throughout his empire.

Our ancestors, and especially at the time they had war with the English, in all their greatest engagements and pitched battles fought for the most part on foot, that they might have nothing but their own force, courage, and constancy to trust to in a quarrel of so great concern as life and honour. You stake (whatever Chrysanthes in Xenophon says to the contrary) your valour and your fortune upon that of your horse; his wounds or death bring your person into the same danger; his fear or fury shall make you reputed rash or cowardly; if he have an ill mouth or will not answer to the spur, your honour must answer for it. And, therefore, I do not think it strange that those battles were more firm and furious than those that are fought on horseback:

> *"Caedebant pariter, pariterque ruebant*
> *Victores victique; neque his fuga nota, neque illis."*

[*"They fought and fell pell-mell, victors and vanquished; nor was flight thought of by either."--AEneid, x. 756.*]

Their battles were much better disputed. Nowadays there are nothing but routs:

> *"Primus clamor atque impetus rem decernit."*

[*"The first shout and charge decides the business."--Livy, xxv. 41.*]

And the means we choose to make use of in so great a hazard should be as much as possible at our own command: wherefore I should advise to choose weapons of the shortest sort, and such of which we are able to give the best account. A man may repose more confidence in a sword he holds in his hand than in a bullet he discharges out of a pistol, wherein there must be a concurrence of several circumstances to make it perform its office, the powder, the stone, and the wheel: if any of which fail it endangers your fortune. A man himself strikes much surer than the air can direct his blow:

> "Et, quo ferre velint, permittere vulnera ventis
> Ensis habet vires; et gens quaecumque virorum est,
> Bella gerit gladiis."

["And so where they choose to carry [the arrows], the winds allow the wounds; the sword has strength of arm: and whatever nation of men there is, they wage war with swords."--Lucan, viii. 384.]

But of that weapon I shall speak more fully when I come to compare the arms of the ancients with those of modern use; only, by the way, the astonishment of the ear abated, which every one grows familiar with in a short time, I look upon it as a weapon of very little execution, and hope we shall one day lay it aside. That missile weapon which the Italians formerly made use of both with fire and by sling was much more terrible: they called a certain kind of javelin, armed at the point with an iron three feet long, that it might pierce through and through an armed man, Phalarica, which they sometimes in the field darted by hand, sometimes from several sorts of engines for the defence of beleaguered places; the shaft being rolled round with flax, wax, rosin, oil, and other combustible matter, took fire in its flight, and lighting upon the body of a man or his target, took away all the use of arms and limbs. And yet, coming to close fight, I should think they would also damage the assailant, and that the camp being as it were planted with these flaming truncheons, would produce a common inconvenience to the whole crowd:

> "Magnum stridens contorta Phalarica venit,
> Fulminis acta modo."

["The Phalarica, launched like lightning, flies through the air with a loud rushing sound."--AEneid, ix. 705.]

They had, moreover, other devices which custom made them perfect in (which seem incredible to us who have not seen them), by which they supplied the effects of our powder and shot. They darted their spears with so great force, as ofttimes to transfix two targets and two armed men at once, and pin them together. Neither was the effect of their slings less certain of execution or of shorter carriage:

[*"Culling round stones from the beach for their slings; and with these practising over the waves, so as from a great distance to throw within a very small circuit, they became able not only to wound an enemy in the head, but hit any other part at pleasure."* —Livy, xxxviii. 29.]

Their pieces of battery had not only the execution but the thunder of our cannon also:

"Ad ictus moenium cum terribili sonitu editos,
pavor et trepidatio cepit."

[*"At the battery of the walls, performed with a terrible noise, the defenders began to fear and tremble."* —Idem, ibid., 5.]

The Gauls, our kinsmen in Asia, abominated these treacherous missile arms, it being their use to fight, with greater bravery, hand to hand:

[*"They are not so much concerned about large gashes—the bigger and deeper the wound, the more glorious do they esteem the combat but when they find themselves tormented by some arrow-head or bullet lodged within, but presenting little outward show of wound, transported with shame and anger to perish by so imperceptible a destroyer, they fall to the ground."* —Livy, xxxviii. 21.]

A pretty description of something very like an arquebuse-shot. The ten thousand Greeks in their long and famous retreat met with a nation who very much galled them with great and strong bows, carrying arrows so long that, taking them up, one might return them back like a dart, and with them pierce a buckler and an armed man through and through. The engines, that Dionysius invented at Syracuse to shoot vast massy darts and stones of a prodigious greatness with so great impetuosity and at so great a distance, came very near to our modern inventions.

But in this discourse of horses and horsemanship, we are not to forget the pleasant posture of one Maistre Pierre Pol, a doctor of divinity, upon his mule, whom Monstrelet reports always to have ridden sideways through the streets of Paris like a woman. He says also, elsewhere, that the Gascons had terrible horses, that would wheel in their full speed, which the French, Picards, Flemings, and Brabanters looked upon as a miracle, "having never seen the like before," which are his very words.

Caesar, speaking of the Suabians: "in the charges they make on horseback," says he, "they often throw themselves off to fight on foot, having taught their horses not to stir in the meantime from the place, to which they presently run again upon occasion; and according to their custom, nothing is so unmanly and so base as to use saddles or pads, and they despise such as make use of those conveniences: insomuch that, being but a very few in number, they fear not to attack a great many." That which I have formerly wondered at, to see a horse made to perform all his airs with a switch only and the reins upon his neck, was common with the Massilians, who rid their horses without saddle or bridle:

> "Et gens, quae nudo residens Massylia dorso,
> Ora levi flectit, fraenorum nescia, virga."

["The Massylians, mounted on the bare backs of their horses, bridleless, guide them by a mere switch."--Lucan, iv. 682.]

> "Et Numidae infraeni cingunt."

["The Numidians guiding their horses without bridles." --AEneid, iv. 41.]

> "Equi sine fraenis, deformis ipse cursus,
> rigida cervice et extento capite currentium."

[*"The career of a horse without a bridle is ungraceful; the neck
extended stiff, and the nose thrust out."--Livy, xxxv. II.*]

King Alfonso,--[*Alfonso XI., king of Leon and Castile, died 1350.*]--
he who first instituted the Order of the Band or Scarf in Spain, amongst
other rules of the order, gave them this, that they should never ride
mule or mulet, upon penalty of a mark of silver; this I had lately out of
Guevara's Letters. Whoever gave these the title of Golden Epistles had
another kind of opinion of them than I have. The Courtier says, that
till his time it was a disgrace to a gentleman to ride on one of these
creatures: but the Abyssinians, on the contrary, the nearer they are to
the person of Prester John, love to be mounted upon large mules, for the
greatest dignity and grandeur.

Xenophon tells us, that the Assyrians were fain to keep their horses
fettered in the stable, they were so fierce and vicious; and that it
required so much time to loose and harness them, that to avoid any
disorder this tedious preparation might bring upon them in case of
surprise, they never sat down in their camp till it was first well
fortified with ditches and ramparts. His Cyrus, who was so great a
master in all manner of horse service, kept his horses to their due work,
and never suffered them to have anything to eat till first they had
earned it by the sweat of some kind of exercise. The Scythians when in
the field and in scarcity of provisions used to let their horses blood,
which they drank, and sustained themselves by that diet:

> "Venit et epoto Sarmata pastus equo."

[*"The Scythian comes, who feeds on horse-flesh"
--Martial, De Spectaculis Libey, Epigr. iii. 4.*]

Those of Crete, being besieged by Metellus, were in so great necessity for drink that they were fain to quench their thirst with their horses urine.--[Val. Max., vii. 6, ext. 1.]

To shew how much cheaper the Turkish armies support themselves than our European forces, 'tis said that besides the soldiers drink nothing but water and eat nothing but rice and salt flesh pulverised (of which every one may easily carry about with him a month's provision), they know how to feed upon the blood of their horses as well as the Muscovite and Tartar, and salt it for their use.

These new-discovered people of the Indies [Mexico and Yucatan D.W.], when the Spaniards first landed amongst them, had so great an opinion both of the men and horses, that they looked upon the first as gods and the other as animals ennobled above their nature; insomuch that after they were subdued, coming to the men to sue for peace and pardon, and to bring them gold and provisions, they failed not to offer of the same to the horses, with the same kind of harangue to them they had made to the others: interpreting their neighing for a language of truce and friendship.

In the other Indies, to ride upon an elephant was the first and royal place of honour; the second to ride in a coach with four horses; the third to ride upon a camel; and the last and least honour to be carried or drawn by one horse only. Some one of our late writers tells us that he has been in countries in those parts where they ride upon oxen with pads, stirrups, and bridles, and very much at their ease.

Quintus Fabius Maximus Rullianus, in a battle with the Samnites, seeing his horse, after three or four charges, had failed of breaking into the enemy's battalion, took this course, to make them unbridle all their horses and spur their hardest, so that having nothing to check their career, they might through weapons and men open the way to his foot, who by that means gave them a bloody defeat. The same command was given by Quintus Fulvius Flaccus against the Celtiberians:

*["You will do your business with greater advantage of your horses'
strength, if you send them unbridled upon the enemy, as it is
recorded the Roman horse to their great glory have often done; their
bits being taken off, they charged through and again back through
the enemy's ranks with great slaughter, breaking down all their
spears."--Idem, xl. 40.]*

The Duke of Muscovy was anciently obliged to pay this reverence to the
Tartars, that when they sent an embassy to him he went out to meet them
on foot, and presented them with a goblet of mares' milk (a beverage of
greatest esteem amongst them), and if, in drinking, a drop fell by chance
upon their horse's mane, he was bound to lick it off with his tongue.
The army that Bajazet had sent into Russia was overwhelmed with so
dreadful a tempest of snow, that to shelter and preserve themselves from
the cold, many killed and embowelled their horses, to creep into their
bellies and enjoy the benefit of that vital heat. Bajazet, after that
furious battle wherein he was overthrown by Tamerlane, was in a hopeful
way of securing his own person by the fleetness of an Arabian mare he had
under him, had he not been constrained to let her drink her fill at the
ford of a river in his way, which rendered her so heavy and indisposed,
that he was afterwards easily overtaken by those that pursued him. They
say, indeed, that to let a horse stale takes him off his mettle, but as
to drinking, I should rather have thought it would refresh him.

Croesus, marching his army through certain waste lands near Sardis, met
with an infinite number of serpents, which the horses devoured with great
appetite, and which Herodotus says was a prodigy of ominous portent to
his affairs.

We call a horse entire, that has his mane and ears so, and no other will
pass muster. The Lacedaemonians, having defeated the Athenians in
Sicily, returning triumphant from the victory into the city of Syracuse,
amongst other insolences, caused all the horses they had taken to be
shorn and led in triumph. Alexander fought with a nation called Dahas,
whose discipline it was to march two and two together armed on one horse,

to the war; and being in fight, one of them alighted, and so they fought on horseback and on foot, one after another by turns.

I do not think that for graceful riding any nation in the world excels the French. A good horseman, according to our way of speaking, seems rather to have respect to the courage of the man than address in riding. Of all that ever I saw, the most knowing in that art, who had the best seat and the best method in breaking horses, was Monsieur de Carnavalet, who served our King Henry II.

I have seen a man ride with both his feet upon the saddle, take off his saddle, and at his return take it up again and replace it, riding all the while full speed; having galloped over a cap, make at it very good shots backwards with his bow; take up anything from the ground, setting one foot on the ground and the other in the stirrup: with twenty other ape's tricks, which he got his living by.

There has been seen in my time at Constantinople two men upon one horse, who, in the height of its speed, would throw themselves off and into the saddle again by turn; and one who bridled and saddled his horse with nothing but his teeth; an other who betwixt two horses, one foot upon one saddle and the other upon another, carrying the other man upon his shoulders, would ride full career, the other standing bolt upright upon and making very good shots with his bow; several who would ride full speed with their heels upward, and their heads upon the saddle betwixt several scimitars, with the points upwards, fixed in the harness. When I was a boy, the prince of Sulmona, riding an unbroken horse at Naples, prone to all sorts of action, held reals--[A small coin of Spain, the Two Sicilies, &c.]--under his knees and toes, as if they had been nailed there, to shew the firmness of his seat.

CHAPTER XLIX

OF ANCIENT CUSTOMS

I should willingly pardon our people for admitting no other pattern or rule of perfection than their own peculiar manners and customs; for 'tis a common vice, not of the vulgar only, but almost of all men, to walk in the beaten road their ancestors have trod before them. I am content, when they see Fabricius or Laelius, that they look upon their countenance and behaviour as barbarous, seeing they are neither clothed nor fashioned according to our mode. But I find fault with their singular indiscretion in suffering themselves to be so blinded and imposed upon by the authority of the present usage as every month to alter their opinion, if custom so require, and that they should so vary their judgment in their own particular concern. When they wore the busk of their doublets up as high as their breasts, they stiffly maintained that they were in their proper place; some years after it was slipped down betwixt their thighs, and then they could laugh at the former fashion as uneasy and intolerable. The fashion now in use makes them absolutely condemn the other two with so great resolution and so universal consent, that a man would think there was a certain kind of madness crept in amongst them, that infatuates their understandings to this strange degree. Now, seeing that our change of fashions is so prompt and sudden, that the inventions of all the tailors in the world cannot furnish out new whim-whams enow to feed our vanity withal, there will often be a necessity that the despised forms must again come in vogue, these immediately after fall into the same contempt; and that the same judgment must, in the space of fifteen or twenty years, take up half-a-dozen not only divers but contrary opinions, with an incredible lightness and inconstancy; there is not any of us so discreet, who suffers not himself to be gulled with this contradiction, and both in external and internal sight to be insensibly blinded.

I wish to muster up here some old customs that I have in memory, some of them the same with ours, the others different, to the end that, bearing in mind this continual variation of human things, we may have our judgment more clearly and firmly settled.

The thing in use amongst us of fighting with rapier and cloak was in practice amongst the Romans also:

> *"Sinistras sagis involvunt, gladiosque distringunt,"*

> *["They wrapt their cloaks upon the left arm, and drew their swords."—De Bello Civili, i. 75.]*

says Caesar; and he observes a vicious custom of our nation, that continues yet amongst us, which is to stop passengers we meet upon the road, to compel them to give an account who they are, and to take it for an affront and just cause of quarrel if they refuse to do it.

At the Baths, which the ancients made use of every day before they went to dinner, and as frequently as we wash our hands, they at first only bathed their arms and legs; but afterwards, and by a custom that has continued for many ages in most nations of the world, they bathed stark naked in mixed and perfumed water, looking upon it as a great simplicity to bathe in mere water. The most delicate and affected perfumed themselves all over three or four times a day. They often caused their hair to be pinched off, as the women of France have some time since taken up a custom to do their foreheads,

> *"Quod pectus, quod crura tibi, quod brachia veilis,"*

> *["You pluck the hairs out of your breast, your arms, and thighs."—Martial, ii. 62, i.]*

though they had ointments proper for that purpose:

> *"Psilotro nitet, aut acida latet oblita creta."*

["She shines with unguents, or with chalk dissolved in vinegar."
--Idem, vi. 93, 9.]

They delighted to lie soft, and alleged it as a great testimony of
hardiness to lie upon a mattress. They ate lying upon beds, much after
the manner of the Turks in this age:

"Inde thoro pater AEneas sic orsus ab alto."

["Thus Father AEneas, from his high bed of state, spoke."
--AEneid, ii. 2.]

And 'tis said of the younger Cato, that after the battle of Pharsalia,
being entered into a melancholy disposition at the ill posture of the
public affairs, he took his repasts always sitting, assuming a strict and
austere course of life. It was also their custom to kiss the hands of
great persons; the more to honour and caress them. And meeting with
friends, they always kissed in salutation, as do the Venetians:

"Gratusque darem cum dulcibus oscula verbis."

["And kindest words I would mingle with kisses."
--Ovid, De Pont., iv. 9, 13]

In petitioning or saluting any great man, they used to lay their hands
upon his knees. Pasicles the philosopher, brother of Crates, instead of
laying his hand upon the knee laid it upon the private parts, and being
roughly repulsed by him to whom he made that indecent compliment:
"What," said he, "is not that part your own as well as the other?"
--[Diogenes Laertius, vi. 89.]--They used to eat fruit, as we do, after
dinner. They wiped their fundaments (let the ladies, if they please,
mince it smaller) with a sponge, which is the reason that 'spongia' is a
smutty word in Latin; which sponge was fastened to the end of a stick, as
appears by the story of him who, as he was led along to be thrown to the
wild beasts in the sight of the people, asking leave to do his business,

and having no other way to despatch himself, forced the sponge and stick down his throat and choked himself.--[Seneca, Ep., 70.] They used to wipe, after coition, with perfumed wool:

"At tibi nil faciam; sed Iota mentula lana."

They had in the streets of Rome vessels and little tubs for passengers to urine in:

"Pusi saepe lacum propter se, ac dolia curta.
Somno devincti, credunt extollere vestem."

["The little boys in their sleep often think they are near the
public urinal, and raise their coats to make use of it."
--Lucretius, iv.]

They had collation betwixt meals, and had in summer cellars of snow to cool their wine; and some there were who made use of snow in winter, not thinking their wine cool enough, even at that cold season of the year. The men of quality had their cupbearers and carvers, and their buffoons to make them sport. They had their meat served up in winter upon chafing dishes, which were set upon the table, and had portable kitchens (of which I myself have seen some) wherein all their service was carried about with them:

"Has vobis epulas habete, lauti
Nos offendimur ambulante caena."

["Do you, if you please, esteem these feasts: we do not like the
ambulatory suppers."--Martial, vii. 48, 4.]

In summer they had a contrivance to bring fresh and clear rills through their lower rooms, wherein were great store of living fish, which the guests took out with their own hands to be dressed every man according to his own liking. Fish has ever had this pre-eminence, and keeps it still, that the grandees, as to them, all pretend to be cooks; and indeed the taste is more delicate than that of flesh, at least to my fancy. But in all sorts of magnificence, debauchery, and voluptuous inventions of effeminacy and expense, we do, in truth, all we can to parallel them; for our wills are as corrupt as theirs: but we want ability to equal them. Our force is no more able to reach them in their vicious, than in their virtuous, qualities, for both the one and the other proceeded from a vigour of soul which was without comparison greater in them than in us; and souls, by how much the weaker they are, by so much have they less power to do either very well or very ill.

The highest place of honour amongst them was the middle. The name going before, or following after, either in writing or speaking, had no signification of grandeur, as is evident by their writings; they will as soon say Oppius and Caesar, as Caesar and Oppius; and me and thee, as thee and me. This is the reason that made me formerly take notice in the life of Flaminius, in our French Plutarch, of one passage, where it seems as if the author, speaking of the jealousy of honour betwixt the AEtolians and Romans, about the winning of a battle they had with their joined forces obtained, made it of some importance, that in the Greek songs they had put the AEtolians before the Romans: if there be no amphibology in the words of the French translation.

The ladies, in their baths, made no scruple of admitting men amongst them, and moreover made use of their serving-men to rub and anoint them:

> "Inguina succinctus nigri tibi servus aluta
> Stat, quoties calidis nuda foveris aquis."

["A slave--his middle girded with a black apron--stands before you, when, naked, you take a hot bath."--Martial, vii. 35, i.]

They all powdered themselves with a certain powder, to moderate their sweats.

The ancient Gauls, says Sidonius Apollinaris, wore their hair long before and the hinder part of the head shaved, a fashion that begins to revive in this vicious and effeminate age.

The Romans used to pay the watermen their fare at their first stepping into the boat, which we never do till after landing:

> "Dum aes exigitur, dum mula ligatur,
> Tota abit hora."

["Whilst the fare's paying, and the mule is being harnessed, a whole hour's time is past."--Horace, Sat. i. 5, 13.]

The women used to lie on the side of the bed next the wall: and for that reason they called Caesar,

> "Spondam regis Nicomedis,"

["The bed of King Nicomedes."--Suetonius, Life of Caesar, 49.]

They took breath in their drinking, and watered their wine

> "Quis puer ocius
> Restinguet ardentis Falerni
> Pocula praetereunte lympha?"

["What boy will quickly come and cool the heat of the Falernian wine with clear water?"--Horace, Od., ii. z, 18.]

And the roguish looks and gestures of our lackeys were also in use amongst them:

> "O Jane, a tergo quern nulls ciconia pinsit,
> Nec manus, auriculas imitari est mobilis albas,
> Nec lingua, quantum sitiat canis Appula, tantum."

["O Janus, whom no crooked fingers, simulating a stork, peck at behind your back, whom no quick hands deride behind you, by imitating the motion of the white ears of the ass, against whom no mocking tongue is thrust out, as the tongue of the thirsty Apulian dog."--Persius, i. 58.]

The Argian and Roman ladies mourned in white, as ours did formerly and should do still, were I to govern in this point. But there are whole books on this subject.

CHAPTER L

OF DEMOCRITUS AND HERACLITUS

The judgment is an utensil proper for all subjects, and will have an oar in everything: which is the reason, that in these Essays I take hold of all occasions where, though it happen to be a subject I do not very well understand, I try, however, sounding it at a distance, and finding it too deep for my stature, I keep me on the shore; and this knowledge that a man can proceed no further, is one effect of its virtue, yes, one of those of which it is most proud. One while in an idle and frivolous subject, I try to find out matter whereof to compose a body, and then to prop and support it; another while, I employ it in a noble subject, one that has been tossed and tumbled by a thousand hands, wherein a man can scarce possibly introduce anything of his own, the way being so beaten on every side that he must of necessity walk in the steps of another: in such a case, 'tis the work of the judgment to take the way that seems best, and of a thousand paths, to determine that this or that is the best. I leave the choice of my arguments to fortune, and take that she first presents to me; they are all alike to me, I never design to go through any of them; for I never see all of anything: neither do they who so largely promise to show it others. Of a hundred members and faces that everything has, I take one, onewhile to look it over only, another while to ripple up the skin, and sometimes to pinch it to the bones: I give a stab, not so wide but as deep as I can, and am for the most part tempted to take it in hand by some new light I discover in it. Did I know myself less, I might perhaps venture to handle something or other to the bottom, and to be deceived in my own inability; but sprinkling here one word and there another, patterns cut from several pieces and scattered without design and without engaging myself too far, I am not responsible for them, or obliged to keep close to my subject, without varying at my own liberty and pleasure, and giving up myself to doubt and uncertainty, and to my own governing method, ignorance.

All motion discovers us: the very same soul of Caesar, that made itself
so conspicuous in marshalling and commanding the battle of Pharsalia, was
also seen as solicitous and busy in the softer affairs of love and
leisure. A man makes a judgment of a horse, not only by seeing him when
he is showing off his paces, but by his very walk, nay, and by seeing him
stand in the stable.

Amongst the functions of the soul, there are some of a lower and meaner
form; he who does not see her in those inferior offices as well as in
those of nobler note, never fully discovers her; and, peradventure, she
is best shown where she moves her simpler pace. The winds of passions
take most hold of her in her highest flights; and the rather by reason
that she wholly applies herself to, and exercises her whole virtue upon,
every particular subject, and never handles more than one thing at a
time, and that not according to it, but according to herself. Things in
respect to themselves have, peradventure, their weight, measures, and
conditions; but when we once take them into us, the soul forms them as
she pleases. Death is terrible to Cicero, coveted by Cato, indifferent
to Socrates. Health, conscience, authority, knowledge, riches, beauty,
and their contraries, all strip themselves at their entering into us, and
receive a new robe, and of another fashion, from the soul; and of what
colour, brown, bright, green, dark, and of what quality, sharp, sweet,
deep, or superficial, as best pleases each of them, for they are not
agreed upon any common standard of forms, rules, or proceedings; every
one is a queen in her own dominions. Let us, therefore, no more excuse
ourselves upon the external qualities of things; it belongs to us to give
ourselves an account of them. Our good or ill has no other dependence
but on ourselves. 'Tis there that our offerings and our vows are due,
and not to fortune she has no power over our manners; on the contrary,
they draw and make her follow in their train, and cast her in their own
mould. Why should not I judge of Alexander at table, ranting and
drinking at the prodigious rate he sometimes used to do?

Or, if he played at chess? what string of his soul was not touched by
this idle and childish game? I hate and avoid it, because it is not play

enough, that it is too grave and serious a diversion, and I am ashamed to lay out as much thought and study upon it as would serve to much better uses. He did not more pump his brains about his glorious expedition into the Indies, nor than another in unravelling a passage upon which depends the safety of mankind. To what a degree does this ridiculous diversion molest the soul, when all her faculties are summoned together upon this trivial account! and how fair an opportunity she herein gives every one to know and to make a right judgment of himself? I do not more thoroughly sift myself in any other posture than this: what passion are we exempted from in it? Anger, spite, malice, impatience, and a vehement desire of getting the better in a concern wherein it were more excusable to be ambitious of being overcome; for to be eminent, to excel above the common rate in frivolous things, nowise befits a man of honour. What I say in this example may be said in all others. Every particle, every employment of man manifests him equally with any other.

Democritus and Heraclitus were two philosophers, of whom the first, finding human condition ridiculous and vain, never appeared abroad but with a jeering and laughing countenance; whereas Heraclitus commiserating that same condition of ours, appeared always with a sorrowful look, and tears in his eyes:

> "Alter
> Ridebat, quoties a limine moverat unum
> Protuleratque pedem; flebat contrarius alter."

> ["The one always, as often as he had stepped one pace from his threshold, laughed, the other always wept." --Juvenal, Sat., x. 28.]

> [Or, as Voltaire: "Life is a comedy to those who think; a tragedy to those who feel." D.W.]

I am clearly for the first humour; not because it is more pleasant to laugh than to weep, but because it expresses more contempt and condemnation than the other, and I think we can never be despised according to our full desert. Compassion and bewailing seem to imply

some esteem of and value for the thing bemoaned; whereas the things we
laugh at are by that expressed to be of no moment. I do not think that
we are so unhappy as we are vain, or have in us so much malice as folly;
we are not so full of mischief as inanity; nor so miserable as we are
vile and mean. And therefore Diogenes, who passed away his time in
rolling himself in his tub, and made nothing of the great Alexander,
esteeming us no better than flies or bladders puffed up with wind, was a
sharper and more penetrating, and, consequently in my opinion, a juster
judge than Timon, surnamed the Man-hater; for what a man hates he lays to
heart. This last was an enemy to all mankind, who passionately desired
our ruin, and avoided our conversation as dangerous, proceeding from
wicked and depraved natures: the other valued us so little that we could
neither trouble nor infect him by our example; and left us to herd one
with another, not out of fear, but from contempt of our society:
concluding us as incapable of doing good as evil.

Of the same strain was Statilius' answer, when Brutus courted him into
the conspiracy against Caesar; he was satisfied that the enterprise was
just, but he did not think mankind worthy of a wise man's concern';
according to the doctrine of Hegesias, who said, that a wise man ought to
do nothing but for himself, forasmuch as he only was worthy of it: and to
the saying of Theodorus, that it was not reasonable a wise man should
hazard himself for his country, and endanger wisdom for a company of
fools. Our condition is as ridiculous as risible.

CHAPTER LI

OF THE VANITY OF WORDS

A rhetorician of times past said, that to make little things appear great was his profession. This was a shoemaker, who can make a great shoe for a little foot.--[A saying of Agesilaus.]--They would in Sparta have sent such a fellow to be whipped for making profession of a tricky and deceitful act; and I fancy that Archidamus, who was king of that country, was a little surprised at the answer of Thucydides, when inquiring of him, which was the better wrestler, Pericles, or he, he replied, that it was hard to affirm; for when I have thrown him, said he, he always persuades the spectators that he had no fall and carries away the prize. --[Quintilian, ii. 15.]--The women who paint, pounce, and plaster up their ruins, filling up their wrinkles and deformities, are less to blame, because it is no great matter whether we see them in their natural complexions; whereas these make it their business to deceive not our sight only but our judgments, and to adulterate and corrupt the very essence of things. The republics that have maintained themselves in a regular and well-modelled government, such as those of Lacedaemon and Crete, had orators in no very great esteem. Aristo wisely defined rhetoric to be "a science to persuade the people;" Socrates and Plato "an art to flatter and deceive." And those who deny it in the general description, verify it throughout in their precepts. The Mohammedans will not suffer their children to be instructed in it, as being useless, and the Athenians, perceiving of how pernicious consequence the practice of it was, it being in their city of universal esteem, ordered the principal part, which is to move the affections, with their exordiums and perorations, to be taken away. 'Tis an engine invented to manage and govern a disorderly and tumultuous rabble, and that never is made use of, but like physic to the sick, in a discomposed state. In those where the vulgar or the ignorant, or both together, have been all-powerful and able to give the law, as in those of Athens, Rhodes, and Rome, and where the public affairs have been in a continual tempest of commotion, to such places have the orators always repaired. And in truth, we shall find few persons in those republics who have pushed their fortunes to any great degree of eminence without the assistance of eloquence.

Pompey, Caesar, Crassus, Lucullus, Lentulus, Metellus, thence took their chiefest spring, to mount to that degree of authority at which they at last arrived, making it of greater use to them than arms, contrary to the opinion of better times; for, L. Volumnius speaking publicly in favour of the election of Q. Fabius and Pub. Decius, to the consular dignity: "These are men," said he, "born for war and great in execution; in the combat of the tongue altogether wanting; spirits truly consular. The subtle, eloquent, and learned are only good for the city, to make praetors of, to administer justice."--[Livy, x. 22.]

Eloquence most flourished at Rome when the public affairs were in the worst condition and most disquieted with intestine commotions; as a free and untilled soil bears the worst weeds. By which it should seem that a monarchical government has less need of it than any other: for the stupidity and facility natural to the common people, and that render them subject to be turned and twined and, led by the ears by this charming harmony of words, without weighing or considering the truth and reality of things by the force of reason: this facility, I say, is not easily found in a single person, and it is also more easy by good education and advice to secure him from the impression of this poison. There was never any famous orator known to come out of Persia or Macedon.

I have entered into this discourse upon the occasion of an Italian I lately received into my service, and who was clerk of the kitchen to the late Cardinal Caraffa till his death. I put this fellow upon an account of his office: when he fell to discourse of this palate-science, with such a settled countenance and magisterial gravity, as if he had been handling some profound point of divinity. He made a learned distinction of the several sorts of appetites; of that a man has before he begins to eat, and of those after the second and third service; the means simply to satisfy the first, and then to raise and actuate the other two; the

ordering of the sauces, first in general, and then proceeded to the
qualities of the ingredients and their effects; the differences of salads
according to their seasons, those which ought to be served up hot, and
which cold; the manner of their garnishment and decoration to render them
acceptable to the eye. After which he entered upon the order of the
whole service, full of weighty and important considerations:

> *"Nec minimo sane discrimine refert,*
> *Quo gestu lepores, et quo gallina secetur;"*

["Nor with less discrimination observes how we should carve a hare,
and how a hen." or, ("Nor with the least discrimination relates how
we should carve hares, and how cut up a hen.)"
⹀Juvenal, Sat., v. 123.]

and all this set out with lofty and magnificent words, the very same we
make use of when we discourse of the government of an empire. Which
learned lecture of my man brought this of Terence into my memory:

> *"Hoc salsum est, hoc adustum est, hoc lautum est, parum:*
> *Illud recte: iterum sic memento: sedulo*
> *Moneo, quæ possum, pro mea sapientia.*
> *Postremo, tanquam in speculum, in patinas,*
> *Demea, Inspicere jubeo, et moneo, quid facto usus sit."*

["This is too salt, that's burnt, that's not washed enough; that's
well; remember to do so another time. Thus do I ever advise them to
have things done properly, according to my capacity; and lastly,
Demea, I command my cooks to look into every dish as if it were a
mirror, and tell them what they should do."
⹀Terence, Adelph., iii. 3, 71.]

And yet even the Greeks themselves very much admired and highly applauded
the order and disposition that Paulus AEmilius observed in the feast he
gave them at his return from Macedon. But I do not here speak of
effects, I speak of words only.

I do not know whether it may have the same operation upon other men that it has upon me, but when I hear our architects thunder out their bombast words of pilasters, architraves, and cornices, of the Corinthian and Doric orders, and suchlike jargon, my imagination is presently possessed with the palace of Apollidon; when, after all, I find them but the paltry pieces of my own kitchen door.

To hear men talk of metonomies, metaphors, and allegories, and other grammar words, would not one think they signified some rare and exotic form of speaking? And yet they are phrases that come near to the babble of my chambermaid.

And this other is a gullery of the same stamp, to call the offices of our kingdom by the lofty titles of the Romans, though they have no similitude of function, and still less of authority and power. And this also, which I doubt will one day turn to the reproach of this age of ours, unworthily and indifferently to confer upon any we think fit the most glorious surnames with which antiquity honoured but one or two persons in several ages. Plato carried away the surname of Divine, by so universal a consent that never any one repined at it, or attempted to take it from him; and yet the Italians, who pretend, and with good reason, to more sprightly wits and sounder sense than the other nations of their time, have lately bestowed the same title upon Aretin, in whose writings, save tumid phrases set out with smart periods, ingenious indeed but far-fetched and fantastic, and the eloquence, be it what it may, I see nothing in him above the ordinary writers of his time, so far is he from approaching the ancient divinity. And we make nothing of giving the surname of great to princes who have nothing more than ordinary in them.

CHAPTER LII

OF THE PARSIMONY OF THE ANCIENTS

Attilius Regulus, general of the Roman army in *Africa*, in the height of
all his glory and victories over the *Carthaginians*, wrote to the Republic
to acquaint them that a certain hind he had left in trust with his
estate, which was in all but seven acres of land, had run away with all
his instruments of husbandry, and entreating therefore, that they would
please to call him home that he might take order in his own affairs, lest
his wife and children should suffer by this disaster. Whereupon the
Senate appointed another to manage his business, caused his losses to be
made good, and ordered his family to be maintained at the public expense.

The elder *Cato*, returning consul from *Spain*, sold his warhorse to save
the money it would have cost in bringing it back by sea into *Italy*; and
being Governor of *Sardinia*, he made all his visits on foot, without other
train than one officer of the Republic who carried his robe and a censer
for sacrifices, and for the most part carried his trunk himself. He
bragged that he had never worn a gown that cost above ten crowns, nor had
ever sent above tenpence to the market for one day's provision; and that
as to his country houses, he had not one that was rough-cast on the
outside.

Scipio AEmilianus, after two triumphs and two consulships, went an
embassy with no more than seven servants in his train. 'Tis said that
Homer had never more than one, *Plato* three, and *Zeno*, founder of the sect
of *Stoics*, none at all. *Tiberius Gracchus* was allowed but fivepence
halfpenny a day when employed as public minister about the public
affairs, and being at that time the greatest man of *Rome*.

CHAPTER LIII

OF A SAYING OF CAESAR

If we would sometimes bestow a little consideration upon ourselves, and employ the time we spend in prying into other men's actions, and discovering things without us, in examining our own abilities we should soon perceive of how infirm and decaying material this fabric of ours is composed. Is it not a singular testimony of imperfection that we cannot establish our satisfaction in any one thing, and that even our own fancy and desire should deprive us of the power to choose what is most proper and useful for us? A very good proof of this is the great dispute that has ever been amongst the philosophers, of finding out man's sovereign good, that continues yet, and will eternally continue, without solution or accord:

> "Dum abest quod avemus, id exsuperare videtur
> Caetera; post aliud, quum contigit illud, avemus,
> Et sitis aequa tenet."

[*"While that which we desire is wanting, it seems to surpass all the rest; then, when we have got it, we want something else; 'tis ever the same thirst"--Lucretius, iii. 1095.*]

Whatever it is that falls into our knowledge and possession, we find that it satisfies not, and we still pant after things to come and unknown, inasmuch as those present do not suffice for us; not that, in my judgment, they have not in them wherewith to do it, but because we seize them with an unruly and immoderate haste:

> "Nam quum vidit hic, ad victum qux flagitat usus,
> Et per quae possent vitam consistere tutam,
> Omnia jam ferme mortalibus esse parata;

> *Divitiis homines, et honore, et laude potentes*
> *Afluere, atque bona natorum excellere fama;*
> *Nec minus esse domi cuiquam tamen anxia corda,*
> *Atque animi ingratis vitam vexare querelis*
> *Causam, quae infestis cogit saevire querelis,*
> *Intellegit ibi; vitium vas efficere ipsum,*
> *Omniaque, illius vitio, corrumpier intus,*
> *Qux collata foris et commoda quomque venirent."*

[*"For when he saw that almost all things necessarily required for subsistence, and which may render life comfortable, are already prepared to their hand, that men may abundantly attain wealth, honour, praise, may rejoice in the reputation of their children, yet that, notwithstanding, every one has none the less in his heart and home anxieties and a mind enslaved by wearing complaints, he saw that the vessel itself was in fault, and that all good things which were brought into it from without were spoilt by its own imperfections."*--Lucretius, vi. 9.]

Our appetite is irresolute and fickle; it can neither keep nor enjoy anything with a good grace: and man concluding it to be the fault of the things he is possessed of, fills himself with and feeds upon the idea of things he neither knows nor understands, to which he devotes his hopes and his desires, paying them all reverence and honour, according to the saying of Caesar:

> *"Communi fit vitio naturae, ut invisis, latitantibus*
> *atque incognitis rebus magis confidamas,*
> *vehementiusque exterreamur."*

[*"'Tis the common vice of nature, that we at once repose most confidence, and receive the greatest apprehensions, from things unseen, concealed, and unknown."*--De Bello Civil, xi. 4.]

CHAPTER LIV

OF VAIN SUBTLETIES

There are a sort of little knacks and frivolous subtleties from which men sometimes expect to derive reputation and applause: as poets, who compose whole poems with every line beginning with the same letter; we see the shapes of eggs, globes, wings, and hatchets cut out by the ancient Greeks by the measure of their verses, making them longer or shorter, to represent such or such a figure. Of this nature was his employment who made it his business to compute into how many several orders the letters of the alphabet might be transposed, and found out that incredible number mentioned in Plutarch. I am mightily pleased with the humour of him,

> *["Alexander, as may be seen in Quintil., Institut. Orat., lib. ii., cap. 20, where he defines Maratarexvia to be a certain unnecessary imitation of art, which really does neither good nor harm, but is as unprofitable and ridiculous as was the labour of that man who had so perfectly learned to cast small peas through the eye of a needle at a good distance that he never missed one, and was justly rewarded for it, as is said, by Alexander, who saw the performance, with a bushel of peas."--Coste.]*

who having a man brought before him that had learned to throw a grain of millet with such dexterity and assurance as never to miss the eye of a needle; and being afterwards entreated to give something for the reward of so rare a performance, he pleasantly, and in my opinion justly, ordered a certain number of bushels of the same grain to be delivered to him, that he might not want wherewith to exercise so famous an art. 'Tis a strong evidence of a weak judgment when men approve of things for their being rare and new, or for their difficulty, where worth and usefulness are not conjoined to recommend them.

I come just now from playing with my own family at who could find out the most things that hold by their two extremities; as Sire, which is a title given to the greatest person in the nation, the king, and also to the vulgar, as merchants, but never to any degree of men between. The women of great quality are called Dames, inferior gentlewomen, Demoiselles, and the meanest sort of women, Dames, as the first. The cloth of state over our tables is not permitted but in the palaces of princes and in taverns. Democritus said, that gods and beasts had sharper sense than men, who are of a middle form. The Romans wore the same habit at funerals and feasts. It is most certain that an extreme fear and an extreme ardour of courage equally trouble and relax the belly. The nickname of Trembling with which they surnamed Sancho XII., king of Navarre, tells us that valour will cause a trembling in the limbs as well as fear. Those who were arming that king, or some other person, who upon the like occasion was wont to be in the same disorder, tried to compose him by representing the danger less he was going to engage himself in: "You understand me ill," said he, "for could my flesh know the danger my courage will presently carry it into, it would sink down to the ground." The faintness that surprises us from frigidity or dislike in the exercises of Venus are also occasioned by a too violent desire and an immoderate heat. Extreme coldness and extreme heat boil and roast. Aristotle says, that sows of lead will melt and run with cold and the rigour of winter just as with a vehement heat. Desire and satiety fill all the gradations above and below pleasure with pain. Stupidity and wisdom meet in the same centre of sentiment and resolution, in the suffering of human accidents. The wise control and triumph over ill, the others know it not: these last are, as a man may say, on this side of accidents, the others are beyond them, who after having well weighed and considered their qualities, measured and judged them what they are, by virtue of a vigorous soul leap out of their reach; they disdain and trample them underfoot, having a solid and well-fortified soul, against which the darts of fortune, coming to strike, must of necessity rebound and blunt themselves, meeting with a body upon which they can fix no impression; the ordinary and middle condition of men are lodged betwixt these two extremities, consisting of such as perceive evils, feel them, and are not able to support them.

Infancy and decrepitude meet in the imbecility of the brain; avarice and profusion in the same thirst and desire of getting.

A man may say with some colour of truth that there is an Abecedarian ignorance that precedes knowledge, and a doctoral ignorance that comes after it: an ignorance that knowledge creates and begets, at the same time that it despatches and destroys the first. Of mean understandings, little inquisitive, and little instructed, are made good Christians, who by reverence and obedience simply believe and are constant in their belief. In the average understandings and the middle sort of capacities, the error of opinion is begotten; they follow the appearance of the first impression, and have some colour of reason on their side to impute our walking on in the old beaten path to simplicity and stupidity, meaning us who have not informed ourselves by study. The higher and nobler souls, more solid and clear-sighted, make up another sort of true believers, who by a long and religious investigation of truth, have obtained a clearer and more penetrating light into the Scriptures, and have discovered the mysterious and divine secret of our ecclesiastical polity; and yet we see some, who by the middle step, have arrived at that supreme degree with marvellous fruit and confirmation, as to the utmost limit of Christian intelligence, and enjoy their victory with great spiritual consolation, humble acknowledgment of the divine favour, reformation of manners, and singular modesty. I do not intend with these to rank those others, who to clear themselves from all suspicion of their former errors and to satisfy us that they are sound and firm, render themselves extremely indiscreet and unjust, in the carrying on our cause, and blemish it with infinite reproaches of violence and oppression. The simple peasants are good people, and so are the philosophers, or whatever the present age calls them, men of strong and clear reason, and whose souls are enriched with an ample instruction of profitable sciences. The mongrels who have disdained the first form of the ignorance of letters, and have not been able to attain to the other (sitting betwixt two stools, as I and a great many more of us do), are dangerous, foolish, and importunate; these are they that trouble the world. And therefore it is that I, for my own part, retreat as much as I can towards the first and natural station, whence I so vainly attempted to advance.

Popular and purely natural poesy

> [*"The term poesie populaire was employed, for the first time, in the French language on this occasion. Montaigne created the expression, and indicated its nature."--Ampere.*]

has in it certain artless graces, by which she may come into comparison with the greatest beauty of poetry perfected by art: as we see in our Gascon villanels and the songs that are brought us from nations that have no knowledge of any manner of science, nor so much as the use of writing. The middle sort of poesy betwixt these two is despised, of no value, honour, or esteem.

But seeing that the path once laid open to the fancy, I have found, as it commonly falls out, that what we have taken for a difficult exercise and a rare subject, prove to be nothing so, and that after the invention is once warm, it finds out an infinite number of parallel examples. I shall only add this one--that, were these Essays of mine considerable enough to deserve a critical judgment, it might then, I think, fall out that they would not much take with common and vulgar capacities, nor be very acceptable to the singular and excellent sort of men; the first would not understand them enough, and the last too much; and so they may hover in the middle region.

CHAPTER LV

OF SMELLS

It has been reported of some, as of Alexander the Great, that their sweat exhaled an odoriferous smell, occasioned by some rare and extraordinary constitution, of which Plutarch and others have been inquisitive into the cause. But the ordinary constitution of human bodies is quite otherwise, and their best and chiefest excellency is to be exempt from smell. Nay, the sweetness even of the purest breath has nothing in it of greater perfection than to be without any offensive smell, like those of healthful children, which made Plautus say of a woman:

> *"Mulier tum bene olet, ubi nihil olet."*

> *["She smells sweetest, who smells not at all."*
> *--Plautus, Mostel, i. 3, 116.]*

And such as make use of fine exotic perfumes are with good reason to be suspected of some natural imperfection which they endeavour by these odours to conceal. To smell, though well, is to stink:

> *"Rides nos, Coracine, nil olentes*
> *Malo, quam bene olere, nil olere."*

> *["You laugh at us, Coracinus, because we are not scented; I would,*
> *rather than smell well, not smell at all."--Martial, vi. 55, 4.]*

And elsewhere:

> *"Posthume, non bene olet, qui bene semper olet."*

*["Posthumus, he who ever smells well does not smell well."
––Idem, ii. 12, 14.]*

I am nevertheless a great lover of good smells, and as much abominate the ill ones, which also I scent at a greater distance, I think, than other men:

> "Namque sagacius unus odoror,
> Polypus, an gravis hirsutis cubet hircus in aliis
> Quam canis acer, ubi latest sus."

["My nose is quicker to scent a fetid sore or a rank armpit, than a dog to smell out the hidden sow."––Horace, Epod., xii. 4.]

Of smells, the simple and natural seem to me the most pleasing. Let the ladies look to that, for 'tis chiefly their concern: amid the most profound barbarism, the Scythian women, after bathing, were wont to powder and crust their faces and all their bodies with a certain odoriferous drug growing in their country, which being cleansed off, when they came to have familiarity with men they were found perfumed and sleek. 'Tis not to be believed how strangely all sorts of odours cleave to me, and how apt my skin is to imbibe them. He that complains of nature that she has not furnished mankind with a vehicle to convey smells to the nose had no reason; for they will do it themselves, especially to me; my very mustachios, which are full, perform that office; for if I stroke them but with my gloves or handkerchief, the smell will not out a whole day; they manifest where I have been, and the close, luscious, devouring, viscid melting kisses of youthful ardour in my wanton age left a sweetness upon my lips for several hours after. And yet I have ever found myself little subject to epidemic diseases, that are caught, either by conversing with the sick or bred by the contagion of the air, and have escaped from those of my time, of which there have been several sorts in our cities and armies. We read of Socrates, that though he never departed from Athens during the frequent plagues that infested the city, he only was never infected.

Physicians might, I believe, extract greater utility from odours than they do, for I have often observed that they cause an alteration in me and work upon my spirits according to their several virtues; which makes me approve of what is said, that the use of incense and perfumes in churches, so ancient and so universally received in all nations and religions, was intended to cheer us, and to rouse and purify the senses, the better to fit us for contemplation.

I could have been glad, the better to judge of it, to have tasted the culinary art of those cooks who had so rare a way of seasoning exotic odours with the relish of meats; as it was particularly observed in the service of the king of Tunis, who in our days--[Muley-Hassam, in 1543.] --landed at Naples to have an interview with Charles the Emperor. His dishes were larded with odoriferous drugs, to that degree of expense that the cookery of one peacock and two pheasants amounted to a hundred ducats to dress them after their fashion; and when the carver came to cut them up, not only the dining-room, but all the apartments of his palace and the adjoining streets were filled with an aromatic vapour which did not presently vanish.

My chiefest care in choosing my lodgings is always to avoid a thick and stinking air; and those beautiful cities, Venice and Paris, very much lessen the kindness I have for them, the one by the offensive smell of her marshes, and the other of her dirt.

CHAPTER LVI

OF PRAYERS

I propose formless and undetermined fancies, like those who publish doubtful questions, to be after a disputed upon in the schools, not to establish truth but to seek it; and I submit them to the judgments of those whose office it is to regulate, not my writings and actions only, but moreover my very thoughts. Let what I here set down meet with correction or applause, it shall be of equal welcome and utility to me, myself beforehand condemning as absurd and impious, if anything shall be found, through ignorance or inadvertency, couched in this rhapsody, contrary to the holy resolutions and prescriptions of the Catholic Apostolic and Roman Church, into which I was born and in which I will die. And yet, always submitting to the authority of their censure, which has an absolute power over me, I thus rashly venture at everything, as in treating upon this present subject.

I know not if or no I am wrong, but since, by a particular favour of the divine bounty, a certain form of prayer has been prescribed and dictated to us, word by word, from the mouth of God Himself, I have ever been of opinion that we ought to have it in more frequent use than we yet have; and if I were worthy to advise, at the sitting down to and rising from our tables, at our rising from and going to bed, and in every particular action wherein prayer is used, I would that Christians always make use of the Lord's Prayer, if not alone, yet at least always. The Church may lengthen and diversify prayers, according to the necessity of our instruction, for I know very well that it is always the same in substance and the same thing: but yet such a privilege ought to be given to that prayer, that the people should have it continually in their mouths; for it is most certain that all necessary petitions are comprehended in it, and that it is infinitely proper for all occasions. 'Tis the only prayer I use in all places and conditions, and which I still repeat instead of

changing; whence it also happens that I have no other so entirely by
heart as that.

It just now came into my mind, whence it is we should derive that error
of having recourse to God in all our designs and enterprises, to call Him
to our assistance in all sorts of affairs, and in all places where our
weakness stands in need of support, without considering whether the
occasion be just or otherwise; and to invoke His name and power, in what
state soever we are, or action we are engaged in, howsoever vicious. He
is indeed, our sole and unique protector, and can do all things for us:
but though He is pleased to honour us with this sweet paternal alliance,
He is, notwithstanding, as just as He is good and mighty; and more often
exercises His justice than His power, and favours us according to that,
and not according to our petitions.

Plato in his Laws, makes three sorts of belief injurious to the gods;
"that there are none; that they concern not themselves about our affairs;
that they never refuse anything to our vows, offerings, and sacrifices."
The first of these errors (according to his opinion, never continued
rooted in any man from his infancy to his old age); the other two, he
confesses, men might be obstinate in.

God's justice and His power are inseparable; 'tis in vain we invoke His
power in an unjust cause. We are to have our souls pure and clean, at
that moment at least wherein we pray to Him, and purified from all
vicious passions; otherwise we ourselves present Him the rods wherewith
to chastise us; instead of repairing anything we have done amiss, we
double the wickedness and the offence when we offer to Him, to whom we
are to sue for pardon, an affection full of irreverence and hatred.
Which makes me not very apt to applaud those whom I observe to be so
frequent on their knees, if the actions nearest to the prayer do not give
me some evidence of amendment and reformation:

> "Si, nocturnus adulter,
> Tempora Santonico velas adoperta cucullo."

["If a night adulterer, thou coverest thy head with a Santonic
cowl."--Juvenal, Sat., viii. 144.--The Santones were the people
who inhabited Saintonge in France, from whom the Romans derived the
use of hoods or cowls covering the head and face.]

And the practice of a man who mixes devotion with an execrable life seems
in some sort more to be condemned than that of a man conformable to his
own propension and dissolute throughout; and for that reason it is that
our Church denies admittance to and communion with men obstinate and
incorrigible in any notorious wickedness. We pray only by custom and for
fashion's sake; or rather, we read or pronounce our prayers aloud, which
is no better than an hypocritical show of devotion; and I am scandalised
to see a man cross himself thrice at the Benedicite, and as often at
Grace (and the more, because it is a sign I have in great veneration and
continual use, even when I yawn), and to dedicate all the other hours of
the day to acts of malice, avarice, and injustice. One hour to God, the
rest to the devil, as if by composition and compensation. 'Tis a wonder
to see actions so various in themselves succeed one another with such an
uniformity of method as not to interfere nor suffer any alteration, even
upon the very confines and passes from the one to the other. What a
prodigious conscience must that be that can be at quiet within itself
whilst it harbours under the same roof, with so agreeing and so calm a
society, both the crime and the judge?

A man whose whole meditation is continually working upon nothing but
impurity which he knows to be so odious to Almighty God, what can he say
when he comes to speak to Him? He draws back, but immediately falls into
a relapse. If the object of divine justice and the presence of his Maker
did, as he pretends, strike and chastise his soul, how short soever the
repentance might be, the very fear of offending the Infinite Majesty
would so often present itself to his imagination that he would soon see
himself master of those vices that are most natural and vehement in him.
But what shall we say of those who settle their whole course of life upon
the profit and emolument of sins, which they know to be mortal? How many
trades and vocations have we admitted and countenanced amongst us, whose
very essence is vicious? And he that, confessing himself to me,

*voluntarily told me that he had all his lifetime professed and practised
a religion, in his opinion damnable and contrary to that he had in his
heart, only to preserve his credit and the honour of his employments, how
could his courage suffer so infamous a confession? What can men say to
the divine justice upon this subject?*

*Their repentance consisting in a visible and manifest reparation, they
lose the colour of alleging it both to God and man. Are they so impudent
as to sue for remission without satisfaction and without penitence?
I look upon these as in the same condition with the first: but the
obstinacy is not there so easy to be overcome. This contrariety and
volubility of opinion so sudden, so violent, that they feign, are a kind
of miracle to me: they present us with the state of an indigestible agony
of mind.*

*It seemed to me a fantastic imagination in those who, these late years
past, were wont to reproach every man they knew to be of any
extraordinary parts, and made profession of the Catholic religion, that
it was but outwardly; maintaining, moreover, to do him honour forsooth,
that whatever he might pretend to the contrary he could not but in his
heart be of their reformed opinion. An untoward disease, that a man
should be so riveted to his own belief as to fancy that others cannot
believe otherwise than as he does; and yet worse, that they should
entertain so vicious an opinion of such great parts as to think any man
so qualified, should prefer any present advantage of fortune to the
promises of eternal life and the menaces of eternal damnation. They may
believe me: could anything have tempted my youth, the ambition of the
danger and difficulties in the late commotions had not been the least
motives.*

*It is not without very good reason, in my opinion, that the Church
interdicts the promiscuous, indiscreet, and irreverent use of the holy
and divine Psalms, with which the Holy Ghost inspired King David. We
ought not to mix God in our actions, but with the highest reverence and
caution; that poesy is too holy to be put to no other use than to
exercise the lungs and to delight our ears; it ought to come from the*

conscience, and not from the tongue. It is not fit that a prentice in
his shop, amongst his vain and frivolous thoughts, should be permitted to
pass away his time and divert himself with such sacred things. Neither
is it decent to see the Holy Book of the holy mysteries of our belief
tumbled up and down a hall or a kitchen they were formerly mysteries, but
are now become sports and recreations. 'Tis a book too serious and too
venerable to be cursorily or slightly turned over: the reading of the
scripture ought to be a temperate and premeditated act, and to which men
should always add this devout preface, 'sursum corda', preparing even the
body to so humble and composed a gesture and countenance as shall
evidence a particular veneration and attention. Neither is it a book for
everyone to fist, but the study of select men set apart for that purpose,
and whom Almighty God has been pleased to call to that office and sacred
function: the wicked and ignorant grow worse by it. 'Tis, not a story to
tell, but a history to revere, fear, and adore. Are not they then
pleasant men who think they have rendered this fit for the people's
handling by translating it into the vulgar tongue? Does the
understanding of all therein contained only stick at words? Shall I
venture to say further, that by coming so near to understand a little,
they are much wider of the whole scope than before. A pure and simple
ignorance and wholly depending upon the exposition of qualified persons,
was far more learned and salutary than this vain and verbal knowledge,
which has only temerity and presumption.

And I do further believe that the liberty every one has taken to disperse
the sacred writ into so many idioms carries with it a great deal more of
danger than utility. The Jews, Mohammedans, and almost all other
peoples, have reverentially espoused the language wherein their mysteries
were first conceived, and have expressly, and not without colour of
reason, forbidden the alteration of them into any other. Are we assured
that in Biscay and in Brittany there are enough competent judges of this
affair to establish this translation into their own language? The
universal Church has not a more difficult and solemn judgment to make.
In preaching and speaking the interpretation is vague, free, mutable, and
of a piece by itself; so 'tis not the same thing.

*One of our Greek historians age justly censures the he lived in, because
the secrets of the Christian religion were dispersed into the hands of
every mechanic, to expound and argue upon, according to his own fancy,
and that we ought to be much ashamed, we who by God's especial favour
enjoy the pure mysteries of piety, to suffer them to be profaned by the
ignorant rabble; considering that the Gentiles expressly forbad Socrates,
Plato, and the other sages to inquire into or so much as mention the
things committed to the priests of Delphi; and he says, moreover, that
the factions of princes upon theological subjects are armed not with zeal
but fury; that zeal springs from the divine wisdom and justice, and
governs itself with prudence and moderation, but degenerates into hatred
and envy, producing tares and nettles instead of corn and wine when
conducted by human passions. And it was truly said by another, who,
advising the Emperor Theodosius, told him that disputes did not so much
rock the schisms of the Church asleep, as it roused and animated
heresies; that, therefore, all contentions and dialectic disputations
were to be avoided, and men absolutely to acquiesce in the prescriptions
and formulas of faith established by the ancients. And the Emperor
Andronicus having overheard some great men at high words in his palace
with Lapodius about a point of ours of great importance, gave them so
severe a check as to threaten to cause them to be thrown into the river
if they did not desist. The very women and children nowadays take upon
them to lecture the oldest and most experienced men about the
ecclesiastical laws; whereas the first of those of Plato forbids them to
inquire so much as into the civil laws, which were to stand instead of
divine ordinances; and, allowing the old men to confer amongst themselves
or with the magistrate about those things, he adds, provided it be not in
the presence of young or profane persons.*

*A bishop has left in writing that at the other end of the world there is
an isle, by the ancients called Dioscorides, abundantly fertile in all
sorts of trees and fruits, and of an exceedingly healthful air; the
inhabitants of which are Christians, having churches and altars, only
adorned with crosses without any other images, great observers of fasts
and feasts, exact payers of their tithes to the priests, and so chaste,
that none of them is permitted to have to do with more than one woman in*

his life--[What Osorius says is that these people only had one wife at a time.]--as to the rest, so content with their condition, that environed with the sea they know nothing of navigation, and so simple that they understand not one syllable of the religion they profess and wherein they are so devout: a thing incredible to such as do not know that the Pagans, who are so zealous idolaters, know nothing more of their gods than their bare names and their statues. The ancient beginning of 'Menalippus', a tragedy of Euripides, ran thus:

> *"O Jupiter! for that name alone*
> *Of what thou art to me is known."*

I have also known in my time some men's writings found fault with for being purely human and philosophical, without any mixture of theology; and yet, with some show of reason, it might, on the contrary, be said that the divine doctrine, as queen and regent of the rest, better keeps her state apart, that she ought to be sovereign throughout, not subsidiary and suffragan, and that, peradventure, grammatical, rhetorical, logical examples may elsewhere be more suitably chosen, as also the material for the stage, games, and public entertainments, than from so sacred a matter; that divine reasons are considered with greater veneration and attention by themselves, and in their own proper style, than when mixed with and adapted to human discourse; that it is a fault much more often observed that the divines write too humanly, than that the humanists write not theologically enough. Philosophy, says St. Chrysostom, has long been banished the holy schools, as an handmaid altogether useless and thought unworthy to look, so much as in passing by the door, into the sanctuary of the holy treasures of the celestial doctrine; that the human way of speaking is of a much lower form and ought not to adopt for herself the dignity and majesty of divine eloquence. Let who will 'verbis indisciplinatis' talk of fortune, destiny, accident, good and evil hap, and other suchlike phrases, according to his own humour; I for my part propose fancies merely human and merely my own, and that simply as human fancies, and separately considered, not as determined by any decree from heaven, incapable of doubt or dispute; matter of opinion, not matter of faith; things which I discourse of according to my own notions, not as I believe, according to God; after a laical, not clerical, and yet always after a very religious manner, as children prepare their exercises, not to instruct but to be instructed.

And might it not be said, that an edict enjoining all people but such as are public professors of divinity, to be very reserved in writing of religion, would carry with it a very good colour of utility and justice ⁓and to me, amongst the rest peradventure, to hold my prating? I have been told that even those who are not of our Church nevertheless amongst themselves expressly forbid the name of God to be used in common discourse, nor so much even by way of interjection, exclamation, assertion of a truth, or comparison; and I think them in the right: upon what occasion soever we call upon God to accompany and assist us, it ought always to be done with the greatest reverence and devotion.

There is, as I remember, a passage in Xenophon where he tells us that we ought so much the more seldom to call upon God, by how much it is hard to compose our souls to such a degree of calmness, patience, and devotion as it ought to be in at such a time; otherwise our prayers are not only vain and fruitless, but vicious: "forgive us," we say, "our trespasses, as we forgive them that trespass against us"; what do we mean by this petition but that we present to God a soul free from all rancour and revenge? And yet we make nothing of invoking God's assistance in our vices, and inviting Him into our unjust designs:

    "Quae, nisi seductis, nequeas committere divis"

    ["Which you can only impart to the gods, when you have gained them over." ⁓Persius, ii. 4.]

the covetous man prays for the conservation of his vain and superfluous riches; the ambitious for victory and the good conduct of his fortune; the thief calls Him to his assistance, to deliver him from the dangers and difficulties that obstruct his wicked designs, or returns Him thanks for the facility he has met with in cutting a man's throat; at the door

of the house men are going to storm or break into by force of a petard,
they fall to prayers for success, their intentions and hopes of cruelty,
avarice, and lust.

> "Hoc igitur, quo to Jovis aurem impellere tentas,
> Dic agedum Staio: 'proh Jupiter! O bone, clamet,
> Jupiter!' At sese non clamet Jupiter ipse."

> ["This therefore, with which you seek to draw the ear of Jupiter,
> say to Staius. 'O Jupiter! O good Jupiter!' let him cry. Think
> you Jupiter himself would not cry out upon it?"--Persius, ii. 21.]

Marguerite, Queen of Navarre,--[In the Heptameron.]--tells of a young
prince, who, though she does not name him, is easily enough by his great
qualities to be known, who going upon an amorous assignation to lie with
an advocate's wife of Paris, his way thither being through a church, he
never passed that holy place going to or returning from his pious
exercise, but he always kneeled down to pray. Wherein he would employ
the divine favour, his soul being full of such virtuous meditations,
I leave others to judge, which, nevertheless, she instances for a
testimony of singular devotion. But this is not the only proof we have
that women are not very fit to treat of theological affairs.

A true prayer and religious reconciling of ourselves to Almighty God
cannot enter into an impure soul, subject at the very time to the
dominion of Satan. He who calls God to his assistance whilst in a course
of vice, does as if a cut-purse should call a magistrate to help him, or
like those who introduce the name of God to the attestation of a lie.

> "Tacito mala vota susurro
> Concipimus."

> ["We whisper our guilty prayers."---Lucan, v. 104.]

There are few men who durst publish to the world the prayers they make to
Almighty God:

"Haud cuivis promptum est, murmurque, humilesque susurros
  Tollere de templis, et aperto vivere voto"

[*"'Tis not convenient for every one to bring the prayers he mutters
out of the temple, and to give his wishes to the public ear.
--"Persius, ii. 6.]*

and this is the reason why the Pythagoreans would have them always public
and heard by every one, to the end they might not prefer indecent or
unjust petitions as this man:

"Clare quum dixit, Apollo!
  Labra movet, metuens audiri: Pulcra Laverna,
  Da mihi fallere, da justum sanctumque videri;
  Noctem peccatis, et fraudibus objice nubem."

[*"When he has clearly said Apollo! he moves his lips, fearful to be
heard; he murmurs: O fair Laverna, grant me the talent to deceive;
grant me to appear holy and just; shroud my sins with night, and
cast a cloud over my frauds."--Horace, Ep., i. 16, 59.--(Laverna
was the goddess of thieves.)]*

The gods severely punished the wicked prayers of OEdipus in granting
them: he had prayed that his children might amongst themselves determine
the succession to his throne by arms, and was so miserable as to see
himself taken at his word. We are not to pray that all things may go as
we would have them, but as most concurrent with prudence.

We seem, in truth, to make use of our prayers as of a kind of jargon, and
as those do who employ holy words about sorceries and magical operations;
and as if we reckoned the benefit we are to reap from them as depending
upon the contexture, sound, and jingle of words, or upon the grave
composing of the countenance. For having the soul contaminated with
concupiscence, not touched with repentance, or comforted by any late
reconciliation with God, we go to present Him such words as the memory

suggests to the tongue, and hope from thence to obtain the remission of our sins. There is nothing so easy, so sweet, and so favourable, as the divine law: it calls and invites us to her, guilty and abominable as we are; extends her arms and receives us into her bosom, foul and polluted as we at present are, and are for the future to be. But then, in return, we are to look upon her with a respectful eye; we are to receive this pardon with all gratitude and submission, and for that instant at least, wherein we address ourselves to her, to have the soul sensible of the ills we have committed, and at enmity with those passions that seduced us to offend her; neither the gods nor good men (says Plato) will accept the present of a wicked man:

> "Immunis aram si terigit manus,
> Non sumptuosa blandior hostia
> Mollivit aversos Penates
> Farre pio et saliente mica."

["If a pure hand has touched the altar, the pious offering of a small cake and a few grains of salt will appease the offended gods more effectually than costly sacrifices."
⁓Horace, Od., iii. 23, 17.]

CHAPTER LVII

OF AGE

I cannot allow of the way in which we settle for ourselves the duration of our life. I see that the sages contract it very much in comparison of the common opinion: "what," said the younger Cato to those who would stay his hand from killing himself, "am I now of an age to be reproached that I go out of the world too soon?" And yet he was but eight-and-forty years old. He thought that to be a mature and advanced age, considering how few arrive unto it. And such as, soothing their thoughts with I know not what course of nature, promise to themselves some years beyond it, could they be privileged from the infinite number of accidents to which we are by a natural subjection exposed, they might have some reason so to do. What an idle conceit is it to expect to die of a decay of strength, which is the effect of extremest age, and to propose to ourselves no shorter lease of life than that, considering it is a kind of death of all others the most rare and very seldom seen? We call that only a natural death; as if it were contrary to nature to see a man break his neck with a fall, be drowned in shipwreck, be snatched away with a pleurisy or the plague, and as if our ordinary condition did not expose us to these inconveniences. Let us no longer flatter ourselves with these fine words; we ought rather, peradventure, to call that natural which is general, common, and universal.

To die of old age is a death rare, extraordinary, and singular, and, therefore, so much less natural than the others; 'tis the last and extremest sort of dying: and the more remote, the less to be hoped for. It is, indeed, the bourn beyond which we are not to pass, and which the law of nature has set as a limit, not to be exceeded; but it is, withal, a privilege she is rarely seen to give us to last till then. 'Tis a lease she only signs by particular favour, and it may be to one only in the space of two or three ages, and then with a pass to boot, to carry

him through all the traverses and difficulties she has strewed in the way
of this long career. And therefore my opinion is, that when once forty
years we should consider it as an age to which very few arrive. For
seeing that men do not usually proceed so far, it is a sign that we are
pretty well advanced; and since we have exceeded the ordinary bounds,
which is the just measure of life, we ought not to expect to go much
further; having escaped so many precipices of death, whereinto we have
seen so many other men fall, we should acknowledge that so extraordinary
a fortune as that which has hitherto rescued us from those eminent
perils, and kept us alive beyond the ordinary term of living, is not like
to continue long.

'Tis a fault in our very laws to maintain this error: these say that a
man is not capable of managing his own estate till he be five-and-twenty
years old, whereas he will have much ado to manage his life so long.
Augustus cut off five years from the ancient Roman standard, and declared
that thirty years old was sufficient for a judge. Servius Tullius
superseded the knights of above seven-and-forty years of age from the
fatigues of war; Augustus dismissed them at forty-five; though methinks
it seems a little unreasonable that men should be sent to the fireside
till five-and-fifty or sixty years of age. I should be of opinion that
our vocation and employment should be as far as possible extended for the
public good: I find the fault on the other side, that they do not employ
us early enough. This emperor was arbiter of the whole world at
nineteen, and yet would have a man to be thirty before he could be fit to
determine a dispute about a gutter.

For my part, I believe our souls are adult at twenty as much as they are
ever like to be, and as capable then as ever. A soul that has not by
that time given evident earnest of its force and virtue will never after
come to proof. The natural qualities and virtues produce what they have
of vigorous and fine, within that term or never,

> "Si l'espine rion picque quand nai,
> A pene que picque jamai,"

["If the thorn does not prick at its birth,
'twill hardly ever prick at all."]

as they say in Dauphin.

Of all the great human actions I ever heard or read of, of what sort
soever, I have observed, both in former ages and our own, more were
performed before the age of thirty than after; and this ofttimes in the
very lives of the same men. May I not confidently instance in those of
Hannibal and his great rival Scipio? The better half of their lives they
lived upon the glory they had acquired in their youth; great men after,
'tis true, in comparison of others; but by no means in comparison of
themselves. As to my own particular, I do certainly believe that since
that age, both my understanding and my constitution have rather decayed
than improved, and retired rather than advanced. 'Tis possible, that
with those who make the best use of their time, knowledge and experience
may increase with their years; but vivacity, promptitude, steadiness, and
other pieces of us, of much greater importance, and much more essentially
our own, languish and decay:

"Ubi jam validis quassatum est viribus aevi
Corpus, et obtusis ceciderunt viribus artus,
Claudicat ingenium, delirat linguaque, mensque."

["When once the body is shaken by the violence of time,
blood and vigour ebbing away, the judgment halts,
the tongue and the mind dote."--Lucretius, iii. 452.]

Sometimes the body first submits to age, sometimes the mind; and I have
seen enough who have got a weakness in their brains before either in
their legs or stomach; and by how much the more it is a disease of no
great pain to the sufferer, and of obscure symptoms, so much greater is
the danger. For this reason it is that I complain of our laws, not that
they keep us too long to our work, but that they set us to work too late.
For the frailty of life considered, and to how many ordinary and natural

rocks it is exposed, one ought not to give up so large a portion of it to childhood, idleness, and apprenticeship.

> *[Which Cotton thus renders: "Birth though noble, ought not to share so large a vacancy, and so tedious a course of education." Florio (1613) makes the passage read as-follows: "Methinks that, considering the weakness of our life, and seeing the infinite number of ordinary rocks and natural dangers it is subject unto, we should not, so soon as we come into the world, allot so large a share thereof unto unprofitable wantonness in youth, ill-breeding idleness, and slow-learning prentisage."]*

29551768R00248

Printed in Great Britain
by Amazon